THE ENGLISH NOVEL

Select Bibliographical Guides

Edited by A. E. DYSON

OXFORD UNIVERSITY PRESS
1974

Oxford University Press, Ely House, London W.1

GLASGOW NEW YORK TORONTO MELBOURNE WELLINGTON
CAPE TOWN IBADAN NAIROBI DAR ES SALAAM LUSAKA ADDIS ABABA
DELHI BOMBAY CALCUTTA MADRAS KARACHI LAHORE DACCA
KUALA LUMPUR SINGAPORE HONG KONG TOKYO

PAPERBACK ISBN 0 19 871027 5
CASEBOUND ISBN 0 19 871033 X

PRINTED IN GREAT BRITAIN
BY RICHARD CLAY (THE CHAUCER PRESS) LTD
BUNGAY, SUFFOLK

CONTENTS

INTRODUCTION

This Guide is intended for those who are embarking on a serious study of English literature. Their first concern is with the obvious questions. Which editions can be recommended, including the authoritative texts, and good cheaper ones? What critics should be read? What biographies exist of the major writers, and can any be described as standard? Are a writer's letters in print? Where do we have to look for full bibliographies? Which books throw light on authors by portraying the background against which they wrote?

Each of the chapters in this book is divided up into sections in which these questions are answered. At the end of each chapter, there is a classified list with bibliographical details of all the books and articles mentioned earlier.

The question of which critics should be read is, perhaps, the most difficult to answer. Differences of opinion naturally flourish. One problem for the student these days is the sheer quantity of criticism published. Any full bibliography bears witness to this, and the effect can be bewildering or even paralysing. Some of the criticism is ephemeral, some for specialists only, some not very good. With so many will-o'-the-wisps, how can a student keep his path?

Each contributor to this Guide has based his selection of critical material on his own experience, but has not merely indulged personal taste. The books and articles cited include those which would figure in any general consensus, and contributors have added the most valuable other articles and books known to them. It is recognized that good work may have been omitted, but a select reading list cannot satisfy everyone, and the sections on BIBLIOGRAPHIES should be complete enough to make amends.

The contributors to this book are concerned with mapping territory, pointing to landmarks, suggesting routes. Such activity is, of course, merely inaugural. The various signposts all point through the door of a library, and once the reader is there the biographies, bibliographies, texts, and works of criticism suggest directions of their own.

New books of importance are reviewed in *The Times Literary Supplement*, the *New York Review of Books* and other leading literary papers, and an eye should be kept on these. Monthly visits to the periodicals room of a good library should be a normal feature of a student's life. He will soon become familiar with the literary journals most frequently listed in this book.

It is becoming increasingly common for important articles from learned journals to be collected together in paperback volumes. These enable the student to own writings which he would otherwise have to borrow from library collections of journals, and which are sometimes difficult to obtain. Some of them will be mentioned in the body of this book, but it may be convenient if I list the most important of the series here.

(a) *Collections of articles on a single author*
   Twentieth Century Views. General Editor, Maynard Mack (Englewood Cliffs, N.J.: Prentice-Hall). Modern critical essays.
   Modern Judgements. General Editor, P. N. Furbank (London: Macmillan). Criticism of the past twenty or thirty years.
   The Critical Heritage Series. General Editor, B. C. Southam (London: Routledge & Kegan Paul; and New York: Barnes & Noble). Reviews and comments from the author's lifetime to today.
   Discussions Of Literature. General Editor, Joseph H. Summers (Boston, Mass.: Heath; and London: Harrap). General critical essays.
   Penguin Critical Anthologies. General Editor, Christopher Ricks (Harmondsworth: Penguin). Criticism from the author's lifetime to today.
(b) *Collections of articles on a single work*
   Macmillan Casebook Series. General Editor, A. E. Dyson (London: Macmillan). About one-third devoted to writings published before 1930, two-thirds to modern criticism.
   Twentieth Century Interpretations. General Editor, Maynard Mack (Englewood Cliffs, N.J.: Prentice-Hall). Mainly recent criticism, in selection.
   Norton Critical Editions (New York: Norton). Text, and selected criticism in section at end.

Students should know where to go for bibliographical information in addition to that which is contained in this book. *The Cambridge Bibliography of English Literature* (edited in four volumes by F. W. Bateson, with a supplementary volume edited by George Watson) is the standard work. It is now being replaced by the *New Cambridge Bibliography of English Literature*, edited by George Watson and Ian Willison, of which two volumes are currently in print. The Modern Language Association of America publishes an annual list of the year's work in English studies in *PMLA*—comprehensive but without commentary. There is also *The Year's Work in English Studies* which is published annually by the English Association (London). This is more selective than the *PMLA* list and has worrying gaps, but it includes commentaries on the works listed, and offers some insight on the varieties of current criticism. Comprehensive and valuable bibliographies are also to be found in the various volumes of the Oxford History of English Literature. Students of literature who are particularly concerned with the historical background might well look for guidance to the appropriate volumes in the Oxford History of England, which, besides being authoritative, contain useful bibliographical material.

A note now on the bibliographical details given in this book. In the REFERENCES section at the end of each chapter, the place and date of publication of a book is almost always that of the most recent edition. Readers should distinguish between *editions* and *impressions*. The copy of a book on a library shelf may well contain the date of an impression printed more recently than the edition listed in this book; but impressions are usually unaltered, or lightly corrected, reprints of the most recent edition.

Books originally published in paperback are given places and dates of publication, but details of paperback *reprints* are not given, because such paperbacks are normally unaltered reprints of the latest hardback editions. They appear in their thousands each year, and readers should consult up-to-date issues of the catalogues *Paperbacks in Print* (U.K.) and *Paperbound Books in Print* (U.S.) to establish which reprints are currently available.

Journals and series cited frequently are customarily referred to by abbreviations of their names, and this practice is followed here. The abbreviations chiefly used are listed on p. x.

A.E.D.

ABBREVIATIONS

AUMLA	*Journal of the Australasian Universities Modern Language Association*
CBEL	*Cambridge Bibliography of English Literature*
DNB	*Dictionary of National Biography*
EIC	*Essays in Criticism*
ELH	*Journal of English Literary History*
HLQ	*Huntington Library Quarterly*
JEGP	*Journal of English and Germanic Philology*
JHI	*Journal of the History of Ideas*
MLN	*Modern Language Notes*
MLQ	*Modern Language Quarterly*
MLR	*Modern Language Review*
MP	*Modern Philology*
N & Q	*Notes and Queries*
NCBEL	*New Cambridge Bibliography of English Literature*
NCF	*Nineteenth-Century Fiction*
OHEL	*Oxford History of English Literature*
PBSA	*Papers of the Bibliographical Society of America*
PMLA	*Publications of the Modern Language Association of America*
PQ	*Philological Quarterly*
RES	*Review of English Studies*
SEL	*Studies in English Literature*
SP	*Studies in Philology*
SR	*Sewanee Review*
TLS	*Times Literary Supplement*
TSLL	*Texas Studies in Language and Literature*
UTQ	*University of Toronto Quarterly*
VS	*Victorian Studies*

1 · BUNYAN   1628–1688

Roger Sharrock

TEXTS
'Here are Sixty Pieces of his Labours and he was Sixty Years of Age',
says his friend and editor Charles Doe, a comb-maker of Southwark,
in 'A Catalogue of Mr. Bunyan's Works' which accompanies the
Folio of 1692. There is still no modern collected edition of Bunyan;
the bulk of these sixty books have remained unreprinted since two
Victorian compilations: *Complete Works*, edited by George Offor, and
Complete Works, edited by Henry Stebbing. Bunyan's reputation is
rightly grounded on his achievement as an imaginative writer in *The
Pilgrim's Progress*, and to a lesser extent in *The Life and Death of Mr.
Badman*, and *The Holy War*; and most biographers and critics have
made use of his spiritual autobiography *Grace abounding to the Chief
of Sinners* in order to elucidate his religious development and trace
the origins of the personality which found full expression in the great
allegories. In short, he has been claimed as a primitive of the novel.
Acknowledgement is sometimes paid to the fact that he is the last
great master of the allegoric mode in the tradition of Dante, Lang-
land, and Spenser; but in an age of proliferating editorial activity he
remains, in respect of his total work, the most neglected of major
English writers. The prose of Milton, Herbert, and Vaughan has
long been available in critical editions, but of most of Bunyan's theological, evangelical, and controversial works there is no modern text
at all. However, this gap will eventually be filled by an edition of the
Miscellaneous Works of John Bunyan under the general editorship of
Roger Sharrock with the assistance of Graham Midgley, T. L.
Underwood, Richard Greaves, and others, to be published by the
Clarendon Press. The first two volumes containing the pamphlets
written against the Quakers and *The Doctrine of the Law and Grace
Unfolded*, Bunyan's most important theological treatise, are due to
appear shortly.

The reader who is not able to gain access to the collections of
Offor and Stebbing may at least find one good example of Bunyan's
exhortatory sermon treatises, *The Heavenly Footman*, in a volume entitled *God's Knotty Log* edited by Henri A. Talon and including also
The Pilgrim's Progress. The emblem book *A Book for Boys and Girls: or,*

Country Rhimes for Children (1928) has been edited by E. S. Buchanan, superseding the earlier facsimile edition by John Brown. Facsimiles of both *Grace Abounding* and *The Pilgrim's Progress* have been produced by Scolar Press.

Offor's edition of the complete works, though hard to come by, is a valuable book. The works are divided as follows: volume i and ii, Experimental, Doctrinal, and Practical; volume iii, Allegorical, Figurative, and Symbolical. Offor put to good use his knowledge as a collector of early Bunyan editions; he aims at accuracy, though he does not collate the texts of minor works and does not always use first editions. He modernizes spelling. His annotations are largely of an evangelical nature, though he records a great number of illuminating Scriptural sources and analogues. His memoir of Bunyan and introduction to *The Pilgrim's Progress* in the third volume are full of historical information. *A Few Sighs from Hell, or, the Groans of a Damned Soul* (1658), *The Strait Gate* (1676), *Come and Welcome to Jesus Christ* (1678), *The Jerusalem Sinner Saved; or, Good News for the Vilest of Men* (1688), *Solomon's Temple Spiritualiz'd* (1688), and *The Water of Life* (1688) may be selected, as well as *The Heavenly Footman* (1698), mentioned above, as treatises which provide evidence of Bunyan's colloquial power as a developing preacher and of his skill in deploying extended images.

Grace Abounding to the Chief of Sinners (1666), written in the middle of Bunyan's first imprisonment, is the indispensable introduction to the creative application of his religious experience which followed. The earlier editions of Edmund Venables and John Brown have now been superseded by that of Roger Sharrock. Where previous editors had reprinted the text of the sixth edition of 1688, this edition is based on the first (1666) with the considerable additions of the third, fifth, and sixth given in the form in which they were first introduced. This, like other modern editions of *Grace Abounding*, also contains *A Relation of the Imprisonment of Mr. John Bunyan* (1765); this work, written before the end of 1661, has not much to say about the course of the imprisonment but gives a graphic account of Bunyan's arrest, examination before the magistrates, and subsequent appearances at quarter-sessions and Bedford assizes.

The standard edition of *The Pilgrim's Progress* (Part One, 1678; Part Two, 1684) is that of J. B. Wharey revised by Roger Sharrock (1960); a second edition of this revision with corrections to the text and some recasting of the introduction has now appeared (1968). In this edition the colloquial, ungrammatical forms which appeared in the first have been restored (they did not pass the printing-house corrector in the later editions which appeared in Bunyan's lifetime). There is a full apparatus of textual variants, an introduction tracing the history of the text through the first twelve editions, and a commentary. This text and that of *Grace Abounding*, without the introductions, textual notes, and commentaries, are available in a single volume in the Oxford Standard Authors series (1966). The Everyman and World's Classics series provide convenient, modernized texts without notes; that in the Penguin English Library offers a text which preserves the marginal notes, though not the marginal Scripture references, an introduction aimed at the general reader, and a few explanatory notes. Another convenient paperback reprint is that introduced by A. K. Adams in the Great Illustrated Classics series.

The next of Bunyan's three great works of entertainment, *The Life and Death of Mr. Badman* (1680), is the one that is least like an allegory and most like a novel, with the names of the characters denoting moral qualities as in some of the personages in the writings of Fielding and Dickens. Over sixty years ago John Brown printed the 1680 text with a few later variants in the same volume as *The Pilgrim's Progress*. The best modern old-spelling edition is that by G. B. Harrison in the World's Classics; it has a short introduction by Bonamy Dobrée, but no notes.

The earlier editions of *The Holy War* (1682) by John Brown and Mabel Peacock are now superseded by James F. Forrest's convenient modern reprint which relies on the first edition and avoids the adulterations of the second; spelling and punctuation are modernized and the notes are few but useful. Critical editions of *The Life and Death of Mr. Badman* and *The Holy War* are still badly needed and will appear under the joint editorship of Roger Sharrock and James F. Forrest in the Oxford edition of the *Miscellaneous Works* referred to above.

It might be convenient to list here those works by Bunyan which are in verse, apart from the songs in *The Pilgrim's Progress* and the prefatory verses to that book and to *The Holy War: Profitable Meditations* (1661), *Prison Meditations* (1665), *Ebal and Gerizim* (1665), *One Thing is Needful* (1665), *A Discourse of the Building, Nature, Excellency and Government of the House of God* (1688), and *A Book for Boys and Girls: or, Country Rhimes for Children* (1686). These works in verse will appear in a single volume edited by Graham Midgley in the Oxford edition.

The following works remained in manuscript until they were printed posthumously by Doe in the Folio of 1692, and subsequently by Chandler and Wilson in the two-volume edition of 1736–7, and in later collections: *An Exposition of the First Ten Chapters of Genesis*; *Of Justification by Imputed Righteousness*; *Paul's Departure and Crown*; *Of the Law and a Christian, Israel's Hope Encouraged*; *The Desire of the Righteous Granted*; *The Saint's Priviledge and Profit*; *Christ a Complete Saviour*; *The Saint's Knowledge of Christ's Love*; *Of the House of the Forest of Lebanon*; and *Of Antichrist and his Ruine*.

CRITICAL STUDIES AND COMMENTARY

While *The Pilgrim's Progress* was constantly reprinted and read, Bunyan's reputation long remained a purely popular one. As Cowper said of him:

> I name not thee, least so despis'd a name,
> Should raise a sneer at thy deserved fame.

As an artisan writing in the language of the market-place he fell outside the Augustan canons of polite literature; and it was unfortunate for his reputation that after his death English Nonconformity soon became liberal and rational, with some loss of sympathy for the heroic Puritan spirit which informs his writings. His uncompromising assurance belongs to the sectarian upsurge of the mid-seventeenth century, rather than to the Restoration: as David Ogg has written, 'Compared with that of his contemporaries, his style is like some strange survival from a more primitive and elemental life' (*England in the Reign of Charles II* (1956), ii. 739). Also the early history of Bunyan's reputation was affected by that cold caution with which the educated public looks upon best-sellers. He had to wait nearly a century and a half for serious critical attention.

This came with the edition of 1830 for which Southey wrote his life. Both Scott and Macaulay made this book the occasion of notable review-essays. The new estimation of Bunyan was influenced by Romantic literary theory; he was seen as an example of the natural genius of the folk as contrasted with the artificial literature of a refined society. The result was a tendency to view Bunyan in isolation from his Puritan environment: thus Coleridge could write: 'The piety of the author was baffled by his genius, and Bunyan of Parnassus had the better of Bunyan of the conventicle' (*Miscellaneous Criticism*, ed. T. M. Raysor (1936), p. 31). Yet he could also acknowledge that *The Pilgrim's Progress* was 'incomparably the best *Summa theologiae evangelicae* ever produced by a writer not miraculously inspired' (*Literary Remains* (1838), iii. 398). Coleridge's numerous scattered comments on the allegory may be found together in R. F. Brinkley, *Coleridge on the Seventeenth Century* (1955).

Critical discussion during the nineteenth century tended to be hagiological, but this period saw the beginnings of genuine scholarly investigation, especially by Nonconformists. A good example is John Jukes, *A Brief History of Bunyan's Church* (1849). Offor's life in the third volume of his edition has already been mentioned. The investigation of sources and analogues was begun by N. Hill in his *The Ancient Poem of G. de Guileville, entitled Le Pélérinage de l'homme, Compared with The Pilgrim's Progress of John Bunyan* (1858). J. B. Grier in *Studies in the English of John Bunyan* (Philadelphia, 1872) was the first in a line of research which has not been followed up as much as one might have expected. John Brown, pastor of Bunyan Meeting at Bedford, wrote what for long remained the standard life, *John Bunyan: His Life, Times and Work* (1885); it is unfortunate that in his revision of 1928, F. M. Harrison had to be content for copyright reasons with the addition of corrective notes and appendices to each chapter of the original. Brown's is a hero-worshipping biography; he makes good use of documents, and is strongest on Bunyan's relation to the Bedford congregation, weakest on his writings. Though deficient as a continuous narrative, his life has more history in it than that of Froude in the English Men of Letters series (1880).

In the period as a whole between Southey's life and 1914 it might be said that the most informed and sympathetic work on Bunyan was done by writers born into the Free Church tradition. Alexander Whyte's *Bunyan Characters* combines a devotional purpose with an understanding of the method of Bunyan's moral portraiture which could not be bettered by modern critical analysis. John Kelman's *The Road: a Study of John Bunyan's Pilgrim's Progress* takes the form of a close examination of the allegory episode by episode; again, while there is a robust acceptance of the Puritan spiritual meanings, this is not divorced from a literary appreciation which often operates through comparisons with other imaginative literature. T. R. Glover's essay in his *Poets and Puritans* may also be mentioned as an example of the inward sympathy of a fellow Nonconformist. In the twentieth century Nonconformist scholars have continued to make contributions in the field of bibliographical and historical research: W. T. Whitley, F. M. Harrison, and H. G. Tibbutt.

Critical attention to Bunyan has increased during the twentieth century, especially in the last twenty years; though, as with the treatment of his text, it is still not in proportion to his importance, and the minor works have been almost wholly neglected. Broadly speaking, critics have ceased to accept the concept so dear to the Romantics and their successors of a natural, uneducated genius; they have seen *The Pilgrim's Progress* against the background of English popular Puritanism and have brought from this source fresh insight into the working of Bunyan's imagination. Source-criticism of a narrower kind, directed to establishing the inspiration for particular episodes in the allegory, was continued by Harold Golder in several articles of which 'Bunyan's Giant Despair' may be mentioned; it has also been continued by D. Gibson's 'On the Genesis of *Pilgrim's Progress*'; a fresh source of comparative study is explored in Roger Sharrock's 'Bunyan and the English Emblem Writers'. Maurice Hussey brings to bear a knowledge of the Puritan attitude to the sin of spiritual ignorance in his 'Bunyan's Mr. Ignorance' (cf. also J. W. Draper's 'Bunyan's Mr. Ignorance'), and of another branch of Puritan literature in 'John Bunyan and the Books of God's Judgements'. But the most exhaustive inquiry into 'sources' in the popular and romance traditions remains J. B. Wharey's *The Sources of Bunyan's Allegories*.

But for the use of scholarship to illuminate our total understanding of Bunyan so that his work is seen in a new light we must turn to William York Tindall's *John Bunyan, Mechanick Preacher*. Tindall sees Bunyan as typical of the class of unordained artisan-preachers who grew up under the Commonwealth; he depicts him as differing only in the superior shrewdness which enabled him to corner the market in various conventional popular forms—the spiritual autobiography, the symbolic fiction, the cautionary moral tale, the millenarian tract. Tindall's examination of these genres, based on a comparative study of a vast range of contemporary material in the Thomason collection and elsewhere, is the most valuable part of his book. His attitude to Bunyan is curiously unsympathetic and hovers between the civilized scepticism of a Gibbon and the levity of a post-Strachey debunker.

Tindall is an innovator, though there is some anticipation of his approach in Gerhard Thiel, *Bunyans Stellung innerhalb der religiosen Strömungen seiner Zeit* (German readers and critics have been continuously interested in Bunyan from the time of the eighteenth-century Pietists). A curious example of a purely hostile and much less informed criticism is Alfred Noyes's essay which appeared in the tercentenary year 1928, and is included in his collection *The Opalescent Parrot*; Noyes censors Bunyan on the score of an inhuman moral rigidity.

Henri A. Talon's *John Bunyan, l'homme et l'oeuvre*, which has been well translated by Barbara Wall, is a full and lively study which attempts to trace the 'inner biography' of Bunyan the religious visionary. Talon profits from the detachment of his French standpoint from the English Puritan tradition, but this does not exclude him from a sympathetic understanding of the heroic passion in Bunyan; he is able to rebut the charges of plagiarism and insincerity. The frequent comparisons with non-English mystical writers are often illuminating.

Roger Sharrock's *John Bunyan* is a concise introduction incorporating the findings of modern scholarship and adding some new ones. Beginning with an account of Puritan England the book passes to a survey of Bunyan's development as convert and pastor of the Bedford congregation, followed by five chapters on the major works (*The Pilgrim's Progress*, Part Two, has a chapter to itself). Sharrock stresses the manner in which the images and 'Scriptures' of *Grace Abounding* are projected into allegorical narrative in *The Pilgrim's Progress*, Part One, and therefore argues for an earlier date for the composition of the latter than had previously been accepted (the argument is developed in detail in the introduction to his Oxford Texts edition). A later book by Sharrock, *The Pilgrim's Progress*, is a short study of the art of the work and of the relationship of the modern reader to Bunyan's naïve imagination.

The criticism of Tindall, Talon, and Sharrock helps to establish a critical portrait of Bunyan that is different in some respects from the figure who received homage in the 1928 tercentenary celebrations. The simple and heroic qualities still stand out (*pace* Tindall); the figure is less isolated, less in Southey's phrase 'a man of one book' (the Authorized Version); he is a man who gave sermons and listened to sermons, who read tracts, popular romances, emblem books, and spiritual lives; a man who had absorbed the robust humour of the homiletic tradition as well as the dignified rhythms of the English Bible. It was possible to understand the epigram of Q. D. Leavis— 'Not Bunyan, but the Puritan tradition wrote Pilgrim's Progress'— without endorsing its exaggeration. The same point is made by F. R. Leavis in his essay in *The Common Pursuit*, an essay which originally appeared as a review of Tindall in *Scrutiny*.

Leavis's later essay (in *Anna Karenina and Other Essays*) is less concerned with Bunyan as the spokesman of a moral tradition than with the universal significance of the seriousness of *The Pilgrim's Progress*, its commitment to 'a power outside ourselves making for righteousness'.

Recent critics have also paid attention to the psychological motivation of Bunyan's conversion. The fear of damnation in his autobiography has been translated into the terms of modern analytical psychology: neurotic obsessions cured by the final integration of his

personality. Of earlier work on these lines mention may be made of
William James's *Varieties of Religious Experience*, E. Marcault's 'Le
Cas Bunyan et le tempérament psychologique', and G. B. Harrison's
John Bunyan: A Study in Personality. Jack Lindsay's *John Bunyan,
Maker of Myths* is of curiosity interest. A more profound understand-
ing of Bunyan's dark night of the soul comes from 'Mark Rutherford'
(William Hale White), who had a Calvinist background, and a
personal knowledge of subjective anguish (see *John Bunyan* and the
comments in his *Last Pages from a Journal*).

An aspect of more recent research has been the exploration of
Calvinist theology in its bearing not only on Bunyan's treatment of
his themes, but on the structure of *The Pilgrim's Progress*. The subject
is briefly treated in Sharrock's article 'Spiritual Autobiography in
The Pilgrim's Progress'. It has been taken further by Wolfgang Iser,
'Bunyans *Pilgrim's Progress*: die kalvinistische Heilsgewissheit und die
Form des Romans' in *Festschrift für Walther Bulst*; and in U. M. Kaufmann, *The Pilgrim's Progress and Traditions in Puritan Meditation*, an
involved but suggestive book which employs a technique similar to
that of L. L. Martz in comparing literary imagery with the imagery
in manuals of devotion. Henri Talon's 'Space and the Hero in *The
Pilgrim's Progress*' may also be mentioned. Awareness of the underlying theological pattern is a strength in Jean Blondel's short booklet,
Allégorie et réalisme dans le Pilgrim's Progress. R. M. Frye, *God, Man and
Satan* is a comparative study of the theological conceptions of Milton
and Bunyan by a critic trained as a theologian. There is a clear and
informed account of Bunyan's theological views by Richard Greaves.

C. S. Lewis's 'The Vision of John Bunyan', reprinted in *They Asked
for a Paper*, contrives to say much in a short compass about the language as well as the vision of Bunyan. Louis Macneice, in his *Varieties
of Parable*, gives a poet's view of Bunyan the creator of images. An
interesting note on the relationship between grammatical variations
and types of vision is Roy Pascal, 'The Present Tense in *The Pilgrim's
Progress*'.

Little separate attention has been devoted to the other major
works, though, as has been seen, the interpretation of *Grace Abounding*
has figured prominently in recent general studies. Exceptions are M.
R. Watson, 'The Drama of *Grace Abounding*' and Barrett S. Mandel,
'Bunyan and the Autobiographer's Artistic Purpose'. There is also
an interesting chapter on Bunyan's autobiographical method in
Joan Webber's *The Eloquent 'I': Style and Self in Seventeenth-Century
Prose* (Wisconsin, 1968). On *The Life and Death of Mr. Badman*
there is S. W. Sachs, *Der typisch-puritanische Ideengehalt in Bunyans Life*

and Death of Mr. Badman; Maurice Hussey has written a general appreciation, 'The Life and Death of Mr. Badman', and Roger Sharrock has shown that one of the cautionary tales told by Wiseman in the book can be traced to a contemporary anecdote of child-murder in 'An anecdote in Bunyan's *Mr. Badman*'. There are articles on *The Holy War* by Sir Charles Firth and D. Lamont; the former shows how closely the military detail of Emanuel's army in the allegory corresponds to the equipment and practice of the Parliamentary armies in the Civil War (see also Firth's *Cromwell's Army*). Sharrock discusses the ancestry of the trial scene in 'The Trial of Vices in Puritan Fiction'.

Of the minor works the neglect is almost total. Bunyan's emblem book *A Book for Boys and Girls* (later called *Divine Emblems*) is discussed in Sharrock's article (1945), and in the final chapter of Rosemary Freeman, *English Emblem Books*. R. L. Greaves has convincingly argued that *Reprobation Asserted*, a harsh statement of the doctrine of predestination in its crudest form, is not by Bunyan.

BIOGRAPHIES

Many of the earlier studies in the last section are critical biographies; this applies to those by Southey, Macaulay, and John Brown, and also to the books by 'Mark Rutherford' and G. B. Harrison. A remarkably balanced and intelligent study, accurate in its historical detail, which is purely biographical in treatment, is that by a Congregationalist scholar G. O. Griffith (*John Bunyan*). John Brown's life was reissued in the tercentenary year with F. M. Harrison's revisions; in this form it has pretensions to the status of an official life; in fact it is more a repository of research and local antiquarian lore. M. P. Willcocks, *Bunyan Calling*, is a popular biography, but a much better one which has digested some of the recent research is Ola E. Winslow, *John Bunyan*.

Joyce Godber's discovery of the bond for Bunyan's release from his second imprisonment in June 1677 is an important piece of research; it establishes that this imprisonment, like his first, must have been in the county gaol, and that its duration was so short as to make it seem unlikely that the First Part of *The Pilgrim's Progress* was written during this confinement ('The Imprisonments of John Bunyan').

No survey, however short, of the interpretation of Bunyan should be without a reference to those imaginative creations which owe something to the inspiration of his work and character. Browning's 'Ned Bratts' in his *Dramatic Idylls*, First Series (1879) might be mentioned. So might Hawthorne's *The Celestial Railroad*.

No manuscript that is indubitably Bunyan's autograph has survived. There are, however, strong grounds for thinking that one of the hands in the minute-book of the gathered church at Bedford is his. Many of the entries between 1672 and 1688, the period when Bunyan was pastor, are in this hand. The document, the oldest dissenting church-book, has been printed in facsimile in a limited edition with an introduction by G. B. Harrison (*The Church Book of Bunyan Meeting*). The original is in the Bunyan Library at Bedford. There is an article on possible Bunyan signatures by T. J. Brown ('English Literary Autographs xxxiii: John Bunyan').

BIBLIOGRAPHIES

The standard bibliography of Bunyan's works is F. M. Harrison, *A Bibliography of the Works of John Bunyan*. The Sotheby Catalogue of the Harmsworth Sale of 1947, when several copies of the 1678 *Pilgrim's Progress* were disposed of, makes interesting reading. F. M. Harrison left a collection of books on Bunyan as well as early editions to Bedford Public Library. The Library published a catalogue in 1938. There is also *A Bunyan Guide* by H. G. Tibbutt in the Elstow Moot Hall Pamphlets, which is sparse in reference but ranges fairly widely.

BACKGROUND READING

The standard histories of the period are Sir Charles Firth, *Oliver Cromwell and the Rule of the Puritans in England*, and David Ogg, *England in the Reign of Charles II*. The course of the persecution of Nonconformists is described in G. R. Cragg, *Puritanism in the Period of the Great Persecution*. R. B. Schlatter, *The Social Ideas of Religious Leaders 1660–1688*, describes the social theories of the various Puritan groups. C. E. Whiting, *Studies in English Puritanism, 1660–1688*, is useful for the lives and ideas of the more extreme sectaries.

Bunyan's two greatest contemporaries in the world of Nonconformity each left personal accounts: the *Journal* of George Fox has been edited by John Nickalls, and there is an Everyman reprint of Richard Baxter, *Reliquiae Baxterianae*. Edmund Calamy's *Account of the Ministers Rejected* may be read in *Calamy Revised* edited by A. G. Matthews, which corrects the biographies. Lucy Hutchinson, *Memoirs of Colonel Hutchinson*, is the story of an individual Puritan written by his wife. *The Puritans*, edited by Perry Miller and T. H. Johnson, is a useful collection of texts.

A good idea of life in a rural community in Bunyan's day may be

gained from Eleanor Trotter, *Seventeenth Century Life in the Country
Parish. The Journeys of Celia Fiennes* (ed. C. Morris) is a first-hand
account by an inveterate traveller of what the roads and towns of
England were like in the late seventeenth century.

For the spiritual life of the Puritans Robert Barclay, *The Inner Life
of the Religious Societies of the Commonwealth* is still informative. So is
The Narrative of the Persecution of Agnes Beaumont, the account of an
episode in which Bunyan was the victim of malicious gossip on
account of his friendship with an attractive member of his congregation. In *The Heart Prepared* Norman Pettit discusses Puritan views
of grace and conversion.

The development of the Puritan ministry is dealt with in William
Haller, *The Rise of Puritanism*, and *Liberty and Reformation in the Puritan
Revolution*; Haller is especially concerned with the growth of the concept of individual freedom of conscience and its impact on political
theory and practice. Wilhelm Schenk, *The Concern for Social Justice in
the Puritan Revolution* is an excellent short monograph which corrects
the excesses of economic interpretation. A different point of view is
expressed with eloquence and learning in Christopher Hill, *Society
and Puritanism before the Civil War*; see also the essays in his *Puritanism
and Revolution*. Geoffrey F. Nuttall, *The Holy Spirit in Puritan Faith and
Experience*, is a specialized study which has a bearing on the literature
of the gathered churches. The same author's *Visible Saints* studies the
rise of the independent congregations to which Bunyan belonged.
The standard *History of Bedfordshire* by Joyce Godber contains information on seventeenth-century church life in the district.

REFERENCES

TEXTS

H. Stebbing, *The Complete Works of John Bunyan* (4 vols., London, 1859).
G. Offor (ed.), *The Complete Works of John Bunyan* (2nd edn., 3 vols., Edinburgh and London, 1860–2).

Grace abounding to the Chief of Sinners (Scolar Press Facsimiles).
The Pilgrim's Progress (Scolar Press Facsimiles).
The Pilgrim's Progress, introduced by A. K. Adams (New York, 1968).

E. S. Buchanan (ed.), *A Book for Boys and Girls: or, Country Rhimes for Children*
(New York, 1928).
J. F. Forrest (ed.), *The Holy War* (Toronto and New York, 1967).
G. B. Harrison (ed.), *The Life and Death of Mr. Badman* (London, 1928).
R. Sharrock (ed.), *Grace Abounding to the Chief of Sinners* (Oxford, 1962).

R. Sharrock (ed.), *The Pilgrim's Progress* (paperback, London, 1965).
—— (ed.), *Grace Abounding and The Pilgrim's Progress* (London, 1966).
A. Talon, (ed.), *God's Knotty Log* (paperback, Cleveland, Ohio, and New York, 1961).
J. B. Wharey (ed.), rev. R. Sharrock, *The Pilgrim's Progress* (2nd edn., Oxford, 1968).

CRITICAL STUDIES AND COMMENTARY

J. Blondel, *Allégorie et réalisme dans le Pilgrim's Progress* (Paris, 1958).
J. Brown, *John Bunyan: His Life, Times and Work* (London, 1885; rev. by F. M Harrison, London, 1928).
R. Browning 'Ned Bratts', *Dramatic Idyls*, 1st ser. (London, 1879).
S. T. Coleridge, in *Coleridge on the Seventeenth Century*, ed. R. F. Brinkley (Durham, N.C., 1955).
J. W. Draper, 'Bunyan's Mr. Ignorance', *MLR* xxii (1927).
Sir C. Firth, *Cromwell's Army* (London, 1912).
—— 'Bunyan's Holy War', *Journal of English Studies*, (1913).
—— *Essays Historical and Literary* (Oxford, 1938).
J. F. Forrest, 'Bunyan's Ignorance and the Flatterer', *SP* lx (1963).
—— 'Mercy with her mirror', *PQ* xlii (1963).
R. Freeman, *English Emblem Books* (London, 1948).
J. A. Froude, *John Bunyan* (London, 1880).
R. M. Frye, *God, Man and Satan* (Princeton, N.J., 1960).
D. Gibson, 'On the Genesis of *Pilgrim's Progress*', *MP* xxxii (1935).
T. R. Glover, *Poets and Puritans* (Cambridge, 1915).
H. Golder, 'Bunyan's Giant Despair', *JEGP* xxx (1931).
R. L. Greaves, 'John Bunyan and *Reprobation Asserted*', *Baptist Quarterly*, xxi (1965).
—— 'John Bunyan and Covenant Thought in the Seventeenth Century', *Church History* (1967).
—— *John Bunyan* (Abingdon, 1969).
J. B. Grier, *Studies in the English of John Bunyan* (Philadelphia, Pa., 1872).
G. B. Harrison, *John Bunyan: a Study in Personality* (London, 1928).
N. Hawthorne, *The Celestial Railroad* (paperback, Signet, New York, 1963).
N. Hill, *The Ancient Poem of G. de Guileville entitled Le Pélérinage de l'homme Compared with the Pilgrim's Progress of John Bunyan* (London, 1858).
M. Hussey, 'Bunyan's Mr. Ignorance', *MLR* xliv (1949).
—— 'The Life and Death of Mr. Badman', *Congregational Quarterly*, xxviii (1950).
—— 'John Bunyan and the Books of God's Judgements', *English* vii (1949).
W. Iser, 'Bunyan's *Pilgrim's Progress*: die Kalvinistische Heilsgewissheit und die Form des Romans' in *Festschrift für Walther Bulst* (Heidelberg, 1960).
J. Jukes, *A Brief History of Bunyan's Church* (London, 1849).
U. M. Kaufmann, *The Pilgrim's Progress and Traditions in Puritan Meditation* (New Haven, Conn., 1966).

J. Kelman, *The Road: A Study of John Bunyan's Pilgrim's Progress* (London, 1915).

D. Lamont, 'Bunyan's *Holy War*: a Study in Christian Experience', *Theology Today*, iii (1946–7).

F. R. Leavis, in *The Common Pursuit* (London, 1953).

—— in *Anna Karenina and other Essays* (London, 1967).

L. D. Lerner, 'Bunyan and the Puritan Culture', *Cambridge Journal*, vii (1954).

C. S. Lewis, 'The Vision of John Bunyan' in *They Asked for a Paper* (London, 1963).

J. Lindsay, *John Bunyan, Maker of Myths* (London, 1937).

T. B. Macaulay, 'John Bunyan', *Edinburgh Review* (December 1830).

L. Macneice, in *Varieties of Parable* (London, 1965).

B. S. Mandel, 'Bunyan and the Autobiographer's Artistic Purpose', *Criticism*, x (1968).

E. Marcault, 'Le Cas Bunyan et le tempérament psychologique' in *Mélanges litteraires de Clermont-Ferrand* (1910).

A. Noyes, *The Opalescent Parrot* (London, 1929).

R. Pascal, 'The Present Tense in *The Pilgrim's Progress*', *MLR* lx (1965).

M. Rutherford (pseud.), *John Bunyan* (London, 1905).

—— *Last Pages from a Journal* (London, 1915).

S. W. Sachs, *Der typisch-puritanische Ideengehalt in Bunyans Life and Death of Mr. Badman* (Leipzig, 1936).

Sir W. Scott, 'John Bunyan', *Quarterly Review* (October 1830).

R. Sharrock, 'Bunyan and the English Emblem Writers', *RES* xxi (1945).

—— 'Spiritual Autobiography in *The Pilgrim's Progress*', *RES* xxiv (1948).

—— 'The Trial of Vices in Puritan Fiction', *Baptist Quarterly*, xix (1951).

—— 'An anecdote in Bunyan's *Mr. Badman*', *TLS* (25 July 1958).

—— *The Pilgrim's Progress* (London, 1966).

—— *John Bunyan* (rev. edn., London, 1968).

G. B. Shaw, in Preface to *Man and Superman* (London, 1903).

H. A. Talon, *John Bunyan: the Man and his Works*, trans. B. Wall (London, 1951).

—— *John Bunyan* (Writers and their Work, London, 1956).

—— 'Space and the Hero in *The Pilgrim's Progress*', *Études anglaises*, xiv (1961).

G. Thiel, *Bunyans Stellung innerhalb der religiosen Strömungen seiner Zeit* (Breslau, 1931).

W. Y. Tindall, *John Bunyan, Mechanick Preacher* (2nd edn., New York, 1967).

M. R. Watson, 'The Drama of *Grace Abounding*', *English Studies*, xlvi (1965).

Joan Webber, *The Eloquent 'I': Style and Self in Seventeenth-Century Prose* (Wisconsin, 1968).

J. B. Wharey, *The Sources of Bunyan's Allegories* (Baltimore, md., 1904).

A. Whyte, *Bunyan Characters*, 4 vols. (Edinburgh, 1893).

BIOGRAPHIES

T. J. Brown, 'English Literary Autographs xxxiii: John Bunyan', *The Book Collector*, ix (1960).

J. Godber, 'The Imprisonments of John Bunyan', *Transactions of the Congregational Historical Society*, xvi (1949).

G. O. Griffith, *John Bunyan* (London, 1927).

G. B. Harrison, *The Church Book of Bunyan Meeting* (London, 1928).

R. Southey, *Life of Bunyan* (London, 1830).

M. P. Willcocks, *Bunyan Calling* (London, 1943).

O. E. Winslow, *John Bunyan* (New York, 1961).

BIBLIOGRAPHIES

F. M. Harrison, *A Bibliography of the Works of John Bunyan* (Oxford Bibliographical Society, 1932).

A catalogue of the Frank Mott Harrison Collection in the Bedford Public Library (Bedford, 1938).

Catalogue of the Harmsworth Trust Library: Ninth Part. Sotheby and Co., 27 January 1947 (London, 1947).

H. G. Tibbutt, *A Bunyan Guide* (Elstow Moot Hall Pamphlets, Bedford, 1952).

W. T. Whitley, *A Baptist Bibliography* (2 vols., London, 1916–22).

BACKGROUND READING

R. Barclay, *The Inner Life of the Religious Societies of the Commonwealth* (London, 1876).

R. Baxter, *Reliquiae Baxterianae* (Everyman, London, 1931).

G. R. Cragg, *Puritanism in the Period of the Great Persecution 1660–1688* (London, 1957).

Sir C. Firth, *Oliver Cromwell and the Rule of the Puritans in England* (rev. edn., London, 1933).

J. Godber, *History of Bedfordshire* (Bedford, 1969).

W. Haller, *The Rise of Puritanism* (New York 1938).

—— *Liberty and Reformation in the Puritan Revolution* (New York, 1953).

G. B. Harrison (ed.), *The Narrative of the Persecution of Agnes Beaumont in 1674* (London, 1929).

C. Hill, *Puritanism and Revolution* (London, 1962).

—— *Society and Puritanism before the Civil War* (London, 1964).

L. Hutchinson, *Memoirs of Colonel Hutchinson* (Everyman, London, 1965).

W. James, *Varieties of Religions Experience* (paperback, Fontana, London, 1960).

A. G. Matthews (ed.), *Calamy Revised* (Oxford, 1934).

P. Miller and T. H. Johnson, *The Puritans* (New York, 1938).

C. Morris (ed.), *The Journeys of Celia Fiennes* (London, 1947).

J. Nickalls (ed.), *The Journal of George Fox* (Cambridge, 1952).

G. F. Nuttall, *The Holy Spirit in Puritan Faith and Experience* (Oxford, 1946).

—— *Visible Saints* (Oxford 1957).

D. Ogg, *England in the Reign of Charles II* (2nd edn., 2 vols., Oxford, 1956).

Norman Pettit, *The Heart Prepared* (New Haven, Conn., 1967).

W. Schenk, *The Concern for Justice in the Puritan Revolution* (London, 1948).

R. B. Schlatter, *The Social Ideas of Religious Leaders, 1660–1688* (London, 1940).

E. Trotter, *Seventeenth Century Life in the Country Parish* (Cambridge, 1919).

C. E. Whiting, *Studies in English Puritanism 1660–1688* (London, 1931).

M. E. Novak

TEXTS

In *A New Family Instructor* (1727), Defoe had one of his characters defend fiction on the grounds that if the work had a moral end, 'then in such Cases, Fables, feigned Histories, invented Tales, and even such as we call Romances, have been allow'd as the most pungent Way of writing or speaking'. Whether the point he wanted to make was social, political, economic, or moral, Defoe usually resorted to a fictional narrative or dialogue to communicate his ideas. Thus any-one attempting to search through Defoe's 550 individual titles for his fictional pieces would find the various editions of his writings hope-lessly inadequate. The work I have quoted is a good example. It contains a series of moral dialogues in which there is some character development that is of interest to anyone writing on Defoe's fiction, yet it appears in no edition of Defoe's writings.

Defoe's best-known novels are included in *The Shakespeare Head Edition of the Novels and Selected Writings of Daniel Defoe* (1927–8). It attempts to reproduce the spelling, punctuation, and capitalization of the works as they appeared in Defoe's time. Unfortunately this edi-tion is frequently inaccurate, and in the case of *Colonel Jack*, the choice of copy text makes it unusable. George Aitken's sixteen-volume edi-tion published in 1895 does not attempt to reproduce Defoe's punc-tuation or even his paragraphing, but it includes *Serious Reflections of Robinson Crusoe, A New Voyage Round the World, Due Preparations for the Plague*, and several other works omitted from *The Shakespeare Head Edition*. More complete than either of these is the twenty-volume edi-tion printed for Thomas Tegg (1840–1), and those wishing to read some of Defoe's semi-fictional works, like *Religious Courtship* or *The Family Instructor*, will have to consult this edition. Of the three editions commonly available in libraries this is the least reliable. Other edi-tions, such as that edited by William Hazlitt (1840–3), have become scarce, or, like that published by Bohn (1854–6), are less complete. A new collected edition is being sponsored by Southern Illinois Press under the editorship of Manuel Schonhorn and Maximillian E. Novak.

Not included in any collected edition is the periodical that Defoe wrote for almost ten years during the reign of Queen Anne, entitled the *Review*. A facsimile edition was edited by Arthur W. Secord in 1938, and a useful index was added by William Payne in 1948. Much of Defoe's best writing for periodicals during the same time that he was writing his fiction appears in the second and third volumes of William Lee's *Daniel Defoe* (1869). Defoe's *Tour Thro' the Whole Island of Great Britain*, edited in an elaborate edition, with an introduction by G. D. H. Cole in 1927, is once again available. A cheaper edition of this work was published by Everyman Library, and an abridgement by Penguin Books in 1971.

Robinson Crusoe, *Moll Flanders*, *Roxana*, *Colonel Jack*, *A Journal of the Plague Year*, and *Captain Singleton* are all available in England and America in inexpensive hardback or paperback. The first part of *Robinson Crusoe*, edited by J. D. Crowley, *Memoirs of a Cavalier*, edited by J. T. Boulton, *Moll Flanders*, edited by George Starr, *Roxana*, edited by Jane Jack, *Colonel Jack*, edited by Samuel Monk, *A Journal of the Plague Year*, edited by Louis Landa, and *Captain Singleton*, edited by Shiv K. Kuman, in the Oxford English Novels series are careful reproductions of the first editions and have useful notes. The Penguin edition of *Robinson Crusoe* (1965) has a sensible introduction by Angus Ross, a glossary, and some notes. Although it changes capitalization, it retains Defoe's punctuation and avoids attempts to divide the work into chapters such as one finds in the Modern Library edition of *Robinson Crusoe* (1948). *A Journal of the Plague Year* (Penguin) and *Captain Singleton* (Everyman) present few textual problems, but *Moll Flanders* was revised in the third edition, and this is commonly used as the copy text. The Oxford World's Classics *Moll Flanders*, however, is based on the first edition on the grounds that there is little evidence that Defoe himself did the revision. Students might wish to compare the two editions before deciding which to use. A recent paperback of *Moll Flanders*, edited by J. Paul Hunter (1970), provide parallel passages of the first and third editions in an appendix, making such a comparison an easy matter.

A warning should be given against using older editions or those by unknown publishers. *Roxana* is sometimes still printed with a continuation first appended in 1745 and certainly not by Defoe. *Robinson Crusoe* was abridged and pirated in the same year it was first printed, and modern abridgements may still be found. It is doubtful that anyone will find one of the many older abridgements of *Moll Flanders* that were so popular in the eighteenth and nineteenth century, but there was one published as late as 1950.

Two good selections from Defoe's poetry and prose have appeared in paperback. *Daniel Defoe*, edited by James Boulton (1965), attempts—by a running commentary and by including brief excerpts from Defoe's longer works—to give an entire picture of the writer and the man. Michael Shugrue's *Selected Poetry and Prose of Daniel Defoe* (1968) includes larger selections from Defoe's journalism and more works in their entirety. I find Shugrue's collection better than Boulton's for a strictly literary approach to Defoe. His decision to print Defoe's excellent and seldom mentioned poem, *The Mock Mourners*, is an indication of his sound judgement, and there is also more material than is provided by Boulton. James Sutherland has added some useful selections to his Riverside edition (1968) of *Robinson Crusoe*. Another volume of selections, edited by Roger Manvell (1953), is too brief to be valuable for serious study.

CRITICAL STUDIES AND COMMENTARY

After speaking of Daniel Defoe's 'extraordinary Genius', William Colepepper stated in 1704 that even 'Mr. De Foe's greatest Enemies wou'd concur . . . That the World has not in any Age produc'd a Man beyond Mr. De Foe, for his miraculous Fancy and lively Invention in all his Writings, both Verse and Prose.' Colepepper was Defoe's friend, and Defoe may have been the person recording this public statement; but it was a fair enough estimate of Defoe's reputation at the time. In 1719, when *Robinson Crusoe* was published, Defoe's enemies had increased, and he was hated by Whig and Tory alike. During the previous year John Read had printed an entire series of letters and poems in his *Weekly Journal* attacking Defoe as a satanic figure. In one of the poems depicting Defoe's voyage to the underworld, Defoe is made to announce himself as '*Satan*'s eldest Son' and demands from Charon special treatment in his voyage over the Styx. Another poem may serve as a paradigm of the kind of abuse Defoe received during the preceding fifteen years:

> This Wretch if possible will cheat Old Nick
> He's so inur'd to Fraudulence and Trick.
> Great *Bulzebube* himself he does outvie,
> For Malice, Treachery, and Audacious Lye.

Yet whatever was said publicly, most of his contemporaries regarded Defoe as an ingenious journalist and a writer who, though lacking classical learning and forced to write quickly and carelessly, had great natural ability and strength. Even Pope, who placed Defoe among the Dunces, confided to Joseph Spence his high opinion of *Robinson Crusoe* and that there was 'something good in all he has writ'.

It was the immediate, international, and continuous success of *Robinson Crusoe* that preserved Defoe's critical reputation. The preface to the sixth German edition, published in 1721, proclaimed that had Defoe written nothing else his eternal fame would be assured. And in the same year, the philosopher, Jean Le Clerc, reviewed the third volume of *Robinson Crusoe* favourably, proclaiming the entire work as a new kind of moral romance that might replace the older forms of fiction—romances of love or novellas of gallantry. In England, Charles Gildon raised his voice against the popular success of Defoe's work, but this lone attack is most useful for suggesting how many people, rich and poor alike, were reading *Robinson Crusoe*.

Defoe's other works of fiction were published in his lifetime without very much critical comment, but it would be a mistake to believe that everything but *Robinson Crusoe* was rediscovered in the nineteenth and twentieth centuries. In fact works that few students read today, like *Religious Courtship* (1722) and *The Family Instructor* (1715, 1718), were still extremely popular in 1840, when William Hazlitt published his life of Defoe, and it is likely that almost everyone in the eighteenth century read them. *Moll Flanders* and *Colonel Jack* are frequently thought of as works popular only with the lower and middle classes. The author of *The Hermit* (1727) grouped these two with *Robinson Crusoe* in this way, as did a couplet in 1729:

> Down in the kitchen, honest Dick and Doll
> Are studying Colonel Jack and Flanders Moll.

Almost all of Defoe's fiction went into several editions throughout the eighteenth century, and the many abridgements and chapbooks made from *Moll Flanders* testify to its numerous readers.

But *Robinson Crusoe* was the only work of fiction to win critical acclaim. It was praised by Rousseau, Dr. Johnson, and Coleridge, whereas works like *Moll Flanders* and *Roxana* would have been regarded as vulgarly realistic by the eighteenth century and as obscene by both that and the following century. Sir Walter Scott advised readers to pass them by 'as we would persons, howsoever otherwise interesting, who may not be in character and manners entirely fit for good society'. As late as 1916, William Trent refused to print excerpts from these novels in his *Daniel Defoe and How to Know Him*. Charles Lamb was the first important critic to find real value in these works for their realism, and he particularly praised *Colonel Jack* for imparting that sense of truth resembling testimony in a law court. Defoe as the master of realistic English fiction—this was to be the role he was to play in works of literary history. Almost every critic quoted by William Hazlitt in 1840 praised Defoe for this single gift, though some foreshadowed future criticism by suggesting his realism was instinctual rather than the result of craft—the product of a failure of the imagination.

In leaving Defoe out of *The Great Tradition* (1948) of the novel and out of good literature in general, F. R. Leavis remarked that everything necessary to be said about Defoe had been said by Leslie Stephen in his *Hours in a Library* in 1874. Perhaps for no better reason than Leavis's powerful influence, much modern criticism seems to have taken its starting point from Stephen's essay. For Stephen, Defoe was not the realistic Flemish painter to whom he was so frequently compared, but rather a photographer capturing everything before him and producing true art only by an occasional accident. Defoe's mental vision, so far from being imaginative, was cold, dry, and precise, and he had so little moral discrimination that he could not tell a villain from a hero. Creating character was beyond him. 'He seems to see in mankind', wrote Stephen, 'nothing but so many million Daniel Defoes.' Behind Stephen's judgements is an attack on Defoe's hero-worshipping biographers, who had praised Defoe as an early proponent of free trade and a profound moralist, even after his activities as a spy and double agent had been revealed. Thus Defoe was a liar and his realism was a lie: 'In other words, he had the most marvellous power ever known of giving verisimilitude to his fictions; or, in other words again, he had the most amazing talent on record for telling lies.' When Q. D. Leavis wrote in her *Fiction and the Reading Public* (1932) that to us, Defoe's 'journalistic arts seem childishly cunning', she was echoing Stephen's attitudes as have all those critics who have viewed Moll Flanders's and Roxana's quest after wealth as a direct reflection of Defoe's low, commercial mind.

Perhaps F. R. Leavis was reacting against Defoe's high reputation with the Bloomsbury group. Virginia Woolf wrote appreciative essays on Defoe: the first in 1919 was reprinted in *The Common Reader* (1924), the second appeared in 1932 in *The Second Common Reader*. Then in 1927 E. M. Forster chose *Moll Flanders* to illustrate his concept of the novel of character in his influential *Aspects of the Novel*. Although Virginia Woolf's essays are slight, they praise Defoe for his psychology and for being a writer who remained 'anonymous'. This was a high compliment for followers of the criticism of T. S. Eliot and the 'New Criticism', and it is not surprising to find Defoe praised for his anonymity by Allen Tate in his 'Techniques of Fiction' published in 1944. Forster's essay was more thorough and remains one of the best studies of Moll's character, since he does not assume that he is dealing with an emanation of Defoe.

Thus modern discussions of Defoe have to be read in terms of a debate over certain key issues: was Defoe a skilled artist capable of writing great fiction, or was he merely a somewhat obtuse journalist, unconcerned with technique but occasionally creating a stroke of art unconsciously or accidentally? Two works which stand apart from this controversy are Arthur W. Secord's *Studies in the Narrative Method of Defoe* (1924) and Sri C. Sen's *Daniel Defoe. His Mind and Art* (1948). Secord's is criticism reduced to an examination of sources, and although the information is useful, his vision of Defoe pasting together bits and pieces of other works is not entirely sound as scholarship or criticism. Sen's response to Defoe is highly personal and sometimes very perceptive, although there are occasional misreadings. To the extent that he praises Defoe as an artist and a thinker he is on the side of the defence, but unlike most recent writers on Defoe, he is not part of the critical debate.

Extremely influential have been two general works on the early English novel, Alan McKillop's *The Early Masters of English Fiction* (1956) and Ian Watt's brilliant and popular work, *The Rise of the Novel* (1957). Every student of Defoe should read these two critics to get a balanced view. McKillop, who credits Defoe with 'genuine artistic intent', has a good critical and scholarly treatment of the entire body of Defoe's fiction. This is the best short study of its kind. Ian Watt's book is more speculative, suggestive, and controversial. Much of what has been written on Defoe since Watt published his book has concentrated on the two works that he chose to illustrate his points, *Robinson Crusoe* and *Moll Flanders*, and on the arguments that Defoe was not, in a modern sense, a conscious artist or an ironist, and that his fiction reflects the new economic individualism of the eighteenth century.

Ian Watt was not the first writer to approach Defoe's fiction through an economic interpretation. Several German critics, particularly Gustav Hübener in 'Der Kaufmann Robinson Crusoe' published in 1920 applied the theories of Max Weber to Defoe, and an article by H. H. Anderson, 'The Paradox of Trade and Morality in Defoe' (1942), provided useful information for critics wishing to deal with Defoe's fiction. But Watt's interpretation, which originally appeared as 'Robinson Crusoe as a Myth', in 1951, showed precisely how important socio-economic themes were to an understanding of Defoe. In his *Economics and the Fiction of Daniel Defoe* (1962), Maximillian E. Novak tried to demonstrate that Defoe was a sophisticated

economist with his own theories and that the economic themes in
Defoe's fiction were not unconscious attitudes explainable by reference to R. H. Tawney, but rather an attempt to dramatize contemporary economic conflicts. He argued that Defoe's attitudes were
different from those of his fictional characters and that the kind of
'paradox' described by Anderson was typical, not of Defoe's muddled
economics, but rather of his method of argument.

Most criticism since then has turned to problems that Ian Watt
ignored. Novak's *Defoe and the Nature of Man* (1963) demonstrated
that Defoe relied upon natural law as an ethical basis in treating
themes like necessity, isolation, love, and courage. And a significant
number of works have attempted to show that *Robinson Crusoe* was
more about Christianity than economics. George Starr, in his *Defoe
and Spiritual Autobiography* (1965) argued convincingly that the very
structure of *Robinson Crusoe* was based on the traditional form of the
spiritual autobiography, and J. Paul Hunter, in *The Reluctant Pilgrim*
(1966), not only agreed with Starr but argued for some other formal
influences from puritan literature as well as an allusive, emblematic
method of great complexity throughout Defoe's fiction. Almost contemporary with these books, several articles have appeared with
similar arguments: William Halewood's 'Religion and Invention in
Robinson Crusoe' (1964); Robert Ayers' '*Robinson Crusoe*: Allusive
Allegorick History' (1967); and Martin J. Greif's 'The Conversion
of Robinson Crusoe' (1966). Starr is more cautious and reliable than
Hunter, who tends to confuse certain techniques that Defoe used
with the central structure of *Robinson Crusoe*. Halewood's essay is
extremely suggestive; Greif's, though published last, adds nothing
new and is often misleading. It was clearly time for a book which
would offer a balanced view of the issues raised during the fifties
and sixties, and in 1971 James Sutherland's *Daniel Defoe: a Critical
Study* provided a sensible overview of Defoe's writings with considerable appreciation of Defoe's artistry.

Robinson Crusoe's experiences on his island have fascinated
writers from Rousseau to Marx. Walter de la Mare's *Desert Islands,
and Robinson Crusoe* (1930) is not so much criticism of Defoe's book as
a brilliant meditation on the subject that inspired Defoe. Somewhat
similar in its interest is Harvey Swados's 'Robinson Crusoe—The
Man Alone' (1958), but those interested in a modest sample of the
kind of psychoanalytic criticism to which Swift has so long been
subject should look at Eric Berne's discussion of Crusoe's anality in
'The Psychological Structure of Space' (1956). Harry Robins's discussion of the way Defoe structured Crusoe's activities on his island

in 'How Smart was Robinson Crusoe?' (1952) is less concerned with
Crusoe's psychology than Defoe's literary techniques. *Twentieth
Century Interpretations of Robinson Crusoe* (1969), edited by Frank Ellis,
is a useful collection of some of the best essays on Defoe's masterpiece.

More than *Robinson Crusoe*, *Moll Flanders* has divided critics over
the question of Defoe's artistry. Ian Watt has discussed some of these
points of view in his essay, 'The Critical Fortunes of *Moll Flanders*'
(1967). This is a clever essay, but it is hardly unbiased. Watt has not
changed his position, and only those who argue against any irony in
Moll Flanders are praised. Actually, this quarrel predates *The Rise of
the Novel*. Mark Schorer's article 'A Study in Defoe: Moral Vision
and Structural Form' (1950) and his introduction to the Modern
Library edition of *Moll Flanders* (1950) argued that Moll's values
were identical with Defoe's and that Defoe lacked both artistic and
moral discrimination; whereas Dorothy Van Ghent in her study,
The English Novel (1953), argued for a 'complex system of ironies' as
the main structural device in Defoe's novel.

Siding with Van Ghent on this question are: Maximillian E.
Novak's 'Moll Flanders' First Love' (1961); Robert Columbus'
'Conscious Artistry in *Moll Flanders*' (1963); Howard L. Koonce's
'Moll's Muddle'; Defoe's Use of Irony in *Moll Flanders*' (1963); and
Novak's 'Conscious Irony in *Moll Flanders*' (1964). Koonce's essay is
probably the best statement of the issues involved; while Novak's
last essay attempts to indicate, on the basis of Defoe's entire writings,
where Defoe was being ironic and where he has been misunderstood.
Arnold Kettle's 'In Defence of Moll Flanders' (1964), attacks Watt
not so much on the grounds of irony as on Defoe's moral awareness
of Moll's world and his ability to render that world in realistic terms.
The best restatement of Ian Watt's position appears in Martin
Price's *To the Palace of Wisdom* (1964), and probably the most radical
offshoot is Denis Donoghue's 'The Values of *Moll Flanders*' (1963).

The problem here has something to do with modern definitions of
irony, for certainly Defoe's contemporaries thought him an ironist.
A contemporary pamphlet has Defoe claim that he will destroy all
his enemies 'by Dint of Irony as I have done'. His opponent exclaims,
'The only Figure in Rhetorick that you are Master of! More thanks
to Nature than Art, who has given it to you, without so much as
letting you know that it is One.' Maximillian E. Novak has dealt
with Defoe's treatment of irony throughout his writings and the reactions of his enemies to it in *The Uses of Irony* (1966).

Two collections reprinting some of these essays have appeared. J.
Paul Hunter's *Moll Flanders* (1970) combines a good text of Defoe's

novel with nearly a hundred pages of criticism. Robert C. Elliott's *Twentieth Century Interpretations of Moll Flanders* has a more complex selection of critical viewpoints. Recently interest has shifted away from the question of irony to investigations of Defoe's narrative techniques. Douglas Brooks's 'Moll Flanders: an Interpretation' (1969) and Novak's 'Defoe's "Indifferent Monitor" ' (1970) argue for Defoe's subtlety as a writer of fiction; while William Piper's 'Moll Flanders as a Structure of Topics' (1969) argues against a complex structure.

Discussions of *Moll Flanders* and *Robinson Crusoe* have occupied most of Defoe's critics, but some attention has been given to the others, particularly *Roxana*. There has been less debate over *Roxana*, and as a result, there has been less duplication. John Henry Raleigh's 'Style and Structure in Defoe's *Roxana*' (1953) is one of the best statements on Defoe's fictional methods. Benjamin's Boyce's 'The Question of Emotion in Defoe' (1953) is a subtle study of Roxana's anxiety. Spiro Peterson's 'The Matrimonial Theme of Defoe's *Roxana*' (1955) argues that *Roxana* is actually a sequel to *Moll Flanders* and that the two heroines represent two different kinds of women and their attitudes toward marriage. Novak's 'Crime and Punishment in *Roxana*' (1966) treats the way in which Defoe unified all the themes of the novel in Roxana's wicked dance before the King. Finally Robert D. Hume's 'The conclusion of Defoe's *Roxana*' (1970) has argued effectively against the idea that the ending is a failure of Defoe's art.

Colonel Jack has attracted the interest of critics interested in Defoe's treatment of the themes of education and gentility. William McBurney's 'Colonel Jacque: Defoe's Definition of the Complete Gentleman' (1962) treats this theme thoroughly—probably better, in fact, than Michael Shinagel's *Daniel Defoe and Middle-Class Gentility* (1968), which, however, has the advantage of providing more background material. That Defoe used *Colonel Jack* to express his distaste for uncontrolled economic individualism is the subject of Novak's 'Colonel Jack's "Thieving Roguing" Trade to Mexico' (1961).

The remainder of Defoe's novels have received little critical attention. Arthur W. Secord's last book, *Robert Drury's Journal* (1961) discussed the work of the title as well as *Memoirs of a Cavalier*, but Secord's method of dealing with Defoe's fiction in terms of sources remained as it was in 1924. Manuel Schonhorn's analysis (1971) of Defoe's tendency in *Captain Singleton* to humanize his pirates and tone down the violence common to pirate narratives has considerable value for changing our notions of Defoe's realism. Gary Scrimgeour's discussion of realism in *Captain Singleton* (1963) is governed by such a limited concept of fictional realism as to be unusable. But Jane Jack has written an excellent article on *A New Voyage Round the World*, and Frank Bastian's 'Defoe's *Journal of the Plague Year* Reconsidered' (1965) suggests an original way of approaching a work that lies between fiction and history. For background reading, Watson Nicholson's *Historical Sources of Defoe's Journal* (1919) is still useful.

Some mention should be made of the *Apparition of Mrs. Veal* and *The Shortest Way with the Dissenters*: the former because it was once thought to be fiction—indeed Defoe's quintessential work of fiction—before it was discovered to be an accurate report of a contemporary event; the latter because Ian Watt has argued that it is actually fiction rather than irony. Manuel Schonhorn's introduction to a collection of pamphlets on Mrs. Veal discusses the problem thoroughly, and Novak's discussion of elements of 'Hoax, Parody, Paradox, Fiction, Irony, and Satire' in *The Shortest Way* contains a summary of that question.

Finally, two works deal with Defoe's attitudes toward fictional form. 'Defoe's Theory of Fiction' (1964) by Novak attempts to bring together all of Defoe's statements about fiction to suggest that Defoe believed realistic fiction was the most effective means of communicating ideas. 'Simon Forecastle's Weekly Journal' (1965) uses Defoe's parody of a seaman's journal to argue Defoe's awareness of fictional techniques.

BIOGRAPHIES AND LETTERS

Few writers can claim to have lived as excitingly as Defoe. Imprisoned perhaps as many as five times, pilloried, and threatened throughout his life with arrest for debt or libel, Defoe has always fascinated his biographers, from Theophilus Cibber in 1753 to John Robert Moore in 1958. But all of these biographers have had the problem of dealing with a great many autobiographical comments scattered throughout his writings, much contrary evidence offered by his enemies, and almost nothing in the form of an intimate correspondence to confirm one or the other. As a result, all of Defoe's biographies are, to some extent, interpretative. Defoe's longest autobiographical piece, *An Appeal to Honour and Justice* (1715), frequently a starting point for his biographers, is available in all editions of Defoe and most selections from his writings. But it is worth paying some attention to the warning of William Minto, the one biographer Defoe failed to enchant: 'Defoe was a great story-teller in more senses than one. We can hardly believe a word that he says about himself without independent confirmation.' Without yielding to

Minto's scepticism, it is only fair to say that the reader should suspect the biographer who places too much trust in Defoe's statements about himself.

The best biography of Defoe is unquestionably James Sutherland's *Defoe*, published originally in 1938 and revised in 1950. This work is reliable in its facts and acute in its judgements on Defoe and his writings. It should be supplemented by John Robert Moore's *Daniel Defoe*. Moore's biography is organized by subject rather than chronologically, but it has a helpful summary of the events of Defoe's life at the back. These two works incorporate almost all the information in earlier biographies with the exception of new facts about Defoe's father contained in Frank Bastian's 'James Foe, Merchant' (1964), about some scandalous attacks on Defoe in Maximillian Novak's 'A Whiff of Scandal in the Life of Daniel Defoe' (1970) and about Defoe's imprisonment in Pat Rogers's 'Defoe in the Fleet Prison' (1971).

Still valuable are: Paul Dottin, *Daniel Defoe et ses romans* (1924); William Lee, *Daniel Defoe* (1869); and Walter Wilson, *Memoirs of the Life and Times of Daniel De Foe* (1830). Lee seems to have had access to newspapers and pamphlets that have disappeared; Wilson provides a somewhat rambling, often irrelevant, historical background and, what is more useful, commentary on works written against Defoe. William Minto's *Daniel Defoe* (1879) adds little to our knowledge but is an excellent antidote to the adulation of Wilson and Lee. A very readable biography containing some helpful comments on Defoe's journalism is William Freeman's *The Incredible Defoe* (1950).

Among those that I would call interpretative biographies, the best are Thomas Wright's *Life of Daniel Defoe*, which was first published in 1894 and revised in 1931, and Alick West's essay on Defoe in *The Mountain in the Sunlight* (1958). The revised version of Wright's work contains commentary on thirty-seven years of Defoe scholarship, some healthy scepticism about the Defoe canon, and useful information on Defoe's relationship with his son-in-law, Henry Baker. But Wright sees Defoe as Robinson Crusoe and Crusoe as Defoe, and almost everything is seen from this perspective. West reads Defoe and his works in Marxist terms and comes to some original, speculative conclusions. Two other biographies seem to me less successful. Brian Fitzgerald's *Daniel Defoe, A Study in Conflict* (1954) attempts something similar to Alick West's Marxist interpretation, but it is less skilful. Michael Shinagel's *Defoe and Middle-Class Gentility* (1968) views Defoe's life in terms of a constant quest after gentility. This does not seem to me a viable thesis, and there are some misreadings as well as wrong information. Shinagel's use of Defoe's *Meditations* as important autobiographical pieces is open to question, but it was worth the effort.

Defoe's correspondence was edited with excellent notes by George Healey in 1955. Most of the letters are to Defoe's patron, Robert Harley, and political rather than personal in nature, but those written from Scotland while Defoe was working as a secret agent are among the best letters of the century. Healey's commentary provides some wonderful insights into the way Defoe could flatter and deceive one of the most astute politicians of the day.

BIBLIOGRAPHIES

The fullest list of Defoe's writings may be found in John Robert Moore's *Checklist of the Writings of Daniel Defoe* (1961). Almost all the works named by Moore may be by Defoe, but there must be close to fifty that are questionable. Although Moore occasionally uses an asterisk to indicate some uncertainty about his ascriptions, there are numerous works identified as Defoe's on the basis of content and style which, unfortunately, cannot be safely ascribed to Defoe. Too much scepticism at this point, however, would be an error. Defoe signed few of his works and sometimes denied authorship of those he did write; and many works not by him were signed with his name to help them sell. It would be a mistake to regard Henry Hutchins's bibliography in the *CBEL* or that by William Trent in the *CHEL* as more conservative. These bibliographies contain works that Defoe *could not* have written; whereas all that can be said of Moore's *Checklist* is that it contains works that Defoe *may not* have written. *NCBEL* contains a bibliography of Defoe based, for the most part, on the Moore *Checklist*, but with some indication of the degree of probability in each ascription.

Anyone wishing to explore all the works ascribed to Defoe will have to work through these bibliographies, the additions to Moore's list in the revision of the *Checklist* in 1962, and his further additions made in his article, 'Defoe Acquisitions at the Huntington Library' (1964). He should add to his list the unquestionably correct attribution of *The Schism Act Explain'd* by B. G. Ivanyi in 1966. And he should consult the *British Museum Catalogue, A Catalog of the Defoe Collection in the Boston Public Library*, ed. J. Alden (1966), and the bibliographies included in the biographies by Walter Wilson, William Hazlitt, William Lee, and Paul Dottin.

Most of the quarrelling concerns Defoe's ephemeral journalism, though enough major works have been involved to cause some heated quarrels. For the student who does not wish to plunge into this morass, I would suggest the brief list of Defoe's important writings in the back of James Sutherland's pamphlet on Defoe in the 'Writers and Their Work' series, number 51, The *NCBEL* contains the best bibliography of modern studies on Defoe and includes a brief section on the more important contemporary attacks on Defoe. For those without access to the *NCBEL*, the old *CBEL* remains the best; but for studies published after 1953 and for a more complete list of titles, it should be supplemented by the annual bibliographies in *PQ*, *PMLA*, *The Years Work in English Studies*, and *Annual Bibliography of English Language and Literature*.

A bibliography of the sources Defoe used in writing about travel is included in Arthur W. Secord's *Studies in the Narrative Method of Daniel Defoe*, and a list of Defoe's writings on economics in Maximillian E. Novak's *Economics and the Fiction of Daniel Defoe*. Among special bibliographical studies are H. C. Hutchins's detailed *Robinson Crusoe and Its Printing, 1719–1731* (1925), and a related work, which contains some interesting observation on Defoe's style, L. L. Hubbard's 'Text Changes in the Taylor Editions of *Robinson Crusoe*' (1928) In 'The Canon of Defoe's Writings' (1956), John Robert Moore explained the rationale behind his *Checklist*. And in 'Defoe's Imaginary Voyages to the Moon' (1966), Rodney M. Baine attempted to show that Moore's listing of several pamphlets as items separate from Defoe's imaginary voyage, *The Consolidator*, was an error. Baine has recently questioned the basis of ascribing works to Defoe in his article 'Chalmers's First Bibliography of Daniel Defoe' (1969), and in his *Daniel Defoe and the Supernatural* (1969) he has argued forcefully against including works like *Duncan Campbell* and *The Dumb Philosopher* in the Defoe canon. Anyone interested in Defoe's reading can consult Helmut Heidenreich's edition of *The Libraries of Daniel Defoe and Phillips Farewell* (1970). Unfortunately the only list of works quoted or mentioned by Defoe in 'D. Defoes und J. Swifts Belesenheit und Literarische Kritik' by W. Gückel and E. Günther (1925) is based on too limited a sample of Defoe's writings to be very useful.

BACKGROUND READING

G. M. Trevelyan wrote, 'When a survey is demanded of Queen Anne's island, of its everyday life far distant from the Mall and yet farther from the sound of war, our thoughts turn to Daniel Defoe, riding solitary on that very quest.' No writer commented so fully on every aspect of his period, and often, when looking in a work on economics or history to explain a point in *Moll Flanders* or *Colonel Jack*, one finds the writer quoting Defoe. And because literary histories frequently base their generalizations about the age on the attitudes of the members of the Scriblerus and Kit-Cat Clubs, it is necessary to turn to historians and economists to discover Defoe's place in his period. An exception to this is Bonamy Dobrée's *English Literature in the Early Eighteenth Century* (1959), in which Defoe is carefully worked into the literary background of his age. Also useful as a general background is the fourth volume of the Pelican Guide to English Literature, *From Dryden to Johnson* (1957), edited by Boris Ford. In addition to a good essay on Defoe by Ian Watt, there are studies of the literary and social background of the time.

Probably the best specific application of the intellectual background to Defoe's fiction is Maximillian E. Novak's *Defoe and the Nature of Man* (1963). The work shows how Defoe's reading in Hobbes, Locke, and Pufendorf influenced his fiction. The opening chapters of Ian Watt's *The Rise of the Novel* (1957) are extremely suggestive on the way the climate of ideas influenced fiction, and George Starr's book, *Defoe and Casuistry* (1967) provides some explanation for the kinds of intellectual debates that pervade Defoe's fiction. As a general background to the thought of Defoe's age, Leslie Stephen's *History of English Thought in the Eighteenth Century*, published almost a century ago, is still indispensable. Basil Willey's *The Eighteenth-Century Background* (1940) limits itself to the theme of nature and is a more manageable work than Stephen's.

There is no adequate study of Defoe's religious thought. The works of Starr and Hunter have revealed the inadequacies of Rudolf Stamm's approach in his article 'Daniel Defoe: an Artist in the Puritan Tradition' (1936), but if we now know more about the way Defoe used religious themes in *Robinson Crusoe*, we are still uncertain about Defoe's total religious outlook. For Defoe's political attitudes, there is a good chapter in Isaac Krannick's *Bolingbroke and His Circle* (1968), which as might be expected, places Defoe in the opposite camp from Bolingbroke. A. E. Levett's essay, 'Daniel Defoe' (1928) underestimates the originality of Defoe's political and social ideas, but it is still useful for emphasizing the importance and pervasiveness of such ideas throughout Defoe's works. The political backgrounds to specific works by Defoe are treated in Mary Campbell's *Defoe's First Poem* (1938) and in John Robert Moore's *Defoe in the Pillory* (1939).

The best history to use in treating Defoe's activities during the reign of Queen Anne is unquestionably G. M. Trevelyan's trilogy,

Blenheim, Ramilies, and *The Peace* (1930–4). Trevelyan used Defoe as a point of departure for the history of the age, and this makes his work especially useful for students of Defoe. During the period in which he was writing his fiction, Defoe was conducting both Whig and Tory newspapers, and no history is capable of providing more than some slight hints of Defoe's real attitude toward the government which paid him to censor the Tory press as a double agent. It is frequently necessary to guess at what Defoe's true response would be, and this is often more consistent on economic and social matters than on politics. William Payne's *Mr. Review* (1947) outlines Defoe's economic ideas as they appeared in the *Review*, and Maximillian E. Novak's *Economics and the Fiction of Daniel Defoe* (1962) argues that Defoe was actually a mercantilist, who wanted to see England expand and progress but was suspicious of capitalistic ventures.

Perhaps the major problem in attempting to place Defoe in his time involves a more precise definition of Defoe's relation with his audience. Many of the traditional assumptions are stated clearly in Q. D. Leavis' *Fiction and the Reading Public* (1932) and in John F. Ross' *Swift and Defoe* (1941). But specific articles like Charles E. Burch's 'Notes on the Contemporary Popularity of Defoe's *Review*' (1937) are rare, and we may never discover in the fragmentary records we have what enabled Defoe to find a style which his contemporaries recognized as original and exciting and which brought the end of the romance and the beginning of the novel.

REFERENCES

TEXTS

(a) Collected Works

The Novels and Miscellaneous Works of Daniel De Foe (20 vols., Oxford, 1840–1).
William Hazlitt (ed.), *The Works of Daniel De Foe* (3 vols., London, 1840–3).
The Novels and Miscellaneous Works of Daniel De Foe (6 vols., London, 1854–6).
George Aitken (ed.), *Romances and Narratives by Daniel Defoe* (16 vols., London 1895).
The Shakespeare Head Edition of the Novels and Selected Writings of Daniel Defoe (14 vols., Oxford, 1927–8).

(b) Selections

J. T. Boulton (ed.), *Daniel Defoe* (London and New York, 1965).
R. Manvell (ed.), *Selections from the Prose of Daniel Defoe* (London, 1953).
M. Shugrue (ed.), *Selected Poetry and Prose of Daniel Defoe* (paperback, New York, 1968).

J. Sutherland (ed.), *Robinson Crusoe and Other Writings* (Boston, Mass., 1968).

(c) Separate Works

J. T. Boulton (ed.) *Memoirs of a Cavalier* (London, 1973).

A. Burgess and C. Bristow (edd.), *A Journal of the Plague Year* (paperback, Harmondsworth, 1966).

G. D. H. Cole (ed.), *A Tour Thro' The Whole Island of Great Britain* (2 vols., London, 1927; rev. D. C. Browning, London, 1963).

J. D. Crowley (ed.) *Robinson Crusoe* (London, 1972).

B. Dobrée and H. Davis (edd.), *Moll Flanders* (London, 1961).

J. P. Hunter (ed.), *Moll Flanders* (paperback, New York, 1970).

J. Jack (ed.), *Roxana, or The Fortunate Mistress* (London, 1964).

S. K. Kumar (ed.), *Captain Singleton* (London, 1969).

L. Landa (ed.), *A Journal of the Plague Year* (London, 1969).

W. Lee (ed.), *Daniel Defoe: His Life and Recently Discovered Writings* (3 vols., London, 1869).

S. H. Monk (ed.), *Colonel Jack* (London, 1965).

P. Rogers (ed.), *A Tour Through the Whole Island of Great Britain* (paperback, Harmondsworth, 1971).

A. Ross (ed.), *Robinson Crusoe* (paperback, Harmondsworth, 1965).

A. W. Secord (ed.), *Review*, Facsimile Text Society, no. 44 (22 vols., New York, 1938); Index W. L. Payne (ed.) (New York, 1948).

G. Starr (ed.), *Moll Flanders* (London, 1971).

J. Sutherland (ed.), *Captain Singleton* (Everyman, (London, 1963).

—— (ed.), *Moll Flanders* (New York, 1959).

CRITICAL STUDIES AND COMMENTARY

H. H. Anderson, 'The Paradox of Trade and Morality in Defoe', *MP* xxxix (1942).

Anonymous preface to *Robinson Crusoe*, trans. L. F. Vischer (6th German edn. Leipzig, 1721).

R. Ayers, '*Robinson Crusoe*: Allusive Allegorick History', *PMLA* lxxxii (1967).

F. Bastian, 'Defoe's *Journal of the Plague Year* Reconsidered', *RES* n.s. xvi (1965).

E. Berne, 'The Psychological Structure of Space', *Psychoanalytic Quarterly*, xxv (1956).

B. Boyce, 'The Question of Emotion in Defoe', *SP* i (1953).

D. Brooks, 'Moll Flanders: an Interpretation', *EIC* xix (1969).

R. Columbus, 'Conscious Artistry in *Moll Flanders*', *SEL* iii (1963).

W. de la Mare, *Desert Islands, and Robinson Crusoe* (London, 1930).

D. Donoghue, 'The Values of *Moll Flanders*', *SR* lxxi (1963).

R. C. Elliott (ed.) *Twentieth Century Interpretations of Moll Flanders* (Englewood Cliffs, N.J., 1970).

F. Ellis (ed.), *Twentieth Century Interpretations of Robinson Crusoe* (Englewood Cliffs, N.J., 1969).

E. M. Forster, *Aspects of the Novel* (London, 1927).

C. Gildon, *Robinson Crusoe Examin'd and Criticis'd*, ed. Paul Dottin (London and Paris, 1923).

M. Greif, 'The Conversion of Robinson Crusoe', *SEL* vi (1966).

W. Halewood, 'Religion and Invention in *Robinson Crusoe*', *EIC* xiv (1964).

W. Hazlitt, 'Life of Defoe', in *Works* (London, 1840–3).

G. Hübener, 'Der Kaufmann Robinson Crusoe', *Englishe Studien*, lix (1920).

R. D. Hume, 'The Conclusion of Defoe's *Roxana*', *Eighteenth-Century Studies*, iii (1970).

J. P. Hunter, *The Reluctant Pilgrim: Defoe's Emblematic Method and Quest for Form in Robinson Crusoe* (Baltimore, Md., 1966).

J. Jack, '*A New Voyage Round the World*, Defoe's Roman à Thèse', *HLQ* xxiv (1961).

A. Kettle, 'In Defence of Moll Flanders', in J. Butt (ed.), *Of Books and Mankind: Essays and Poems Presented to Bonamy Dobrée* (London, 1964).

H. L. Koonce, 'Moll's Muddle: Defoe's Use of Irony in *Moll Flanders*', *ELH* xxx (1963).

J. Le Clerc, *Bibliotheque ancienne et moderne*, xv (1721).

F. R. Leavis, *The Great Tradition* (London and New York, 1948).

Q. D. Leavis, *Fiction and the Reading Public* (London, 1932).

P. Longueville, *The Hermit* (London, 1727).

W. McBurney, 'Colonel Jacque: Defoe's Definition of the Complete Gentleman', *SEL* ii (1962).

A. D. McKillop, *The Early Masters of English Fiction* (Lawrence, Kans., 1956)

W. Nicholson, *The Historical Sources of Defoe's Journal of the Plague Year* (Boston, Mass., 1919).

M. E. Novak, 'Moll Flanders' First Love', *Papers of Michigan Academy of Science, Arts, and Letters*, xlvi (1961).

—— 'Colonel Jack's "Thieving Roguing" Trade to Mexico and Defoe's Attack upon Economic Individualism', *HLQ* xxiv (1961).

—— *Economics and the Fiction of Daniel Defoe* (Berkeley, Calif., 1962).

—— *Defoe and the Nature of Man* (Oxford, 1963).

—— 'Defoe's Theory of Fiction', *SP* lxi (1964).

—— 'Conscious Irony in *Moll Flanders*', *College English*, xxvi (1964).

—— 'Simon Forecastle's Weekly Journal', *TSLL* vi (1965).

—— 'Defoe's Use of Irony', in H. T. Swedenberg (ed.) *The Uses of Irony* (Los Angeles, Calif., 1966).

—— 'Crime and Punishment in Defoe's *Roxana*', *JEGP* lxv (1966).

—— 'Defoe's *Shortest Way with the Dissenters*: Hoax, Parody, Paradox, Fiction, Irony, and Satire', *MLQ* xxvii (1966).

—— 'Defoe's "Indifferent Monitor" ': the Complexity of Moll Flanders', *Eighteenth-Century Studies*, iii (1970).

—— 'A Whiff of Scandal in the Life of Daniel Defoe', *HLQ* xxxiv (1970).

S. Peterson, 'The Matrimonial Theme of Defoe's *Roxana*', *PMLA* lxx (1955).

W. Piper, 'Moll Flanders as a Structure of Topics', *SEL* ix (1969).

M. Price, *To the Palace of Wisdom* (New York, 1964).

J. H. Raleigh, 'Style and Structure in Defoe's *Roxana*', *University of Kansas City Review*, xx (1953).

J. Read, *The Weekly Journal*, 8 November 1718, 22 November 1718.

H. Robins, 'How Smart Was Robinson Crusoe?', *PMLA* lxvii (1952).

Pat Rogers, 'Defoe in the Fleet Prison', *RES* xxii (1971).

M. Schonhorn (ed.), *Accounts of the Apparition of Mrs. Veal*, by Daniel Defoe *et al.*, Augustan Reprint Society, no. 115 (Los Angeles, Calif., 1965).

—— 'Defoe's *Captain Singleton*: A Reassessment with Observations', *Papers on Language and Literature* vii (1971).

M. Schorer, 'A Study in Defoe: Moral Vision and Structural Form', *Thought*, xxv (1950).

Sir Walter Scott, 'Defoe', *Miscellaneous Works*, iv (Edinburgh, 1880).

G. J. Scrimgeour, 'The Problem of Realism in Defoe's *Captain Singleton*', *HLQ* xxvii (1963).

A. W. Secord, *Studies in the Narrative Method of Defoe* (Urbana, Ill., 1924).

—— *Robert Drury's Journal* (Urbana, Ill., 1961).

S. C. Sen, *Daniel Defoe. His Mind and Art* (Calcutta, 1948).

M. Shinagel, *Defoe and Middle-Class Gentility* (Cambridge, Mass., 1968).

J. Spence, *Observations, Anecdotes and Characters of Books and Men*, ed. J. M. Osborn (2 vols., Oxford, 1966).

G. Starr, *Defoe and Spiritual Autobiography* (Princeton, N.J., 1965).

L. Stephen, 'Defoe's Novels', *Hours in a Library* (3 vols., London, 1874–9).

James Sutherland, *Daniel Defoe a Critical Study* (Boston, 1971).

H. Swados, 'Robinson Crusoe—The Man Alone', *Antioch Review*, xviii (1958)

A. Tate, 'Techniques of Fiction', *SR* lii (1944).

W. Trent, *Daniel Defoe and How to Know Him* (New York, 1916).

D. Van Ghent, *The English Novel: Form and Function* (New York, 1953).

I. Watt, 'Robinson Crusoe as a Myth', *EIC* i (1951).

—— *The Rise of the Novel* (Berkeley, Calif., 1957).

—— 'The Critical Fortunes of *Moll Flanders*', *Eighteenth-Century Studies*, i (1967).

V. Woolf, *The Common Reader* (London, 1924).

—— *The Second Common Reader* (London, 1932).

BIOGRAPHIES AND LETTERS

F. Bastion, 'James Foe, Merchant, Father of Defoe', *N & Q* (March, 1964).

T. Cibber, *Lives of the Poets of Great Britain and Ireland to the time of Dean Swift* (5 vols., London, 1753); vol. iv contains a life of Defoe.

D. Defoe, 'An Appeal to Honour and Justice', in J. Boulton (ed.), *Defoe* (London, 1965).

P. Dottin, *Daniel Defoe et ses romans* (3 vols., Paris, 1924).

B. Fitzgerald, *Daniel Defoe. A Study in Conflict* (London, 1954).

W. Freeman, *The Incredible Defoe* (London, 1950).

G. Healey (ed.), *The Letters of Daniel Defoe* (Oxford, 1955).

W. Lee, *Daniel Defoe: His Life and Recently Discovered Writings* (3 vols., London, 1869).

W. Minto, *Daniel Defoe* (London, 1879).

J. R. Moore, *Daniel Defoe, Citizen of the Modern World* (Chicago, 1958).

M. Shinagel, *Defoe and Middle-Class Gentility* (Cambridge, Mass., 1968).

J. Sutherland, *Defoe* (London, 1938; rev. edn., 1950).

A. West, *The Mountain in the Sunlight* (London, 1958).

W. Wilson, *Memoirs of the Life and Times of Daniel De Foe* (3 vols., London, 1830).

T. Wright, *The Life of Daniel Defoe* (London, 1894; rev. edn., 1931).

BIBLIOGRAPHIES

J. Alden (ed.), *A Catalog of the Defoe Collection in the Boston Public Library* (Boston, Mass., 1966).

R. M. Baine 'Defoe's Imaginary Voyages to the Moon', *PMLA* lxxxi (1966).

—— 'Chalmers's First Bibliography of Daniel Defoe', *TSLL* x (1969).

—— *Daniel Defoe and the Supernatural*, (Athens, Ga., 1969).

P. A. Brown *et al.* (edd.), 'Annual Bibliography', *PMLA* lxxii (1957—).

R. S. Crane *et al.* (edd.), 'English Literature, 1660–1800: A Current Bibliography', *PQ* (4 vols., 1926–60, bound; Princeton, N.J., 1950, 1962).

W. Gückel and E. Günther, 'D. Defoes und J. Swifts Belesenheit und Literarische Kritik', *Palaestra*, 149 (Leipzig, 1925).

W. Hazlitt, 'Chronological Catalogue of the Works of Daniel Defoe', in *The Works of Daniel Defoe* (3 vols., London, 1840–1843).

H. Heidenreich (ed.), *The Libraries of Daniel Defoe and Phillips Farewell* (Berlin, 1970).

L. L. Hubbard, 'Text Changes in the Taylor Editions of *Robinson Crusoe*', *PBSA* xx (1928).

H. C. Hutchins, 'Daniel Defoe', in F. W. Bateson (ed.), *CBEL* ii (Cambridge, 1941).

—— *Robinson Crusoe and Its Printing 1719–1731* (New York, 1925).

B. G. Iványi, 'Defoe's Prelude to the Family Instructor', *TLS* 7 April 1966.

S. Lee *et al.* (edd.), *The Years Work in English Studies*, The English Association, i–xlvi (1919–65).

W. Lee, 'A Chronological Catalogue of Daniel Defoe's Works', in *Daniel Defoe: His Life and Recently Discovered Writings*, i (3 vols., London, 1869).

J. R. Moore, 'The Canon of Defoe's Writings', *Library*, 5th ser. xi (1956).

—— *A Checklist of the Writings of Daniel Defoe* (Bloomington, Ind., 1961; rev. 1962).

—— 'Defoe Acquisitions at the Huntington Library', *HLQ* xxviii (1964).

M. E. Novak, *Economics and the Fiction of Daniel Defoe*, (Berkeley, Calif., 1962).

—— 'Daniel Defoe', in George Watson (ed.), *NCBEL* ii (Cambridge, 1969).

E. A. Peers *et al.* (edd.), *Annual Bibliography of English Literature*, The Modern Humanities Research Association, i–xli (1921–66).

J. M. S. Tompkins and H. W. Husbands, 'Daniel Defoe', in George Watson (ed.), *CBEL* v (Cambridge, 1957).

W. Wilson, 'Catalogue of De Foe's Works', *Memoirs of the Life and Times of Daniel De Foe* (3 vols., London, 1830).

BACKGROUND READING

C. E. Burch, 'Notes on the Contemporary Popularity of Defoe's *Review*', *PQ* xvi (1937).

M. Campbell, *Defoe's First Poem* (Bloomington, Ind., 1938).

B. Dobrée, *English Literature in the Early Eighteenth Century* (Oxford, 1959).

B. Ford (ed.), *From Dryden to Johnson*, Pelican Guide to English Literature, iv (Harmondworth, 1956).

I. Kramnick, *Bolingbroke and His Circle*, (Cambridge, Mass., 1968).

A. E. Levett, 'Daniel Defoe', in F. J. C. Hearnshaw (ed.), *The Social and Political Ideas of Some Thinkers of the Augustan Age* (London, 1928).

J. R. Moore, *Defoe in the Pillory and Other Studies* (Bloomington, Ind., 1939).

W. L. Payne, *Mr. Review* (New York, 1947).

J. F. Ross, *Swift and Defoe* (Berkeley, Calif., 1941).

R. Stamm, 'Daniel Defoe: an Artist in the Puritan Tradition', *PQ* xv (1939).

G. Starr, *Defoe and Casuistry* (Princeton, N.J., 1971).

L. Stephen, *History of English Thought in the Eighteenth Century* (2 vols., London and New York, 1876).

G. M. Trevelyan, *England under Queen Anne* (3 vols., London, 1930–4).

B. Willey, *The Eighteenth-Century Background* (London, 1940).

3 · SWIFT 1667–1745

Louis A. Landa

TEXTS

Jonathan Swift, a controversial figure during his life, remains to this day the subject of extended controversy. Perhaps no aspects of this great satirist have proved more troublesome than that of determining the canon and the texts, the problem, that is, of distinguishing with confidence his authentic works from the many false attributions, and the related problem, equally difficult, of establishing authoritative printed versions which represent precisely what Swift wrote and how he wished it to come down to posterity. Although these are problems for the specialized scholar, they are worth mentioning in order to warn all prospective readers of Swift to exercise caution. Any edition of Swift's writings which happens to be available should not be accepted automatically as satisfactory. A good rule of thumb is to avoid editions printed in the eighteenth and nineteenth centuries. The twentieth century, which takes pride in having refined the principles and practices of editing, is more to be trusted, though not always. Fortunately we now have a standard edition of Swift's prose works, reliably edited by Herbert Davis, with occasional assistance from three other Swift scholars. This is the Shakespeare Head Edition, published at Oxford, in fourteen volumes (1939–68). The Introductions to the volumes in this edition, taken collectively, present a valuable, informative account of various aspects of Swift's life and times and of the circumstances which prompted him to write particular works. For our present purposes, confined to his prose fiction, the two relevant volumes are volume i (containing *A Tale of A Tub* and *The Battle of the Books*) and volume xi (containing *Gulliver's Travels*). These are the works of Swift which are distinctively narrative in method and have some of the qualities we ordinarily associate with prose fiction.

These three works have often been reprinted. The standard edition of *A Tale of a Tub* and *The Battle of the Books* is the one prepared by A. C. Guthkelch and D. Nichol Smith, 2nd edn., 1958. Of the many editions this has the fullest annotation of the texts and in the Introduction there is the most complete account of sources, circumstances of composition, and other important related matters. For ordinary

purposes the reprinting of these works in some easily available anthologies, such as those listed under REFERENCES below, will serve. A
definitive, fully annotated edition of *Gulliver's Travels* remains to be
done; but a number of inexpensive editions are generally acceptable
for student use. Two of the more extensively annotated are those
edited by Arthur E. Case (1938), and Louis A. Landa (1960). Editions with fewer annotations or none are available in abundance,
prepared by Peter Dixon, Philip Pinkus, Martin Price, Ricardo
Quintana, Edward Rosenheim, J. F. Ross, Miriam Kosh Starkman,
and C. L. Jenkins (with an Introduction by Donald Greene).

CRITICAL STUDIES AND COMMENTARY

Of the making of books about Swift there is no end. As might be
expected, *Gulliver's Travels* is the focus of critical attention. In the
second half of the eighteenth century and throughout the nineteenth
century, and even well into the twentieth century, critical comment
was very often conditioned by two striking aspects of Swift's personality, his presumed insanity and his misanthropy. The result was a
crude and invalid reading of the work in which faulty biographical
evidence was brought to bear in interpreting *Gulliver's Travels* and,
simultaneously and conversely, *Gulliver's Travels* was brought to bear
in interpreting the man. In Swiftian criticism these were the decades
of disapproval of both the man and his work, primarily on ethical
and religious grounds, even though his genius was recognized. The
development of this criticism has been treated at length by Donald
M. Berwick in *The Reputation of Jonathan Swift, 1781–1882* (1941),
and briefly by Merrel D. Clubb, in 'The Criticism of Gulliver's
"Voyage to the Houyhnhnms", 1726–1914', *Stanford Studies in
Language and Literature* (1941), and by Milton Voigt, in *Swift and the
Twentieth Century* (1964), Chapter I, pp. 3–27. A notable strain in the
criticism of the nineteenth century particularly was the tendency to
view *Gulliver's Travels*, especially Part IV, as the product of a diseased
mind, a view rejected by the informed critics of the twentieth century
as naïve and unsound. Nevertheless, echoes of this view persist today
in a different guise more congenial to these times: the psychoanalysts
have seized upon *Gulliver's Travels* as a document which reveals, in
their opinion, that Swift was neurotic or schizoid or obsessive, and
that implicit in the *Travels* is evidence of such neurotic traits as coprophilia, voyeurism, exhibitionism, mysophobia, impotency, anal
eroticism, and narcissistic gratification. Two of these studies may be
mentioned with a caution that reputable Swift critics consider them
and similar pyschoanalytic interpretations with great scepticism, and

regard them as vitiated frequently by the failure of the psychoanalyst to have full or accurate knowledge of Swift, or to take into account the literary and intellectual traditions which nourished Swift and which explain more convincingly both him and his masterpiece: Phyllis Greenacre's *Swift and Carroll: A Psychoanalytic Study of Two Lives* (1955), and Dr. Benjamin Karpman, 'Neurotic Traits of Jonathan Swift as Revealed by *Gulliver's Travels*: A Minor Contribution to the Problem of Psychosexual Infantalism and Coprophilia', *Psychoanalytic Review*, xxix (1942), 26–45, 165–84.

A fundamental objection, among others, to studies of this nature is that the literary work is converted into a medical case-history; and that the commentators repeat, in extreme form, what might be called the biographical fallacy of nineteenth-century critics, the tendency to identify Lemuel Gulliver, a literary character, with his creator, Jonathan Swift. Much of the recent commentary is a reaction to earlier crude attempts to identify the two. It is now a truism in Gulliverian criticism that Gulliver is *not* Swift, that he is a *persona* to be viewed independently of the author of *Gulliver's Travels*. An influential, pioneering article by Ricardo Quintana, ('Situational Satire: A Commentary on the Method of Swift', set the tone for many later studies by insisting that Gulliver is a fully realized character moving about in a fully realized world. After the appearance of this article a trend appeared in the criticism. It can be characterized by the word *formal*. The critics who find this approach congenial wish to avoid or reduce the emphasis earlier critics had placed on the biographical or social or intellectual background; or perhaps it is fairer to say that they wish to use historical background with more sophistication. But fundamentally their intention is to explicate the work in terms of its formal qualities, such as theme, structure, character, situation, and satiric and other rhetorical devices. Several books in this category are worth mentioning as typical. They illustrate well how the highly refined and subtle analysis of the literary work itself, so characteristic of modern criticism, can yield fruitful results: Martin Price, *Swift's Rhetorical Art: A Study in Structure and Meaning* (1953); John M. Bullitt, *Jonathan Swift and the Anatomy of Satire: A Study of Satiric Technique* (1953); William E. Ewald, *The Masks of Swift* (1954); Edward W. Rosenheim, *Swift and the Satirist's Art* (1963).

One important result of this intense critical gaze has been the preoccupation with the 'character' of Lemuel Gulliver. This is logical enough since he is to the *Travels* what Hamlet is to Shakespeare's play. What is Gulliver, who is he? The most frequent answer is that he is a *persona*, a fictive device manipulated by Swift for narrative and satiric purposes, not to be considered as we consider a character or developed personality in a novel. This matter is canvassed with great keenness in Robert C. Elliott's *The Power of Satire: Magic, Ritual, Art* (1960), where we are told that 'Swift does not create a sense of reality about Gulliver. Gulliver is not a character in the sense that Tom Jones, say, is a character. He has the most minimal subjective life ...' (p. 200). But when Mr. Elliott analyses Gulliver, the very language itself suggests that Gulliver is in fact a personality, capable of satiric insight, of embarrassment, of the desire to ingratiate himself. A number of critics have not resisted the temptation to give Gulliver a subjective life; they have at times seen Lemuel Gulliver, or at least written about him, as though he is an integrated personality with motives, attitudes, impulses, and feelings grounded in experience. The worst offender in this respect is the author of an article which has the merit of being a pioneering effort to distinguish between Swift and Gulliver, John B. Moore's 'The Role of Gulliver' (1928). It may be that the critics who have ruled out an historical approach —an interpretation of the 'character' of Gulliver in terms of the intellectual and social background—are faced with special difficulties. It is possible that the *formal* approach cannot deal adequately with the relation between *persona* and character. The problem is pondered with great interest by Ian Watt, in 'The Ironic Tradition in Augustan Prose from Swift to Johnson'. Here we find a persuasive suggestion, that in Part IV of the *Travels* Swift has involved Gulliver in situations which, though they were intended to represent abstract issues, do actually provoke intense emotional participation by readers, to the extent that Lemuel Gulliver is transformed from *persona* into character. Swift has unwittingly turned a puppet into a human being. In simple terms the issue tacitly under debate is the extent to which Swift has endowed Gulliver with a psyche either by design or by accident. Occasionally the discussions leave the impression that we are to accept him as a man with a continuous life-history, but this is an unstated rather than an acknowledged assumption—and much too naïve for all but a few. It may be said, perhaps incautiously, that Swift is not interested in Gulliver as a *man* but as a representation of *mankind*, of human nature. He is a flexible 'character' (as distinct from a personality), whose fundamental function is philosophical or intellectual, and as such is constantly being manipulated to represent a diversity of views or ideas being satirically explored, a device, a kind of domestic and foreign observer, around whom and through whom the satire ceaselessly flows. He is, of course, functional in carrying on the narrative; but the significant order of reality which he represents has not to do with flesh and blood but with the allegorical and the abstract.

The 'rediscovery' of Lemuel Gulliver—a fully realized character (in Quintana's phrase) not to be identified with Jonathan Swift—has led some critics to the very opposite of the traditional view that Gulliver is the mouthpiece of Swift's pessimism and misanthropy. Swift, the argument is, has presented us with a deluded and dehumanized Gulliver, himself the object of Swift's satire. Such is the 'final comedy' of Part IV of the *Travels*, as John F. Ross calls it in his article 'The Final Comedy of Lemuel Gulliver'. Or as Samuel Holt Monk remarks: 'Swift directs his savage, comic gaze straight at Gulliver and his insane pretensions'; see Monk's 'The Pride of Lemuel Gulliver', reprinted in *Eighteenth-Century English Literature: Modern Essays in Criticism*, ed. James L. Clifford (New York, 1959). In this view we are asked to believe that it is not Swift but Gulliver who has turned away from humanity to darkness or madness or intolerable pride. He, not Swift, is the misanthrope, and as such is the object of Swift's satire. For an effective challenge to this view one should turn to Ronald S. Crane's essay 'The Houyhnhnms, the Yahoos, and the History of Ideas', in *Reason and the Imagination: Studies in the History of Ideas, 1600–1800*, ed. J. A. Mazzeo (1962). As a preliminary to the recent interpretations of Part IV, which has come to be considered the crucial part of the *Travels*, one may turn to the summary of earlier interpretations in Merrel D. Clubb's 'The Criticism of Gulliver's "Voyage to the Houyhnhnms", 1726–1914'. There exists an interesting parallel over a period of two centuries in the respective critical interpretations of Lemuel Gulliver and the Houyhnhnms: just as Gulliver was thought to be the spokesman for Swift, so the Houyhnhnms were almost invariably considered to be an expression of Swift's utopian views. The tradition has been that the land of the noble horses represented an ideal commonwealth, to which man could aspire, but which he had miserably failed to attain. Now with the view of Gulliver as a satiric butt, the Houyhnhnms, as well, have come under indictment as unacceptably stolid and cold—not an allegorization of ideal norms for man, but actually repellent—and themselves the embodiment of pride, even of two of the most dangerous of all eighteenth-century heterodoxies, deism and stoicism. Critics who maintain this view vary, but they have in common a central thesis: Gulliver, they assert, has radically misinterpreted the true nature of the Houyhnhnms (as have most critics and readers of the past) by absurdly accepting them as ideal beings. Swift, we are told, did not intend them to be so taken. Among the proponents of this theory in one form or another is Kathleen Williams, who set it forth in an article, 'Gulliver's Voyage to the Houyhnhnms', and later incorporated it into her book, *Jonathan Swift and the Age of Compromise* (1958) (see especially pages 154–209). Similar interpretations may be found in the articles, already mentioned, by Ross and Monk. Even Irvin Ehrenpreis, the eminent biographer of Swift, fell in with this group temporarily by suggesting in his *The Personality of Jonathan Swift* (1958), pp. 99 ff., that the Houyhnhnms combine deistic and stoic views of human nature. A convincing rejection of this point of view came from George Sherburn in a notable article, 'Errors concerning the Houyhnhnms', and from Ronald S. Crane, 'The Rationale of the Fourth Voyage', in *Jonathan Swift: Gulliver's Travels*, ed. R. A. Greenberg (1961), pp. 300–7. And Ehrenpreis, after further consideration, recanted his earlier view, in 'The Meaning of Gulliver's Last Voyage'. Here he concludes that the Houyhnhnms may be accepted as 'ideal patterns where Swift is setting them off against man's irrationality, and as comic figures where he is smiling at the whole project of bestowing concrete life upon unattainable abstractions'. Thus Ehrenpreis mediates between the two broad views, the traditional one that the Houyhnhnms represent utopian ideals and the recent one that they are the objects of Swift's satire, a compromise which Miss Williams would probably accept.

Of the many other strains in Gulliverian commentary we must confine ourselves to two. One of these is observable in several commentators who have endeavoured to show that the *Travels* reflect in some important respects Swift's thinking as a Christian divine. Here the assumption is that a man who was an active clergyman for a quarter of a century before writing *Gulliver's Travels* would almost inevitably inject some of his professional ideas into the book. This too is a view with a long tradition. It was stated as early as 1755, by Swift's relation and biographer, Deane Swift, in *An Essay upon the Life, Writings, and Character of Dr. Jonathan Swift*. The Christian conception of the evil nature of man, Deane Swift asserted, is the 'groundwork of the whole satyre contained in the voyage to the Houyhnhnms'. In 1926 this general viewpoint was interestingly restated by T. O. Wedel in 'On the Philosophical Background of *Gulliver's Travels*', and again, more elaborately, by Louis A. Landa, in 1946: 'A good case can be made for Part IV of *Gulliver* as being in its implications Christian apologetics, though of course in non-theological terms; in a sense it is an allegory which veils human nature and society as a Christian divine views them. It is by [extension] a defence of the doctrine of redemption and man's need of grace'; see

'Jonathan Swift: The Critical Significance of Biographical Evidence' in *English Institute Essays, 1946* (1947). Three other commentators, not content with a purely formal approach, have cogently applied a biographical and historical approach in an attempt to demonstrate that Christian strains are present in the *Travels*. The first of these is Ernest Tuveson, whose article, 'Swift: the Dean as Satirist' is supplemented by two articles of unusual interest, Roland M. Frye's 'The Yahoos and the Christian Symbols of Sin', and Donald Greene's significant, more general study of the pervasiveness of Augustinian views of man's nature in eighteenth-century thought: 'Augustinianism and Empiricism: A Note on Eighteenth-Century English Intellectual History'. These commentators do not argue that the *Travels* is a religious work: they see it as secular, in which a distinctly Christian view of human nature is present. But Ronald S. Crane, the foremost proponent of a formal approach (though he often richly uses an historical approach), rejects an interpretation of the work in these terms. He finds no evidence, internal or external, that Swift so conceived the *Travels* (see 'The Rationale of the Fourth Voyage', already referred to).

The critics who have been concerned with the intellectual aspect of *Gulliver's Travels* as distinct from its artistry have in recent years been giving attention to Part III. In the past Part III has often been dismissed as episodic and ineffective, with scant attention paid to its substance. But now we have come to see that Swift's treatment of science in this portion of the book is of very special interest. He was living in the age of Boyle and Newton, in the period of exciting scientific investigations which became the basis for our modern science; and Swift's assimilation and use of scientific ideas for his satiric purposes are particularly evident in Part III. The old notion that he had an antipathy for science, stemming from his student days at Trinity College, Dublin, has been discarded. It is more likely that any presumed aversion to science (and it is only a presumption) rose out of an uneasiness, shared with many contemporaries, that science was receiving emphasis and support at the expense of moral philosophy (the contemporary phrase for ethics or the knowledge of man); or it may be that he reacted against the excessive claims in some quarters for what science could accomplish. Like his contemporaries, Swift felt that the study of man—of human nature—was the proper study of mankind. But his age was the witness of many impractical, speculative, and trivial experiments, often carried on by the most highly respected scientists under the aegis of the Royal Society. These abuses or corruptions of science became the objects of satire from the inception of the Royal Society at the Restoration; and Swift should be seen as only one of many literary men who laughed at the pretensions of some scientists and some experiments. A useful introduction to the subject is George R. Potter's 'Swift and Natural Science', but the most brilliant and extended studies of this aspect of *Gulliver's Travels* are Marjorie H. Nicolson's *The Microscope and English Imagination*, a monograph in Smith College Studies in Modern Languages, and her article (with Nora Mohler), 'The Scientific Background of Swift's *Voyage to Laputa*'. Both have been reprinted in Miss Nicolson's book, *Science and Imagination* (paperback, 1956).

The other two works by Swift with which we are concerned, *A Tale of A Tub* and *The Battle of the Books*, are the subject of critical analysis in the general studies already mentioned, those by Quintana, Price, Ewald, Kathleen Williams, Elliott, and E. W. Rosenheim, as well as others. In addition, Quintana has provided for *A Tale* a useful, brief survey of the variety of critical approaches in recent criticism: see his 'Emile Pons and the Modern Study of Swift's *A Tale of a Tub* (1965)'. The alleged indecencies and irreverence of the work, which preoccupied critics in the eighteenth and nineteenth centuries, now receive little attention. It is the complexity, allusiveness, and brilliancy of *A Tale* which today seem more striking, as well as its rich intellectual substance. Of the many discussions of Swift's satiric effectiveness in this early piece one can profitably begin with Quintana's *Swift: An Introduction* (1955); then, for a more elaborate analysis, one should follow with Edward Rosenheim's *Swift and the Satirist's Art* (1963). If one is to understand *A Tale* and *The Battle of the Books* in their historical and cultural aspects, one must turn to the distinguished study by Richard Foster Jones, *Ancients and Moderns: A Study in the Background of the 'Battle of the Books'* (1936), where the controversy over ancient and modern cultures, a matter of supreme importance to the seventeenth and eighteenth centuries, is elaborately treated in its scientific and other phases. Since these two works by Swift are part of that controversy, the background supplied by Jones is vital. For most students the abridged version, supplied by Jones himself, in *The Seventeenth Century: Studies in the History of English Thought and Literature from Bacon to Pope*, will serve; or one may turn to a briefer treatment of the subject by Anne Burlingame, '*The Battle of the Books' in its Historical Setting* (1920).

The two major strains in *A Tale*, the satire of what Swift and many of his contemporaries conceived to be corruptions in religion and learning, have been examined often and fully in many articles and in several books. One of the more effective studies of Swift's attack on the abuses of learning is Miriam Kosh Starkman's highly specialized but readable and informative book, *Swift's Satire on Learning in 'A Tale of a Tub'* (1950). Mrs. Starkman reveals Swift's essential conservatism in her analysis of his reaction to the Moderns, to their faith in the new experimental science of the Royal Society and to their belief in progress and innovation. She is particularly illuminating in distinguishing the various Swiftian antipathies to a number of cultural aspects of modernity which he considered erroneous or dangerous or absurd and therefore proper targets for satiric indictment—materialism, pedantry, Epicureanism, and Cartesianism, among others.

Mrs. Starkman's critical commentary on the satire of learning in *A Tale* has its complement in Philip Harth's examination of the other phase of the book—the religious—in *Swift and Anglican Rationalism: The Religious Background of 'A Tale of a Tub'* (1961). For generations Swift was accused of having passed beyond the bounds of orthodoxy: *A Tale*, many critics complained, is irreverent and impious, even obscene—a banter upon the religion of Jesus Christ, so one of Swift's contemporaries called it. Disturbed by such accusations in his own day Swift defended himself in an 'Apology' introduced into the fifth edition of the work in 1710: he maintained that he was exercising the valid functions of the satirist in exposing the follies and errors in religion, not religion itself. In our times the sincerity of this 'Apology' is generally accepted (with occasional dissent), though of course the intolerance of his age, which Swift embodied, is rejected. For the critic of the twentieth century the religious controversies of the seventeenth century constitute an historical fact which, when used by a literary author, is to be viewed with detachment and subjected to critical assessment like any other fact. Harth's book is an example of the distance that modern criticism of *A Tale* has travelled from the older kind. Harth has profited from the ingenious and sophisticated methods of others, but unlike some of them he hesitates to impose unity or a thesis on this exceedingly complex work. He takes literally Swift's remark in the 'Apology' of 1710, that the work is concerned with abuses in religion and in learning; and for him this duality indicates the nature and structure of *A Tale*: two separate subjects, with different backgrounds, each given distinct treatment. Harth, whose concern is with the religious aspect of the work, emphasizes what is too often forgotten, that *A Tale of a Tub* in fact derives from the seventeenth century, and that we must look for its meaning to Swift's assimilation of rationalistic currents of thought in the Anglicanism of the Restoration period. From his reading of the Anglican rationalists, such divines as made up the groups known as Cambridge Platonists and Latitudinarians (who in their turn stemmed from Richard Hooker), Swift drew both the substance and the method of his religious satire in *A Tale*. Although he added dimensions to what he drew from these sources, Swift, so Mr. Harth argues, uses for his satiric intentions the ideas and rhetorical conventions of these polemical divines, the very ideas and methods that they themselves had used earlier in attacking Catholicism, Non-conformity, atheism, and scepticism.

BIOGRAPHIES AND LETTERS

The biographies of Swift written in the eighteenth and nineteenth centuries are being replaced by the massive, detailed, critical biography by Ehrenpreis, to be complete in three volumes, two of which have now appeared. The title of this work indicates its wide scope: *Swift the Man, His Works, and His Age*. For the casual student or reader of Swift this excellent biography may be on a scale too extensive, but it is now the final authority on biographical matters. If other biographies are used, they should be corrected or supplemented by reference to Ehrenpreis. Note too that it contains valuable critical comment on Swift's works and background as well as biographical matters. Ehrenpreis has given us another book of great value, *The Personality of Jonathan Swift* (1958), not strictly biographical, but significantly and incidentally so, in that it discusses three puzzling aspects of Swift with which every biographer must cope: first, Swift's relations with the two women who played the most important roles in his life (the Stella and Vanessa of his letters and poetry); secondly, the alleged obscenity of his writings; and thirdly, his old age and mental decay. The main purpose of this brief work is to show how Swift's personality is reflected in his writing; and thus what we have is a combination of biography and criticism. But we may well take the book as meeting the demand made by George Sherburn in a highly influential article, 'Methods in Books about Swift'. In this indispensable article Sherburn pleaded for biographers and critics to avoid the customary theatrical and sensational treatment of the facts of Swift's life and personality which for generations had coloured and distorted critical interpretations. Ehrenpreis examined coolly, in the light of the established facts, the aspects of Swift which so often in the past have been exploited for melodramatic effects, and he gives a picture of Swift in sensible and acceptable terms. Sherburn's article and Ehrenpreis's *The Personality of Swift* go far in dispelling many of the myths and legends which have kept us from seeing Swift plainly.

By far the best brief introduction to Swift, the man and his works, is Ricardo Quintana's *Swift: An Introduction* (1955). This is a critical biography by a distinguished scholar whose writings on Swift, the result of many years of patient study and reflection, have been highly influential. The first chapter is a summary of Swift's life, and the remaining chapters consider particular phases of his career mingled with analyses of the works relevant to these phases. It is a sound and readable account which serves well as a point of departure for specific aspects of Swift or for more elaborate general treatment, such as may be found in Quintana's excellent *The Mind and Art of Swift* (1936), a vade-mecum which is a landmark in modern Swift studies. Obviously no single book can adequately treat all phases of Swift's long, complex career. For a fuller treatment one has to turn to more specialized studies. Since these are likely to be more formidable than many students will tolerate, the few mentioned here are presented with diffidence. Swift's relations with Esther Johnson, the Stella of his verse and of his fascinating *Journal to Stella*, are examined sensibly by Herbert Davis in a pleasant, brief book, *Stella: A Gentlewoman of the Eighteenth Century* (1942), reprinted in Davis's collection: *Jonathan Swift: Essays on his Satire and Other Studies* (1964). If one wishes to understand more fully Swift's career as a churchman, one may turn to Louis A. Landa's *Swift and the Church of Ireland* (1954). For an excellent account of Swift's activities and writings on behalf of Ireland we have Oliver Ferguson's *Swift and Ireland* (1962). Swift's brilliant four years in England, from 1710 to 1714, when he was the leading journalist of Queen Anne's last ministry and the associate of eminent statesmen and of other writers, have been treated by Bertrand Goldgar in *The Curse of Party: Swift's Relations with Addison and Steele* (1961). And for that inescapable subject, the perennial preoccupation of the critics, Swift's 'madness', one should turn to an article by Sir Walter Russell Brain, a distinguished medical scientist, and later first Lord Brain, who published an informed and persuasive explanation: 'The Illness of Dean Swift'. This authoritative study, along with Ehrenpreis's, chapters on 'Madness' and 'Old Age' in *The Personality of Jonathan Swift*, where Brain's views are incorporated, gives the facts of Swift's final years. It is now accepted that Swift was not insane in a *medical* sense even though he was declared *legally* incompetent (at the age of nearly 75) to manage his person or his affairs, as a result of a petition by friends who realized that his failing memory and understanding necessitated a guardian. He was, it is true, sinking into physical and mental lethargy, showing the ravages of illness and old age, suffering from Ménière's syndrome (which affected his balance and his hearing) and from orbital cellulitis (which affected his vision). He appears also to have suffered a stroke in 1742, at the age of 75, which affected his speech. But these were deteriorative organic factors, not insanity, though the interesting diagnosis made by Dr. Brain does not rule out mental and emotional factors interwoven with or intensified by the neurological aspects of Swift's case; nor does it ignore the presence in Swift of strong obsessional qualities.

Any discussion of Swift's biographers inevitably leads to mention of his letters, a primary source of multitudinous facts of his life on which the biographer must depend. The correspondence has been brought together in five volumes, edited by Harold Williams, who annotated the letters extensively, depending in part on his own wide knowledge of Swift and his times, and in part on the knowledge of F. Elrington Ball, whose edition of Swift's correspondence is incorporated into the Williams edition, 1963–5. Although Swift is not ranked with the greatest of the letter-writers, many of his letters have wit and charm; and they are consistently revealing and interesting. Unless one dips into the correspondence one is likely to miss aspects of an elusive and fascinating personality not wholly observable in the formal works. Particularly one should read some of the most revealing of all his letters, those he wrote to Esther Johnson, which disclose a tender and intimate side of Swift not found elsewhere. These too have been edited by Harold Williams: *Jonathan Swift: Journal to Stella* (2 vols., Oxford, 1948). And finally we may at this point make a passing reference to Swift's poetry, though its relevance will not be immediately evident. The fact is that an extraordinary number of his poems are biographical, and often reveal the man in a way the prose works do not. They are frequently effusions of a personal nature, revealing what he felt about his friends, or his enemies, or about social or public events. Collectively they are vital for a full understanding of the man. The authoritative edition is that by Harold Williams (3 vols., Oxford, 1958). A brief study by Maurice Johnson, *The Sin of Wit: Jonathan Swift as a Poet* (1950), offers a good introduction to the subject and may be supplemented by Herbert Davis's 'Swift's View of Poetry' and his 'Alecto's Whip', both in Davis's excellent collection, *Jonathan Swift: Essays on his Satire and Other Studies* (paperback, 1964).

BIBLIOGRAPHIES

The foregoing account refers to relatively few of the literally hundreds of books and articles devoted to Swift. Two bibliographical lists in print covering the periods 1895–1945 and 1945–65 mention respectively 573 and 659, the great majority of which are articles, although a formidable number are books. Clearly anyone confronting this mass of criticism needs guidance. Fortunately there are useful bibliographical aids. If one wishes to consult critical works published in the eighteenth and nineteenth centuries, one may turn to H. Teerink's *A Bibliography of the Writings of Jonathan Swift*, (2nd edn.) edited by Arthur H. Scouten (1963), pp. 405–31. This lists the more important critical studies up to 1895; and it may be supplemented for the period 1781–1882 by the bibliography in Donald M. Berwick's *The Reputation of Jonathan Swift, 1781–1882* (1941). For the period 1895 to 1945 consult *Jonathan Swift: A List of Critical Studies published from 1895 to 1945* (1945), by Louis A. Landa and James Edward Tobin, and for the period 1945–65 consult *A Bibliography of Swift Studies, 1945–1965* (1967), by James J. Stathis. The first of these is merely a list without description of the contents of the books or articles mentioned, though it does indicate which of the titles are likely to be most useful. The compilation by Stathis contains a brief descriptive statement appended to the titles listed. Another useful list has been compiled by Claire Lamont—'A Checklist of Critical and Biographical Writings on Jonathan Swift, 1945–1965', in *Fair Liberty was all his Cry: A Tercentenary Tribute to Jonathan Swift, 1667–1745,* ed. A. N. Jeffares (1967). The indispensable bibliographical aid is Milton Voigt's *Swift and the Twentieth Century* (1964), an excellent and wide ranging analysis and assessment both of the trends in Swift criticism and of scores of individual books and articles, major and minor. Voigt's first chapter is a useful survey of nineteenth-century criticism. The value of this book as a survey and analysis of twentieth-century criticism cannot be overestimated. Three brief but useful surveys may be mentioned: Herbert Davis, 'Recent Studies of Swift: A Survey'; Ricardo Quintana, 'A Modest Appraisal: Swift Scholarship and Criticism, 1945–65', in *Fair Liberty was all his Cry: A Tercentenary Tribute to Jonathan Swift, 1667–1745,* ed. A. Norman Jeffares (1967); and George Mayhew, 'Recent Swift Scholarship', in *Jonathan Swift, 1667–1967: A Dublin Tercentenary Tribute,* edd. Roger McHugh and Philip Edwards, (1967).

BACKGROUND READING

No one has attempted to treat in a single book the background of *Gulliver's Travels* in all of its aspects, but many of the books and articles already mentioned have background materials interwoven in the discussion. One short chapter in Quintana's *The Mind and Art of Swift* (1936), is entitled 'History and Background of the Book';

but it can only indicate briefly a few aspects of the intellectual and literary background which influenced Swift. Nevertheless, this chapter and the one titled 'Controlling Ideas' will suggest how formidable *Gulliver's Travels* is and how deeply rooted it is in its times. The most obvious point to be made about the literary background is the impact on Swift of the many earlier accounts of imaginary voyages. This literary genre had existed from the time of the Greek author, Lucian (*c*. A.D. 115–*c*. 200), and flourished in Swift's time, both on the Continent and in England; it was often, as in Swift, the vehicle of satire and social comment. A good introduction to the imaginary voyage and its vogue may be found in Philip R. Gove's *The Imaginary Voyage in Prose Fiction* (1941), and in William A. Eddy's *Gulliver's Travels: a Critical Study* (1923). Eddy's book, which is to be used cautiously when it concerns itself with Swift's sources, is nevertheless useful in displaying the variety of imaginary voyages (to the sun, the moon, to strange lands of strange beasts, to utopian communities, etc.) which are in the background of the *Travels*. Particularly for the background of Part IV of *Gulliver* with its ideal commonwealth of horses (though their idealism is now called into question in some quarters), one can read a brief study of extraordinary interest by George Boas, *The Happy Beast in French Thought of the Seventeenth Century* (1933). Here the beast fable, specifically as it grew out of rhetorical conventions and was related to the paradox, is examined. A whole theriophilic literature which depended on paradox existed, and it helps to explain the element of intellectual play in Part IV of *Gulliver*, an element often completely overlooked by critics of a solemn complexion. Since the basic point in Part IV is the paradox that beast is superior to man, it can be illuminating to observe how traditionally the paradox had been exploited by authors before Swift. The book by Boas, complemented by Henry Knight Miller's article, 'The Paradoxical Encomium with Special Reference to its Vogue in England, 1600–1800', (1956), may give the reader a new perspective in his appreciation of *Gulliver*. Also useful for Part IV is Arthur O. Lovejoy's ' "Pride" in Eighteenth-Century Thought', in his book, *Essays in the History of Ideas* (1948). For the scientific background the brilliant study by Marjorie Nicolson, *Science and Imagination* (1956), is indispensable. To this should be added R. F. Jones's 'The Background of the Attack on Science in the Age of Pope', in *Pope and His Contemporaries: Essays Presented to George Sherburn*, ed. James L. Clifford and Louis A. Landa (1949). The political milieu, so important in Parts I and II, is treated by Arthur Case in *Four Essays on 'Gulliver's Travels'* (1945), pp. 69–96. This may be supplemented by Chapter IV ('Whigs and Tories in Queen Anne's Day') in A. S. Turberville's *English Men and Manners in the Eighteenth Century* (paperback, 1961), and Chapters III–VIII in William Thomas Laprade's *Public Opinion and Politics in Eighteenth Century England* (1936). A pioneering article, still informative and differing somewhat from the interpretations offered by Arthur Case, is C. H. Firth's 'The Political Significance of *Gulliver's Travels*', (reprinted in his *Essays Historical & Literary* (1938), pp. 210–41). For more complete aspects of the political scene, we have Keith Feiling's *A History of the Tory Party, 1640–1714* (1924); G. N. Clark's *The Later Stuarts 1660–1714* (1934); and Basil Williams's, *The Whig Supremacy, 1714–1760* (1939). A pleasant, more general article touching politics, church, and social conditions, all reflected in *Gulliver's Travels*, is J. G. Simms's 'Ireland in the Age of Swift', in *Jonathan Swift: A Dublin Tercentenary Tribute, 1667–1967*, edd. Roger McHugh and Philip Edwards (1967). Finally, for aspects of the ethical and religious background, and current theories of human nature, one may consult the articles, already referred to, by T. O. Wedel, Roland Frye, and Donald Greene.

The background of *A Tale of A Tub* and *The Battle of the Books* is amply presented in R. F. Jones's *Ancients and Moderns* and Anne Burlingame's *The Battle of the Books in its Historical Setting*, both already mentioned; and again in the studies devoted specifically to *A Tale*, as those by Starkman and Harth particularly.

REFERENCES

TEXTS

(*a*) *Collected works*

H. J. Davis (ed.), *The Prose Works of Jonathan Swift* (14 vols., Oxford, 1939–68); the standard edition.

J. Horrell (ed.), *The Collected Poems of Jonathan Swift* (2 vols., London, and Cambridge, Mass., 1958).

H. J. Davis (ed.), *Swift: Poetical Works* (London, New York, and Toronto, 1967).

H. Williams (ed.), *The Poems of Jonathan Swift* (3 vols., 2nd edn., Oxford, 1968); the standard edition.

(*b*) *Selections*

W. A. Eddy (ed.), *Gulliver's Travels, A Tale of a Tub, The Battle of the Books* (Oxford, 1956).

A. C. Guthkelch and D. Nichol Smith (edd.), *A Tale of a Tub* [*and*] *The Battle of the Books* (2nd edn., Oxford, 1958); the standard edition.

J. Hayward (ed.), *Selected Prose Works of Jonathan Swift* (London, 1949).

L. A. Landa (ed.), *Gulliver's Travels and Other Writings* (Boston, Mass., 1960).

P. Pinkus (ed.), *Jonathan Swift: A Selection of his Works* (Toronto, London, and New York, 1965).

R. Quintana (ed.), *Gulliver's Travels and Other Writings* (New York, 1958).

E. Rosenheim (ed.), *Jonathan Swift: Selected Prose and Poetry* (New York, 1959).

M. K. Starkman (ed.), *Swift: Gulliver's Travels and Other Writings* (New York 1962).

C. Van Doren (ed.), *The Portable Swift* (New York, 1948; 2nd edn., London, 1968).

(c) Separate works

A. E. Case (ed.), *Gulliver's Travels* (New York, 1938).

P. Dixon and J. Chalder (edd.), *Gulliver's Travels* (Harmondsworth and Baltimore, Md., 1967).

R. A. Greenberg (ed.), *Gulliver's Travels: An Annotated Text with Critical Essays* (New York, 1961).

R. B. Heilman (ed.), *Gulliver's Travels* (New York, 1950; 2nd edn., 1969).

C. L. Jenkins and D. Greene (edd.), *Gulliver's Travels* (New York and Toronto, 1971).

L. A. Landa (ed.), *Gulliver's Travels* (Boston, Mass., 1960; London, 1965).

M. Price (ed.), *Gulliver's Travels* (Indianapolis, Ind., and New York, 1963).

P. Quennell (ed.), *Gulliver's Travels* (London, 1952).

J. F. Ross (ed.), *Gulliver's Travels* (New York, 1948).

H. Williams (ed.), *Gulliver's Travels: The Text of the First Edition, with an Introduction, Bibliography and Notes* (London, 1926).

—— (ed.), *Gulliver's Travels* (London, 1900).

CRITICAL STUDIES AND COMMENTARY

D. M. Berwick, *The Reputation of Jonathan Swift, 1781–1882* (Philadelphia, Pa., 1941).

J. M. Bullitt, *Jonathan Swift and the Anatomy of Satire: A Study of Satiric Technique* (Cambridge, Mass., 1953).

A. E. Burlingame, '*The Battle of the Books*' in its Historical Setting (New York, 1920).

A. E. Case, *Four Essays on 'Gulliver's Travels'* (Princeton, N.J., 1945).

R. S. Crane, 'The Rationale of the Fourth Voyage', in R. A. Greenberg (ed.), *Jonathan Swift: Gulliver's Travels*, (paperback, New York, 1961).

—— 'The Houyhnhnms, the Yahoos, and the History of Ideas', in J. A. Mazzeo (ed.), *Reason and the Imagination: Studies in the History of Ideas, 1600–1800* (New York and London, 1962).

M. D. Clubb, 'The Criticism of Gulliver's "Voyage to the Houyhnhnms 1726–1914",' in *Stanford Studies in Language and Literature* (1941).

H. J. Davis, 'Swift's View of Poetry' and 'Alecto's Whip', in *Jonathan Swift: Essays on His Satire and Other Studies* (paperback, New York, 1964).

—— *The Satire of Jonathan Swift* (New York, 1947).

I. Ehrenpreis, *The Personality of Jonathan Swift* (London, 1958).

—— 'The Meaning of Gulliver's Last Voyage', *Review of English Literature*, iii (1962).

R. C. Elliott, *The Power of Satire: Magic, Ritual, Art* (Princeton, N.J., 1960).

W. E. Ewald, *The Masks of Swift* (Cambridge, Mass., 1954).

R. M. Frye, 'The Yahoos and the Christian Symbols for Sin', *JHI* xv (1954).

D. Greene, 'Augustinianism and Empiricism: A Note on Eighteenth-Century English Intellectual History', *Eighteenth-Century Studies*, i (1967).

P. Harth, *Swift and Anglican Rationalism: The Religious Background of 'A Tale of A Tub'* (Chicago, 1961).

M. Johnson, *The Sin of Wit: Jonathan Swift as a Poet* (Syracuse, N.Y. 1950).

R. F. Jones, *Ancients and Moderns: A Study in the Background of the 'Battle of the Books'* (St. Louis, Mo., 1936; 2nd edn., 1961).

L. A. Landa, 'Jonathan Swift: The Critical Significance of Biographical Evidence', in *English Institute Essays, 1946* (New York, 1947).

F. R. Leavis, 'The Irony of Swift', *Scrutiny*, ii (1934); reprinted in *Determinations* (London, 1934).

S. H. Monk, 'The Pride of Lemuel Gulliver', *SR* lxiii (1955).

J. B. Moore, 'The Role of Gulliver', *MP* xxv (1928).

M. Nicolson (with N. Mohler), 'The Scientific Background of Swift's *Voyage to Laputa*', *Annals of Science*, ii (1937); reprinted in Professor Nicolson's *Science and Imagination* (1956). See also 'Swift's "Flying Island" in the Voyage to Laputa', *Annals of Science*, ii (1937).

—— *The Microscope and English Imagination*, Smith College Studies in Modern Languages, xvi, no. 4 (Northampton, Mass., 1935); reprinted in *Science and Imagination* (1956). See pp. 193–9 and *passim*.

G. R. Potter, 'Swift and Natural Science', *PQ* xx (1941).

M. Price, *Swift's Rhetorical Art: A Study in Structure and Meaning* (New Haven, Conn., and London, 1953).

R. Quintana, *The Mind and Art of Jonathan Swift* (London and New York, 1936).

—— 'Situational Satire: A Commentary on the Method of Swift', *UTQ* xvii (1948).

—— *Swift: An Introduction* (London, New York, and Toronto, 1955).

E. W. Rosenheim, jun., *Swift and the Satirist's Art* (Chicago, 1963).

J. F. Ross, 'The Final Comedy of Lemuel Gulliver', *Studies in the Comic*, University of California Publications in English, no. 8 (1941).

G. Sherburn, 'Errors concerning the Houyhnhnms', *MP* lvi (1958).

—— 'Methods in Books about Swift', *SP* xxxv (1938).

M. K. Starkman, *Swift's Satire on Learning in 'A Tale of a Tub'* (Princeton, N.J., 1950).

E. Tuveson, 'Swift: the Dean as Satirist', *UTQ* xxii (1953).

I. Watt, 'The Ironic Tradition in Augustan Prose from Swift to Johnson', in *Restoration and Augustan Prose*, William Andrews Clarke Memorial Library: Seminar Papers (July 1956).

T. O. Wedel, 'On the Philosophical Background of *Gulliver's Travels*', *SP* xxiii (1926).

K. Williams, 'Gulliver's Voyage to the Houyhnhnms', *ELH* xviii (1951).

Each of the following titles is a collection of essays or articles by various critics. For the most part these are reprinted studies from many sources.

A. Jeffares, (ed.), *Fair Liberty was all his Cry: A Tercentenary Tribute to Jonathan Swift, 1667–1745* (London, Melbourne, Toronto, New York, 1967); contains 19 studies, 4 not previously printed.

R. McHugh and P. Edwards (edd.), *Jonathan Swift, 1667–1967: A Dublin Tercentenary Tribute* (Dublin, 1967); contains 11 studies previously unprinted.

E. Tuveson (ed.), *Swift: A Collection of Critical Essays* (Englewood Cliffs, N.J., 1964); contains 10 reprinted studies.

BIOGRAPHIES AND LETTERS

F. E. Ball (ed.), *The Correspondence of Jonathan Swift, D.D.*, (6 vols. London, 1910–14).

W. R. Brain (Sir), 'The Illness of Dean Swift', *Irish Journal of Medical Science*, 6th ser. (1952).

H. J. Davis, *Stella: A Gentlewoman of the Eighteenth Century* (New York, 1942); reprinted in Davis's *Jonathan Swift: Essays on his Satire and Other Studies* (paperback, New York, 1964).

I. Ehrenpreis, *The Personality of Jonathan Swift* (London, 1958); chs. 1, 6, 7.

—— *Swift the Man, His Works, and His Age:* vol. 1, *Mr. Swift and his Contemporaries;* vol. 11, *Dr. Swift* (London, 1962, 1967); in progress. This is the standard biography.

O. Ferguson, *Jonathan Swift and Ireland* (Urbana, Ill., 1962).

B. Goldgar, *The Curse of Party: Swift's Relations with Addison and Steele* (Lincoln, Neb., 1961).

P. Greenacre, *Swift and Carroll: A Psychoanalytic Study of Two Lives* (New York, 1955).

B. Karpman, 'Neurotic Traits of Jonathan Swift as Revealed by *Gulliver's Travels*: A Minor Contribution to the Problem of Psychosexual Infantilism and Coprophilia', *Psychoanalytic Review*, xxix (1942).

L. A. Landa, *Swift and the Church of Ireland* (Oxford, 1954).

D. Swift, *Essay upon the Life, Writings, and Character of Dr. Jonathan Swift* (London, 1755).

H. Williams (ed.), *Jonathan Swift: 'Journal to Stella'* (2 vols., Oxford, 1948).

—— (ed.), *The Correspondence of Jonathan Swift* (5 vols., Oxford, 1963–5).

BIBLIOGRAPHIES

D. M. Berwick, *The Reputation of Jonathan Swift, 1781–1882* (Philadelphia, Pa., 1941); see pp. 163–7.

H. J. Davis, 'Recent Studies of Swift: A Survey', *UTQ* vii (1938).

C. Lamont, 'A Checklist of Critical and Biographical Writings on Jonathan Swift, 1945–1965', in A. N. Jeffares (ed.), *Fair Liberty was all his Cry: A Tercentenary Tribute to Jonathan Swift, 1667–1745* (London, Melbourne, Toronto, and New York, 1967).

L. A. Landa and J. E. Tobin, *Jonathan Swift: A List of Critical Studies published from 1895 to 1945* (New York, 1945).

G. Mayhew, 'Recent Swift Scholarship', in R. McHugh and P. Edwards, (edd.), *Jonathan Swift, 1667–1967: A Dublin Tercentenary Tribute* (Dublin, 1967).

R. Quintana, 'A Modest Appraisal of Swift Scholarship and Criticism, 1945–65', in A. N. Jeffares (ed.), *Fair Liberty was all his Cry.*

—— 'Emile Pons and the Modern Study of Swift's *A Tale of a Tub*', *Études anglaises*, xviii (1965).

J. J. Stathis, *A Bibliography of Swift Studies, 1945–1965* (Nashville, Tenn., 1967).

H. Teerink, *A Bibliography of the Writings of Jonathan Swift*, 2nd edn., revised and corrected by A. H. Scouten, (Philadelphia, Pa., 1963).

M. Voigt, *Swift and the Twentieth Century* (Detroit, Mich., 1964).

BACKGROUND READING

G. Boas, *The Happy Beast in French Thought of the Seventeenth Century* (Baltimore, Md., 1933).

A. Burlingame. See under CRITICAL STUDIES.

A. Case. See under CRITICAL STUDIES.

G. N. Clark, *The Later Stuarts, 1660–1714* (Oxford, 1934).

W. A. Eddy, *Gulliver's Travels: A Critical Study* (Princeton, N.J., 1923).

K. Feiling, *A History of the Tory Party 1640–1714* (Oxford, 1924; reissued, 1951).

C. H. Firth, 'The Political Significance of *Gulliver's Travels*', *Proceedings of the British Academy*, ix (1919–20).

P. R. Gove, *The Imaginary Voyage in Prose Fiction* (New York, 1941).

R. F. Jones. See under CRITICAL STUDIES.

W. T. Laprade, *Public Opinion and Politics in Eighteenty-Century England to the Fall of Walpole* (New York, 1936; reprinted 1971).

A. O. Lovejoy, ' "Pride" in Eighteenth-Century Thought', *MLN* xxxvi (1921); reprinted in revised form in his *Essays in the History of Ideas* (Baltimore, Md., 1948).

H. K. Miller, 'The Paradoxical Encomium with Special Reference to its Vogue in England, 1600–1800', *MP* liii (1956).

M. Nicolson, *Science and Imagination* (paperback, Ithaca, N.Y., London, 1956).

J. G. Simms, 'Ireland in the Age of Swift', in R. McHugh and P. Edwards (edd.), *Jonathan Swift, 1667–1967: A Dublin Tercentenary Tribute* (Dublin, 1967).

A. S. Turberville, *English Men and Manners in the Eighteenth Century: An Illustrated Narrative* (paperback, New York, 1957); see ch. 4, 'Whigs and Tories in Queen Anne's Day'.

B. Williams, *The Whig Supremacy, 1714–1760* (Oxford, 1939).

(See also under CRITICAL STUDIES AND COMMENTARY the essays by Donald Greene, Roland Frye, and T. O. Wedel.)

4 · RICHARDSON 1689–1761

John Carroll

TEXTS

In 1739 Samuel Richardson owned a thriving printing-house, and, in his fiftieth year, seemed the very model of the poor but industrious apprentice whose virtue had been amply rewarded. During that year, he was commissioned by two booksellers 'to give them a little book (which, they said, they were often asked after) of familiar letters on the useful concerns in common life', *Letters Written to and for Particular Friends* (often closer to character sketches or short stories than to model letters, and edited by Brian W. Downs under the title *Familiar Letters on Important Occasions*) was published in 1741. But the completion of the book was delayed when, in writing two letters on the plight of a servant girl endangered by her master's attentions, he recalled a story he had heard many years before of a beautiful maid who had turned the lust of a squire into marital love. He began writing *Pamela* in November 1739 and published it a year later.

Its blend of naïveté and sophistication won immediate popularity. In a remark that may well have contained a hint of irony, Alexander Pope commented that this novel would do more good than many volumes of sermons. Another reader proclaimed that if all other books were to be burned, this work, next to the Bible, ought to be preserved; and young ladies in fashionable places held up copies of the novel to show one another that they were as modish in their reading as in their dress. Indeed, one of the most remarkable qualities of Richardson has been his ability to command interest from a widely varied audience, from the 'young, the ignorant, and the idle', as Johnson described typical novel-readers in the eighteenth century, to writers and critics as diverse as the Marquis de Sade, William Hazlitt, Jane Austen, Lord Macaulay, and Gertrude Stein.

Richardson's situation as a novelist was unique. Since he printed his own works, he could directly oversee each edition of his work, altering and adding material as he wished and using typography to create the effects he desired. Thus, for example, italic type and punctuation are used with care and imagination to establish the rhythm of his characters' voices, emphasize his didactic aims, or suggest the flow of his characters' ideas.

It is therefore of considerable importance to have exact reproductions of Richardson's texts. In 1971 T. C. D. Eaves and Ben
Kimpel reprinted the first edition of the first part of the novel—the
only reprint of that edition now available. In their introduction, as
well as in an article on the revisions of the novel, they discuss the
thoroughness with which Richardson altered the text in later
editions. The general effect of these changes is to give the novel an
air of greater 'correctness'. The editors state that Richardson made
Pamela's style 'more suitable to her status as an ideal figure' in the
later editions. They add, 'The gain in "correctness" is more than offset by a loss in spontaneity.' This reprinting of the first edition now
makes it possible to see the novel with all its initial faults and freshness. An edition of Part One, with a most perceptive introduction by
W. M. Sale, was also published in 1958.

Pamela was so popular that other authors published 'sequels'.
Partly to drive these spurious works off the market, Richardson
produced a continuation of the novel that showed his heroine as an
exemplary wife and mother. The only modern edition that prints
both Part One and its sequel is that of the Everyman Library, which
has an excellent introduction by M. Kinkead-Weekes.

At present, there is no reprinting of the first edition of *Clarissa*. An
unabridged edition of *Clarissa*, which modernizes spelling, punctuation, and typography, is available in Everyman's Library. As several
scholars have shown, *Clarissa* was also revised extensively after the
first edition; once again it is open to question whether these revisions
are in fact improvements. Abridged editions of this novel (in Modern
Library and Houghton Mifflin paperback) have undoubtedly made
the story familiar to twentieth-century readers who do not have the
stamina to read a novel which, in its first edition, ran to over 2,500
pages, but abridgement sacrifices that plethora of detail which at
once arouses impatience and builds suspense.

In 1971 the 1902 edition of the complete novels of Richardson,
edited by W. L. Phelps, was reprinted. A separate edition of *Sir
Charles Grandison* is published in the Oxford English Novels series,
edited with an introduction by Jocelyn Harris, and the novel may
also be bought as a separate part of the Phelps edition. The edition
of Richardson's complete novels used by most scholars is that of the
Shakespeare Head Press, which appeared in a limited edition between 1929 and 1931. This edition provides generally reliable texts,
and acknowledges the versions of the novels in Richardson's lifetime
from which they are printed.

As criticism of fiction comes to depend increasingly on a precise, close reading of the text, the kind of scrupulous care hitherto exercised in editing poetry and drama must also be used in editing fiction. In Richardson's case, this kind of editing is particularly important. He is notorious for his prolixity, but a wealth of invention does not necessarily mean a poverty of craftsmanship. E. M. Forster praised Richardson as a novelist who, despite his copious flow, never permitted the intrusion of a word that was out of place. The statement would have pleased Richardson since he always welcomed—with more than ordinary zest—exclamations of delight and approval. But for Richardson the praise would not have been unexpected. In his notes for a preface to *Clarissa* he wrote 'Judges will see, that, long as the work is, there is not one digression, not one Episode, not one Reflection, but what arises naturally from the Subject, and makes for it, and to carry it on.'

Highly interesting essays on Richardson's methods of revising his fiction have been published by M. Kinkead-Weekes, R. C. Pierson and T. C. D. Eaves and Ben Kimpel. From these discussions of Richardson's revisions of his work, an important and lively question has arisen: should one read his earliest version, as it went from manuscript to type, retaining the freshness of the creative intention, or should one read the version which represents his later reactions to his own work and the criticism he had heard? The changes are so extensive that one might argue the third edition of *Clarissa* is a somewhat different novel from the first edition. Only when the texts are placed side by side can the critic make his decision—and at best the decision will be arguable.

CRITICAL STUDIES AND COMMENTARY

The ideal reader of Richardson's novels in the eighteenth century lived in a remote country house and had the time and inclination to live with his characters day after day and to peruse every word of his fiction with the care of a participant in the action. Richardson found this ideal reader in Lady (Dorothy) Bradshaigh. She began writing to him during the serial publication of *Clarissa* to plead for a happy ending to the novel, and their correspondence continued to his death. Lady Bradshaigh read with a care and passion that would flatter any writer, and with a certain innocence and abandon that enabled Richardson to tutor her in the fine points of his fiction. Many of Richardson's most revealing comments on his novels appear in letters to her and other friends.

In truth, from the very beginning of his writing career Richardson was blessed with readers and critics who perceived what he was attempting in his technique and were sympathetic—to the point of idolatry—with his overt moralizing. In a letter to Richardson, which was printed as prefatory material to *Pamela*, J .B. de Freval not only praised the teachings of the novel but commended the epistolary form for its vividness and dramatic qualities.

So much adulation is, of course, an invitation to attack. In *Pamela–Shamela* B. Kreissman surveys the contemporary reactions to the novel in the forms of parodies, burlesques, and criticism, and gives an account of the reputation of the novel to our own time. Fielding's *Shamela*, the most famous of the parodies, is a boisterous, ribald attack on the style and the morality of the novel. This attack continues in *Joseph Andrews* where, in the opening and concluding chapters, Fielding ridicules Pamela's obsession with chastity and her tendency to measure the rewards of virtue in material terms.

In the preface to his sister's novel *David Simple*, Fielding argued that the epistolary form is not well suited to the novel. But even Fielding was deeply and favourably impressed by *Clarissa*, which he praised in a letter to Richardson as well as in print. Unquestionably, *Clarissa* is Richardson's finest work, a novel in which the attempted seduction of the heroine by Lovelace becomes a battle between classes, sexes, and the heavenly and diabolical. In *Sir Charles Grandison* Richardson portrayed a perfect gentleman to complement his drawing of the ideal lady in *Clarissa*—and also, perhaps, to offset the popularity Fielding had won for the scapegrace Tom Jones. With *Sir Charles Grandison* he moved from tragedy to comedy of manners, and it is highly significant that Jane Austen, whose 'knowledge of Richardson's works was such as no one is likely again to acquire' knew 'every circumstance narrated in *Sir Charles Grandison*'.

Criticism of Richardson in eighteenth-century England concerned itself far more with his morality than with his techniques, yet the loving attention to the slightest gesture and the minute fact to be found in, say, James Boswell and Laurence Sterne, may well be indirect tributes to his craftsmanship. Perhaps the most acute comment on the novelist by a contemporary is that of Samuel Johnson, who remarked of Clarissa that 'there is always something which she prefers to truth'. Johnson thereby touched on the subtle way in which morality and the epistolary form interact. Richardson's characters always profess openness of heart, yet this demand for absolute frankness is also an invitation to conceal emotions and impulses from themselves and thereby from their friends.

Richardson's work had an enormous influence on the Continent; Rousseau, de la Clos, de Sade, Goethe, Pushkin, Balzac, George

Sand, and de Musset testify to his popularity by direct praise, allu-sion, or the indirect praise of imitation. This popularity and influence have been traced carefully in such works as L. Price's 'On the Recep-tion of Richardson in Germany', and B. A. Facteau's *Les Romans de Richardson sur la scène française*.

The best critical essay on Richardson by a contemporary is Denis Diderot's 'Éloge de Richardson'. Since a man is not upon oath in a eulogy, one expects praise, but the adulation of Diderot nevertheless startles by its very extravagance. In the midst of this praise, however, Diderot elaborates on Richardson's masterly use of detail, on the range of styles at his command and on his perception of the darker regions of the mind in a way that illuminates both the novelist's artistry and his psychology.

Until the beginning of the nineteenth century, Richardson and Fielding shared honours as the foremost English novelists. In *Fielding the Novelist*, a work that traces the reputations of the two rivals up to the twentieth century, F. T. Blanchard notes a marked decline in Richardson's reputation in the early 1800s. The sheer length of his works began to daunt and to weary an increasing number of readers. He began to seem old-fashioned and, as the Victorian age came nearer, viciously immoral. Laetitia Matilda Hawkins, for instance, dismissed him to the lowest depths by writing that 'Rousseau was decent compared to Richardson'.

Yet in the romantic period Richardson received perceptive criti-cism from Coleridge, Scott, and Hazlitt. In his *Biographia Literaria* (Chapter 23), Coleridge captures the essence of Richardson's world by referring to the 'self-involution and dream-like continuity' of his work and to his 'morbid consciousness of every thought and feeling in the whole flux and reflux of the mind'. Scott's brief life of Richard-son is a judicious appraisal of the novels showing that they had received his careful, generally sympathetic attention. Hazlitt devotes merely a few pages to Richardson in *English Comic Writers*, but these pages contain a wealth of critical observations. His remark that the novels have 'the romantic air of a pure fiction, with the literal minuteness of a common diary' is not only a finely compressed des-cription of their qualities but suggests why Richardson's novels are at once so rich and baffling to the critic. Hazlitt goes on to praise the design of Richardson's work—of *Pamela*, he remarks that 'it would seem as if a step lost, would be as fatal here as in a mathematical demonstration'—and also touches on a most important flaw, Richardson's tendency to confound 'his own point of view with that of the immediate actors in the scene'.

In the Victorian period, one can find many writers who praise Richardson in brief comments or allusions. Ruskin, Macaulay, Tennyson, and Stevenson admired his fiction, but there are few extended works of criticism that shed new or different light on these novels. Leslie Stephen's essay on Richardson, while occasionally grudging in its praise, nevertheless suggests the reasons for Richardson's power over readers in his own day and over the few who read him in the nineteenth century: 'He is so keenly in earnest, so profoundly interested about his characters, so determined to make us enter into their motives, that we cannot help being carried away. . . . He is always, as it were, writing at high pressure and under a sense of responsibility.'

The first book-length studies of Richardson in English came at the turn of the century in the critical biographies of Clara Thomson and Austin Dobson, which will be discussed in the next section. During the first two decades of this century, theses and scholarly articles on Richardson began to appear with frequency. Some of these—such as W. P. Uhrström's *Studies on the Language of Richardson*—are still helpful to the Richardsonian scholar, but very few are indispensable and some misleading. E. Poetzsche's *Samuel Richardsons Belesenheit*, for example, used literary quotations and allusions in Richardson's novels and letters in an attempt to show the range of his reading. As subsequent scholars have pointed out, many of these quotations were simply taken from such books as Edward Bysshe's *Art of English Poetry* and the *Thesaurus Dramaticus*, compilations of 'beauties' from poetry and drama that Richardson thumbed through when he wanted to brighten a passage with verses from Dryden or Otway or Lee.

Controversies also began in the early part of the century about 'influences' on Richardson, particularly his relation to French fiction. Richardson did not, in fact, know French—although this did not necessarily mean that he was ignorant of continental novels in translation. At any rate, Richardson himself always disclaimed indebtedness to anybody. He asserted in his letters that he thought of *Pamela* as a 'new species of writing'. Robert A. Day's *Told in Letters: Epistolary Fiction before Richardson* is quite valuable in helping to gain perspective on these claims. Day bases his work, which is both critical and historical, on an examination of over 200 epistolary novels that appeared in England between 1660 and 1740. This survey shows, as he remarks, that 'pre-Richardsonian epistolary fiction developed by fits and starts to a point where Richardson's work may be viewed historically as the culmination of a process of development rather

than as a literary eruption'. But while Richardson used techniques
that had already been exploited, it is impossible to establish any real
connection, in terms of direct influence, between these earlier novels
and Richardson's. As Day says, *Pamela* 'was a crystallization of many
tendencies of its age'. For further information on the epistolary novel
in the century, the student may consult F. G. Black's 'The Technique of Letter Fiction in English from 1740 to 1800' and G. Singer's
Epistolary Novel.

In *Samuel Richardson and the Dramatic Novel*, Ira Konigsberg has
attempted to show that there was a significant relation between the
style, themes, and techniques of contemporary drama and Richardson's work. There are indeed similarities, but these similarities *remain*
similarities and the influences *possible* influences. Richardson may
not have been quite as original as he thought, but neither previous
fiction nor drama explains how he produced these works, any more
than pre-Shakespearian drama really explains the genius Shakespeare brought to the theatre.

Some of the most interesting, if not always the most convincing,
essays on Richardson in recent years have explored the psychological
implications of his themes and characters. Many have found pre-
Freudian revelations of hidden and perverse sexual drives, particularly in *Clarissa*. These studies are, in effect, further explorations of
Diderot's comment that 'il porte le flambeau au fond de la caverne'.
In 1933 Mario Praz's *The Romantic Agony* drew attention to Clarissa
as an archetypal suffering virgin, a highly influential figure in a
drama of sadism and masochism that haunts Western literature.
Morris Golden (in *Richardson's Characters*) takes up this theme and
treats the conflicts in the novels as projections of Richardson's own
psyche, conflicts in which there is an interaction between sadistic and
masochistic impulses. Dorothy Van Ghent's essay on *Clarissa* in *The
English Novel* suggests that the heroine typifies a kind of female de-
bility—created by the myths of Puritanism and bourgeois family
life—that invites sadistic attack. And Leslie Fiedler in *Love and Death
in the American Novel* argues that *Clarissa*, 'pays allegiance to that
secret religion of the bourgeoisie in which tears are considered a truer
service of God than prayers, the Pure Young Woman replaces Christ
as the savior, marriage becomes the equivalent of bliss eternal, and
the Seducer is the only Devil'. This is all very exciting, not to say
sensational, but what is generally missing from such studies is
acknowledgement of Richardson's own awareness of this 'secret
religion'; his realization, as Sir Charles Grandison says, that 'Men
and Women are devils to one another'; and his insistence that the

most infinitely scrupulous care must be exercised in observing one's emotions and impulses. He also realizes that such scrupulosity invites self-delusion, particularly in those characters who strive to reach the highest form of goodness available to them. A more sober study than Fiedler's—and one, indeed, that anticipated many of his remarks on Richardson by over twenty years—is *Pamela's Daughters* by R. P. Utter and G. B. Needham. This book begins with Pamela as the progenetrix of heroines in English and American fiction, traces her lineage into the twentieth century, and shows how her characteristics (modesty, sense, and sensibility) have been the subject of continuing variations. This is a most useful and entertaining work.

A power struggle is, of course, always going on in Richardson's heroines between impulse and conscience, and there are also continuous battles between man and woman. Just as important in some ways are the struggles between classes. For Richardson, both the middle-class, in its materialism, and the aristocracy, in its freedom from economic and moral constraints, are often at odds with the unique being who tries to live by the sanctions of another world. The social background of the novels—and its effect on the characters' motives, decisions, and conduct—has been most thoroughly and cogently treated by Ian Watt in *The Rise of the Novel*. Also indispensable is W. M. Sale's essay 'From *Pamela* to *Clarissa*', which discusses Richardson's effort to work out a *modus vivendi* between upper and lower classes in the first novel and his transition in *Clarissa* to a viewpoint that questioned the ultimate compatibility of the two castes. Norman Rabkin's '*Clarissa*: A Study in the Nature of Convention' discusses Richardson's presentation of the struggle between the characters' instincts and eighteenth-century ideals of decorum, and in 'Clarissa's Coffin' Alan Wendt interestingly treats moral and religious themes in the novel. An article that helpfully places *Clarissa* in the context of eighteenth-century politics and economics is Christopher Hill's 'Clarissa Harlowe and Her Times'. Hill contends that the real theme of the novel is 'the effect on individuals of property marriage', and he shows that Lovelace is not only a rebel against moral convention but a radical in his political views. Good as it is, this article fails to encompass the astonishingly diverse qualities of *Clarissa*.

Until quite recently, Richardson's sexual mythology and social commentary had received much more attention than his technique. The structural skills of Richardson in *Pamela* have been briefly but convincingly described by M. Kinkead-Weekes in his introduction to the Everyman Library edition and by Ian Watt in *The Novelist As*

Innovator (a collection of essays edited by W. Allen). F. W. Hilles, in 'The Plan of *Clarissa*', has shown how precisely Richardson disposed the various parts of the action and controlled the centre of narration in each section of that novel. Richardson's handling of the epistle, as a means of manipulating point of view, had long been deplored as a clumsy device that obtruded itself on the attention, exacting a heavy price in credulity. A. D. McKillop's 'Epistolary Technique in Richardson's Novels' emphasizes the way in which letters are used to further plot as well as to exploit the possibilities of multiple points of view; this monograph is indispensable to the student of Richardson's technique. A. M. Kearney's '*Clarissa* and the Epistolary Form' is a stimulating essay on the novel in which this device is used to best advantage.

Richardson's style has been easily dismissed by some critics as awkward, colloquial, and lacking in that grace and balance we associate with Augustan prose. In fact, Richardson commanded an astonishingly diverse range of styles, from the prattle of Pamela to the verbal pyrotechnics of Lovelace. W. Farrell's 'The Style and the Action in *Clarissa*' raises important points about the different levels of style in this novel, and Kearney's 'Richardson's *Pamela*: the Aesthetic Case' discusses, among other important points, the intrusion of the authorial voice on which Hazlitt had commented. Aside from these specialized studies, the discussions of Richardson's work as a whole by R. F. Brissenden (in the 'Writers and Their Work Series') and by Kearney (in the 'Profiles in Literature' series) are compact introductions that may be read profitably even by those familiar with the novels.

Several of the essays already mentioned in this section have been reprinted in *Samuel Richardson: A Collection of Critical Essays* edited by John Carroll; this book gives a representative view of twentieth-century criticism on Richardson's novels. Rosemary Cowler's *Twentieth Century Interpretations of 'Pamela'* surveys important commentaries on the Richardsonian novel that still provokes the most extreme reactions from critics.

Cynthia Griffin Wolff's *Samuel Richardson and the Eighteenth-Century Puritan Character* discusses his conception of character, his literary devices for rendering character, and possible sources in Puritan literature that may have influenced his work. Christian Pons's *Richardson et la littérature bourgeoise en Angleterre* traces Richardson's literary and 'sentimental' heritage and also provides useful critical commentary on his works. In 'Richardson and Romance' Margaret Dalziel gives one of the most provocative and persuasive studies of his debt to the prose romances, a form with which his novels have close affinities, though he despised and disliked the styles and conventions of this predecessor to the novel.

Since 1950 over 100 items on Richardson have appeared in print—ranging from brief notes to book-length studies. In recent years the most notable change has been in the direction of treating Richardson as a genius perfectly aware of what he was doing rather than as an 'unconscious genius'. Critics are now less burdened with the assumption, espoused by Joseph Wood Krutch in *Five Masters*, that Richardson must be accorded greatness only while one enumerates all of the reasons why he should not be great.

BIOGRAPHIES AND LETTERS

The first full-length biographies of Richardson were by Clara Thomson (1900) and Austin Dobson (1902). Both are more satisfactory as biographers than critics. Brian W. Downs's *Richardson* succeeds in being concise and comprehensive in its treatment of Richardson's artistry. Downs is particularly good in his discussion of the tradition of sentimentalism. Paul Dottin's *Samuel Richardson. Imprimeur de Londres* is a detailed analysis of the man and his works, but it is marred by a style that, in trying to be animated, becomes arch.

The standard biography is now *Samuel Richardson* by Eaves and Kimpel. A thoroughly scrupulous work of scholarship, this book not only presents all the facts available on Richardson's life but traces the compositions, receptions, and alterations of his novels. A. D. McKillop's *Samuel Richardson: Printer and Novelist* is also an indispensable work. McKillop is particularly helpful in tracing the genesis of the novels and their subsequent influence. (His essay on Richardson in *Early Masters of English Fiction* is also highly valuable as a synthesis of McKillop's views on all three novels.) The definitive account of Richardson's career as a printer is that of W. M. Sale in *Samuel Richardson, Master Printer*. This work lists many of the books printed by Richardson.

All of the biographies of Richardson depend to a great extent on his voluminous correspondence. The bulk of his surviving letters is in the Forster Collection of the Victoria and Albert Museum, where it fills six fat folio volumes. Mrs. Anna Laetitia Barbauld edited this correspondence in a six-volume edition at the beginning of the nineteenth century. The introduction, partly based on material she garnered from those who knew Richardson, is still of importance, and her choice of material from Richardson's correspondence is, generally speaking, judicious. Her transcriptions and datings are occasionally inaccurate, however, and she gives no indication of where she has deleted material. An edition of *Selected Letters of Samuel Richardson* was published in 1964. The purpose of this volume, edited by John Carroll, was to include letters which illuminated the themes, characters, and craftsmanship of his novels and which revealed something of his personality.

In 1969 William C. Slattery edited the correspondence between Richardson and Johannes Stinstra, the Dutch translator of *Clarissa*. This collection of material, which includes the most important of Richardson's autobiographical letters, is particularly useful because Slattery has also included Stinstra's prefaces to various sections of his translation. Although heavily moralistic, these prefaces contain acute commentaries on Richardson's methods as a novelist and are also highly indicative of the ways in which a European contemporary reacted to these works.

BIBLIOGRAPHY

W. M. Sale's *Samuel Richardson: A Bibliographical Record* describes the editions of the novels in Richardson's lifetime and gives accounts of the editions of his minor works. Sale also presents important material on the history of the writing and publication of these works. By its very nature, this book is of more importance to the scholar than to the student.

F. Cordasco's *Richardson, A List of Critical Studies, 1896–1946* is outdated and, in addition, has many errors. Although published in 1936, the bibliography in McKillop's *Samuel Richardson* is still valuable since it refers to many works which, though not primarily about Richardson, contain significant comments on his fiction. Pons's *Richardson et la littérature bourgeoise en Angleterre* also contains an extensive bibliography. The *CBEL* as well as the annual bibliographies of *PMLA*, *PQ*, and the Modern Humanities Research Association provide useful sources of information on works about Richardson.

BACKGROUND READING

Basil Williams's *The Whig Supremacy, 1714–1760* covers the political, social, and economic milieu in which Richardson wrote. For a more detailed view of the matrix from which Richardson's characters emerged, G. E. Mingay's *English Landed Society in the Eighteenth Century* is a dependable and engaging work. The details of daily living in this period are discussed from a variety of perspectives in *Johnson's England*, edited by A. S. Turberville. Leslie Stephen's

English Thought in the Eighteenth Century is still a useful, though not a completely reliable, guide to the intellectual world in which Richardson lived, and Basil Willey's *Eighteenth-Century Background* may also be read profitably. R. S. Crane's 'Suggestions Toward a Genealogy of the Man of Feeling' is a most important essay providing a general view of the development of the doctrines behind the sentimental movement. Since contemporary ideals of decorum are so significant in Richardson's work, J. E. Mason's *Gentlefolk in the Making* is helpful background reading for these novels.

Of course, nothing supersedes a thorough knowledge of the literature of Richardson's own age. Contemporary novels, dramas, and letters (as well as sermons) establish the very form and pressure of Richardson's times.

REFERENCES

TEXTS

(a) Collected works

W. L. Phelps (ed.), *Pamela, Clarissa, Sir Charles Grandison* (London, 1902; reprinted New York, 1971).

W. King and A. Bott (edd.), *Pamela, Clarissa, Sir Charles Grandison* (Oxford, 1929–31).

(b) Separate works

R. F. Brissenden (ed.), *Clarissa: Preface, Hints of Prefaces, and Postscript* (Los Angeles, 1964).

J. A. Burrell (abridged), *Clarissa* (Modern Library, New York, 1950).

J. Butt (intro.), *Clarissa* (Everyman, London and New York, 1962).

B. Downs (ed.), *Familiar Letters on Important Occasions* (London, New York, and Toronto, 1928).

T. C. D. Eaves and B. Kimpel (edd.), *Pamela* (paperback, Boston, Mass., 1971).

J. Harris (ed.), *Sir Charles Grandison* (3 vols., London, New York, and Toronto 1972).

M. Kinkead-Weekes (intro.), *Pamela* (Everyman, London and New York, 1965).

W. M. Sale (intro.), *Pamela* (New York, 1958).

G. Sherburn (abridged), *Clarissa* (paperback, Houghton Mifflin, Boston, Mass., 1962).

CRITICAL STUDIES AND COMMENTARY

F. G. Black, 'The Technique of Letter Fiction in English from 1740 to 1800', *Harvard Studies in Philology*, xv (1933).

F. T. Blanchard, *Fielding the Novelist* (New Haven, Conn., 1926).

R. F. Brissenden, *Samuel Richardson* (London, New York, and Toronto, 1958).

J. Carroll. *Samuel Richardson: A Collection of Critical Essays* (Englewood Cliffs, N.J., 1969).

S. T. Coleridge, *Coleridge's 'Biographia Literaria'*, ed. J. Shawcross (2 vols., Oxford and New York, 1907).

R. Cowler, *Twentieth Century Interpretations of 'Pamela'* (Englewood Cliffs, N. J., 1969).

M. Dalziel, 'Richardson and Romance,' *AUMLA* xxxiii (1970).

R. A. Day, *Told in Letters: Epistolary Fiction before Richardson* (Ann Arbor, Mich., 1966).

D. Diderot, 'Éloge de Richardson', *Oeuvres complètes*, ed. J. Assezat (Paris, 1875).

T. C. D. Eaves and B. Kempel, 'The Composition of *Clarissa* and its Revisions before Publication', *PMLA* lxxxiii (1968).

T. C. D. Eaves and B. Kempel, 'Richardson's Revisions of Pamela', *Studies in Bibliography*, xx (1967).

B. A. Facteau, *Les Romans de Richardson sur la scène française* (Paris, 1927).

W. Farrell, 'The Style and the Action in *Clarissa*', *Studies in English Literature 1500–1900*, iii (1963).

L. Fiedler, *Love and Death in the American Novel* (paperback, New York, 1967).

H. Fielding, *Joseph Andrews and Shamela*, ed. M. Battestin (paperback, Boston, Mass., 1961).

M. Golden, *Richardson's Characters* (Ann Arbor, Mich., 1963).

W. Hazlitt, *English Comic Writers* (London, 1951).

C. Hill, 'Clarissa Harlowe and Her Times', *EIC* v (1955).

F. W. Hilles, 'The Plan of *Clarissa*', *PQ* xlv (1966).

A. Kearney, '*Clarissa* and the Epistolary Form', *EIC* xvi (1966).

—— 'Richardson's *Pamela*: the Aesthetic Case', *Review of English Literature*, vii (1966).

—— *Samuel Richardson* (paperback, London and New York, 1968).

M. Kinkead-Weekes, '*Clarissa* Restored?', *RES* n.s. x (1959).

I. Konigsberg, *Samuel Richardson and the Dramatic Novel* (Lexington, Ken., 1968).

B. Kreissman, *Pamela–Shamela* (Lincoln, Nebr., 1960).

J. W. Krutch, *Five Masters* (Bloomington, Ind., 1959).

A. D. McKillop, 'Epistolary Technique in Richardson's Novels', *Rice Institute Pamphlets* (Houston, Texas, 1951); reprinted in *Studies in the Literature of the Augustan Age* ed. R. C. Baye (Ann Arbor, Mich., 1966).

R. C. Pierson, 'The Revisions of Richardson's *Sir Charles Grandison*', *Studies in Bibliography*, xxi (1968).

E. Poetzsche, *Samuel Richardsons Belesenheit* (Kiel, 1908).

C. Pons, *Samuel Richardson et la Littérature bourgeoise en Angleterre* (Aix-en-Provence, n.d.).

M. Praz, *The Romantic Agony* (2nd edn., London, 1970).

L. Price, 'On the Reception of Richardson in Germany', *JEGP* xxv (1926).

N. Rabkin, '*Clarissa*: A Study in the Nature of Convention, *ELH* xxiii (1956).

W. M. Sale, 'From *Pamela* to *Clarissa*', in *The Age of Johnson*, ed. F. W. Hilles (New Haven, Conn., 1964).

G. F. Singer, *The Epistolary Novel: its Origin, Development, Decline and Residuary Influence* (Philadelphia, Pa., 1933).

Sir W. Scott, *Lives of the Novelists* (London and New York, 1910).

L. Stephen, 'Samuel Richardson' in *Hours in a Library* (London, 1892).

W. P. Uhrström, *Studies on the Language of Richardson* (Uppsala, 1907).

R. P. Utter and G. B. Needham, *Pamela's Daughters* (New York, 1937).

D. Van Ghent, 'On *Clarissa Harlowe*' in *The English Novel* (New York, 1967).

I. Watt, *The Rise of the Novel* (Berkeley, Calif., 1960).

—— 'Samuel Richardson' in *The Novelist as Innovator*, ed. W. Allen (London, 1965).

A. Wendt, 'Clarissa's Coffin', *PQ* xxxix (1960).

C. G. Wolff, *Samuel Richardson and the Eighteenth-Century Puritan Character* (Hamden, Conn., 1972).

BIOGRAPHIES AND LETTERS

A. L. Barbauld (ed.), *Correspondence of Samuel Richardson* (London, 1804; reprinted New York, 1968).

J. Carroll (ed.), *Selected Letters of Samuel Richardson* (Oxford, 1964).

A. Dobson, *Samuel Richardson* (London, 1902; reprinted Detroit, Mich., 1968).

P. Dottin, *Samuel Richardson, Imprimeur de Londres* (Paris, 1931).

B. Downs, *Richardson* (London, 1928; reprinted New York, 1968).

T. C. D. Eaves and B. Kimpel, *Samuel Richardson: A Biography* (Oxford, 1971).

A. D. McKillop, *Samuel Richardson: Printer and Novelist* (Chapel Hill, N.C., 1936; reprinted Hamden, Conn., 1960).

—— *Early Masters of English Fiction* (paperback, Lawrence, Kans., 1968).

W. M. Sale, *Samuel Richardson, Master Printer* (Ithaca, N.Y., 1950).

W. Slattery, *The Richardson-Stinstra Correspondence and Stinstra's Prefaces to Clarissa* (Carbondale, Ill., London, and Amsterdam, 1969).

C. L. Thomson, *Samuel Richardson* (London, 1900).

BIBLIOGRAPHIES

F. Cordasco, *Richardson: a List of Critical Studies 1896–1946* (Brooklyn, N.Y., 1948).

W. M. Sale, *Samuel Richardson: a Bibliographical Record of His Literary Career* (New Haven, Conn., 1936; reprinted Hamden, Conn., 1968).

ANNUAL BIBLIOGRAPHIES

PQ
PMLA
Modern Humanities Research Association

BACKGROUND READING

R. S. Crane, 'Suggestions toward a Genealogy of the "Man of Feeling" ', *ELH* i (1934).

J. E. Mason, *Gentlefolk in the Making* (Philadelphia, Pa., 1935).

G. E. Mingay, *English Landed Society in the Eighteenth Century* (London and Toronto, 1963).

Sir L. Stephen, *English Thought in the Eighteenth Century* (New York, 1962).

A. S. Turberville (ed.), *Johnson's England* (Oxford, 1952).

B. Willey, *The Eighteenth-Century Background* (London, 1961).

B. Williams, *The Whig Supremacy, 1714–1760* (Oxford, 1952).

Martin C. Battestin

EXCEPT perhaps at New Scotland Yard and the Old Vic, Fielding is today primarily remembered neither as one of London's greatest reforming justices nor—to invoke Shaw's pleasant extravagancy, who had not seen the recent production of *The Covent-Garden Tragedy* at the National Theatre—as 'the greatest dramatist, with the single exception of Shakespeare, produced by England between the Middle Ages and the nineteenth century'. Although the theatre was Fielding's first love and the magistracy the arduous preoccupation of his last years, he is today generally remembered for a handful of novels: for *Jonathan Wild the Great* (1743) and *Amelia* (1751), and most especially for *Joseph Andrews* (1742) and his masterpiece, *Tom Jones* (1749). With these works—which Fielding himself preferred to call 'histories' or 'biographies', or, more grandly, 'comic epic poems in prose'—the modern British novel came into its own as an art form. What is more, as Kingsley Amis remarked some fifteen years ago and as the spate of criticism since then amply attests, no other novelist of the eighteenth century has worn so well.

Properly, then, the focus of the present survey is Fielding's fiction, as it has been the subject of recent critical analysis and revaluation from a variety of perspectives. Though interesting in and for themselves, Fielding's plays, journals, and social pamphlets will be considered here only as they illuminate the themes and techniques of the novels.

TEXTS

Since 1762, the date of Arthur Murphy's original collection, a number of editions of Fielding's works have been published, most of them elegantly introduced and as casually put together by the belletrists of the nineteenth century—by, to mention only the most prominent names, Thomas Roscoe (1840), Leslie Stephen (1882), George Saintsbury (1893), Edmund Gosse (1898–9), and W. E. Henley (1903). Of these collections, none is either complete or textually reliable, though the Henley edition, lately reprinted (16 vols., 1967), is more comprehensive and hence less objectionable than any of the others. The need for a definitive edition of Fielding's works is therefore acute; happily, however, it will be met over the next several years as the volumes of the recently projected Wesleyan Edition are completed and published. Launched in 1967 with the publication of *Joseph Andrews* (ed. M. C. Battestin), the Wesleyan Edition will eventually make all of Fielding's writings available in reliable, old-spelling texts; the apparatus to each volume—in addition to the general introduction, which will treat such matters as the circumstances and date of composition and the history of the printing and publication of the work—will include explanatory annotations and lists of variant readings. Textually, the entire edition is being prepared under the supervision of Fredson T. Bowers, with specific editorial responsibilities delegated as follows: the plays, E. V. Roberts; the journals and related political pamphlets, W. B. Coley; the *Miscellanies*, including *Jonathan Wild the Great* and *A Journey from This World to the Next*, H. K. Miller; the social and legal tracts, M. R. Zirker; miscellaneous works, including *Shamela*, S. W. Baker; *Tom Jones*, Bowers and Battestin; *Amelia*, Battestin.

While we await the completion of the Wesleyan project, the study of Fielding will presumably continue apace, for which purpose a number of useful editions of individual works are already available. For the plays the following editions are particularly noteworthy: *The Tragedy of Tragedies*, ed. J. T. Hillhouse (1918) or ed. L. J. Morrissey (1970); *The Author's Farce*, ed. C. B. Woods (1966); *The Historical Register for the Year 1736*, ed. W. W. Appleton (1967); *The Grub-Street Opera*, ed. E. V. Roberts (1968); and *Pasquin*, ed. O. M. Brack, *et al.* (1973). For the periodicals: *The True Patriot*, ed. M. Locke, in facsimile (1964); and *The Covent-Garden Journal*, ed. G. E. Jensen (1915). For the fiction: *Shamela and Joseph Andrews*, ed. Battestin (1961), ed. D. Brooks (1970), or ed. Baker (1973); *Jonathan Wild*, ed. J. H. Plumb (1962), or, together with *The Journal of a Voyage to Lisbon*, ed. Saintsbury (1932); *Amelia*, ed. Saintsbury (1930). At present there is no entirely satisfactory edition of *Tom Jones*, though numerous inexpensive reprints of the novel are available, the most useful of these being R. P. C. Mutter's (1966), based on the third edition, and Baker's (1973), based on the more authoritative fourth edition; both versions include explanatory annotations. One year after the publication of the Wesleyan *Tom Jones*, Battestin will bring out in the Riverside series a modernized paperback edition of the novel with full notes addressed to the general reader. Several other inexpensive reprints of *Tom Jones* are worth mentioning for their introductions by such distinguished critics as George Sherburn (1950), A. R. Humphreys (1962), and Frank

Kermode (1964). Despite their scholarly imperfections, three editions of Fielding's miscellaneous minor works deserve notice: these are *The Female Husband and Other Writings*, ed. C. E. Jones (1960), a slim collection of several fugitive items, including Fielding's satiric poem, *The Masquerade*, and a selection of his epilogues; *The Lover's Assistant*, ed. Jones (1961), the Dublin reprint of Fielding's *Ovid's Art of Love Paraphrased*; and *The Journal of a Voyage to Lisbon*, ed. H. E. Pagliaro (1963). Finally, I. Williams has recently published (1970) a useful collection of Fielding's own criticism culled from his journals and fiction.

CRITICAL STUDIES AND COMMENTARY

In his own century as in ours, Fielding suffered from the criticisms of those who either misunderstood his fiction or found it not very much to their taste. The blue-stockinged apostles of Richardson were no less severe with Fielding than F. R. Leavis has been (1948), and Dr. Johnson's preference for the author of *Clarissa*, 'who knew how a watch was made', over Fielding, who could merely 'tell the hour by looking on the dial-plate', anticipated by two centuries Ian Watt's distinction (1957)—drawn to Fielding's disadvantage—between Richardson's technique of 'formal realism' and Fielding's 'realism of assessment'. In Fielding's day began that sanctimonious disparagement of his works on moral grounds that we have come to think of as peculiarly 'Victorian'. Readers condemned him for the 'lowness' of his themes—his preoccupation with the adventures (chiefly sexual) of footmen and foundlings, country wenches and Mayfair demi-reps. To Richardson, for example, *Joseph Andrews* was merely a 'lewd and ungenerous engraftment' on *Pamela*, and *Tom Jones* was a work so immoral, as he had heard, that he would not risk contaminating his mind by reading it. Fielding's political enemies, the hired scribblers of *Old England*, had read it, however, and throughout 1749 gleefully subjected his masterpiece to a merciless barrage of sarcasm and vituperation—a programme of abuse which culminated in December of that year when 'Orbilius', their colleague in pseudonymous invective, published his *Examen* of the novel. Indeed, when earthquakes shook London in the spring of 1750, a writer in *Old England* proposed that these terrible events were signs of God's displeasure at the enthusiastic reception accorded to *Tom Jones*.

But, as the very stridency of these attacks testifies, Fielding's fiction was received by a numerous and, for the most part, an approving audience. In the novelist's lifetime, *Joseph Andrews* went through five editions totalling 10,500 copies, and *Tom Jones*, of which the first edition was bought up before the announced date of publication (10 February 1749), was reprinted three times before the year was out, the four editions together comprising 10,000 copies. By the time *Amelia* was ready for publication, Fielding's reputation was in fact so solidly established that his bookseller, anticipating a general run on the novel, made arrangements for printing 8,000 copies, an extraordinary number for the time. As might be expected from this evidence, if Fielding's enemies were outspoken in damning his art and his morals, there were other readers ready to praise him—Elizabeth Carter and the Abbé Desfontaines, for instance, who delighted in *Joseph Andrews*; Boswell, who defended *Tom Jones* against Dr. Johnson; and, eventually, even the good Doctor himself, who at last came round to Fielding's side, pronouncing *Amelia* 'the most pleasing of all the romances'.

Of all the contemporary appreciations of Fielding's achievement, however, most significant was the anonymous *Essay on the New Species of Writing founded by Mr. Fielding* (1751); this pamphlet, possibly by Francis Coventry, is now readily available in the edition by A. D. McKillop (1962). A further aid to those interested in reviewing Fielding's early reception at first hand is the recent anthology, *Fielding: The Critical Heritage*, edd. R. Paulson and T. Lockwood (1968). The standard and indispensable account of the reception of Fielding's novels and of his changing reputation from the beginnings through the early decades of the present century is, however, F. T. Blanchard's exhaustive survey, *Fielding the Novelist* (1926). In Blanchard may be found convenient summaries of the views of such influential critics as Lord Monboddo, Beattie, Coleridge, Hazlitt, Scott, Thackeray, and Taine, to name only a few. Here one may trace, with a mixture of amusement and dismay, the evolution of the Victorian estimate of Fielding, which presented him as at once the greatest craftsman and the most debauched moralist among the writers of English fiction—a view, it is pleasant to note, which in 1896 led to the publication of an edition of *Tom Jones* expurgated by the novelist's grand-daughter! The most eloquent, and therefore the most damaging, of Fielding's Victorian critics was William Makepeace Thackeray, that lionized custodian of the public taste and morality, who in his review of the Roscoe edition (*The Times*, 2 September 1840) and in his subsequent lecture in *The English Humourists* (1853) distinguished between Fielding's consummate artistry in *Tom Jones*—'the most astonishing production of human ingenuity'—and what he regarded as the novelist's deplorable sense of morality, 'blunted' by a life wasted in taverns, gaming houses, and brothels. The subject of 'Thackeray's Injustice to Fielding' has been succinctly treated by Ralph Rader (1957) and earlier by Cross and Blanchard.

Before the criticism of Fielding's fiction could progress very far beyond mere exclamations of astonishment that such a 'literary providence' could be the attribute of such a coarse mind, Fielding's moral and intellectual character had to be redeemed from the aspersions and misrepresentations of his early biographers. For this good work we are indebted to W. L. Cross, whose *History of Henry Fielding* (1918) remains after half a century the standard life. Though Cross's biography has its faults—which, as we shall see, are by no means inconsiderable—yet the image of Fielding it presented served to restore him to respectability, as it were, and prepared the way for the current revaluation of his thought—moral, religious, social, and political. While Cross avoided any systematic analysis of Fielding's ethical views, he declared his opinion that the novelist's constant theme of an active benevolism was to be associated with the doctrines of Shaftesbury. For three decades thereafter critics such as Digeon (1923), Swann (1929), and Joesten (1932) improbably defined Fielding's moral philosophy as a mixture of deism and neo-stoicism, though Fielding had himself ridiculed these systems in the character of Square in *Tom Jones*. To Digeon, in fact, the relative failure of *Amelia*, its cheerless and rather maudlin didacticism, was the regrettable result (he supposed) of Fielding's latter-day conversion from deism to Christianity.

The flaw in this interpretation was pointed out by James A. Work in a seminal article, 'Henry Fielding, Christian Censor' (1949), which defined the Christian content of *The Champion* and proposed its general pertinence to Fielding's subsequent writings. Following this lead in *The Moral Basis of Fielding's Art* (1959), M. C. Battestin presented the first comprehensive analysis of Fielding's ethical and religious thought, demonstrating Fielding's debt to the rationalist, Latitudinarian tradition within the Church and, through an explication of *Joseph Andrews*, suggesting the relevance of this background to an understanding of the themes and structure of Fielding's fiction. Also useful—indeed indispensable—to anyone wishing to come to terms with the intellectual content of Fielding's works is H. K. Miller's admirable commentary on the *Miscellanies* (1961), that collection of essays in verse and prose in which Fielding defines such concepts as 'good-nature', 'greatness', and 'liberty' or discusses the characters of men. More recently, in *Fielding's Moral Psychology* (1966) Morris Golden has explored what he calls the theme of the 'enclosed self' in Fielding's fiction, finding a tension in the novels between the philosophies of Locke and Mandeville on the one hand and of Shaftesbury and the Latitudinarians on the other. A stimulating, if not very scholarly, contribution to the current reappraisal of Fielding's morality is J. Middleton Murry's essay 'In Defence of Fielding' (1956). Two excellent studies of Fielding's social thought have served to deepen, and in important ways to qualify, our understanding of his ethics: these are George Sherburn's article, 'Fielding's Social Outlook' (1956), and M. R. Zirker's monograph, *Fielding's Social Pamphlets* (1966), which, by revealing the fundamental conservatism of Fielding's attitude toward the poor, defines the limits of his doctrine of benevolism. Finally, one of the most important books on Fielding in recent years, G. W. Hatfield's *Fielding and the Language of Irony* (1968), examines the ways in which Fielding's concern for the moral health of society was inextricably connected with his self-conscious concern with language, the medium of his art itself and the sole means of communicating and perpetuating the moral wisdom of the past.

These studies, which share the common assumption that Fielding was, to use Sherburn's phrase, 'fundamentally a moralist', may be said to mark the main direction Fielding criticism has taken during the past decade. Sensing a certain awkwardness in the attempt to represent England's greatest comic novelist as the earnest exponent of morality and social order, other critics have chosen to stress the witty, playful side of Fielding's art: W. B. Coley, for example, in 'The Background of Fielding's Laughter' (1959) and especially Andrew Wright in *Henry Fielding: Mask and Feast* (1965). Though they proceed from a dubious premiss that confuses thematic considerations with those of tone and texture—i.e. since comedy by definition is not 'serious', Fielding's comic novels cannot have a serious moral purpose—these essays nevertheless have the salutary effect of directing our attention towards Fielding's comedy, its methods and techniques. Several other critics since the war have done just this—among them A. R. Humphreys, 'Fielding's Irony: Its Methods and Effects' (1942); W. R. Irwin, 'Satire and Comedy in the Works of Henry Fielding' (1946); and A. E. Dyson, 'Satiric and Comic Theory in Relation to Fielding' (1957). Of the various distinguishing features of Fielding's comic art none has received so much attention of late as the related questions of his irony and his use of an omniscient, intrusive narrator. Besides Hatfield's book mentioned above, G. R. Levine in *Henry Fielding and the Dry Mock* (1967) enumerates Fielding's ironic devices and discusses their function in the early works, including *Joseph Andrews* and *Jonathan Wild;* and in her rather more interesting study of irony in *Tom Jones* (1965) Eleanor Hutchens focuses on the types of oblique verbal irony which Fielding introduced into the English novel. The nature and function of Fielding's self-conscious narrator, another of his influential contributions to the art of novel-writing, have been the subject of brilliant analyses by Wayne Booth in 'The Self-Conscious Narrator in Comic Fiction before *Tristram Shandy*' (1952) and *The Rhetoric of Fiction* (1961), and of some astute, if unsympathetic, criticism by Ian Watt in his now classic study, *The Rise of the Novel* (1957). Equally illuminating on Fielding's methods of characterization is J. S. Coolidge, 'Fielding and "Conservation of Character"' (1960), who traces the shift from the 'type' characters of the early novels to the more 'realistic' figures of *Amelia*. Other books concerned in general with the theory and art of Fielding's fiction are: E. M. Thornbury, *Henry Fielding's Theory of the Comic Prose Epic* (1931), with a useful appendix reprinting the auction catalogue of Fielding's library; M. Johnson, *Fielding's Art of Fiction* (1961), a collection of essays on various devices in *Shamela*, *Joseph Andrews*, *Tom Jones*, and *Amelia*; S. Sacks, *Fiction and the Shape of Belief* (1963), an example of the so-called 'Chicago School' of neo-Aristotelian criticism, using Fielding to demonstrate the perhaps self-evident premiss that a novelist's beliefs are 'expressed in the judgments he conveys of his characters, their actions, and their thoughts'; and M. Irwin, *Fielding: The Tentative Realist* (1967), a rather perverse and finally irrelevant study of Fielding's fictional development.

For the non-specialist, a readable and perceptive introduction to Fielding's art of fiction is Robert Alter's *Fielding and the Nature of the Novel* (1968), an often brilliant anatomy (and defence) of Fielding's achievement, relating *Joseph Andrews* and *Tom Jones* to a tradition of the 'art-novel' extending from Cervantes to Joyce, Gide, and Nabokov. Especially valuable as sound, general introductions to Fielding are John Butt's excellent essay in the series 'Writers and Their Work' (1954, rev. edn., 1959) and A. D. McKillop's chapter on the novels in *The Early Masters of English Fiction* (1956). Designed to acquaint the reader with a broad selection of the best recent criticism on Fielding, R. Paulson's 'Spectrum' anthology (1962) reprints more than a dozen stimulating essays, most of them mentioned in the present survey.

The studies we have reviewed so far comprise a full selection of the most illuminating and provocative criticism written in the effort to define the general character of Fielding's art and thought. We may turn now to those essays which have been concerned more narrowly with particular works of his fiction.

On *Shamela* (1741): it was C. B. Woods's careful scholarship which demonstrated Fielding's authorship of this brilliant travesty beyond any reasonable doubt (1946). The place *Shamela* holds in the colourful history of the reception of *Pamela* is fully delineated in A. D. McKillop's *Samuel Richardson* (1936) and B. Kreissman's *Pamela–Shamela* (1960). There are no extensive analyses of Fielding's parody —perhaps because his basic joke needs no explaining—but in their introductions to editions of the work S. W. Baker (1953), Watt (1956) and Battestin (1961) identify the targets of Fielding's satire and discuss the reasons for his impatience, moral and aesthetic, with Richardson's novel. M. Johnson's *Fielding's Art of Fiction*, mentioned above, includes an interesting critique of Fielding's parodic method; and in an elaborate and ingenious essay, E. Rothstein has analysed the 'framework' devices that introduce the travesty (1968).

On *Joseph Andrews* (1742): Battestin's explication of the novel's themes and structure in *The Moral Basis of Fielding's Art* may be supplemented by H. Goldberg's in *The Art of 'Joseph Andrews'* (1969), which explores Fielding's debt to the comic romance tradition. Maynard Mack's preface to the Rinehart edition (1948) is an excellent general essay. In two other essays, D. Taylor traces the development of Joseph as hero (1957) and M. Spilka discusses the ways in which Fielding's comedy is resolved in the night adventures at Booby Hall (1953). The argument of the famous preface is the subject of a thoughtful analysis by Goldberg (1964); and the digressions of the novel—long an irritation to post-Coleridgean (or rather post-Jamesian) advocates of organic unity—have been defended and explained by Goldberg (1966) and D. Brooks (1968), among others. In 'Fielding's Revisions of *Joseph Andrews*' (1963) Battestin discusses the extensive changes introduced into the second edition and provides a full sample of the variant readings.

On *Jonathan Wild the Great* (1743): the standard study of Fielding's sources and of the background of his themes is W. R. Irwin, *The Making of Jonathan Wild* (1941), while J. E. Wells's early article (1913) is basic to an understanding of Fielding's political purpose in the book. In an interpretation of the 'moral allegory' of *Jonathan Wild* (1957), A. Wendt treats the antithetical relationship between Wild and Heartfree in the light of Fielding's Preface to the *Miscellanies*, defining the opposition between greatness and goodness. Until recently *Jonathan Wild* rarely elicited the sort of serious critical interest that has illuminated Fielding's other fiction; since 1965, however, more than a half-dozen articles on the book have appeared, perhaps the most notable of these being W. J. Farrell's 'The Mock-Heroic Form of *Jonathan Wild*' (1966) and J. Preston's 'The Ironic Mode: A Comparison of *Jonathan Wild* and *The Beggar's Opera*' (1966).

On *Amelia* (1751): the relative failure of Fielding's last novel from an aesthetic point of view has continued to puzzle his critics, though perhaps it is just here that Wright's emphasis upon the playfulness of Fielding at his best is most helpful. But if Fielding had 'gone soft' by the time of *Amelia*, as F. R. Leavis has put it, he nevertheless appears in that book as a skilful, ambitious craftsman and as a moralist of weighty substance. These aspects of the novel have been treated by G. Sherburn in his excellent essay, 'Fielding's *Amelia*: An Interpretation' (1936); by A. R. Towers in '*Amelia* and the State of Matrimony' (1954); by A. Wendt in 'The Naked Virtue of Amelia' (1960); by S. W. Baker in 'Fielding's *Amelia* and the Materials of Romance' (1962); and most recently by D. S. Thomas in 'Fortune and the Passions in Fielding's *Amelia*' (1965), a perceptive reading of the book based on a thorough understanding of Fielding's intellectual debt to the Christian humanist tradition.

Tom Jones, of course, is Fielding's masterpiece, the book on which his reputation stands and, Dr. Leavis's cavils notwithstanding, one of the monuments of the 'great tradition' of English fiction. Most of the general studies mentioned earlier naturally address themselves to *Tom Jones*, but there is much other criticism besides. For the non-specialist an excellent introduction is I. Ehrenpreis's monograph (1964), containing sound and stimulating discussions of Fielding's themes and techniques. This useful volume may be supplemented by M. C. Battestin's anthology of critical essays on the novel (1968), including essays by Watt (on Fielding's 'realism of assessment'), Empson (on his moral perceptiveness), Wright (on his delight in artifice), R. S. Crane (on the intricate architecture of the plot), Booth (on the intrusive narrator), and Alter (on Fielding's style); an appendix provides a fairly comprehensive bibliography of other recent criticism. Of the articles reprinted in this collection two at least require the attention of every serious student of the novel: these are Empson's spirited and brilliant 'defence' of Fielding's achievement (1958) and Crane's exhaustive neo-Aristotelian anatomy of Fielding's famous plot (1950). Though not based on the sort of rigorous historical scholarship that is necessary if the assumptions of Fielding's art and thought are to be properly estimated, two other essays by Dorothy Van Ghent (1953) and Robert Alter (1964) are none the less extremely readable and perceptive. Fielding's style and his use of the devices of classical rhetoric to enhance his comedy and to advance his moral themes are the subjects of two excellent articles by H. K. Miller (1966, 1970). Coley has a most interesting discussion of Gide's remarks on the moral content and narrative method of the novel (1959). With respect to the didactic purpose of *Tom Jones*, J. Preston has argued that Fielding's theme is the necessity of forming accurate moral judgements (1966). In two complementary essays Battestin discusses the meaning of design in the novel (1970) and the techniques by which Fielding conveys the central correlative themes of prudence and *sophia* (1968). In two other essays he interprets the episode of gypsies as a satiric parable against Jacobitism (1967) and he evaluates the Osborne–Richardson film of the novel as an adaptation of Fielding's art and his meaning (1966). The revisions of the novel are described by G. E. Jensen (1937), who, however, errs in supposing that the third, rather than the fourth, edition is more authoritative.

An interesting, and rather important, aspect of Fielding's career as a novelist is the nature of his personal relationship and professional rivalry with Samuel Richardson, the author whose first novel, *Pamela* (1740), prompted Fielding to try his own hand at a very different kind of fiction. Inevitably, this topic finds a prominent place in such standard, comprehensive studies as those by Cross, Blanchard, and McKillop (*Samuel Richardson*, 1936) already cited. The basic account, however, is McKillop's early article, 'The Personal Relations between Fielding and Richardson' (1931), which should be read in conjunction with Fielding's famous letter to his rival on the subject of *Clarissa*, a fascinating document discovered by E. L. McAdam and published in 1949. Also relevant are R. E. Moore's 'Dr. Johnson on Fielding and Richardson' (1951), F. Kermode's provocative essay in critical discrimination, 'Richardson and Fielding' (1950), and O. Jenkins's recent article, 'Richardson's *Pamela* and Fielding's "Vile Forgeries" ' (1965), a defence of Richardson suggesting that the continuation of *Pamela* was written, in part at least, to answer Fielding's ridicule of the novel in *Shamela*. An unusual and quite refreshing approach to the subject is that taken by W. Park in 'Fielding *and* Richardson' (1966), which argues that, despite their obvious differences, these two founders of the modern English novel were in some important ways very much alike.

Since Fielding's fiction often bears the marks of his early training as a dramatist, we may conclude this section by citing a few general studies of his plays. Still perhaps the best of these—which is not to say that it is very penetrating or profound—is by F. W. Bateson in

English Comic Drama, 1700–50 (1929). Three other critics, W. H. Rogers (1943), L. P. Goggin (1952), and J. P. Hunter (1972), have examined the techniques of Fielding's drama; and in *Comedy and Society from Congreve to Fielding* (1959), J. Loftis views the plays against the background of social history.

BIOGRAPHIES AND LETTERS

Within the last half-century Cross (1918) and F. H. Dudden (1952) produced voluminous lives of Fielding, yet neither of these works can be considered definitive. Admittedly, the obstacles in the way of Fielding's biographers have been formidable. Arthur Murphy, who gave us the only contemporary account of Fielding's life (1762), was no Boswell: though he had known Fielding personally and had the opportunity to seek information from the novelist's family and friends, Murphy used the occasion of his 'Essay' merely to flaunt his own meagre wit and two-penny learning; so as not 'to disturb the Manes of the dead', he avoided relating the incidents of Fielding's life, and in the course of the entire essay the only dates he supplied are those of his subject's birth and death. When one considers the further fact that only twenty of Fielding's letters are generally known to have survived (they have not been collected), the dearth of primary materials on which to base a dependable biography becomes lamentably clear.

Though Fielding was one of the most prominent public and literary figures of his age, his life, except in its broadest outlines, remains obscure, clouded by the misrepresentations of his enemies and the extravagant speculations of his friends. As we have already remarked, Cross's heroic labour of love remains the standard biography. Yet, though the product of much painstaking research, Cross's life is more an apology than an objective work of scholarship; in it the discernible facts of Fielding's career are too often ignored or distorted so as not to contradict the author's complimentary hypotheses. In order to restore Fielding to respectability among the upholders of propriety Cross idealized his subject, presenting him as a paragon rather than a man. More than a generation later, Dudden had the opportunity to repair these faults and to add to our knowledge of the facts of Fielding's career. Instead, though it contains long and sometimes illuminating discussions of Fielding's works and of the relevant historical backgrounds, Dudden's mammoth biography is little more than a servile imitation of Cross, written from the same assumptions and perpetuating the same errors of fact and interpretation. At present, therefore, there is no satisfactory major life of Fielding, nor is there—despite the numerous popular biographies that have been published—a reliable, briefer life suitable for the non-specialist reader.

Since the publication of Cross's work, several scholars have contributed to our knowledge and understanding of particular aspects of Fielding's life. An accurate and comprehensive study of his legal career is still needed, but B. M. Jones's *Henry Fielding, Novelist and Magistrate* (1933) is a beginning, and in two important articles A. B. Shepperson (1954) and W. B. Coley (1965) supply a good deal of new information relevant to Fielding's appointments to the magistracy. In 'Fielding's Changing Politics and *Joseph Andrews*' (1960), Battestin challenged Cross's characterization of Fielding as a staunch and unswerving antagonist of the prime minister, Sir Robert Walpole. Indeed, Isobel Grundy's publication (1972) of some early poems by Fielding has served to point the need for a complete reassessment of his political attitudes and loyalties during the 1730s: in these poems Fielding openly supports Walpole's party while satirizing the Scriblerus group of Tory wits. Finally, in 'Fielding and "Master Punch" in Panton Street' (1966), Battestin reconstructs an amusing episode of 1748 in which Fielding appears as impresario of a puppet theatre.

BIBLIOGRAPHY

A comprehensive, descriptive bibliography of Fielding's works is included in Cross, who, however, admits several unauthentic items to the canon while excluding other works now known to be by Fielding. In this respect, as in most others, Dudden merely duplicates Cross. Some of these errors are corrected by R. C. Jarvis in his series of notes, 'Fielding and the "Forty-Five" ' (1956–7).

Useful bibliographies of secondary works on Fielding are provided by Blanchard and by F. Cordasco (1948). (For corrections and additions to Cordasco, see the review in *PQ* (1950).) An exhaustive checklist of works by and about Fielding is included in the *NCBEL*. Sections on Fielding are contained in the annual bibliographies of current scholarship published by *PMLA* and *PQ*.

BACKGROUND READING

Though, as he observed of *Don Quixote*, Fielding's own novels may be regarded as histories of 'the world in general', they are also very much the product of England's Augustan Age. With this fact in mind, many of the critics already cited have been careful to place his fiction in its historical context, demonstrating the ways in which a book like *Tom Jones*, for example, gives imaginative expression to contemporary ideas, issues, and events. The student who wishes a broader acquaintance with this background may turn to a number of basic general studies. On the political history of the period, for example, W. E. H. Lecky's *History of England in the Eighteenth Century* (1878–90) provides an excellent detailed survey, which may be supplemented by Basil Williams's *The Whig Supremacy 1714–60* (1939), J. B. Owen's *The Rise of the Pelhams* (1957), and J. H. Plumb's biography of Robert Walpole (1956–61). Some informative accounts of English society in Fielding's day are A. S. Turberville, *English Men and Manners in the 18th Century* (1926); G. M. Trevelyan, *Illustrated English Social History*, vol. iii (1951); M. D. George, *England in Transition* (1931) and *London Life in the Eighteenth Century* (1925); and H. Phillips, *Mid-Georgian London* (1964).

On the history of ideas—the philosophical and religious milieu which helped to condition Fielding's thought—Leslie Stephen's *History of English Thought in the Eighteenth Century* (1876) remains a standard work, and Basil Willey's companion studies of the seventeenth- and eighteenth-century backgrounds (1934, 1946) comprise a stimulating and readable introduction to the subject. For an incisive survey of the Church in the period, see G. R. Cragg, *The Church and the Age of Reason 1648–1789* (1960). In religion Fielding subscribed to the optimistic doctrines of the Low Church, Latitudinarian divines whose views on human nature, together with those of Shaftesbury, profoundly influenced the benevolist movement and the so-called school of sensibility. For a definition of the Latitudinarian position, the pioneering and indispensable essay is R. S. Crane's 'Suggestions toward a Genealogy of the "Man of Feeling" ' (1934); also useful is R. N. Stromberg's *Religious Liberalism in Eighteenth Century England* (1954). Finally, two excellent studies that will help in a general way to familiarize the student with the climate of life and thought in which Fielding wrote are (for the non-specialist) A. R. Humphreys's *The Augustan World* (1954) and (for the specialist) J. W. Johnson's *The Formation of English Neoclassical Thought* (1967).

REFERENCES

TEXTS

(a) Collected works

A. Murphy (ed.), *The Works of Henry Fielding, Esq.; With the Life of the Author* (4 and 8 vols., London, 1762).

T. Roscoe (ed.), *The Works of Henry Fielding, Complete in One Volume, With Memoir of the Author* (London, 1840).

L. Stephen (ed.), *The Works of Henry Fielding, Esq. Edited with a Biographical Essay* (10 vols., London, 1882).

G. Saintsbury (ed.), *The Works of Henry Fielding* (12 vols., London 1893).

E. Gosse (ed.), *The Works of Henry Fielding, With an Introduction* (12 vols., Westminster and New York, 1898–9).

W. E. Henley (ed.), *The Complete Works of Henry Fielding, Esq. With an Essay on the Life, Genius and Achievement of the Author* (16 vols., New York and London, 1903; reprinted New York, 1967).

W. B. Coley (executive ed.), *The Wesleyan Edition of the Works of Henry Fielding* (Oxford and Middletown, Conn., 1967—); in progress.

(b) Separate works

W. W. Appleton (ed.), *The Historical Register for the Year 1736 and Eurydice Hissed* (paperback, Lincoln, Nebr., 1967).

S. W. Baker (ed.), *Joseph Andrews and Shamela* (paperback, New York, 1973).

—— (ed.), *Tom Jones* (paperback, New York, 1973).

M. C. Battestin (ed.), *The History of the Adventures of Joseph Andrews* (Wesleyan Edition, Oxford, and Middletown, Conn., 1967).

—— (ed.), *Joseph Andrews and Shamela* (paperback, Boston, Mass., 1961, and London, 1965).

—— and F. Bowers (edd.), *The History of Tom Jones, a Foundling* (Wesleyan Edition, Oxford and Middletown, Conn., 1973).

O. M. Brack, Jr., W. Kupersmith, and C. A. Zimansky (edd.), *Pasquin* (paperback, Iowa City, 1973).

D. Brooks (ed.), *Joseph Andrews and Shamela* (paperback, London and New York, 1970).

J. T. Hillhouse (ed.), *The Tragedy of Tragedies, or The Life and Death of Tom Thumb the Great* (New Haven, Conn., 1918).

A. R. Humphreys (ed.), *The History of Tom Jones* (2 vols. paperback, London and New York, 1962).

G. E. Jensen (ed.), *The Covent-Garden Journal* (2 vols. New Haven, Conn., and London, 1915; reprinted New York, 1964).

C. E. Jones (ed.), *The Female Husband and Other Writings* (paperback, Liverpool, 1960).

—— (ed.), *The Lovers Assistant, or New Art of Love (1760)*, Augustan Reprint Society Publications, No. 89 (paperback, Los Angeles, Calif., 1961).

F. Kermode (ed.), *The History of Tom Jones* (paperback, New York, 1964).

M. Locke (ed.), *The True Patriot: and The History of Our Own Times* (University, Ala., 1964, and London, 1965).

H. K. Miller (ed.), *Miscellanies, Volume One* (Wesleyan Edition, Oxford and Middletown, Conn., 1972).

L. J. Morrisey (ed.), *Tom Thumb and the Tragedy of Tragedies* (paperback, Edinburgh, 1970).

R. P. C. Mutter (ed.), *The History of Tom Jones* (paperback, Harmondsworth, 1966).

H. E. Pagliaro (ed.), *The Journal of a Voyage to Lisbon* (New York, 1963).

J. H. Plumb (ed.), *The Life of Mr. Jonathan Wild the Great* (paperback, New York, 1962).

E. V. Roberts (ed.), *The Grub-Street Opera* (paperback, Lincoln, Nebr., 1968).

G. Saintsbury (ed.), *Amelia* (2 vols., London, 1930; reprinted).

—— (ed.), *Jonathan Wild the Great and The Journal of a Voyage to Lisbon* (London, 1932; new edn., paperback, 1964).

G. Sherburn (ed.), *The History of Tom Jones a Foundling* (paperback, New York, 1950; reprinted).

I. Williams (ed.), *The Criticisms of Henry Fielding* (New York, 1970).

C. B. Woods (ed.), *The Author's Farce* (paperback, Lincoln, Nebr., 1966).

CRITICAL STUDIES AND COMMENTARY

R. Alter, *Fielding and the Nature of the Novel* (Cambridge, Mass., 1968).

—— 'The Picaroon Domesticated', in *Rogue's Progress: Studies in the Picaresque Novel* (Cambridge, Mass., 1964).

S. W. Baker (ed.), *An Apology for the Life of Mrs. Shamela Andrews* (Berkeley and Los Angeles, Calif., 1953).

—— 'Fielding's *Amelia* and the Materials of Romance', *PQ* xli (1962).

F. W. Bateson, 'Henry Fielding', in *English Comic Drama, 1700–50* (Oxford, 1929).

M. C. Battestin, 'Fielding's Definition of Wisdom: Some Functions of Ambiguity and Emblem in *Tom Jones*', *ELH* xxxv (1968).

—— 'Fielding's Revisions of *Joseph Andrews*', *Studies in Bibliography*, xvi (1963).

—— (ed.), *Joseph Andrews and Shamela* (paperback, Boston, Mass., and London, 1965).

—— *The Moral Basis of Fielding's Art: A Study of 'Joseph Andrews'* (Middletown, Conn., 1959; reprinted 1964).

—— 'Osborne's *Tom Jones*: Adapting a Classic', *The Virginia Quarterly Review*, xlii (1966); reprinted in W. R. Robinson (ed.), *Man and the Movies* (Baton Rouge, La., 1967).

—— (ed.), *Tom Jones: A Collection of Critical Essays* (Englewood Cliffs., N.J., 1968).

—— 'Tom Jones and "His *Egyptian* Majesty": Fielding's Parable of Government', *PMLA* lxxxii (1967).

—— '*Tom Jones*: The Argument of Design', in H. K. Miller, E. Rothstein, and G. Rousseau (edd.), *The Augustan Milieu* (Oxford, 1970).

F. T. Blanchard, *Fielding the Novelist: A Study in Historical Criticism* (New Haven, Conn., 1926; reprinted).

W. C. Booth, *The Rhetoric of Fiction* (Chicago, 1961; paperback).

—— 'The Self-Conscious Narrator in Comic Fiction before *Tristram Shandy*', *PMLA* lxvii (1952).

D. Brooks, 'The Interpolated Tales in *Joseph Andrews* Again', *MP* lxv (1968).

J. Butt, *Fielding*, Writers and Their Work, No. 57 (London, 1954; revised 1959).

W. B. Coley, 'The Background of Fielding's Laughter', *ELH* xxvi (1959).

—— 'Gide and Fielding', *Comparative Literature*, xi (1959).

J. S. Coolidge, 'Fielding and "Conservation of Character" ', *MP* lvii (1960).

[F. Coventry], *An Essay on the New Species of Writing Founded by Mr. Fielding*, (*1751*), ed. A. D. McKillop, Augustan Reprint Society Publications, No. 95 (Los Angeles, Calif., 1962).

R. S. Crane, 'The Plot of *Tom Jones*', *Journal of General Education*, iv (1950); revised as 'The Concept of Plot and the Plot of *Tom Jones*', in Crane (ed.), *Critics and Criticism Ancient and Modern* (Chicago, 1952).

W. L. Cross (see under BIOGRAPHIES AND LETTERS).

A. Digeon, *Les Romans de Fielding* (Paris, 1923); trans. *The Novels of Fielding* (London, 1925).

A. E. Dyson, 'Satiric and Comic Theory in Relation to Fielding', *MLQ* xviii (1957).

—— *The Crazy Fabric* (London, 1965).

I. Ehrenpreis, *Fielding: Tom Jones* (London, 1964; Woodbury, N.Y., 1965).

W. Empson, 'Tom Jones', *The Kenyon Review*, xx (1958).

W. J. Farrell, 'The Mock-Heroic Form of *Jonathan Wild*', *MP* lxiii (1966).

L. P. Goggin, 'Development of Techniques in Fielding's Comedies', *PMLA* lxvii (1952).

H. Goldberg, *The Art of 'Joseph Andrews'* (Chicago, Ill., and London, 1969).

—— 'Comic Prose Epic or Comic Romance: The Argument of the Preface to *Joseph Andrews*', *PQ* xliii (1964).

—— 'The Interpolated Stories in *Joseph Andrews* or, "the History of the World in General" Satirically Revised', *MP* lxiii (1966).

M. Golden, *Fielding's Moral Psychology* (Amherst, Mass., 1966).

G. W. Hatfield, *Henry Fielding and the Language of Irony* (Chicago, 1968).

A. R. Humphreys, 'Fielding's Irony: Its Methods and Effects', *RES* xviii (1942).

J. P. Hunter, 'Fielding's Reflexive Plays and the Rhetoric of Discovery', *Studies in the Literary Imagination* v (1972).

E. Hutchens, *Irony in 'Tom Jones'* (University, Ala., 1965).

M. Irwin, *Henry Fielding: The Tentative Realist* (Oxford, 1967).

W. R. Irwin, *The Making of 'Jonathan Wild': A Study in the Literary Method of Henry Fielding* (New York, 1941; reprinted).

—— 'Satire and Comedy in the Works of Henry Fielding', *ELH* xiii (1946).

O. Jenkins, 'Richardson's *Pamela* and Fielding's "Vile Forgeries" ', *PQ* xliv (1965).

G. E. Jensen, 'Proposals for a Definitive Edition of Fielding's *Tom Jones*', *Library*, xviii (1937).

M. Joesten, *Die Philosophie Fieldings* (Leipzig, 1932).

M. Johnson, *Fielding's Art of Fiction: Eleven Essays on 'Shamela', 'Joseph Andrews'. 'Tom Jones', and 'Amelia'* (Philadelphia, Pa., 1961).

F. Kermode, 'Richardson and Fielding', *Cambridge Journal*, iv (1950).

B. Kreissman, *Pamela–Shamela: A Study of the Criticisms, Burlesques, Parodies, and Adaptations of Richardson's 'Pamela'* (paperback, Lincoln, Nebr., 1960).

F. R. Leavis, *The Great Tradition: George Eliot, Henry James, Joseph Conrad* (London, 1948).

G. R. Levine, *Henry Fielding and the Dry Mock: A Study of the Techniques of Irony in His Early Works* (The Hague, 1967).

J. Loftis, *Comedy and Society from Congreve to Fielding* (Stanford, Calif., 1959).

E. L. McAdam, 'A New Letter from Fielding', *The Yale Review*, xxxviii (1949).

M. Mack (ed.), *The History of the Adventures of Joseph Andrews* (paperback, New York, 1948).

A. D. McKillop, 'Henry Fielding', in *The Early Masters of English Fiction* (Lawrence, Kans., 1956).

—— 'The Personal Relations between Fielding and Richardson', *MP* xxviii (1931).

—— *Samuel Richardson, Printer and Novelist* (Chapel Hill, N.C., 1936; reprinted).

H. K. Miller, *Essays on Fielding's 'Miscellanies': A Commentary on Volume One* (Princeton, N.J., 1961).

—— 'Some Functions of Rhetoric in *Tom Jones*', *PQ* xlv (1966).

—— 'The Voices of Henry Fielding: Style in *Tom Jones*', in Miller, Rothstein, and Rousseau (edd.), *The Augustan Milieu* (Oxford, 1970).

R. E. Moore, 'Dr. Johnson on Fielding and Richardson', *PMLA* lxvi (1951).

J. M. Murry, 'In Defence of Fielding', in *Unprofessional Essays* (London, 1956).

W. Park, 'Fielding *and* Richardson', *PMLA* lxxxi (1966).

R. Paulson (ed.), *Fielding: A Collection of Critical Essays* (paperback, Englewood Cliffs., N.J., 1962).

—— and T. Lockwood (edd.), *Fielding: The Critical Heritage* (paperback, London, 1968).

J. Preston, 'The Ironic Mode: A Comparison of *Jonathan Wild* and *The Beggar's Opera*', *EIC* xvi (1966).

—— '*Tom Jones* and "the Pursuit of True Judgment" ', *ELH* xxxiii (1966).

R. Rader, 'Thackeray's Injustice to Fielding', *JEGP* lvi (1957).

W. H. Rogers, 'Fielding's Early Aesthetic and Technique', *SP* xl (1943).

E. Rothstein, 'The Framework of *Shamela*', *ELH* xxxv (1968).

S. Sacks, *Fiction and the Shape of Belief: A Study of Fielding with Glances at Swift, Johnson and Richardson* (Berkeley and Los Angeles, Calif., 1964).

G. Sherburn, 'Fielding's *Amelia*: An Interpretation', *ELH* iii (1936).

—— *The Rise of the Novel: Studies in Defoe, Richardson and Fielding* (Berkeley and Los Angeles, Calif., and London, 1957).

J. E. Wells, 'Fielding's Political Purpose in *Jonathan Wild*', *PMLA* xxi (1913).

M. Spilka, 'Comic Resolution in Fielding's *Joseph Andrews*', *College English*, xv (October 1953).

G. R. Swann, 'Fielding and Empirical Realism', in *Philosophical Parallelism in Six English Novelists: The Conception of Good, Evil and Human Nature* (Philadelphia, Pa., 1929).

D. Taylor, jun., 'Joseph as Hero in *Joseph Andrews*', *Tulane Studies in English*, vii (1957).

W. M. Thackeray, *The English Humourists of the Eighteenth Century*, Lecture v (London, 1853); available in Everyman's Library edition.

D. S. Thomas, 'Fortune and the Passions in Fielding's *Amelia*', *MLR* lx (1965).

E. M. Thornbury, *Henry Fielding's Theory of the Comic Prose Epic* (Madison, Wis., 1931; reprinted).

A. R. Towers, '*Amelia* and the State of Matrimony', *RES* n.s. v (1954).

D. Van Ghent, 'On *Tom Jones*', in *The English Novel: Form and Function* (New York, 1953).

I. P. Watt (ed.), *An Apology for the Life of Mrs. Shamela Andrews* (*1741*), Augustan Reprint Society Publications, no. 57 (Los Angeles, Calif., 1956).

—— *The Rise of the Novel: Studies in Defoe, Richardson and Fielding* (Berkeley, and Los Angeles, Calif., and London, 1957).

J. E. Wells, 'Fielding's Political Purpose in *Jonathan Wild*', *PMLA* xxi (1913).

A. Wendt, 'The Moral Allegory of *Jonathan Wild*', *ELH* xxiv (1957).

—— 'The Naked Virtue of Amelia', *ELH* xxvii (1960).

C. B. Woods, 'Fielding and the Authorship of *Shamela*', *PQ* xxv (1946).

J. A. Work, 'Henry Fielding, Christian Censor', in F. W. Hilles (ed.), *The Age of Johnson: Essays Presented to Chauncey Brewster Tinker* (New Haven, Conn., 1949).

A. Wright, *Henry Fielding: Mask and Feast* (Berkeley and Los Angeles, Calif., and London, 1965).

M. R. Zirker, jun., *Fielding's Social Pamphlets: A Study of 'An Enquiry into the Causes of the Late Increase of Robbers' and 'A Proposal for Making an Effectual Provision for the Poor'* (Berkeley and Los Angeles, Calif., 1966).

BIOGRAPHIES AND LETTERS

M. C. Battestin, 'Fielding and "Master Punch" in Panton Street', *PQ* xlv (1966).

—— 'Fielding's Changing Politics and *Joseph Andrews*', *PQ* xxxix (1960).

W. B. Coley, 'Fielding's Two Appointments to the Magistracy', *MP* lxiii (1965).

W. L. Cross, *The History of Henry Fielding* (3 vols., New Haven, Conn., 1918; reprinted 1964).

F. H. Dudden, *Henry Fielding: His Life, Works and Times* (2 vols., Oxford, 1952; reprinted London, 1966).

I. Grundy, 'New Verse by Henry Fielding', *PMLA* lxxxvii (1972).

B. M. Jones, *Henry Fielding, Novelist and Magistrate* (London, 1933).

A. Murphy, 'Essay on the Life and Genius of Henry Fielding, Esq.;' in J. E. Wells, Fielding's *Works* (4 and 8 vols., London, 1762).

A. B. Shepperson, 'Additions and Corrections to Facts about Fielding', *MP* li (1954).

BIBLIOGRAPHY

F. T. Blanchard (see under CRITICAL STUDIES AND COMMENTARY).

F. Cordasco, *Fielding: A List of Critical Studies Published from 1895 to 1946* (Brooklyn, 1948).

W. L. Cross (see previous section).

F. H. Dudden (see previous section).

R. C. Jarvis, 'Fielding and the "Forty-Five" ', *N & Q* n.s. iii–iv (September, November 1956, January 1957).

BACKGROUND READING

G. R. Cragg, *The Church and the Age of Reason, 1648–1789* (paperback, Harmondsworth, 1960; rev. edn. 1966).

R. S. Crane, 'Suggestions toward a Genealogy of the "Man of Feeling" ', *ELH* i (1934).

M. D. George, *England in Transition* (London, 1931; rev. edn., paperback, Harmondsworth, 1953).

——— *London Life in the Eighteenth Century* (London, 1925; paperback, Harmondsworth, 1965).

A. R. Humphreys, *The Augustan World: Life and Letters in Eighteenth-Century England* (London, 1954).

J. W. Johnson, *The Formation of English Neo-Classical Thought* (Princeton, N.J., 1967).

W. E. H. Lecky, *The History of England in the Eighteenth Century* (London, 1878–90).

J. B. Owen, *The Rise of the Pelhams* (London, 1957).

H. Phillips, *Mid-Georgian London* (London, 1964).

J. H. Plumb, *Sir Robert Walpole* (2 vols., London, 1956–61).

L. Stephen, *History of English Thought in the Eighteenth Century* (2 vols. London, 1876; 3rd rev. edn., paperback, 1963).

R. N. Stromberg, *Religious Liberalism in Eighteenth-Century England* (Oxford, 1954).

G. M. Trevelyan, *Illustrated English Social History*, vol. iii (London, 1951).

A. S. Turberville, *English Men and Manners in the Eighteenth Century* (Oxford, 1926; rev. edn. 1929).

B. Willey, *The Seventeenth-Century Background: Studies in the Thought of the Age in Relation to Poetry and Religion* (London, 1934).

——— *The Eighteenth-Century Background: Studies on the Idea of Nature in the Thought of the Period* (London, 1946).

B. Williams, *The Whig Supremacy 1714–60* (Oxford, 1939; 2nd edn., rev. by C. H. Stuart, 1962).

Duncan Isles

AT the outset of this survey, special attention must be drawn to three particularly indispensable works to which frequent reference will be made: Lodwick Hartley's *Laurence Sterne in the Twentieth Century* (referred to by the cue-title *Hartley*); *Laurence Sterne: A Collection of Critical Essays*, ed. John Traugott, Twentieth Century Views series (cue-title *TCV*); and *The Winged Skull: Papers from the Laurence Sterne Bicentenary Conference*, edd. Arthur H. Cash and John M. Stedmond (cue-title *WS*). *Hartley*, described in the Bibliographies section below, is the standard guide to Sterne criticism up to 1968. *TCV* is the best available collection of its kind, containing eight of the most influential critical studies published between 1929 and 1962, together with a thoughtful introduction by Traugott. *WS*'s five sections include Sterne's literary career, sources, prose style, techniques, and influence. Taken as a whole, it provides the best single means of sampling the preoccupations, scope, and standard of present-day Sterne criticism.

For their generous assistance in the preparation of the following discussion, my warmest thanks are due to Professor Lodwick Hartley and Dr. Richard Davies.

TEXTS

A modern collected edition of Sterne's works is in progress, under the general editorship of Melvyn New. In the meantime, the standard collected editions remain Wilbur Cross's twelve-volume *Works and Life*, and the seven-volume unannotated Shakespeare Head. The most useful selected edition is Douglas Grant's Reynard, which includes Sterne's own *Memoirs of Mr. Laurence Sterne*, and excerpts from the sermons and letters, in addition to the major works. Ian Jack's Oxford English Novels volume gives fully annotated scholarly texts of *A Sentimental Journey*, *The Journal to Eliza*, and *A Political Romance*. The best inexpensive paperback editions of both *Tristram Shandy* and *A Sentimental Journey* are Graham Petrie's Penguins. Gardner Stout has provided a superb definitive edition of *A Sentimental Journey*. The standard scholarly edition of *Tristram Shandy* remains that of James Work, but advanced students should supplement its textual treatment and annotation by reference to Ian Watt's excellent Riverside edition.

CRITICAL STUDIES AND COMMENTARY

In the interests of coherence, intelligibility, and ease of reference, the following system of sub-division has been adopted in this section.

The first sub-section (*The Eighteenth and Nineteenth Centuries*) begins by referring to works which will enhance the reader's understanding of earlier criticism and provide information concerning Sterne's reputation and influence throughout the period. It goes on to give a very brief summary of eighteenth- and nineteenth-century critical tendencies.

The second sub-section (*The Twentieth Century*) is devoted to critical studies up to 1971. For the particular benefit of non-specialist students whose time for reading secondary material is severely limited, initial selection has been made of a 'core' of introductory studies. These should help the reader to follow the main lines of interest manifested in present-day Sterne criticism, and to understand the underlying developments in modern literary theory on which they are based. The sub-section continues by examining the most important book-length critical studies of Sterne's works. It ends with a highly selective survey of shorter critical essays, considered under the categories of Sterne's sources, philosophy, and literary techniques.

The third and final sub-section (*Sterne and Modern Literature*) discusses criticism of his modern influence.

The Eighteenth and Nineteenth Centuries

The status and interpretation of Sterne's works within this period is reflected in contemporary critical discussion, and in their literary influence both in Britain and overseas. It should be emphasized that some degree of familiarity with contemporary literary theory is an essential prerequisite to the study of early critical analyses of Sterne's works, especially as his own contributions to the theory of prose fiction are of such importance. In this field, J. W. H. Atkins gives the best introductory guide to eighteenth-century theory. Wimsatt and Brooks's *Neoclassical Criticism* provides further discussion which is both more detailed and more controversial, and René Wellek's *Later Eighteenth Century* is the standard scholarly work. The only major published study specifically related to criticism of the eighteenth-century novel is J. B. Heidler's.

Readers who are particularly interested in Sterne's eighteenth-
and nineteenth-century reception and influence have been well
served by modern scholarship. Reprints of eighteenth-century reviews are to be found in Bartlett and Sherwood's *English Novel*,
George Barnett's *Eighteenth-Century British Novelists on the Novel*, and
(particularly) Ioan Williams's *Novel and Romance*. Alan Howes's indispensable *Yorick and the Critics* gives an excellent detailed account of
Sterne's English reputation from 1760 to 1868. J. C. T. Oates's
Shandyism and Sentiment (dealing with Sterneian imitations) displays
an unusual gift for combining erudition with entertainment, and
should certainly be read by all Sterne enthusiasts. Detailed and
illuminating discussion relating to various aspects of Sterne's influence will be found in such works as James Foster's *History of the Pre-
Romantic Novel in England*; Robert Mayo's *English Novel in the Magazines*; A. B. Shepperson's *Novel in Motley*; and J. M. S. Tomkins's
Popular Novel in England. Eighteenth- and nineteenth-century British
authors in whose works scholars claim to detect Sterne's influence
include Burns, Mackenzie, Southey, Byron, Dickens, Bulwer-Lytton,
and Thackeray. Sterne's foreign reception and influence has received
a great deal of study, particularly in Germany. *WS* gives excellent
brief surveys relating to Germany (Bernhard Fabian), Italy (Paul
Kirby), North America (Lodwick Hartley), and Japan (Natsuo
Shumuta). References to discussions of Sterne's alleged influence on
a wide variety of individual foreign authors (Rousseau, Diderot,
Stendhal, Goethe, Heine, Tolstoi, Pushkin, and many more) will be
found in *Hartley*.

When considering Sterne's sensational and controversial impact
upon the reading public of his own day, it is important to remember
that *Tristram Shandy* was originally published in five instalments
between December 1759 and January 1767. Apart from creating a
certain amount of suspense, this instalment system had important
repercussions on the novel's critical reception. For example, its
novelty waned with each successive instalment, whereas admiration
of its pathos correspondingly increased. It was as controversial as it
was popular and fashionable. Its novelty, wit, pathos, and good-
natured satire were praised, but many readers disliked its seeming
oddity, incoherence, and—particularly, in view of Sterne's profes-
sion—obscenity. *A Sentimental Journey* (February 1768) outstripped
Tristram Shandy in popularity, and was particularly appreciated for
its sentimentality and pathos. Both works were widely and un-
successfully imitated.

Sterne's popularity remained high throughout the remainder of the century, although John Ferriar's scrutiny of his literary borrowings (*Illustrations of Sterne*) added the charge of plagiarism to the other adverse criticisms. In the first half of the nineteenth century, Sterne's status as a popular writer inevitably dwindled, but he was read appreciatively by many of his fellow-writers, including Coleridge, Hazlitt, Scott, De Quincey, Lamb, Carlyle, Leigh Hunt, Bulwer-Lytton, and Dickens. It was from among these writers that the most important critical comments came. The most perceptive of these comments were made in Coleridge's 1818 lecture on the nature of wit and humour. Coleridge considered Sterne as a humorist alongside Cervantes, Shakespeare, and Rabelais, and gave a shrewd analysis of Sterne's comic effects, and use of digressions. Hazlitt, too, in his *Lectures on the English Comic Writers* (delivered in the winter of 1818–19), praised Sterne's prose style and characterization, emphasizing his achievement as a humorist rather than as a master of pathos. Sir Walter Scott, in the introductory essay of his edition of *Tristram Shandy* (Ballantyne's Novelist's Library series, 1823), praised Sterne's original genius, although he disapproved of his affectation and tasteless ribaldry. Later in the century, Leigh Hunt's *Essay on Wit and Humour* (1846) defined humour—along the lines of Coleridge and Hazlitt—as the result of incongruity. Within this tradition, Hunt ranked Uncle Toby as the greatest of all humorous characters, and saw *Tristram Shandy* as the outstanding example of a book which combined wit and humour with profound wisdom. Howes claims this evaluation to be 'not an isolated phenomenon, but rather an indication of the critical sentiment of the time'. The opposite approach to Sterne, which saw him as a contemptible hypocrite who wrote insincere, maudlin, and indecent novels, was also widespread, however. Thackeray (whose own relationship with Sterne's works was complex, as Howes points out) gave this hostile approach its most memorable expression in his *Lectures on the English Humourists* (delivered in 1851).

By the late nineteenth and early twentieth centuries, Sterne's works were accepted as 'classics', but tended to be a minority taste among the general reading public. Scholars performed valuable ground-work in biography, editing, and influence-study. The critical assessments of the time were, however, gravely impeded by their apparent inability to differentiate between the novelist's personality and those of his narrators. It seems to have been generally accepted that Sterne was Tristram and/or Yorick, and that the narrator's attitudes and statements were to be taken at their face-value, thereby precluding the possibility of recognizing, or responding to, irony.

The Twentieth Century

During the first forty years of the present century, we see the gradual emergence of a more sophisticated approach to Sterne criticism. Growing awareness of *Tristram Shandy's* and *A Sentimental Journey's* inner coherence, and of their author's artistry, self-discipline, and careful utilization of his predecessors, is apparent in the criticism of (among others) Virginia Woolf and Sir Herbert Read. The late 1930s witnessed a series of extremely important critical advances in the work of Kenneth MacLean, Theodore Baird, W. B. C. Watkins (*TCV*), and Rufus Putney, all pointing in various ways toward Sterne's artistry in such matters as the manipulation of contemporary literary conventions and expectations; the conscious use of careful plot-construction; and the use of irony and significant detail.

The next thirty years (up to 1970) witnessed an astonishing increase in the volume, erudition, and subtlety of published discussion. This critical debate has not, of course, been conducted in a vacuum, but in the context of similar, and closely related, activity in the fields of eighteenth-century studies (particularly Swift criticism) and literary theory. It is now generally accepted that Tristram and Yorick (like Swift's Hack and Gulliver) are deliberately contrived entities, to be judged as fictional characters; that Sterne's attitude toward them and their philosophies is complex and ambiguous (though there is an infinite range of critical emphasis within the spectrum bounded by Sterne's allegedly sympathetic, playful admiration for any given character on the one hand, and his merciless concealed ridicule on the other); and that Sterne is in some way a serious and profound thinker as well as a comedian.

(a) Introductory Studies

The best initial introduction to Sterne studies is Alan McKillop's *Early Masters of English Fiction* (*TCV*). In his analysis of Sterne's techniques, achievements, and relationship with other writers, McKillop makes comprehensive use of modern approaches in a manner which is uniformly sensible and well balanced. Sterne's relationship with other past and contemporary writers (such as Cervantes, Rabelais, Locke, Swift, Pope, and Richardson), and with current literary genres and traditions (including the 'conventional' novel form, 'learned wit', the mock-heroic, and the burlesque), is carefully examined. He is seen as neither a simple moralist nor a simple satirist, but as a writer who draws our attention to the mixture of admirable and laughable characteristics in any given object, character, or concept. Thus, 'the old learning, the old pompous rhetoric, and the new science are taken to be ludicrous and important at the same time. They can be absurd and significant.' Similarly, feeling or 'sentiment' is seen as 'inevitable and admirable, the glory of human nature, but at the same time ludicrous.' The mixed attributes of Sterne's characters (including his narrators) enable them to be contrasted both favourably and unfavourably with the world about them. Tristram is a humorist writing about humorists, sharing some of the ludicrous aspects of his subjects (such as his father's comic pedantry), but at the same time retaining 'a control that can be described as partly rational and partly social'. In *A Sentimental Journey*, the narrator Yorick is 'a comic figure representing at the same time sentimentalism and the ultimate refinement or attenuation of the comedy of humors', so that sentimentalism itself is simultaneously sympathized with and laughed at.

With regard to *A Sentimental Journey*, McKillop should be supplemented by the critical introduction to Stout's edition (see TEXTS). Developing McKillop's sensible remarks about the character of Yorick, Stout suggests that Yorick's good-natured sentimentalism is fundamentally admirable, but (as is inevitable in an imperfect world) comically flawed. Yorick's shortcomings are being continually exposed in his Quixotic dealings with his fellow-men. He is sufficiently perceptive and self-conscious to be both aware of and ruefully amused at his failings. In general, *A Sentimental Journey* is regarded as a kind of 'parable', or 'fable', illustrating the perplexities involved in the potentially successful struggle to obey one of the eighteenth century's favourite moral imperatives, '*Know thyself.*'

Tristram Shandy and *A Sentimental Journey* are so demanding and absorbing in themselves that it is easy for readers to ignore the literary qualities of Sterne's sermons and correspondence. Here, the best introductions are the appropriate chapters of James Downey's *Eighteenth Century Pulpit* (which, for detailed study, must be supplemented by Lonsing Hammond's admirably thorough investigation) and Howard Anderson's *Familiar Letter in the Eighteenth Century*. Downey regards the sermons as the most extreme example of contemporary preachers' efforts 'to rid the form of the sermon of the last vestigial influence of classical oratory.' They come 'closer to passing over entirely into the field of literature than [those of] any other preacher of the eighteenth century.' Their literary devices include a style that is 'a surprising mixture of simplicity and majesty'; liberal use of contrast, drama, and digression; a strong rhetorical attempt to exploit the congregation's emotions; and a particularly significant tendency toward fictionalizing Scriptural characters in order to reveal their thoughts in stream-of-consciousness fashion. Anderson similarly demonstrates the literary self-consciousness of Sterne's correspondence. 'His generous and subtle imagination enabled him to express his feeling for others in a style most likely to ensure their sympathetic response.' Dramatic techniques (such as dramatizing the act of writing and placing the reader *in medias res*) are used to create a sense of immediacy. Other familiar ground shared by the letters and novels includes Sterne's carefully contrived verbal associations (often obscene, and always adjusted to the recipient's intellectual capacity) and his assumption of the *persona* of a wittily indecisive wise fool.

For any reader wishing to relate Sterne's works to those of his predecessors and contemporaries, the best introductory study remains D. W. Jefferson's '*Tristram Shandy* and the Tradition of Learned Wit' (*TCV*). Here, it is argued that the novel has an underlying coherent form, and belongs within a tradition of 'learned wit' exemplified by Rabelais and carried on by Swift. This wit is characteristically directed towards learned topics, is marked by an 'elasticity in moving from the serious to the flippant', was eventually destroyed by 'a middle-class spirit in religion and morals', and had in Sterne its last great practitioner. The appropriate sections of Ian Watt's *Rise of the Novel* and (particularly) Martin Price's *To the Palace of Wisdom* are valuable in relating Sterne to other contemporary novelists. According to Watt, Sterne fits into the tradition of 'formal realism' in the development of the novel, finding 'a way of reconciling Richardson's realism of presentation with Fielding's realism of assessment'. Price's complex and absorbing analysis initially relates *Tristram Shandy* to two other works published in the same years as Sterne's first two volumes. The works are Johnson's *Rasselas* and Voltaire's *Candide*, and all three together are seen to manifest a tendency toward a form of prose fiction that 'denies the possibility of resolution.' This is a development of Fielding's 'novel of flagrantly contrived resolution', where characters like Tom Jones and Booth 'lack the strength to master their situations'. *Candide* embodies comic rejection of reliance on rational systems, and indicates the cultivation of eccentricity and impulse as a refuge from rationality. Like Voltaire, Johnson 'distrusts man's hope that he can understand ... providence and, even more, man's assumption that he has understood it.' *Tristram Shandy* takes up the same themes of human ineffectuality and the unreliability of 'systems and forms'. Tristram, consciously suffering from 'the malady of association', is a failed and hesitant version of Fielding's securely ironic narrator. He welcomes the accidental, and reacts to death, grief, and formality by the flight to France in Volume vii. Sterne's emphasis is on man creating his own joy ('Viva la joia'); the 'erotic energy' of the peasant dance is the alternative to Maria's grief.

One of the most useful categories of introductory studies that can be mentioned here is that which correlates modern literary theory and the development of Sterne criticism. The three works which appear to have had the most formative influence in this respect are Northrop Frye's *Anatomy of Criticism*; Stuart Tave's *Amiable Humorist*; and Wayne Booth's *Rhetoric of Fiction*. In addition to these, if the reader wishes to see a present-day example of the most sophisticated theories of prose fiction being applied to Sterne's art, he should turn to Robert Gorham Davis's 'Sterne and the Delineation of the Modern Novel' (*WS*). Frye's examination of prose style sees Sterne as 'the chief master of prose *melos* [that is, Aristotelian 'music', as opposed to *opsis*, or spectacle] before the development of "stream of consciousness" techniques'. His other major categorization of Sterne comes in his celebrated analysis of 'fiction' (used to describe literature designed to be read rather than spoken or enacted) and prose-fictional genres. *Tristram Shandy* emerges as the most successful combination of the realistic 'novel' and the stylized satirical 'anatomy'.

Stuart Tave's *Amiable Humorist* is principally concerned with the evolution of complex fictional characters who are neither purely heroic nor purely ridiculous, but are simultaneously comic and sympathetic. Such characters are employed in two-way satire, in which the 'amiable humorist' character exposes the weaknesses of society by his positive qualities, while his own weaknesses are exposed by the norms of society. A very persuasive argument seeks to validate this concept and to place Don Quixote, Parson Adams, and the characters of *Tristram Shandy* within the 'amicable humorist' tradition.

Wayne Booth's *Rhetoric of Fiction* is indispensable. Its scope is vast, covering prose fiction of all countries and periods, and the work is widely regarded as the best study of narrative technique that has yet been made. It contains a detailed and convincing analysis of the various formal traditions (including particular kinds of comic novels, essay-collections and miscellaneous satires which employ deliberately comic narrators) lying behind *Tristram Shandy*. Tristram is presented as a dramatized character in his own right, completely independent of Sterne. He is a typically human mixture of ridiculous and sympathetic attributes. As a story-teller, he is seen by the reader as a comic failure, his desperate and incompetent efforts to control his material supplying a high proportion of the novel's comic effects. On the other hand, Sterne, the creator behind the scenes, succeeds in combining this illusion of chaos with the achievement of a unified work of art. This unity resides primarily in the personality of Tristram himself. In addition, Booth claims that, as far as Sterne is concerned, *Tristram Shandy* is a completed work.

Davis's 'Sterne and the Delineation of the Modern Novel' applies to Sterne the ideas that have emerged in the theoretical discussion of the novel in the 1960s. His radical claim is that *Tristram Shandy* 'demonstrates more fully and translucently the basic ontology of the novel, the sense of what the novel really is or does, . . . than any single modern novel'. In support of his vision of Sterne the master theorist, Davis produces a brilliant and compact analysis of some of the central theoretical characteristics involved in the creation and reading of prose fiction. Sterne's creative and philosophical relationship with Goethe, Kierkegaard, Joyce, Beckett, Faulkner, Butor, Robbe-Grillet, and—particularly—Thomas Mann is also examined.

(b) Book-length Critical Studies

Of the major critical analyses published up to 1959, the most challenging and influential is John Traugott's *Tristram Shandy's World*, which is concerned with Sterne's use of both Locke and the devices of formal rhetoric. Traugott argues that Sterne uses 'Locke's terminology and logic with a solemn mock-devotion', exploiting—and even at certain points burlesquing—his ideas. With regard to Sterne's rhetoric, it is suggested that the central problem dealt with in *Tristram Shandy* is that of communication.

The 1960s saw the emergence of at least four sophisticated, well-written English critical studies, namely: Arthur Cash's *Sterne's Comedy of Moral Sentiments*; John Stedmond's *Comic Art of Laurence Sterne*; William Piper's *Laurence Sterne*; and Melvyn New's *Laurence Sterne as Satirist*. Cash's work is the standard study of *A Sentimental Journey*. It examines the *Journey* in the light of the sermons, and identifies Sterne's ethical rationalism as its underlying moral basis. Stedmond's *Comic Art* has strong claims to be the best comprehensive critical study of Sterne to have appeared so far. Its first part gives an extremely thorough survey of Sterne's prose style; narrative and satiric technique; relationship with (and borrowings from) other writers; and use of a wide range of conventions (such as rhetoric and 'learned wit'). Stedmond deals particularly well with Sterne's technique of playing with the reader's expectations; his relationship to Rabelais, Burton, Erasmus, Browne, and Swift; and his deliberate juxtaposition of several contrasting prose styles. The second part of Stedmond's study offers a detailed, systematic analysis of *Tristram Shandy* and *A Sentimental Journey*, together with a discussion of the Sermons. Tristram is seen as a fully-dramatized narrator (as suggested by Booth), and a 'clown-author'. He is a paradoxically wise fool, 'a comic portrait of the artist, and a comic analogue of the human predicament', obsessed by words and the problem of communication, and at the mercy of stray impulses. In varying degrees, Walter, Toby, and Tristram are all 'dunces' in the *Dunciad* tradition, whereas Yorick comes closest to the norm of desirable human behaviour. *A Sentimental Journey*, it is claimed, blends comedy and benevolistic morality. Yorick is a self-consciously comic figure (but no clown) whom Sterne gently mocks.

Like Stedmond, Piper places particular emphasis on Sterne's works in the context of their own time. Tristram and Yorick appear in the company of Swift's Hack and Gulliver, Addison's Spectator, and Johnson's Rambler, as self-conscious narrators who are publically and socially oriented to serve their creators' satiric purposes. Sterne's conversational style is allied to that of Swift, Addison, Johnson, and Wilkes. Tristram's central problem is allegedly that most of the material that he particularly wants to discuss in public is 'profoundly unsuitable to social communication' by virtue of its oddity, painful unpleasantness, or obscenity. Piper's interpretation of *A Sentimental Journey* is optimistic; in the smiling European milieu (as opposed to the claustrophobic four-mile radius of the Shandy world), Yorick functions as an empirical teacher of the nature and benefits of sentiment. His inconsistency, self-love, and tendency toward over-sentimentality may appear absurd, but this is counter-balanced by his charm, good nature, candour, frequent intelligence, and self-knowledge. He therefore emerges with 'the dignity that comes with public, grace, honesty, and intelligence'.

In sharp contrast to this approach, New presents us with an austere Swiftian view of *Tristram Shandy*. His almost diagrammatically simple thesis can best be summed up in his own words: '*Tristram Shandy* is not a psychological novel, but a satire, and thus finds its coherence not in human consciousness, but in satiric target and satiric attack. . . . Sterne's satiric attack is twofold. In the first place, he satirizes the creative urge in man, in so far as it results in "creations" wholly inadequate to the purposes they were intended to serve. Second, Sterne attacks the desire to promulgate these follies and failures, the insistence upon converting one's neighbours to one's point of view. ... Ultimately ... [Sterne attacks] the attitude of pride and self-sufficiency with which men offer, from their frail bodies and pitiable minds, solutions to the universe. The final sin is taking oneself and one's ideas more seriously than either warrants. The final virtue is humility.' New mounts a magnificent defence of his position in both general and particular terms. He builds an initial foundation on a study of eighteenth-century theology and philosophy and modern critical theory. Here, he emphasizes Sterne's religious orthodoxy; the relationship between orthodoxy and classical satire (which depends on the pre-existence of a clearly-defined body of norms); and the nature of the satire (the primary objective of which is attack). New then defends his case in a detailed interpretation of *Tristram Shandy*; in which Toby is the ridiculous *miles gloriosus*; Walter the *philosophus gloriosus*; and Tristram the proud, self-indulgent Dunce who not only casts all rigorous moral and artistic standards aside in the riding of his hobby-horse (which is *Tristram Shandy* itself) but attempts to debauch his readers by encouraging them to ride with him.

William V. Holtz's *Image and Immortality* is the first major Sterne study of the 1970s. Holtz provides a provocative and erudite discussion of the relationship between pictorial and literary expression in the eighteenth century. He examines the relationship of Sterne's theories to Hogarth's, and contends that *Tristram Shandy* strives to unite the pictorial and the literary.

(c) Critical Essays
Sources

'To see Sterne as untypical of his age, as an oddity, and to think of him as a prophet crying out in the sterile wilderness of the eighteenth century about the stream of consciousness or exsitentialism is absurd.' This statement of Clarence Tracy's is the theme of much current Sterne scholarship, and is nowhere better illustrated than in the essay from which the quotation is taken, namely, 'As Many Chapters as Steps' (*WS*), where Tracy examines the relationship between biography and novel-writing in Sterne's time. Louis Landa's 'Shandean Homunculus' brilliantly elucidates *Tristram Shandy* by reference to contemporary scientific theory. Similarly, Cash's 'Birth of Tristram Shandy' relates the obstetrical techniques and instruments of John Burton the man-midwife to appropriate passages (so to speak) in the novel. Robert Alter's '*Tristram Shandy* and the Game of Love' considers the function of the convention of sexual wit as both a source of imaginative pleasure and an 'instrument of epistemological critique'. Another important aspect of contemporary thought is perceptively examined in Graham Petrie's 'Rhetoric as Fictional Technique in *Tristram Shandy*' and 'A Rhetorical Topic in *Tristram Shandy*'. The latter provides an extremely impressive close analysis of Sterne's borrowings (from Bacon and Burton), and his treatment of rhetoric, in Walter Shandy's lament for Bobby's death. Sterne's relationship to the fine arts has received considerable attention by such scholars as Frederick Antal, R. F. Brissenden, and William Holtz. With regard to Sterne and contemporary writers, the appropriate chapter of Robert Paulson's *Satire and the Novel* contributes a particularly important detailed comparison of *Tristram Shandy*, *A Tale of a Tub*, and *The Memoirs of Martinus Scriblerus*.

Philosophy

Of all the currently fashionable aspects of Sterne criticism, discussion of his philosophy and its sources is perhaps the most specialized, and can certainly be highly perplexing. Any reader whose interests lie in this direction is strongly advised to obtain prior first-hand knowledge of the philosophical works involved, supplemented by some introductory study of those works written by a professional philosopher. A. S. Pringle-Pattison's edition of Locke's *Essay concerning Human Understanding* will be found particularly useful, supplemented by such introductory works as Basil Willey's *Eighteenth-Century Background and English Moralists*, R. I. Aaron's *John Locke*, and C. R. Morris's *Locke, Berkeley, Hume*. The central concentration of Sterne criticism in this field has been upon the relationship between Sterne and Locke; its present tendency is toward viewing this relationship in an increasingly sophisticated and ambiguous light. Traugott's important book, discussed above, was preceded by chapters in K. MacLean's pioneering *John Locke and English Literature of the Eighteenth Century* and John Laird's *Philosophical Incursions into English Literature*. After Traugott comes Robert Griffin's 'Tristram Shandy and Language', Cash's 'Lockean Psychology of *Tristram Shandy*', Ernest Tuveson's *Reason and the Imagination* (which sees both Locke and Sterne attacking traditional attitudes), and Howard Anderson's 'Associationism and Wit in *Tristram Shandy*'. With regard to Sterne and modern philosophy, the best series of essays is to be found in *The Winged Skull*, particularly Jean-Jacques Mayoux's 'Variations on the Time-sense'; Robert Davis's 'Sterne and the Delineation of the Modern Novel' (discussed above); Denis Donoghue's 'Sterne, Our Contemporary'; and Helene Moglen, 'Laurence Sterne and the Contemporary Vision'.

Techniques

However sophisticated our awareness of Sterne's literary and philosophical *milieux* may become, no reader of either *Tristram Shandy* or *A Sentimental Journey* can fail to be aware of entering the presence of works of genius that are in many respects unique. Detailed critical analysis, then, must always occupy the front line in Sterne studies. In recent years, for example, the traditional claim that Sterne's prose style is 'conversational' has come under increasingly critical scrutiny. In this respect, the *Winged Skull* essays of Eugene Hnatko and Louis Milic are an interesting contrast in approach and methodology. Hnatko intelligently uses traditional methods, coming to conclusions which modify the 'conversational' approach without fundamentally challenging it. His main claim is that Sterne's style is 'conversationalistic' (manipulating language and typography to create the *illusion* of conversational atmosphere), rather than conversational. Milic's more radical approach (based on information-theory and statistical analysis) virtually rejects the validity of 'conversational' as a critical term. His information-theory suggests that the effectiveness of stylistic devices will decrease as their novelty wears off; his statistics indicate that Sterne was aware of this difficulty, and, with each successive instalment of *Tristram Shandy*, varied the frequency and nature of his devices.

With regard to Sterne's use of narrative technique and structure, the major studies already referred to are usefully supplemented in Dorothy Van Ghent's *English Novel* and John Preston's *Created Self*. Sterne's manipulation of time in *Tristram Shandy* is currently attracting a great deal of critical attention. The complexities that can be produced by correlating the pasts, presents, and futures, real and fictional, of Sterne, Tristram, his characters, the eighteenth-century reader, and the modern reader, become hopelessly mind-boggling. One cannot help suspecting that at least part of Sterne's purpose in making Tristram half-aware of the problem was simply to lure us into insoluble conundrums. The pioneer time-study is contained in A. A. Mendilow's *Time and the Novel* (*TCV*). Benjamin Lehman's 'Of Time, Personality, and the Author' (*TCV*) is also important, and present-day approaches can best be sampled in the *Winged Skull* essays referred to in our discussion of philosophical criticism.

Another major area of technical discussion is the extent to which the structure of *Tristram Shandy* was planned in advance by Sterne, with particular reference to the problem of whether it is complete in its present form or was accidentally terminated by Sterne's loss of interest, or death. Booth's previously discussed claim that the work was both planned and completed has won widespread acceptance. Two particularly interesting modifications to his view have recently been put forward in *The Winged Skull*. Marcia Allentuck relates *Tristram Shandy* to the technique of '*il non finito*', whereby the artist deliberately leaves a work (like a sketch or a torso) 'incomplete' in the conventional sense, for artistic effect. R. F. Brissenden's persuasive discussion suggests a two-stage evolution in composition. Thus, *Tristram Shandy* was *begun* primarily as a Scriblerian satire against pedantry (with a strong local flavour), and continued in this vein for the first twenty chapters. Thereafter, Sterne became involved with his characters, and radically changed his direction in theme and character-development. Brissenden's evidence, derived from discrepancies in characterization between the 'first' and 'second' parts, is impressive.

Sterne and Modern Literature

It is a commonly-held belief that Sterne's novels were written two hundred years ahead of their time. Paradoxically, however, relatively little thorough scrutiny appears to have been devoted to his influence on, and affinity to, twentieth-century writers and art-forms, compared with the vast amount of work that has been done on his links with his own time. The greatest amount of study in the modern field appears to have concentrated on Sterne's importance to Virginia Woolf, James Joyce, and Thomas Mann (see *Hartley* for details). A fresh line of enquiry is seen in Graham Petrie's 'Note on the Novel and the Film', which relates Sterne's flashbacks and verbal images to the techniques of the modern cinema. The recent publication of *The Winged Skull* gives ample evidence that interest in this area of exploration is increasing. Robert Davis's consideration of modern novels and the cinema in 'Sterne and the Delineation of the Modern Novel' has already been discussed. Jean-Jacques Mayoux draws an interesting analogy between Uncle Toby and Faulkner's Reverend Hightower, 'whose personal time-flow has been stopped', and relates Sterne to the cinema. A. Owen Aldridge contributes an excellent detailed study of Sterne's influence on the Brazilian novelist Machado de Assis's *Epitaph for a Small Winner*. Finally, Helene Moglen's 'Laurence Sterne and the Contemporary Vision' establishes his relevance to modern philosophy and literature: 'Sterne the philosopher looks ahead to some aspects of the thought of Bergson, James, and Freud, the three major philosophical influences on the modern novel. In this way, Sterne the novelist anticipates contemporary literary themes and narrative techniques.' Her examination of Sterne's intellectual links with the modern philosophers (especially Bergson) leads to detailed discussion of the relationship of Sterne's techniques and preoccupations to those of Proust, Gide, Joyce, Virginia Woolf, and Mann. Her final remarks on *Tristram Shandy* provide a singularly appropriate conclusion to any survey of Sterne criticism:

There is, of course, always the danger that the contemporary reader will find more in this ambiguous and paradoxical work than its author could himself have conceived. The greater danger is that we should, in our pride of complexity, forget the joy and the love of Sterne's work, for Sterne was, above all, an apostle of these. The final irony which we should consider, therefore, is this: he who wrote a work that seems to us so prophetic in its awareness of multiplicity, so incisive in its ironic vision, so brilliant in its complexity of execution, was a confirmed believer in the simplest of truths.

BIOGRAPHIES AND LETTERS
Biographies
It is now realized that Sterne's method of using dramatized narrators in his works creates a formidable barrier between Sterne's own personality and his would-be biographers—the opinions of Tristram or Yorick cannot simply be assumed to be Sterne's own. An even worse obstacle is created by the fact that Sterne by no means confined the use of his narrators to his works; his public behaviour deliberately encouraged the public to identify him with his characters. As Hartley puts it, then, 'The task of extracting the "real" Sterne is not entirely dissimilar to one of the better known labors of Heracles.' This labour is currently being undertaken by Arthur Cash. In the meantime, the standard biography is Wilbur Cross's *Life and Times of Laurence Sterne*.

The biographical section of Fluchère's *Laurence Sterne* (not included in Barbara Bray's abridged translation) helps to bring together the results of the biographical researches that have been undertaken since the publication of Cross's third edition in 1929. As opposed to original biographical research (which systematically attempts to recover information), we have available a great number of biographical interpretative essays (attempting to utilize known information in a more significant way) and 'popular' biographies. Overton James's *Relation of 'Tristram Shandy' to the Life of Sterne* makes a brave and conscientious attempt to work out the relationship between Sterne and his narrators. The biographical sections of Work's introduction to *Tristram Shandy*, and Stout's to *Sentimental Journey* (see TEXTS) are well worth reading. Of the many 'popular' biographies,

Lodwick Hartley's *Laurence Sterne* (a revised version of his earlier *This is Lorence*) can be recommended.

Letters

Sterne's letters were not only brutally 'edited' after his death—many being destroyed or ruthlessly censored—by his daughter Lydia and others, but also extensively and skilfully forged. Despite these difficulties, Lewis Curtis's patient scholarship has provided us with an excellent standard edition of the letters, with admirable annotated texts and extensive introductory material. Since the appearance of his edition, several additional letters have been published (see Hartley). *The Journal to Eliza* is readily obtainable in Jack's edition of *A Sentimental Journey*, and there is a useful selection of letters in Grant Reynard edition. Literary criticism of Sterne's correspondence has already been discussed in the CRITICAL STUDIES section.

BIBLIOGRAPHIES

The best guide to Sterne studies in general is Lodwick Hartley's *Laurence Sterne in the Twentieth Century*. The first section of this work contains a lucid summary and critical appraisal of the work that has been done in major areas of Sterne studies (biography, criticism of *Tristram Shandy* and *A Sentimental Journey*, the letters, the sermons and Sterne's literary reputation and influence), concluding with a general summary of what twentieth-century Sterne scholarship has achieved. This section should be read by all Sterne students. The second, and more specialized, section is a very full annotated bibliography of Sterne studies which discusses each item listed and provides references to the most important reviews of the major items. The first edition of this work (1966) covers the period 1900–65; this has now been superseded by the second revised and extended edition (1968).

Apart from Hartley's work, the main bibliographies of Sterne criticism that are available outside the general eighteenth-century works of reference are: the valuable checklists by Monkman, Oates, and Hartley in *WS*; Francesco Cordasco's *Laurence Sterne: A List of Critical Studies from 1896 to 1946*; and the bibliographies of Cross's *Life and Times of Sterne* and Fluchère's *Laurence Sterne*. Detailed lists of Sterne's publications will, of course, be found in *NCBEL* and the *British Museum General Catalogue of Printed Books*. As for all other authors of the 1660–1800 period, the standard annual annotated bibliography of Sterne studies is 'English Literature, 1660–1800: A Current Bibliography' which has appeared annually in the *Philological Quarterly* since 1926. These bibliographies are periodically collected, indexed, and re-published in book form as *English Literature 1660–1800: A Bibliography of Modern Studies*; so far, the bibliographies of the period 1926–70 have been thus collected. In keeping up with current Sterne studies between issues of the *Philological Quarterly* bibliography, the reviews and lists which appear in each issue of such periodicals as the *Johnsonian News Letter*, *Eighteenth-Century Studies*, and the *Review of English Studies* are particularly useful.

BACKGROUND READING

In coming to terms with Sterne's art, the most important form of 'background reading' must obviously be the close study of other eighteenth-century writers (particularly Swift and the novelists), for which guidance is given in the appropriate essays in the present work and its companion volumes. Next to this, the most useful supplementary activity is the study of eighteenth-century philosophy, and the reading of major critical studies of the eighteenth-century novel in general. Appropriate works in these fields have been recommended throughout the course of discussion in the CRITICAL STUDIES section. Detailed reference to wider background studies of eighteenth-century life and thought will be found in the standard bibliographies of the period (see BIBLIOGRAPHIES section). For their combination of erudition and entertainment, particularly warm recommendation can be given to the following recent books on eighteenth-century life: Ian Watt's *Augustan Age*; Donald Greene's *Age of Exuberance*; A. F. Scott's *Every One a Witness*; George Rudé's *Hanoverian London*; and Alfred Cobban's superbly-illustrated *Eighteenth Century*.

REFERENCES

TEXTS

(a) Collected works

W. L. Cross (ed.), *The Works and Life of Laurence Sterne* (12 vols., New York, 1904).

The Shakespeare Head Edition of the Writings of Laurence Sterne (7 vols., Oxford, 1926–7).

D. Grant (ed.), *Sterne: Memoirs of Mr. Laurence Sterne; The Life and Opinions of Tristram Shandy; A Sentimental Journey; Selected Sermons and Letters* (Reynard Library series, London, 1950).

(b) Separate works

I. Jack (ed.), *A Sentimental Journey through France and Italy* to which are added *The Journal to Eliza* and *A Political Romance*, (Oxford English Novels series, London, 1968).

G. Petrie (ed.), *The Life and Opinions of Tristram Shandy Gentleman* (Penguin paperback, Harmondsworth, 1967).

—— (ed.), *A Sentimental Journey through France and Italy* (Penguin paperback, Harmondsworth, 1967).

G. D. Stout, jun. (ed.), *A Sentimental Journey through France and Italy by Mr. Yorick* (Berkeley and Los Angeles, Calif., 1967).

I. Watt (ed.), *The Life and Opinions of Tristram Shandy, Gentleman* (Riverside paperback, Boston, Mass., 1965).

J. A. Work (ed.), *The Life and Opinions of Tristram Shandy, Gentleman* (New York, 1940).

CRITICAL STUDIES AND COMMENTARY

Abbreviations

TCV. J. Traugott (ed.), *Laurence Sterne: A Collection of Critical Essays*, Twentieth Century Views series (Englewood Cliffs, N.J., 1968).

WS. A. H. Cash and J. M. Stedmond (edd.), *The Winged Skull: Papers from the Laurence Sterne Bicentenary Conference* (Kent, Ohio, and London, 1971).

R. I. Aaron, *John Locke* (3rd edn., Oxford, 1971).

A. O. Aldridge, 'From Sterne to Machado de Assis', *WS*.

M. Allentuck, 'In Defense of an Unfinished *Tristram Shandy*', *WS*.

R. Alter, '*Tristram Shandy* and the Game of Love', *American Scholar*, xxxvii (1968).

H. Anderson, 'Sterne's Letters: Consciousness and Sympathy', in Anderson et al. (edd.), *The Familiar Letter in the Eighteenth Century* (Lawrence, Kans., and London, 1966).

—— 'Associationism and Wit in *Tristram Shandy*', *PQ* xlviii (1969).

F. Antal, 'The Moral Purpose of Hogarth's Art', *Journal of the Warburg and Courtauld Institutes*, xv (1952).

J. W. H. Atkins, *English Literary Criticism 17th and 18th Centuries* (London, 1951).

T. Baird, 'The Time-Scheme of *Tristram Shandy* and a Source', *PMLA* li (1936).

G. L. Barnett (ed.), *Eighteenth-Century British Novelists on the Novel* (New York, 1968).

L. C. Bartlett and W. R. Sherwood (edd.), *The English Novel: Background Readings* (Philadelphia, Pa., and New York, 1967).

W. C. Booth, *The Rhetoric of Fiction* (Chicago and London, 1961).

R. F. Brissenden, 'Sterne and Painting', in J. Butt (ed.), *Of Books and Humankind* (London, 1964).

—— ' "Trusting to Almighty God": Another Look at the Composition of *Tristram Shandy*', *WS*.

A. H. Cash, 'The Lockean Psychology of *Tristram Shandy*', *ELH* xxii (1955).

—— *Sterne's Comedy of Moral Sentiments: The Ethical Dimension of the 'Journey'*, MHRA Monograph; Duquesne Studies Philological Series, vi (Pittsburgh, Pa., 1966).

A. H. Cash 'The Birth of Tristram Shandy: Sterne and Dr. Burton', in R. F Brissenden (ed.), *Studies in the Eighteenth Century* (Canberra, 1968).

——and J. M. Stedmond, (edd.), *The Winged Skull*.

S. T. Coleridge, 'Wit and Humour', *Lectures of 1818*, ix, in T. M. Raysor (ed.), *Coleridge's Miscellaneous Criticism* (London, 1936).

R. G. Davis, 'Sterne and the Delineation of the Modern Novel', *WS*.

D. Donoghue, 'Sterne, Our Contemporary', *WS*.

J. Downey, *The Eighteenth Century Pulpit* (Oxford, 1969).

B. Fabian, 'Tristram Shandy and Parson Yorick among some German Greats', *WS*.

J. Ferriar, *Illustrations of Sterne* (2 vols., London, 1812).

J. R. Foster, *History of the Pre-Romantic Novel in England*, MLAA Monograph Series, xvii (New York and London, 1949).

N. Frye, *Anatomy of Criticism: Four Essays* (Princeton, N.J., 1957).

R. J. Griffin, 'Tristram Shandy and Language', *College English*, xxii (1961).

L. van der H. Hammond, *Lawrence Sterne's 'Sermons of Mr. Yorick'*, Yale Studies in English, cviii (New Haven, Conn., and London, 1948).

L. Hartley, 'The Dying Soldier and the Love-lorn Virgin: Notes on Sterne's Early Reception in America', *WS*.

William Hazlitt, *Lectures on the English Comic Writers*, in P. P. Howe (ed.), *Complete Works* (21 vols., vol. vi, London and Toronto, 1931).

J. B. Heidler, *The History, from 1700 to 1800, of English Criticism of Prose Fiction*, University of Illinois Studies in Language and Literature, xiii (Urbana, Ill., 1928).

E. Hnatko, 'Sterne's Conversational Style', *WS*.

W. V. Holtz, *Image and Immortality: A Study of 'Tristram Shandy'* (Providence, R.I., 1970).

A. B. Howes, *Yorick and the Critics: Sterne's Reputation in England, 1760–1868*, Yale Studies in English, cxxxix (New Haven, Conn., and London, 1958).

J. H. Leigh Hunt, *Wit and Humour* (London, 1846).

D. W. Jefferson, '*Tristram Shandy* and the Tradition of Learned Wit', *EIC*, i (1951); amended version, '*Tristram Shandy* and its Tradition', in B. Ford (ed.), *From Dryden to Johnson* (Pelican Guide to English Literature, iv, Harmondsworth, 1957); original version reprinted in *TCV*.

P. F. Kirby, 'Sterne in Italy', *WS*.

J. Laird, *Philosophical Incursions into English Literature* (Cambridge, 1946).

L. A. Landa, 'The Shandean Homunculus: The Background of Sterne's "Little Gentleman" ', in C. Camden (ed.), *Restoration and Eighteenth-Century Literature* (Chicago, 1963).

B. H. Lehman, *Studies in the Comic* (Berkeley, 1941); *TCV* reprints chapter, 'Of Time, Personality, and the Author: A Study of *Tristram Shandy*'.

J. Locke, *An Essay concerning Human Understanding*, ed. A. S. Pringle-Pattison (Oxford, 1924).

A. D. McKillop, *The Early Masters of English Fiction* (Lawrence, Kans., and London, 1956); *TCV* reprints Sterne section (with amended footnotes).

K. MacLean, *John Locke and English Literature of the Eighteenth Century* (New Haven, Conn., and London, 1936).

R. D. Mayo, *The English Novel in the Magazines 1740–1815* (Evanston, Ill., and London, 1962).

J.-J. Mayoux, 'Variations on the Time-Sense in *Tristram Shandy*', *WS*.

A. A. Mendilow, *Time and the Novel* (London and New York, 1952); *TCV* reprints excerpt, 'The Revolt of Sterne', with amended notes.

L. T. Milic, 'Information Theory and the Style of *Tristram Shandy*', *WS*.

H. Moglen, 'Laurence Sterne and the Contemporary Vision', *WS*.

Sir C. R. Morris, *Locke, Berkeley, Hume* (Oxford, 1931).

M. New, *Laurence Sterne as Satirist: A Reading of 'Tristram Shandy'* (Gainesville, Fla., 1969).

J. C. T. Oates, *Shandyism and Sentiment, 1760–1800* (Cambridge, 1968).

R. Paulson, *Satire and the Novel in Eighteenth-Century England* (New Haven, Conn., and London, 1967).

G. Petrie, 'A Note on the Novel and the Film: Flashbacks in *Tristram Shandy* and *The Pawnbroker*', *Western Humanities Review*, xxi (1967).

—— 'Rhetoric as Fictional Technique in *Tristram Shandy*', *PQ* xlviii (1969).

—— 'A Rhetorical Topic in *Tristram Shandy*', *MLR* lxv (1970).

W. B. Piper, *Laurence Sterne*, Twayne English Authors Series (New York, 1965).

J. Preston, *The Created Self: The Reader's Role in Eighteenth-Century Fiction* (London, 1970).

M. Price, *To the Palace of Wisdom: Studies in Order and Energy from Dryden to Blake* (New York, 1964).

R. D. S. Putney, 'The Evolution of *A Sentimental Journey*', *PQ* xix (1940).

—— 'Laurence Sterne: Apostle of Laughter', in F. W. Hilles (ed.), *The Age of Johnson* (New Haven, Conn., and London, 1949); reprinted in J. L. Clifford (ed.), *Eighteenth-Century English Literature* (New York, 1959).

Sir H. E. Read, *Collected Essays in Literary Criticism* (2nd edn., London, 1951).

—— *English Prose Style* (rev. edn., London, 1952).

Sir Walter Scott, *The Lives of the Novelists*, (Everyman, London and New York, 1910); first published as prefatory memoirs in *Ballantyne's Novelist's Library* (10 vols., London, 1821–4).

A. B. Shepperson, *The Novel in Motley: A History of the Burlesque Novel in English* (Cambridge, Mass., 1936).

N. Shumuta, 'Laurence Sterne and Japan', *WS*.

J. M. Stedmond, *The Comic Art of Laurence Sterne: Convention and Innovation in 'Tristram Shandy' and 'A Sentimental Journey'* (Toronto, 1967).

—— and A. H. Cash (ed.), *The Winged Skull*.

S. M. Tave, *The Amiable Humorist: A Study in the Comic Theory and Criticism of the Eighteenth and Early Nineteenth Centuries* (Chicago, 1960).

W. M. Thackeray, *The English Humourists of the Eighteenth Century*, in G. Saintsbury (ed.), *The Oxford Thackeray* (London, 1908).

J. M. S. Tomkins, *The Popular Novel in England 1770–1800*, Methuen University Paperbacks edn., with new Introduction (London, 1969).

C. Tracy; 'As Many Chapters as Steps', *WS*.

J. L. Traugott, *Tristram Shandy's World: Sterne's Philosophical Rhetoric* (Berkeley and Los Angeles, Calif., 1954); *TCV* reprints excerpt, 'The Shandean Comic Vision of Locke'.

—— (ed.), *Laurence Sterne: A Collection of Critical Essays (TCV)*.

E. Tuveson, 'Locke and Sterne', in J. A. Mazzeo (ed.), *Reason and the Imagination* (New York and London, 1962).

D. Van Ghent, *The English Novel: Form and Function* (New York, 1953).

W. B. C. Watkins, *Perilous Balance: The Tragic Genius of Swift, Johnson and Sterne* (Princeton, N.J., 1939); *TCV* reprints excerpt, 'Yorick Revisited'.

I. Watt, *The Rise of the Novel: Studies in Defoe, Richardson, and Fielding* (London, 1957).

R. Wellek, *The Later Eighteenth Century* (London, 1955); vol. i of *A History of Modern Criticism: 1750–1950*.

B. Willey, *The Eighteenth-Century Background* (London, 1940).

—— *The English Moralists* (London, 1964).

I. Williams (ed.), *Novel and Romance 1700–1800: A Documentary Record* (London, 1970).

W. K. Wimsatt and C. Brooks, *Neo Classical Criticism* (London, 1970); vol. ii of *Literary Criticism: A Short History* (new four-volume edn.).

V. Woolf, *The Common Reader: Second Series* (London, 1932).

BIOGRAPHIES AND LETTERS

W. L. Cross, *The Life and Times of Laurence Sterne* (3rd rev. edn., New Haven, Conn., and London, 1929).

L. P. Curtis, *Letters of Laurence Sterne* (Oxford, 1935).

H. Fluchère, *Laurence Sterne, de l'homme à l'œuvre: Biographie critique et essai d'interprétation de 'Tristram Shandy'* (Paris, 1961); critical section translated by Barbara Bray, as *Laurence Sterne: From Tristram to Yorick, An Interpretation of 'Tristram Shandy'* (London, 1965).

L. Hartley, *Laurence Sterne: A Biographical Essay* (Chapel Hill, N.C., 1968).

O. P. James, *The Relation of 'Tristram Shandy' to the Life of Sterne*, Studies in English Literature, xxii (The Hague, 1966).

BIBLIOGRAPHIES

British Museum General Catalogue of Printed Books: Photo-lithographic edition to 1955 (London, 1959–66); *Ten-Year Supplement, 1956–1965* (London, 1968); *Five-Year Supplement, 1966–1970* (London, 1971–   ).

CBEL, ed. F. W. Bateson (4 vols., Cambridge, 1940): main Sterne entry, vol. ii (1660–1800), by L. P. Curtis, covers the period up to 1936; vol. v (Cambridge, 1957) supplements the Sterne entry up to 1954. *CBEL* is now being replaced by *NCBEL* (*q.v.* below), but is not entirely superseded, as *NCBEL* is organized differently and is more selective.

F. Cordasco, *Laurence Sterne: A List of Critical Studies from 1896 to 1946*, Eighteenth Century Bibliographical Pamphlets, iv (Brooklyn, N.Y., 1948).

Eighteenth-Century Studies, edd. R. H. Hopkins and D. Greene; published quarterly by the University of California Press, Berkeley.

L. Hartley, *Laurence Sterne in the Twentieth Century: An Essay and a Bibliography of Sternean Studies 1900–1968* (rev. edn., Chapel Hill, N.C., 1968).

—— 'American Editions of Laurence Sterne to 1800: A Checklist', *WS*.

Johnsonian News Letter, edd. J. L. Clifford and J. H. Middendorf; published quarterly from Columbia University, New York.

L. A. Landa *et al.*, (edd.), *English Literature 1660–1800: A Bibliography of Modern Studies . . . compiled for 'Philological Quarterly'* (6 vols., Princeton, N.J., and London, 1950–72); covers the period 1926–70.

K. Monkman and J. C. T. Oates, 'Towards a Sterne Bibliography: Books and Other Materials Displayed at the Sterne Conference', *WS*.

NCBEL, ed. G. Watson. Superb Sterne entry by J. C. T. Oates, in vol. ii, 1660–1800 (Cambridge, 1971). Gives bibliographies of Sterne's works; Sterneana (including songs); and a selective bibliography of critical studies up to 1969.

J. C. T. Oates, 'Maria and the Bell: Music of Sternian Origin', *WS*; cf. Oates, *Shandyism and Sentiment*, listed in CRITICAL STUDIES AND COMMENTARY.

PQ, ed. C. A. Zimansky; published quarterly by the University of Iowa, Iowa City. Each July issue contains the annual current eighteenth-century bibliography, entitled *English Literature 1660–1800* up to 1970, now re-organized and entitled *The Eighteenth Century*.

RES, ed. J. B. Bamborough; published quarterly by the Clarendon Press, Oxford.

BACKGROUND READING

A. B. C. Cobban, *The Eighteenth Century: Europe in the Age of Enlightenment* (London, 1969).

D. Greene, *The Age of Exuberance: Backgrounds to Eighteenth-Century English Literature* (New York, 1970).

G. Rudé, *Hanoverian London 1714–1808* (London, 1971).

A. F. Scott (ed.), *Every One a Witness: The Georgian Age* (London, 1970).

I. Watt (ed.), *The Augustan Age: Approaches to its Literature, Life, and Thought* (Greenwich, Conn., 1968).

7 · SMOLLETT 1721–1771

Lewis M. Knapp

TEXTS

Like Fielding, Goldsmith, and Johnson, Smollett was a remarkably versatile author. He produced poems, plays, translations of Le Sage, Cervantes, and Fénelon, and contributed to the translation of the works of Voltaire. He also wrote a tremendous amount of history, that of England and other countries, all widely read in the eighteenth century. Initiated by him was the *Critical Review*, to which he contributed numerous important reviews, most of them still unidentified. He was and is, however, best known as a novelist. His novels were printed in a great many separate editions after *Roderick Random* was published in 1748. Some twenty years after his death, collected editions of the novels began to appear. At Edinburgh in 1790, there was published a six-volume edition, now rare, called *Miscellaneous Works*, containing his plays and poems, his *Travels through France and Italy*, and all of his novels except *The History and Adventures of an Atom*, first attributed to him about 1769, and included in later sets of his works. From 1796 to 1820, a Scotsman, Dr. Robert Anderson, prepared for publication seven standard editions of Smollett's *Miscellaneous Works*, each in six volumes; and in 1797, Dr. John Moore, a distant relation of Smollett, arranged for the publishing of an eight-volume edition of his works.

In the nineteenth century editions included a set of five volumes in 1809, with Rowlandson's illustrations; many editions of the *Miscellaneous Works*, edited by T. Roscoe; and numerous editions of the *Works*, edited by David Herbert. Other editions were prepared by J. P. Browne, W. E. Henley, and G. E. B. Saintsbury. Many single-volume publications of Smollett's novels, edited by T. Roscoe, became available from 1841 to 1889. Several collections of Smollett's works, edited by G. H. Maynadier, were published in New York from 1902 to 1911. An elegantly printed, limited edition of his novels was published in 1925–6 at Oxford by Basil Blackwell, publisher to the Shakespeare Head Press. No paperback publication of Smollett's novels as a set has yet been undertaken.

Editions of single novels (especially *Roderick Random*, *Peregrine Pickle*, and *Humphry Clinker*) have been extremely numerous for more than two centuries, and at least one of these has been translated into the languages of Germany, France, Holland, Denmark, Sweden, Italy, Poland, Czechoslovakia, and Estonia. (Fielding's *Tom Jones* and Goldsmith's *Vicar of Wakefield* have also been read in many languages. For information on translations of eighteenth-century novels, consult the *CBEL* under the headings of various writers. For extensive data on the European translations of Smollett's historical works and novels, consult Eugène Joliat's excellent book, *Smollett et la France*, 1935.)

Recent editions of Smollett's fiction have been printed by the Oxford University Press (Oxford English Novels): *The Adventures of Peregrine Pickle*, a reprint of the first edition, edited by James L. Clifford (1964, and now available in a paperback); *The Expedition of Humphry Clinker*, edited by Lewis M. Knapp (1966), and now available in paperback; and *The Adventures of Ferdinand Count Fathom*, edited by Damian Grant (1971). *The Expedition of Humphry Clinker*, edited by André Parreaux (1968), is available in a paperback, as is the same novel edited by Angus Ross (Penguin English Library, 1967). There have been a few other paperbacks but these are of little use for students because they usually lack introductions or notes.

CRITICAL STUDIES AND COMMENTARY

As a preface to critical studies of Smollett written after his death in 1771, I shall attempt to summarize aspects of his reputation during his lifetime. In 1748, immediately following the publication of *Roderick Random*, he acquired sudden popularity as a novelist at the age of twenty-seven. This was not enlarged by the publication of *Peregrine Pickle* in 1751, a year after he received his medical degree. Where he practised medicine, for how long, and with what success, are problems still unsolved. It is clear, however, that Smollett never concentrated on writing novels. About 1747 he prepared his translation of Le Sage's *Gil Blas*, and by 1748 he was working on his translation of Cervantes's *Don Quixote*, printed in 1755. He had also spent much time writing and revising *The Regicide*, never staged, but published in 1749.

Smollett's third novel, *The Adventures of Ferdinand Count Fathom*, was available early in 1753. This did not increase his popularity as a novelist, and his next novel, *The Adventures of Sir Launcelot Greaves*, was not written until 1760, when it appeared serially in the *British Magazine*, which he edited. Before this Smollett had worked incredibly fast on his *Complete History of England*, published 1757–8, and on other historical projects. By 1760 Smollett was in poor health, but he must have become well known as a versatile writer, and especially as a reviewer in the *Critical Review*, which had had many readers since it first appeared in 1756. His reputation as an historian was also widespread.

After the death of his only child, Elizabeth, in April 1763, Smollett and his wife resided in Nice, France, from 1763 to 1765. His *Travels through France and Italy*, published in 1766, added to his reputation as a versatile writer. In 1768 he went to Italy. His most popular novel, *The Expedition of Humphry Clinker*, was printed in June 1771, a few months before his death.

This novel revived and increased Smollett's notable reputation after his death. Until the 1830s there were only a very few novels (probably Fielding's *Tom Jones*, and Goldsmith's *The Vicar of Wakefield*) more widely read than *Roderick Random* and *Humphry Clinker*. From 1771 to the 1830s, the latter appeared in about forty separate editions, including an American imprint in 1813, as well as German, Dutch, Danish, Russian, and French translations.

It is certain that Smollett's reputation declined at an increasing rate during the whole Victorian era. Many readers and critics alluded to and stressed what they regarded as 'coarseness' in his novels, a comparative lack of structure, and an implied lack of moral emphasis. It is likely, however, that his reputation has increased constantly in recent decades. To determine just when and where it began seems impossible. Obviously, in the last few decades, much more research and critical writing on Smollett have been done, which have stimulated older critics as well as students. Some of this writing has thrown light on Smollett's moral purposes, and has shown that his best fiction is not utterly deficient in structure, and that he does not indulge in obscenity.

In Smollett's *Plays and Poems* (London, 1777), there are only very limited critical comments (brief generalizations) concerning his writing. The same is true for the account of Smollett in the first volume of his *Miscellaneous Works*, printed in Edinburgh in 1790.

Dr. John Moore, the author of the novels *Mordaunt* and *Zeluco*, and whose edition of Smollett's works has already been mentioned, was associated with Smollett in Paris in 1750, and in Glasgow in 1766, and preserved some of Smollett's letters. However, concerning Smollett's writings his comments were both generalized in form and limited in scope. 'The romances of Dr. Smollett', he declared, 'are not so much distinguished for the invention of the story, as for strong masculine humour, just observations on life, and a great variety of original characters.' Assuming, as later readers and critics have done (see James R. Foster's 'Smollett and the *Atom*') that Smollett wrote the *Atom*, Moore made this statement:

In this performance Smollett combines the manner of Swift and Rabelais: while in many parts he equals their humour, he has not always avoided their indelicacy . . . Prejudice has certainly guided his pencil in drawing the portraits or rather caricatures . . . some of which do the greatest injustice to the originals for whom they were intended; yet the performance, on the whole, affords new proofs of the humour, wit, learning, and powerful genius of the painter: and . . . no political allegory has been executed with equal wit and pleasantry since the days of Arbuthnot.

Dr. Moore was the last of Smollett's critics ever to have corresponded with him or met him. About 1795, Dr. Robert Anderson began his series of intermingled biographical accounts and criticisms which first appeared in a very brief form in *Works of the British Poets, with Prefaces, Biographical and Critical* (1795). During twenty-five years Anderson altered and lengthened both his biographical and his critical accounts of Smollett in biographies and editions of his works, published in 1796, 1800, 1803, 1806, 1811, 1817, and 1820. Anderson's criticisms of Smollett were extremely general, and sometimes partly contradictory; he merely mentioned the 'beauty and universality' of Smollett's genius; the 'utility and elegance' of his works; 'force and vitality' of his mind; and the 'independence of his spirit'. Anderson also alluded vaguely to Smollett's learning in Greek and Roman literature, in science, politics, philosophy, and in ancient and modern history. Like many nineteenth-century commentators, Anderson was disturbed by what he regarded as Smollett's frequent violence and indelicacy, though he recognized a moral purpose in his writings. In his comments on *Roderick Random*, he asserted that it would be safer to conceal some scenes from 'youthful inexperienced readers'. Concerning the memoirs of Lady Vane in *Peregrine Pickle*, Anderson felt that Smollett had, 'with justice, been thought low, indelicate, and immoral'.

In marked contrast to such assertions, Anderson cited (in his 'Life of Smollett') from his own personal correspondence with a clergyman in Massachusetts the following:

I record here, with pleasure, the testimony of the Rev. Dr. John Elliot, a clergyman of great worth and learning, in the State of Massachusetts, to the good tendency of these fictitious narratives, as it affords me at once an opportunity of reflecting on the friendship of the correspondent whose words I transcribe, and of shewing the high estimation in which the novels of Smollett are held by men of education and piety in the United States. 'Smollett was always a favorite author with me. When I was at college his novels were in every one's hand, as a sweet relaxation from severer studies; and these taught us more of human nature than we could learn from grave lessons on the ancient and modern schools. A brother of mine died some years ago, of a lingering complaint, who had serious views, a belief in future glory, and a steady apprehension of dying, yet every day would read *Peregrine Pickle*. As long as he lived he said he meant to be cheerful. A hearty laugh drove away pain; and Smollett could make him laugh when nothing else could'.

The writer of this unusual tribute to the comic scenes in *Peregrine Pickle*, the Revd. Dr. John Elliot, graduated from Harvard in 1772 and became a member of the Massachusetts Historical Society. In that Society about 1800, there were some letters *to* Smollett, copies of which Anderson gratefully received from Elliot.

Anderson's generalizations about Smollett's novels included a few contrasts between him and 'the moral, the sublime, the pathetic but tiresome Richardson', and 'the ingenious, the humorous, the diffuse Fielding with all his wit, learning and knowledge of mankind'. Although Anderson objected to the youthful profligates in some of Smollett's novels, and insisted that sailors, rogues, misanthropes, gamblers, and duellists were among Smollett's favourite characters, he consistently believed that his novels contained a moral tendency. He also declared that after perusing the 'wire-drawn history of *Clarissa*, and the diffusive narrative of *Tom Jones*, we never quit them with as much reluctance as we feel in closing the pages of Smollett, who, with less regularity of able, and without introducing so many observations of a moral tendency, or so much of what may be called fine writing, possesses, in an eminent degree, the art of fascinating and riveting the mind'.

In the century and a half since 1820, there have been many comparisons and contrasts between the varied achievements of Richardson, Fielding, Smollett, and Sterne. About 1821 Smollett's works received some important criticism from Sir Walter Scott in his *Lives of the Novelists*, which includes accounts of Richardson, Fielding, Goldsmith, Johnson, Sterne, and later novelists. Scott regarded *Roderick Random* as an imitation of Le Sage, and also believed that its many early readers imagined that more of its characters than Smollett intended were portraits of living personages. *Peregrine Pickle* was, according to Scott, 'more finished', and 'more sedulously laboured into excellence', with a 'much wider range of character and incident' than in *Roderick Random*. Concerning *Count Fathom*, Scott felt that it contained too much moral depravity, and yet despite that fact, he

asserted that it was impossible to deny his applause over its 'wonderful knowledge of life and manners'. Scott was relatively uninterested
in *Launcelot Greaves*, but he rated *Humphry Clinker* as Smollett's most
pleasing composition. The most significant portion of Scott's essay on
Smollett was his comparison of Smollett and Fielding. Fielding, in
Scott's opinion, possessed a 'higher and purer taste', and 'more
elegance of composition and expression'. Furthermore, Fielding's
heroes and heroines Scott appraised as higher and more pleasing
characters. And yet in the final pages of his essay on Smollett, Scott
declared: 'If Fielding had superior taste , the palm of more brilliancy
of genius, more inexhaustible richness of invention, must in justice be
awarded to Smollett.' And Scott also insisted that although *Tom
Jones* was a masterpiece, Smollett's *Roderick Random*, *Peregrine Pickle*,
and *Humphry Clinker* each far excelled *Joseph Andrews* or *Amelia*.
Despite Scott's realization that Smollett's novels lack very formal
structure, he concluded his appraisal of Smollett in 1821 by the
following paragraph:

Upon the whole, the genius of Smollett may be said to resemble that of
Rubens. His pictures are often deficient in grace; sometimes coarse, and
even vulgar in conception; deficient in keeping, and in the due subordination of parts to each other; and intimating too much carelessness on the part
of the artist. But these faults are redeemed by such richness and brilliancy of
colours; such a profusion of imagination—now bodying forth the grand and
terrible—now the natural, the easy, and the ludicrous; there is so much of
life, action, and bustle, in every group he has painted; so much force and
individuality of character—that we readily grant to Smollett an equal rank
with his great rival Fielding, while we place both far above any of their
successors in the same line of fictitious composition.

In the period before 1832, in addition to the three Scotsmen,
Moore, Anderson, and Scott, there were many leading writers who
admired Smollett. Among them were Wordsworth, Coleridge,
Hazlitt, Byron, Lamb, and Leigh Hunt. Their praise of Smollett,
cited in the fourth chapter of Boege's *Smollett's Reputation as a Novelist*,
did not contain technical criticism, but it was enthusiastic. These
writers, of course, were not novelists, and their most memorable
criticism dealt with subjects other than prose fiction.

Among famous Victorians, Thomas Carlyle and Charles Dickens
both gave Smollett superlative praise. Both, when very young, read
Roderick Random and *Humphry Clinker* and recalled that experience
years later with great delight. In their writings are many allusions to
Smollett.

By the middle of the nineteenth century Smollett's reputation had begun to diminish. Thackeray was partially responsible for this. He emphasized his belief that Fielding was superior to Smollett, though in his *The English Humourists of the Eighteenth Century* (Lecture v, on Hogarth, Smollett, and Fielding) he concluded his remarks on Smollett by the following assertion: 'The novel of "Humphry Clinker" is, I do think, the most laughable story that has ever been written since the goodly art of novel-writing began. Winifred Jenkins and Tabitha Bramble must keep Englishmen on the grin for ages yet to come; and in their letters and the story of their loves there is a perpetual fount of sparkling laughter as inexhaustible as Bladud's well.' Thackeray, however, complained of the weak structure of *Roderick Random* as contrasted with the excellent organization of *Tom Jones*.

In the Victorian period, a few writers and critics gradually increased their opposition to what they called the occasional coarse and brutal data in Smollett's fiction. John Ruskin emphasized this, but nevertheless he enjoyed reading *Humphry Clinker*. This very popular novel Matthew Arnold's father, Dr. Thomas Arnold, Headmaster of Rugby, read fifty times, as he told his student, Arthur Penrhyn Stanley, later Dean of Westminster. David Hannay, in his biography of Smollett (1887), called attention to what he regarded as brutality and human cruelty in episodes in *Roderick Random* and *Peregrine Pickle*, but nevertheless he praised these novels and stressed their popularity. The Scotsman, Oliphant Smeaton, in his biography of Smollett (1897, chapter 10), made a very elementary analysis of Smollett's indebtedness to French and Spanish literature, and of his growing genius in creating characters of permanent appeal. Smeaton did not deal with Smollett's coarseness, but in his attempt to illuminate Smollett's personality, he cited phrases from unpublished letters attributed to Smollett. After seventy years, not one of these letters has been located, and it is practically certain, therefore, that the extracts were inventions or fabrications by Smeaton, who indulged in similar activities in his biography of Allan Ramsay, published in 1896.

In the 1890s, toward the end of the Victorian period, George E. B. Saintsbury, an historian, and, as V. S. Pritchett describes him, a 'booksoaked critic', wrote biographical and limitedly critical introductions to Smollett's *Roderick Random*, *Peregrine Pickle*, *Count Fathom*, *Launcelot Greaves*, and *Humphry Clinker*. In dealing with Smollett's *Roderick Random*, Saintsbury compared him with Fielding. At the end of the introduction to *Humphry Clinker*, this novel was given high praise in general terms, and Smollett was called a 'man of genius'. It is possible that Saintsbury produced a slight increase in Smollett's student-readers and in his general popularity.

Similar results may well have followed an edition of Smollett's works in twelve volumes (1899–1901), with an Introduction to *Roderick Random* and short 'Bibliographical Notes' by William Ernest Henley, and other notes by Thomas Seccombe. Henley's criticism of Smollett (and also of Fielding) is available in his *Essays*. Henley was frequently inaccurate and excessively extreme in stating his dislike of Smollett's personality. Oddly enough, he was also extravagant in his praise of Smollett's literary achievements. In volume xii of this edition there is a 'Bibliographical Note' by Thomas Seccombe, the author of an excellent biographical article on Smollett, published in *The Dictionary of National Biography*. Seccombe also contributed to Henley's edition an introduction to Smollett's *Travels Through France and Italy*, which was enlarged and published in separate editions of the *Travels* in 1907 and [1919], in the World's Classics. The edition of Smollett's works with notes by Henley and Seccombe is not easily available at present. Equally scarce is the collection in twelve volumes with an Introduction by G. H. Maynadier. Maynadier was a mild critic expressing more praise than dislike, but his essays added little to previous generalizations about Smollett as a novelist. In the rare Shakespeare Head Edition of Smollett's Novels (1925) there are some helpful bibliographical and textual notes at the end of each novel (*Launcelot Greaves* excepted). In contrast to such limited editions there frequently appeared, in the Victorian period and in the early 1900s, numerous reprints of Smollett's works in one or in two volumes such as those containing his memoirs and pieces of criticism by Sir Walter Scott, Thomas Roscoe, and David Herbert. Similar volumes of Fielding's works appeared along with Smollett's in this period.

In the last half-century there has been an increasing biographical and critical interest in all of the leading eighteenth-century novelists —Defoe, Richardson, Fielding, Smollett, and Sterne. The most important recent works on Smollett will now be considered in more or less chronological sequence.

In 1925 Yale University Press published Howard Swazey Buck's *A Study in Smollett, chiefly 'Peregrine Pickle'*, and in 1927 his *Smollett as Poet*. These books contain a small amount of literary criticism, stressing Smollett's artistic weakness in his relative lack of structure, but praising 'the finer emotional feeling' of his novels, an effect also found in some of his poetry. Buck also commented on what some of Smollett's readers have regarded as his more or less coarse material:

The coarseness and realism in his novels of which we hear so much, are pushed to the point of extravagance where they cease to be true, and are in themselves a kind of romance. In these vivid, grotesque pages of his we are lost, almost from first to last, in a world of the imagination. These pages, moreover, are animated by a fertility of incident, a speed, energy and vigor of development which I believe are quite without parallel in the English novel. These prose qualities are what in poetry would be called 'fire' or 'passion'—palpably the spirit which blows through *The Tears of Scotland* and the *Ode to Independence*. It is true that ... this warmth is often nearer the warmth of anger than of love and tenderness; but it is in no case the mere hardness and callousness which Henley would have us see as Smollett's fatal weakness; ... I believe justice has never been done [to] the finer emotional feeling of Smollett's novels.

This is perhaps the beginning in our century of new concepts of Smollett's so-called coarseness condemned by some of the earlier critics.

In 1926 Herbert Read, the brilliant literary critic and poet, wrote a notable chapter on Smollett in his *Reason and Romanticism, Essays in Literary Criticism*. Read declared that Smollett's style surpassed Fielding's, and toward the end of his chapter deals with the general problem of indecency or coarseness, the presence of which several early critics of Smollett had denounced. 'As a matter of fact,' Read asserted,

Smollett is never obscene or blasphemous, nor in any but a limited sense pornographical or erotic ... Smollett is not sensual; it is almost our complaint that he is not sensual enough. In short, his indiscretions are confined to the coprological kind: that is to say, they hover round certain daily physical acts to which we are all subject, but of which only the neurotic are ashamed ... There is every difference between the matter-of-fact narrative of Smollett and the equivocal suggestions of Sterne ... he is everywhere masculine and healthy, direct and unfurtive.

These statements by Herbert Read have produced new attitudes toward Smollett's realism and style.

Accounts of Smollett containing thoughtful criticism are to be found in Oliver Elton's *Survey of English Literature 1730–1780*, (1928), and Ernest A. Baker's *History of the English Novel*, vol. iv (1930). Elton regarded Smollett in relation to *Roderick Random* as 'an angry observer of mankind'. In this novel Smollett drew pictures, as Elton states it, with 'the honesty of Hogarth, and with something of his power'. Smollett's language, according to Elton, 'as is often truly said, is surer, and more rapid and direct than Fielding's' with minor exceptions. Baker also praised Smollett as a 'prince among story-tellers' although he lacked Elton's enthusiasm for *Roderick Random*, and stated that his style, although vigorous, incisive, and fluent, was 'almost destitute of grace and elegance'. Baker, in his final paragraph demonstrates similarities between Swift and Smollett in that both writers were 'extremely sensitive and tender-hearted', and 'exceptional in their anxiety about personal cleanliness in an age that was pretty lax in such matters'. Baker's final generalizations are as follows:

The hater of filth will be the foulest in his stigmatization of foulness. The most sensitive will be the most outrageous in exposing horror and suffering. An irritable man like Smollett, or a man of fierce indignation like Swift, naturally, when he gets into a rage, flings out with just those things that he finds most nauseating and repulsive. In neither case was it prurience. The most probable explanation of both men's offences against literary decency seems to be this.

Students of modern psychology will find all this worth investigating in greater detail.

Critical appraisals of Smollett published since 1930, like those of Fielding, have increased in number and occasionally in range and value. All students of Smollett should read Louis L. Martz's *The Later Career of Tobias Smollett*, which deals brilliantly with Smollett's work and style in his historical publications, and also with the contents and style of *Launcelot Greaves*, the *Atom*, and *Humphry Clinker*. Another very useful book, George M. Kahrl's *Tobias Smollett, Traveler-Novelist*, contains at the end of the final chapter, two valuable comparisons: (1) the style of travel books and that of Smollett; (2) the styles of Fielding and Smollett. No ambitious student of these two novelists should fail to read V. S. Pritchett's *The Living Novel*: Pritchett's criticism of Smollett is outstanding, and among other original statements is one which points out links between Smollett and Joyce. Fred W. Boege's *Smollett's Reputation as a Novelist* (1947) contains a remarkable and accurate mass of data concerning the varying status of Smollett from the eighteenth century down to 1947. In Lewis M. Knapp's biography of Smollett (1949), there is in chapter 16 a brief critical survey of Smollett's creative writing limited to his novels. An important criticism of Smollett is found in an excellent book, *The Early Masters of English Fiction* by Alan Dugald McKillop (1956). An article by Albrecht B. Strauss, 'On Smollett's Language: A Paragraph in *Ferdinand Count Fathom*', is one of the best in recent years. Another, by Milton Orowitz, 'Smollett and the Art of Caricature', should also be studied. A clear and definite appraisal of

M. A. Goldberg's *Smollett and the Scottish School* (1959) is difficult, as is shown by the anonymous reviewer of it in *TLS*, 6 November 1959. A short article by William Bowman Piper, 'The Large Diffused Picture of Life in Smollett's Early Novels', is well worth reading. Donald Bruce's *Radical Doctor Smollett* (1964) is non-scholarly, often inaccurate, and occasionally unjust to Fielding. However, some of Bruce's assertions about Smollett are stimulating, but they should often be modified. A commendable book, despite some odd *errata*, is Robert Giddings's *The Tradition of Smollett* (1967) which includes a chapter on the picaresque tradition.

Rogue's Progress, Studies in the Picaresque Novel, by Robert Alter, contains a chapter called 'The Picaroon as Fortune's Plaything', dealing with *Roderick Random*. This is reprinted in a paperback volume, *Essays on the Eighteenth-Century Novel*, edited by Robert Donald Spector. In *Satire and the Novel in Eighteenth-Century England*, by Ronald Paulson, there is a sophisticated chapter, 'Smollett: The Satirist as a Character Type'. Two articles by Philip Stevick, 'The Augustan Nose' and 'Stylistic Energy in the Early Smollett', are well worth reading, as are Sheridan Baker's '*Humphry Clinker* as Comic Romance' in *Essays on the Eighteenth-Century Novel*, and Paul-Gabriel Boucé's 'Les Procédés du comique dans *Humphry Clinker*'.

The most complete study of Smollett ever published is *Les Romans de Smollett, Étude critique* by Paul-Gabriel Boucé (1971)—now being translated into English. It deals not only with all of his novels (except *The History and Adventures of an Atom* which may or may not be Smollett's), but also with his life, his personality, his literary realism, his structure of the comic, and his literary style. In Chapter II, 'Smollett's Personality', Boucé includes his violent emotions, his generosity, his hatred of war, his intellectual passion, his religion and Puritanism, his love of independence, and his moralism. Readers and students of Smollett should examine carefully the final pages, entitled 'General Conclusions', which mention former views of Smollett's personality which have been corrected in the last fifty years.

Tobias Smollett, Bicentennial Essays, edited by George S. Rousseau and Paul-Gabriel Boucé (1971), contains critical essays by ten Smollett scholars.

BIOGRAPHIES AND LETTERS

The earliest short and incomplete accounts of Smollett's life were combined with critical comments, as has already been shown in the section dealing with CRITICAL STUDIES. References have already been given to biographical data in Smollett's *Plays and Poems*; his *Miscellaneous Works*; John Moore's *Works of Smollett*; Robert Anderson's numerous editions of his works; and Sir Walter Scott's *Lives of the Novelists*.

Later in the nineteenth century there were published other biographies of Smollett by Robert Chambers, David Hannay, Oliphant Smeaton, and Thomas Seccombe. A biography by Lewis Melville, which appeared in 1926, is extremely inaccurate in many respects. Arnold Whitridge's *Tobias Smollett, A Study of His Miscellaneous Works* contains both biography and criticism. In 1949, *Tobias Smollett, Doctor of Men and Manners* by Lewis M. Knapp was published. This is known as the standard biography.

For 200 years Smollett's letters have gradually been printed in a great variety of periodicals, books, and articles, usually biographical. The chief contributors to the publication of Smollett's letters have been Dr. Robert Anderson, Dr. John Moore, Joseph Irving, Edward S. Noyes, Henry W. Meikle, Lewis M. Knapp, and Lawrence Fitzroy Powell. In the *Letters of Tobias George Smollett, A Supplement to the Noyes Collection*, collected and edited by Francesco Cordasco (1950), there are five letters attributed to Smollett later acknowledged by Cordasco to be forgeries. These are letters 19, 26, 29, 30, and 31.

BIBLIOGRAPHIES

There are the following technical bibliographies: (1) Luella F. Norwood, 'A Descriptive Bibliography of the Creative Works of Tobias Smollett'; (2) Franklin B. Newman, 'A Consideration of the Bibliographical Problems Connected with the First Edition of *Humphry Clinker*'.

There are numerous bibliographies referring in general to Smollett's works, and to usually unclassified aspects of his life. A useful bibliography of items in the British Museum, prepared by John P. Anderson, appeared in Hannay's biography of Smollett. Noyes included in his edition of Smollett's letters a list of books. In Joliat's *Smollett et la France* are two bibliographies, one on the translations of Smollett's works, and the other a general bibliography. Claude E. Jones added bibliographies to his *Smollett Studies*, and Boege concluded his *Smollett's Reputation as a Novelist* with an impressive select bibliography. Immediately following this appeared two others by Cordasco, one in 1947 and the other in 1948. These are entitled *Smollett Criticism* and include 373 items. At the end of Knapp's biography of Smollett is a brief selected list of books and articles, most of which contain important bibliographical data. There are very short bibliographies in Carmine R. Linsalata's *Smollett's Hoax: Don Quixote in English*, in Goldberg's *Smollett and the Scottish School*, and in Bruce's *Radical Doctor Smollett*.

BACKGROUND READING

Selections from the novels of Defoe, Richardson, and Fielding should be found helpful in evaluating Smollett's comparative lack of structure, his characterization, and his other techniques, as well as his psychological effects. To read Le Sage's *Gil Blas* in French or in Smollett's translation is instructive; also the study of Cervante's *Don Quixote*, though most students will find this task easiest in Smollett's translation, as the Spanish of Cervantes is very difficult. A familiarity with eighteenth-century picaresque techniques is necessary in order to judge what has been written recently on this subject, as well as to understand the picaresque in Smollett's novels. A knowledge of the types of satire utilized by Dryden, Swift, and Pope will assist the understanding of Smollett's satire. Smollett's type-characters appear to be occasionally derived from Shakespeare, Ben Jonson, or Restoration writers: there is a useful essay by George M. Kahrl, 'The Influence of Shakespeare on Smollett'.

For the appreciation of Smollett's references to London, André Parreaux's *Smollett's London* is recommended.

It is often difficult to realize the Scottish quality of Smollett's sense of the comic. There is an excellent book, *The Scot in History* by Wallace Notestein, containing information on the early Scottish traditions of various types of humour.

REFERENCES

TEXTS

(a) Collected works

R. Anderson (ed.), *Miscellaneous Works with Memoirs of his Life and Writings* (6 vols., Edinburgh, 1796, 1800, etc.).

Dr. J. Moore (ed.), *Works with Memoirs of his Life* (8 vols., London, 1797).

Miscellaneous Works (5 vols., Edinburgh, 1809); illustrated by Rowlandson.

T. Roscoe (ed.), *Miscellaneous Works* (London, 1841).

D. Herbert (ed.), *Works* (Edinburgh, 1870).

J. P. Browne (ed.), *Works* (8 vols., 1872).

W. E. Henley and T. Seccombe (edd.), *Works* (12 vols., London and New York, 1899–1901).

G. Saintsbury (ed.), *Works* (12 vols., Edinburgh, London, and Philadelphia, Pa., 1895).

G. H. Maynadier (ed.), *Works* (12 vols., New York and Boston, Mass., 1902).
Novels (Shakespeare Head edition, 11 vols., Oxford, 1925–6).

(b) Separate works

J. L. Clifford (ed.), *The Adventures of Peregrine Pickle* a reprint of the first edition (1751) (London, 1964).

D. Grant (ed.), *The Adventures of Ferdinand Count Fathom* (London, 1971).

L. M. Knapp (ed.), *The Expedition of Humphry Clinker* (London, 1966).

A. Parreaux (ed.), *The Expedition of Humphry Clinker* (Boston, Mass., 1968).

A. Ross (ed.), *The Expedition of Humphry Clinker* (Penguin, Harmondsworth, 1967).

T. Seccombe (ed.), *Travels through France and Italy* (World's Classics, London, 1919).

CRITICAL STUDIES AND COMMENTARY

R. Alter, *Rogue's Progress, Studies in the Picaresque Novel* (Cambridge, Mass., 1964).

E. A. Baker, *History of the English Novel*, vol. iv (London, 1930).

S. Baker, 'Humphry Clinker as Comic Romance' in *Essays on the Eighteenth-Century Novel*, ed. R. D. Spector (Bloomington, Ind., 1965), 154–64.

F. W. Boege, *Smollett's Reputation as a Novelist* (Princeton, N.J., 1947).

P.-G. Boucé, 'Les Procédés du comique dans *Humphry Clinker*', *Études anglaises* (1966).

—— *Les Romans de Smollett, Étude critique* (Paris, 1971).

D. Bruce, *Radical Doctor Smollett* (Boston, Mass., 1965).

H. S. Buck, *A Study in Smollett, chiefly Peregrine Pickle* (New Haven, Conn., 1925).

—— *Smollett as Poet* (New Haven, Conn., 1927).

Dr. J. Elliot. For his and his brother's love for *Peregrine Pickle*, see R. Anderson's *Miscellaneous Works of Tobias Smollett, M.D.* (6 vols., Edinburgh, 1806), i, 134; and Anderson's *Miscellaneous Works of Tobias Smollett, M.D.* (6 vols., Edinburgh, 1820), i, 126.

O. Elton, *Survey of English Literature 1730–1780* (2 vols., London, 1928), i, 204–16.

R. Giddings, *The Tradition of Smollett* (London, 1967).

M. A. Goldberg, *Smollett and the Scottish School* (Albuquerque, N. Mex., 1959).

D. Hannay. See under BIOGRAPHIES AND LETTERS.

E. Joliat, *Smollett et la France* (Paris, 1935).

G. M. Kahrl, *Tobias Smollett, Traveler-Novelist* (Chicago, 1945).

A. D. McKillop, *The Early Masters of English Fiction* (Lawrence, Kans., 1956).

L. L. Martz, *The Later Career of Tobias Smollett* (New Haven, Conn., 1942; 1967).

G. H. Maynadier, 'Introduction' to *The Works of Tobias Smollett* (12 vols., Boston Mass., 1902).

M. Orowitz, 'Smollett and the Art of Caricature', *Spectrum*, vol. ii, pp. 155–67 (Santa Barbara, Calif., 1958).

R. Paulson, 'Satire in the Early Novels of Smollett', *JEGP* lix (1960).

—— *Satire and the Novel in Eighteenth-Century England* (New Haven, Conn., 1967); ch. 5 deals with Smollett.

W. B. Piper, 'The Large Diffused Picture of Life in Smollett's Early Novels', *SP* lx (1963).

V. S. Pritchett, *The Living Novel* (New York, 1947); see 'The Shocking Surgeon', pp. 32–7.

H. Read, *Reason and Romanticism, Essays in Literary Criticism* (London, 1926).

G. S. Rousseau and P.-G. Boucé (edd.), *Tobias Smollett, Bicentennial Essays Presented to Lewis M. Knapp* (New York, 1971).

Sir W. Scott. See under BIOGRAPHIES AND LETTERS.

T. Seccombe. Account of Smollett in *DNB*.

O. Smeaton, *Tobias Smollett* (Edinburgh, 1897).

A. P. Stanley, See his *Life and Correspondence* by R. Prothero (2 vols., New York, 1894), i, 65, for the account of Dr. Thomas Arnold's reading of *Humphry Clinker*.

P. Stevick, 'The Augustan Nose', *UTQ* xxxiv (1965).

—— 'Stylistic Energy in Early Smollett', *SP* lxiv (1967).

A. B. Strauss, 'On Smollett's Language: A Paragraph in *Ferdinand Count Fathom*', in *Style in Prose Fiction, Columbia University English Institute Essays, 1958* (New York, 1959), pp. 25–54.

W. M. Thackeray, *The English Humourists of the Eighteenth Century* (2nd rev. edn., London, 1953).

BIOGRAPHIES AND LETTERS

R. Chambers, *Smollett: His Life and a Selection from his Writings* (London and Edinburgh, 1867).

F. Cordasco, *Letters of Tobias George Smollett, A Supplement to the Noyes Collection* (Madrid, 1950).

D. Hannay, *Life of Tobias George Smollett* (London, 1887).

J. Irving, *Some Account of the Family of Smollett of Bonhill; with A Series of Letters Hitherto Unpublished, Written by Dr. Tobias Smollett, Author* (Dumbarton, printed for private circulation, 1859).

L. M. Knapp, *Tobias Smollett, Doctor of Men and Manners* (Princeton, N.J., 1949; reprinted New York, 1963).

—— (ed.), *The Letters of Tobias Smollett* (Oxford, 1970).

H. W. Meikle, 'New Smollett Letters', *TLS* (24 and 31 July 1943).

Lewis Melville, *The Life and Letters of Tobias Smollett* (London, 1926).

E. S. Noyes, *The Letters of Tobias Smollett, M.D.* (Cambridge, Mass., 1926).

L. F. Powell, 'William Huggins and Smollett', *MP* xxxiv (1936); letters of Smollett to Huggins and Gatehouse.

Sir W. Scott, *The Lives of the Novelists* (New York, 1872).

T. Seccombe. See under CRITICAL STUDIES.

O. Smeaton, *Tobias Smollett* (Edinburgh, 1897).

A. Whitridge, *Tobias Smollett, A Study of his Miscellaneous Works* (New York, 1925).

BIBLIOGRAPHIES

J. P. Anderson, Bibliography in David Hannay's *Life of Tobias George Smollett* (London, 1887).

F. W. Boege. See under CRITICAL STUDIES.

D. Bruce. See under CRITICAL STUDIES.

F. Cordasco, *Smollett Criticism, 1925–1945: A Compilation* (Brooklyn, N.Y., 1947).

—— *Smollett Criticism, 1770–1924: a Bibliography, Enumerative and Annotative* (Brooklyn, N.Y., 1948).

M. A. Goldberg. See under CRITICAL STUDIES.

E. Joliat. See under CRITICAL STUDIES.

C. E. Jones, *Smollett Studies* (Berkeley, Calif., 1942).

C. R. Linsalata, *Smollett's Hoax: Don Quixote in English* (Stanford, Calif., 1956).

F. B. Newman, 'A Consideration of the Bibliographical Problems Connected with the First Edition of *Humphry Clinker*', *PBSA* xliv (1950).

L. F. Norwood, 'A Descriptive Bibliography of the Creative Works of Tobias Smollett' (Yale University dissertation, 1931).

E. S. Noyes. See under BIOGRAPHIES AND LETTERS.

BACKGROUND READING

G. M. Kahrl, 'The Influence of Shakespeare on Smollett', reprinted from the Parrott Presentation Volume (Princeton, N.J., 1935).

W. Notestein, *The Scot in History, A Study of the Interplay of Character and History* (New Haven, Conn., 1947); chapters 28 and 29.

A. Parreaux, *Smollett's London* (Paris, 1965).

W. E. K. Anderson

TEXTS

The Great Unknown in his own day, Scott has become the Great
Unread in ours. Yet to omit Scott entirely from our reading list is
scarcely prudent, for it leaves not so much a gap in our knowledge as
a chasm across our understanding of the age. His contemporaries
read Scott avidly and compared him to Shakespeare; the booksellers
placed orders for his next novel before it was even begun, and he
could command a royalty of £4,000 on a first impression of 8,000
copies. The rest of the century is littered with cheap, collected,
illustrated editions of his works. Balzac, Tolstoy, Emily Brontë, and
Hardy acknowledge a debt to Scott. His influence is apparent on
Victorian architecture and Victorian life as well as on Victorian
fiction. Whatever one feels about Scott the novelist, he is there and
cannot be ignored.

His works ranged along the shelves of a library are undeniably a
daunting prospect. The novels stretch to forty-eight volumes; there
are twelve volumes of the collected poetry, and a further thirty of
miscellaneous prose works—and that still leaves out his personal
writings, the twelve volumes of his letters and a journal of 700 pages.
His range is quite astonishing. He made his name as a collector of
ballads, burst into fame as the poet of *The Lay of the Last Minstrel*,
Marmion, and the rest, then amassed a fortune from the novels which
he began writing at the age of forty-two. But he was also a historian,
the author of a massive *Life of Napoleon* and of a *History of Scotland*; a
successful children's writer; a neglected and under-regarded critic;
the editor of Dryden and Swift, and a contributor to numerous
magazines and journals, principally to the *Quarterly*, which he was
instrumental in founding and which, from 1826, his son-in-law
edited. Scott was a professional writer who wrote books for money.
As he was always short of money—firstly to buy, build on, and en-
large his country estate of Abbotsford, and later to pay off the debt
of nearly £130,000 with which he was saddled by the failure of his
publishers in the financial crash of 1826—he seldom stopped writing.
He had always one, and often two major works in hand; and the day
after one novel was finished another, if not already under way, was

begun. The first question, then, is not 'What should I read *about* Scott?' but 'What should I read *of* Scott?'

The logical place to begin is where Scott the novelist began, with *Waverley*. Although in many ways a disappointing novel it is a good introduction to Scott. It is an unconscionable time in beginning—it bursts into life only when Waverley comes back from the Highlands, and that is half-way through—but it has the double interest of showing a novelist struggling to find his own particular style, and of illustrating most of the things which Scott does best. There is a conflict between two opposing views of life; there are some great scenes, in court and on the field of battle; there are historical figures convincingly portrayed in supporting roles, swiftly realized minor characters, and major characters motivated by courage, loyalty, and honour. The pattern for the best of the novels that follow is carved out here.

Old Mortality (the most perversely titled of all Scott's works, named after a character who appears only in the introduction) is a better-organized novel and may perhaps be the better starting-place for someone who has not read anything by Scott. Set in Scotland in Covenanting times it evokes the period brilliantly and is surpassed by none of the other novels in its clashes of character—Claverhouse against Covenanters—and the drama of its best scenes. Had the ending been more convincing this would have been Scott's masterpiece; with the last chapters as they are it is still Scott at his best, even if that best could have been better.

The ending of *Rob Roy* is similarly marred, but Scott is a comic novelist and this is his great comic novel of Fairservice and Bailie Jarvie. It is important too for its theme, carefully worked out in terms of Credit against Honour, the modern world against the romantic past. Victory, contrary to the popular misconception about Scott, goes to the moderns—as it does later in *Redgauntlet*, which ends, almost alone among Scott's best novels, when and as it should.

The Heart of Mid-Lothian, however, has been the favourite of the critics, and it is easy to see why. The plot is a good plot; the theme of justice is as relevant to our day as to Scott's. The central character, Jeanie Deans, is strong enough to meet the demands of her position, and the way in which the historical Porteous Riots interact with the personal sufferings of the Deans family is richly satisfying. Many critics take exception to the last third of the novel, but strictly speaking it is the last quarter which disappoints them. *The Heart of Mid-Lothian* was planned as a three-volume novel and expanded to four; in the first edition, volume three concludes with Jeanie's interview with the Queen, and as far as this the novel is an undoubted master-piece. If only one novel is to be read, this is probably the one to choose. It is not entirely representative of Scott, however, and for a balanced picture it should be supplemented by the short stories at least, collected for World's Classics by Lord David Cecil, and prefer-ably by *Old Mortality* and *Redgauntlet*.

The five novels mentioned so far are all 'Scotch Novels', and apart from *Redgauntlet*, which belongs to 1824, were among the first written. The best of the remaining novels are also Scottish in setting, for Scott, in common with other novelists, wrote best when closest to his own experience. The second rank of his novels consists of *Guy Mannering*, *The Antiquary*, *The Bride of Lammermoor* (which many would place in the first rank), *A Legend of Montrose* and *The Fair Maid of Perth*. Bringing up the rear, a considerable distance behind, are the romances, of which the most readable are *Ivanhoe*, *Quentin Durward*, *The Fortunes of Nigel*, and *Woodstock*.

There is no standard scholarly edition of Scott's novels. The com-plete editions mentioned in the Bibliography have Scott's own intro-ductions and notes written for the first collected edition, the *Magnum Opus* as he called it, which began to appear in 1829, and the Border Edition has editorial introductions by Andrew Lang. The cheaper editions, published by Everyman, Collins, and Nelson, include only the more popular novels. A few novels are available in paperback, principally but not exclusively from Signet Books and Everyman.

CRITICAL STUDIES AND COMMENTARY

Scott's popularity has waxed and waned over the years; critical opinion has remained more or less constant. Many of the nineteenth-century reviews of Scott's novels are well worth attention, therefore, as they lay down lines of thought that have been taken up by later generations of critics. These are now available in John Hayden's useful compendium, *Scott: the Critical Heritage*, which ranges from Jeffrey on *Marmion* to reviews or comments by Sydney Smith, Cole-ridge, Goethe, Wordsworth, Macaulay, Balzac, Newman, Bagehot, Henry James, and Ruskin. For further discussion of Scott's critics nothing is likely to replace Hillhouse's *Waverley Novels and their Critics*, which is an admirable account of Scott's effect on his own and later generations.

Three at least of the nineteenth-century criticisms of Scott should be read. The first is Scott's own anonymous review of *Tales of My Landlord*, in which he defends his portraits of the extremist Covenan-ters in *Old Mortality* against the attack made on them by the Revd.

Thomas McCrie, but admits that his novels have some glaring
deficiencies:

... Whatever merit individual scenes and passages may possess, (and none
has been more ready than ourselves to offer our applause), it is clear that
their effect would be greatly enhanced by being disposed in a clear and continued narrative ... In addition to the loose and incoherent style of the
narration, another leading fault in these novels is the total want of interest
which the reader attaches to the character of the hero. Waverley, Brown, or
Bertram in Guy Mannering, and Lovel in the Antiquary, are all brethren of
a family; very aimiable and very insipid sort of young men ... His chief
characters are never actors, but always acted upon by the sport of circumstances, and have their fates uniformly determined by the agency of the
subordinate persons ...

Scott is as severe on himself as any of his critics.

The second criticism that should be read is Walter Bagehot's
assessment of Scott's whole achievement, in an article on various
editions of the Waverley Novels which first appeared in the *National
Review* in 1858. It outlines Scott's real strengths and may justly be
considered the best Victorian essay on Scott.

The third is Carlyle, who should be read as devil's advocate. To
Carlyle 'The great fact about [the Waverley Novels] is, that they
were faster written and better paid for than any other books in the
world.' His memorable attack on the novels, condemning Scott for
the triviality of his mind as well as for his grasping commercialism,
is a small part of his long review of Lockhart's *Life of Scott*, salted a
little, perhaps, by the memory of Scott's discourtesy in failing to
acknowledge his kindness in forwarding a letter and medal from
Goethe. The burden of his complaint is worth quoting as it is still the
chief criticism of those who dismiss Scott. It is that 'these famed
books are altogether addressed to the every-day mind; that for any
other mind there is next to no nourishment in them'. They serve, in
short, no purpose except that of 'harmlessly amusing indolent languid men'—and that is not enough:

But after all, in the loudest blaring and trumpeting of popularity, it is ever
to be held in mind, as a truth remaining true forever, that literature *has* other
aims than that of harmlessly amusing indolent languid men: or if Literature
have them not, then Literature is a very poor affair. ... Under this head
there is little to be sought or found in the Waverley Novels. Not profitable
for doctrine, for reproof, for edification, for building up or elevating, in any
shape! The sick heart will find no healing here, the darkly struggling heart
no guidance: the Heroic that is in all men no divine awakening voice. We
say, therefore, that they do not found themselves on deep interests, but on

comparatively trivial ones: not on the perennial, perhaps not even on the lasting.

The grave charge that Scott has nothing to say is an untrue one, but a fertile untruth from which has grown some admirable recent criticism stating the case for Scott as a novelist of theme as well as of plots and characters.

Modern critics of Scott—and Scott has been short of readers, but never of critics—may be loosely divided into three schools of thought. The first may be called the catholic critics, who like all the Scottish novels at least, and are willing to judge them by criteria which are not necessarily appropriate to other novelists. They usually rank *Old Mortality* and *Redgauntlet* as high as *The Heart of Mid-Lothian*. The second school, the puritans, tend to give serious consideration only to *The Heart of Mid-Lothian* and the short stories, which have the formal and thematic unity that they approve. The third school, the un-believers, dismiss Scott entirely.

Of this persuasion is E. M. Forster, whose *Aspects of the Novel* con-tains an attack on Scott not less devastating and much more witty than Carlyle's. Scott 'is seen to have a trivial mind and a heavy style. He cannot construct. He has neither artistic detachment nor passion, and how can a writer who is devoid of both, create characters who will move us deeply?' To prove his assertion that Scott cannot even tell a story, he takes *The Antiquary*—Scott's favourite among the novels—and deftly tears the plot into absurd fragments. Scott is plainly not E. M. Forster's kind of novelist. Nor, indeed, is he F. R. Leavis's: Scott's place in *The Great Tradition* is in a footnote. 'Wander ing Willie's Tale' and 'The Two Drovers' are mentioned with approval, but on the larger issues he finds Scott wanting:

He made no serious attempt to work out his own form and break away from the bad tradition of the eighteenth-century romance. Of his books, *The Heart of Mid-Lothian* comes the nearest to being a great novel, but hardly *is* that, too many allowances and deductions have to be made. Out of Scott a bad tradition came. . . .

As an answer to the unbelievers there is no long critical work, no 'novel by novel' survey of the whole sweep of Scott's achievement; but there are articles, chapters, and essays, and some good recent books on selections of the novels. The traditional case—one might even say the classic case—for Scott, is made out best in an extended essay by Lord David Cecil. This is not easily come by, and it may be helpful, therefore, to have its main conclusions summarized here.

There is nothing half-hearted about Lord David Cecil's defence of

Scott, for he is a worshipper, and is untroubled by doubts about Scott's place in the Pantheon. 'He is a very great novelist indeed: and so far from not being serious, touched depths and heights often that most English novelists never touch at all.' If he does not appeal to everyone it is because 'his merits do not lie open for every eye to see, especially the sort of eye with which people are taught to regard novels nowadays. One must learn to appreciate him.' He defines his range as 'all that part of experience which concerns man as a product of his local environment and his historic past', his subjects as those aspects of life 'which peculiarly illustrate its connection with the past', and his themes as the conflict 'between an individual tempera- ment and a tradition; or sometimes between the representatives of one tradition and another'. He is surely right to emphasize as he does Scott's range, for a novelist has a right to be judged on what he does rather than on what he fails to do. Scott's range hardly touches the usual subjects of the novel; it 'leaves out all that vast, varied area of human activity and interest we call private life; all man's preoccupa- tions as an individual, pursuing his individual happiness, his personal hopes, fears and problems and pleasures and weaknesses and aspi- rations'. And if that is much to lose it extends, in compensation, into the regions of romance and the supernatural and even into 'the heroic tragedy of epic and saga and ballad'. Lord David believes that within his range Scott is supreme. He likes the grand scale on which he works, the skill with which he tells a story, the simple but not superficial characters who resemble those of Shakespeare rather than Dickens in the way their comic side never becomes their whole character. Lord David, however, loves Scott well this side of idolatry, and he knows how much escapes his 'powerful, negligent grasp'. He recognizes the lack of form and proportion, the conventionality of his plots, the lifelessness of his heroines and the 'impeccable, incredible, indistinguishable young men' who are his heroes. Worst of all Scott frequently wrote outside his true range, so that 'as serious novels *Ivanhoe* and the rest of them are failures'.

The same enthusiasm for his subject, which sends the reader in the end back to the novels themselves, informs David Daiches's admir- able essay, 'Scott's Achievement as a Novelist'. This is more readily attainable and is the best single short introduction to Scott. For Daiches, as for all Scott's most perceptive critics from his own day until ours, the Scottish novels are those on which his reputation must stand or fall, and his essay confines itself to these works. It states much of the traditional case for Scott, but its particular value is that it goes on from there to answer by implication the objection, which stems from Carlyle, that Scott is a romantic and unconcerned with life as it is really lived. Daiches argues convincingly that Scott's best novels at least are 'anti-romantic'. *Rob Roy* and *Redgauntlet*, for instance, where the forces of the old world and the old ways are in the end impotent against the new world of commercial power and prosperity, show that heroic action 'is, in the last analysis, neither heroic nor useful, and that man's destiny, at least in the modern world, is to find his testing time not amid the sound of trumpets but in the daily struggles and recurring crises of personal and social life'. Furthermore Scott is concerned with real issues. He has no philosophy of history, but he does use history to illuminate aspects of man's fate which have a relevance beyond the immediate historical setting. 'Fanaticism, superstition, pedantry—these and qualities such as these are always with us, and Scott handles them again and again.' The key to Scott, Daiches believes, is the conflict in his personality between prudent Briton and passionate Scot, and between love of the past and belief in the present, a conflict from which emerges all his greatest work. A host of other observations—on his style, his plots, his heroes—are tossed off in the course of this breathtaking and exhilarating scamper through Scott.

Thomas Crawford's short but useful book on Scott in the 'Writers and Critics' series deals with all the facets of his work, with the ballads, poems, and lesser romances, as well as with the best of the Scottish novels. There is some account of Scott's life and a personal assessment of his character, which was marked, Crawford thinks, by 'a refusal to put art first, and a disastrous compromise with the market'. There are two chapters on the novels in general—one on 'Intentions and Themes', the other on 'Character, Metre, Style'— and a whole chapter on *The Heart of Mid-Lothian* which, along with two short stories, 'The Highland Widow' and 'The Two Drovers', he agrees with Leavis in finding Scott's best work.

Two more recent books deal intelligently with Scott's best novels. A. O. S. Cockshut divides his study, *The Achievement of Walter Scott*, into two parts. In the first he discusses Scott's literary personality, the workings of cause and effect in the novels and the relationship of the medievalist and the entertainer. In the second he writes on five of the novels: *Waverley, Old Mortality, Rob Roy, The Heart of Mid-Lothian*, and *Redgauntlet*. This is the best book yet published on these particular novels. Close behind comes D. D. Devlin's *The Author of Waverley*, a critical study with useful chapters on 'Scott and Fiction' and 'Scott and History' leading to an analysis of *Waverley, A Legend of Montrose, Rob Roy, The Bride of Lammermoor*, and *Redgauntlet*.

A number of chapters on Scott in histories of literature or of the novel are not to be despised, since they either summarize received opinion or contain new insights of their own. In the first category comes Walter Allen's Penguin, *The English Novel*, whose account, since it covers most of the novels, is inevitably hasty, but is none the less a sound introduction to Scott, whom Allen discusses at greater length in *Six Great Novelists*. 'Scott is one of the great imperfect novelists,' he warns the reader, 'and his imperfections are exactly those most offensive to present day taste.'

In the second category there is Ian Jack's chapter on 'The Waverley Romances' which stresses, as the title suggests, the romantic element in the novels—the complicated intrigues, villainous foreigners, and the young heroes of mysterious origins—and associates Scott interestingly with the contemporary concept of the picturesque. Arnold Kettle, who is of the 'short stories and *Heart of Mid-Lothian* only' persuasion, has an admirable study of that novel in his paperback. He scores some good points in passing. He notes that Scott's range is wider than that of any of his predecessors, even Fielding, and draws attention to his humour, which is not wit but a 'sense of the comic clash between characters working within different sets of assumptions'; he believes that Scott 'is not a writer we can afford to despise' and forecasts a revival of his fortunes.

In his chapter on Scott in *The Living Novel*, V. S. Pritchett praises *The Heart of Mid-Lothian*, 'The Highland Widow', and 'The Two Drovers'; but even if this choice should begin to seem unoriginal his commentary is not, and he ranges widely and wittily over the other novels. He does not find many of the heroines alluring—'Miss Bellenden in her castle stands like a statue and talks like an epitaph' —and he thinks Scott's history not real history but merely 'the settled, the collectable, the antique'. He reminds us that Scott totally avoids the sentimentality of Dickens and is 'one of the great comic writers'.

The best remaining criticism is on particular aspects of his work rather than on the full range of his achievement. Donald Davie's *Heyday of Sir Walter Scott*, a book whose main concern is to show the influence of Scott on Pushkin, Fenimore Cooper, and others, is important for its commentary on *Waverley*, which, as the first of a successful line, surely merits all the attention it receives here. It is a convincing defence of Waverley himself—'a strong portrait of a weak or weakish character'—and of the structure and theme of the novel. Davie relates the early chapters to the rest and stresses the historical insights: 'It shows the victory of the un-heroic (the English

Waverley) over the heroic (the Scottish MacIvor); it shows that this was inevitable and on the whole welcome, yet also sad.' David Craig, in *Literature and the Scottish People*, a book on the whole unfriendly to Scott, challenges his merits as a historical novelist and deplores his lack of interest in the life around him as material for fiction. His views on Scott's treatment of religious extremism in *Old Mortality* and *The Heart of Mid-Lothian* are of interest to anyone studying those novels, although Scott seems to answer some of his criticism in the review of *Tales of my Landlord* in the *Quarterly* mentioned above. A different insight into Scott's historical vision is provided by Georg Lukács in *The Historical Novel*, which attempts to show that Scott the high Tory shared a Marxist view of history. The argument would be more convincing did it not rely on the premiss that the events of *Waverley* (1745) occur *before* those of *Rob Roy* (1715).

Comment on other aspects of Scott's life and work is provided by the Sir Walter Scott Lectures which are given every two years at the University of Edinburgh. The 1950 volume, collected by W. L. Renwick, is invaluable. Edwin Muir advances the intriguing psychological theory 'that the disastrous outcome of Scott's affair with Williamina and the resolution with which he put her memory behind him contracted the scope of his imagination and made it impossible for him to describe love'. G. M. Young approves the excellence of his descriptions of 'the scenery of action', for instance in the account of the battle of Drumclog in *Old Mortality* where 'Scott set an example and a standard which some of his successors, professed historians, may have reached, but none, I think, has ever surpassed.' Scott, he submits, filled the past with real, speaking people; he realized, and helped others to realize, that history is concerned with an entire culture. Grierson, in another of the lectures, surveys the sub-literary undergrowth out of which the Waverley Novels grew, and concludes that 'Scott's closest affinities are, after all, not with the romantic and terror novels of his age, but with the older masters, Fielding and Smollett.' Another of his essays, 'Lang, Lockhart and Biography', throws light not only on Lockhart's manipulations, but also on Scott's financial affairs.

Recent years have seen a revival of interest in Scott, with a flurry of critical articles as well as the occasional book. The tendency, since Daiches's essay appeared in 1951, has been to treat Scott with the sort of detailed attention already accorded to some other writers. That this can be dangerous is clear. Scott is a great writer but a straightforward one. The merits and demerits of his work are on the whole obvious, and he did not weigh his words carefully enough to justify the kind of analysis which is appropriate to the work of Henry James. The best modern criticism, however, has been willing to recognize that preconceptions about what a novel ought to be stand in the way of an appreciation of Scott, and that it is better to take him instead on his own terms. On the theme of *The Heart of Mid-Lothian*, 'the nature of justice as it is in any age', Robin Mayhead is worth reading, although his defence of Scott as artist perhaps tries too hard to press Scott into a mould which he obstinately refuses to fit. Stewart Gordon on *Waverley*, Joseph Duncan on the Anti-Romantic in *Ivanhoe*, and Robert Gordon on *The Bride of Lammermoor* should also be mentioned. These articles have been reprinted in *Walter Scott*, edited by D. D. Devlin, a useful selection of recent criticism that does not include, unfortunately, two articles—'Scott's *Redgauntlet*' by David Daiches and 'Scott and *Redgauntlet*' by D. D. Devlin—which must be read by anyone who believes, as these two critics clearly do, that *Redgauntlet* is as great a novel as *The Heart of Mid-Lothian*.

The other important recent collection of essays is *Scott's Mind and Art*, edited by Norman Jeffares. Besides being a convenient source for the criticism of Bagehot, Daiches, and Lukács already mentioned, it contains two particularly fine essays by David Murison and F. A. Pottle. Murison's 'The Two Languages of Scott' is an admirable guide to Scott's use of his native language. Pottle's well-known essay, in which he draws a distinction between Boswell's powers of almost total recall and Scott's 'imaginative memory', is of value far beyond the study of those two authors alone.

BIOGRAPHIES AND LETTERS

For all but two of the numerous Lives of Scott there is one main source—Lockhart's *Life*, which was published five years after Scott's death. It is one of the great biographies. Probably no biographer, not even Boswell, has known his subject better. Lockhart was married to Scott's daughter Sophia; he knew most of Scott's friends; he spent his summers at Chiefswood on the Abbotsford estate; he was the sole member of the family with whom Scott discussed his literary concerns. Of these advantages, and of his access to Scott's papers after his death, Lockhart made full use. He has been caught out since, of course, in errors and omissions of various kinds. Some of his facts are wrong, the occasional person is misnamed or left unnamed, and, what is more important, he can be shown to have manipulated some of his quotations from Scott's letters, omitting paragraphs without comment and even running together letters of different dates. But the faults are small beside the massive achievement of the work as a whole. Carlyle objected that the *Life* was not so much a biography as the materials for a biography, but its loosely-woven texture, which allows Scott and Scott's friends to tell the story in their own words wherever possible, today appears its chief merit. Despite its occasional inaccuracies it is an invaluable source of information about Scott's life from month to month, a good book to read right through, but also, thanks to its extended chapter-headings and index, a handy work of reference for anyone interested in a particular aspect of Scott's life.

Only two other biographies of Scott are indispensable. The first is *Sir Walter Scott, Bart.*, written by Professor Grierson after he had seen through the press the Centenary Edition of Scott's *Letters*. Many of these letters were not known to Lockhart, and others he chose not to use; in effect they provided Grierson with a complete picture of Scott's life which enabled him to write a new biography, confirming the truth of Lockhart's account in many places but correcting him in others and adding considerably to our total knowledge of Scott.

The other is Edgar Johnson's two-volume *Sir Walter Scott: the Great Unknown*. Over fifteen years Professor Johnson read and sifted everything written by Scott and about Scott: the result is the most painstaking and thorough of all the accounts of Scott's life. It is not the most readable biography of Scott, but it is the most authoritative. It is, and is likely to remain, the work of reference to which we turn for the date of any event important in Scott's life or for the confirmation of any fact that is known about it.

In time for 1970, Arthur Melville Clark published *Sir Walter Scott: the formative years*. The date was carefully chosen, for it is Melville Clark's contention that Scott was born not in 1771 but in 1770, and that we should therefore have celebrated his bicentenary a year earlier than we did. His redating of Scott's birth has not convinced the generality of scholars, and his argument should be read in conjunction with Dr. Corson's refutation of it in *The Scotsman* for 26 December 1970. The book sheds light, though, into several hitherto unconsidered corners of Scott's early life.

Of the one-volume Lives of Scott by many hands, quarried for the most part from Lockhart, the most readable is John Buchan's *Sir Walter Scott*. Buchan had an instinctive understanding of his subject (he was after all, like Scott, a man of action, a man of letters, and a writer of popular fiction with a Scottish flavour), and his book is full of fine insights into the man and the novels.

Other biographies of Scott can safely be left undisturbed. The student who is interested should go next to the memoirs of those who knew Scott, which genuinely add their mite to the sum of our know-ledge of him.

The Letters of Sir Walter Scott mentioned above fill nearly 5,000 pages, and even at that they omit almost half the letters which are now known to be in existence. No doubt other men have written as many letters, but it is unusual for so many to have survived. The reason, however, is clear. From 1802 at least, when *The Minstrelsy of the Scottish Border* was published, Scott was a fellow of some mark and likelihood whose letters were not to be thrown away; later he was the foremost literary man of the age, and his letters were curiosities to be treasured, with signatures—to judge by the number which have been cut off—considerably in demand. Grierson's edition is not complete, nor is it always accurate. The conjectural dating of some letters is suspect, and the discovery of originals has shown that some of the copies he had to use were careless approximations only; some early letters came to light only after the volume to which they belonged had been published, and had to be placed instead in an appendix. Worst of all, the only index (until Dr. Corson's projected work is published) remains on cards in the National Library of Scotland. But when all that is said, Grierson's edition is still a vast and valuable collection of Scott's own letters. In one sense they are disappointing, for references to the novels are few and discussions of literary theory almost nonexistent. But in other ways they are rewarding. Their lively style, the pervasive humour and occasional revealing indiscretion bring us closer to Scott than Lockhart's *Life*, and help to account for the affection which he almost universally inspired. The letters he received have also been preserved, and more than 6,000 of them are bound up in Scott's private letter-books. Although they include letters from most of the great men and great writers of his age, only selections have been published. Wilfred Partington's *Private Letter-Books* and *Sir Walter's Postbag* are entertaining, but of limited value to the scholar.

The final source of our knowledge of Scott the man is his own journal, which he began late in life in 1825, and carried on—although at times intermittently—until a few months before his death in 1832. It is unfortunate that the only years for which we have Scott's own account are his latest and his earliest, described in *The Journal* and the fragment of Autobiography at the beginning of Lockhart's *Life*. *The Journal*, however, is a moving book and a remarkable record of courage in adversity. Within a few weeks of taking it up Scott was bankrupt; a few months later he lost his wife; as time goes on he himself is writing more and more compulsively to pay off his debts after a first, second, and then a third stroke. Tait's edition is textually superior to the original edition by David Douglas, but as Tait died with his labours unfinished the notes and index are far from adequate. The new edition, the work of the present writer, attempts to establish a text and to provide the reader with the information that he needs about the people and events of the *Journal* years.

BIBLIOGRAPHIES

Dr. James Corson's *Bibliography of Scott* is comprehensive and unusually helpful on anything written before 1943; and since so much that was so good was written in the nineteenth century or—through the stimulus of the centenary of Scott's death—in the 1930s, it is not as out-of-date as this might sound. What is more, it covers not only books and periodicals relating to Scott but even quite obscure newspaper articles. The author, who knows more about Scott than any other man living, has read virtually everything that he lists and is able to comment helpfully on many of the entries. This remains, and is likely to remain, the standard bibliography of Scott.

To find a complete account of recent writing about Scott it is necessary to sift the usual standard works of reference. The Bibliography in Ian Jack's British Council *Sir Walter Scott*, however, is helpful up until the end of 1957; there is a good select bibliography in D. D. Devlin's *Sir Walter Scott*, published in 1968, and Professor Edgar Johnson lists a number of works that are not mentioned by either of these earlier writers in the Bibliography of *Sir Walter Scott: the Great Unknown*.

BACKGROUND READING

It is easy to forget at how many points Scott touched his age. He was an important figure in the Romantic Movement. His collection of ballads, *The Minstrelsy of the Scottish Border*, came out only four years after *Lyrical Ballads*; his novels fanned the interest of his own age and the next in the Gothic, the medieval, and the picturesque; the *Demonology* and several of the novels reflect the romantic interest in the supernatural. Scott popularized—more effectively than Wordsworth, because more people read him—the taste for wild scenery. The house in which he lived, the 'Conundrum Castle' of Abbotsford, was etched and described for dozens of publications, and had its effect on the architecture and interior decoration of the Victorian age which Scott did not quite live to see. Furthermore, Scott was not only Britain's foremost novelist, but also one of her leading poets: he declined the laureateship in 1813. He was the personal friend of Byron, Southey, Moore, Campbell, and Wordsworth, as well as of Edinburgh lawyers and London politicians, of Peel, and Wellington, and the King himself. To his contemporaries Scott seemed to bestride the narrow world. Any background reading on the Romantic Movement or on the early years of the nineteenth century is directly or indirectly, therefore, the background to Scott.

There is, however, a dualism which sets him a little apart from the others. He is part Scot, part European; an educated man, familiar with Italian, German, and English literature, yet drawing inspiration from the primitive culture of Scotland's past. His debt to Scottish *literature* as opposed to Scottish life is, it is true, small, once due tribute has been paid to the influence of the Border ballads, but it can be traced with the help of Kurt Wittig's *Scottish Tradition in Literature* (a good factual account of his predecessors) and Edwin Muir's *Scott and Scotland* (the acutest assessment of their influence on his work). Muir's book is a sensitive exploration by a Scottish poet of the effect on Scott (himself pulled two ways by his 'riotous imagination' and his 'practical sense') of a tradition in which realism had always coexisted with fantasy. For Scottish life at the time, especially for the civilized and stimulating environment of Edinburgh at the end of its golden age, the choice might fall on Cockburn's *Memorials of His Time* (for a contemporary view), Douglas Young's *Edinburgh in the Time of Sir Walter Scott* (for its wealth of factual detail) and Professor Youngson's *Making of Classical Edinburgh*, a brilliant account of the town's expansion which is of wider than architectural interest.

Scott is, lastly, an important figure in the history of the novel, even if at this distance of time he is not the colossus he appeared to his own age. His achievement cannot be fully measured without some awareness of the novel as he found it. For him the great tradition came from the picaresque novelists; he refers again and again to Cervantes and Le Sage, the great originators, and to Fielding and Smollett, the fathers of 'the minor romance or English novel'. He had read most of the novels written in the late eighteenth century—indeed *The Journal* indicates that he remained a confirmed, if rapid, reader of novels until the end of his life—and traces of the influence of Horace Walpole, Mrs. Radcliffe, and Scott's own friend Maria Edgeworth can be found in his best as well as in his less good work. To understand the novel as Scott saw it, one could do no better than dip into *Don Quixote* and *Gil Blas*, *Tom Jones*, *Peregrine Pickle*, and *Tristram Shandy*, *The Castle of Otranto*, *The Mysteries of Udolpho*, and *Castle Rackrent*.

REFERENCES

TEXTS

(*a*) *The Novels*

Collected Editions of the Waverley Novels:
  Border Edition, A. Lang (ed.), (London, 1892–4).
  Century Scott (London, 1898).
  Dent Library Edition (London and Toronto, 1931).
  Edinburgh Edition (Edinburgh, 1901–3).
  —and many more too numerous to list.
Cheap Editions of individual novels are published by
  Collins New Classics
  Everyman's Library
  Nelson Classics.
Paperback Editions of some novels are obtainable, principally in
  Everyman Paperbacks
  Signet Books.

(*b*) *Other works*

Lord D. Cecil (ed.), *Short Stories of Sir Walter Scott* (World's Classics, London, 1934).
J. L. Robinson (ed.), *Poetical Works of Sir Walter Scott* (London, 1904).
Sir W. Scott, *Miscellaneous Prose Works* (Edinburgh, 1834–40; 1871).
I. Williams (ed.), *Sir Walter Scott on Novelists and Fiction* (London, 1968); a collection of Scott's essays, reviews, and prefaces.

CRITICAL STUDIES AND COMMENTARY

W. Allen, *The English Novel* (Penguin, Harmondsworth, 1954; New York, 1955).
—— *Six Great Novelists* (London, 1955).
W. Bagehot, 'The Waverley Novels', in M. St. John Stevas (ed.), *Collected Works* (London, 1965); or in A. N. Jeffares (ed.), *Scott's Mind and Art* (Edinburgh, 1969); or in J. O. Hayden (ed.), *Scott: the Critical Heritage* (London, 1970).
T. Carlyle, 'Sir Walter Scott' in *Scottish and Other Miscellanies* (Everyman, London and New York, 1964); or (an extract only) in J. O. Hayden (ed.).
Lord D. Cecil, *Sir Walter Scott* (London, 1933).
A. O. S. Cockshut, *The Achievement of Walter Scott* (London, 1969).
D. Craig, '*The Heart of Mid-Lothian*: its Religious Basis', *EIC* viii (1958).
—— *Literature and the Scottish People* (London and New York, 1961).
T. Crawford, *Scott* (paperback, Edinburgh, 1965).
D. Daiches, 'Scott's Achievement as a Novelist', in *Literary Essays* (Edinburgh 1956); or in D. D. Devlin (ed.), *Walter Scott* (London, 1968); or in A. N. Jeffares (ed.).
—— 'Scott's *Redgauntlet*', in *From Jane Austen to Joseph Conrad*, edd. R. C. Rathburn and M. Steinmann (Minneapolis, 1958).

D. Davie, *The Heyday of Sir Walter Scott*, (London, 1961).

D. D. Devlin, 'Scott and *Redgauntlet*', *Review of English Literature*, iv (1963).

—— (ed.), *Walter Scott* (London, 1968).

—— *The Author of Waverley* (London, 1971).

J. E. Duncan, 'The Anti-Romantic in *Ivanhoe*', *NCF* ix (1955).

E. M. Forster, *Aspects of the Novel* (London, 1927; New York, 1947).

R. C. Gordon, '*The Bride of Lammermoor*: a novel of Tory Pessimism', *NCF* xii (1957); or i D. D. Devlin (ed.).

S. S. Gordon, '*Waverley* and the "Unified Design" ', *ELH* xviii (1951); or in D. D. Devlin (ed.).

H. J. C. Grierson, 'Lang, Lockhart and Biography', in *Essays and Addresses* (London, 1940).

—— 'The Man and the Poet' and 'History and the Novel', in W. L. Renwick (ed.), *Sir Walter Scott Lectures* (Edinburgh and Chicago, 1950).

J. O. Hayden (ed.), *Scott: the Critical Heritage* (London, 1970).

W. Hazlitt, 'Sir Walter Scott' in *The Spirit of the Age* (World's Classics, London, 1904); or in J. O. Hayden (ed.).

J. T. Hillhouse, *The Waverley Novels and their Critics* (Minneapolis, Minn., and London, 1936; New York, 1967).

I. Jack, *Sir Walter Scott* (London, 1958).

—— *English Literature 1815–1832* (London, 1963).

A. N. Jeffares (ed.), *Scott's Mind and Art* (Edinburgh, 1969).

F. Jeffrey, *Contributions to the Edinburgh Review* (London, 1844); or D. Nicol Smith (ed.), *Jeffrey's Literary Criticism* (London, 1910); or in J. O. Hayden (ed.).

A. C. Kettle, *An Introduction to the English Novel* (2nd edn., London and New York, 1967).

F. R. Leavis, *The Great Tradition* (London, 1948; New York, 1963).

G. Lukács, *The Historical Novel* (trans. H. and S. Mitchell, London, 1962); or (an extract only) in A. N. Jeffares (ed.).

R. Mayhead, '*The Heart of Mid-Lothian*: Scott as Artist', *EIC* vi (1956); or in D. D. Devlin (ed.).

E. Muir, 'Walter Scott: the Man' and 'Walter Scott: the Writer', in W. L. Renwick (ed.).

David Murison,' The Two Languages of Scott', in A. N. Jeffares (ed.).

F. A. Pottle, The Power of Memory in Boswell and Scott', in A. N. Jeffares (ed.).

V. S. Pritchett, *The Living Novel* (London, 1946; New York, 1964).

W. L. Renwick (ed.), *Sir Walter Scott Lectures 1940–1948* (Edinburgh and Chicago, 1950).

Sir W. Scott, 'Tales of My Landlord', *Quarterly Review*, xvi (1817); or in J. O. Hayden (ed.).

G. M. Young, 'Scott and the Historians', in W. L. Renwick (ed.).

BIOGRAPHIES AND LETTERS

W. E. K. Anderson (ed.), *The Journal of Sir Walter Scott* (Oxford, 1972).

J. Buchan, *Sir Walter Scott* (London and New York, 1932).

A. Melville Clark, *Sir Walter Scott: the formative years* (Edinburgh and London 1969).

J. C. Corson, 'Birth of the last minstrel: vital years in debate', in *The Scotsman*, 26 December 1970.

H. J. C. Grierson *et al.* (eds.), *The Letters of Sir Walter Scott* (London, 1932–7).

—— *Sir Walter Scott, Bart. A New Life supplementary to, and corrective of, Lockhart's Biography* (London, 1938).

E. Johnson, *Sir Walter Scott: the Great Unknown* (2 vols., New York and London, 1970).

J. G. Lockhart, *The Life of Sir Walter Scott* (2nd edn., Edinburgh, 1839; Edinburgh Edition, Edinburgh, 1902; Everyman, London and New York, 1906).

W. Partington, *The Private Letter-Books of Sir Walter Scott* (London, 1930).

—— *Sir Walter's Post Bag* (London, 1932).

BIBLIOGRAPHIES

J. C. Corson, *Bibliography of Scott: A Classified and Annotated List of Books and Articles relating to his Life and Works, 1797–1940* (Edinburgh and New York, 1943).

Other select Bibliographies will be found in

D. D. Devlin (ed.), *Walter Scott* (London, 1968).

I. Jack, *Sir Walter Scott* (paperback, London, 1958).

E. Johnson, *Sir Walter Scott: the Great Unknown* (2 vols., New York and London, 1970).

BACKGROUND READING

H. Cockburn, *Memorials of his Time* (Edinburgh, 1909).

E. Muir, *Scott and Scotland* (London, 1936; New York, 1938).

K. Wittig, *The Scottish Tradition in Literature* (Edinburgh and Chester Springs, 1961).

D. Young, *Edinburgh in the Time of Sir Walter Scott* (Norman, Okla., 1965).

A. J. Youngson, *The Making of Classical Edinburgh* (Edinburgh and Chicago, 1966).

9 · JANE AUSTEN 1775–1817

B. C. Southam

TEXTS

Readers of Jane Austen are well catered for. The novels are available in a wide range of modern editions, several with helpful notes and introductions designed specifically for student use. Fortunately, the texts of the original editions are fairly sound and we are not faced with a legacy of bibliographical problems. There are very few debatable readings, and these are relatively unimportant. The only textual nicety concerns the original publication of the novels in three-volume sets (*Sense and Sensibility, Pride and Prejudice, Emma, Mansfield Park*) or in two-volume sets (*Northanger Abbey* and *Persuasion*). It has been argued that Jane Austen intended the volume-division to play a part in the structural design of the novels, and hence to affect our experience in reading them. Thus some modern editions make a point of indicating these divisions through the system of chapter-numbering.

The text to which all students will want to refer is the Oxford edition prepared by R. W. Chapman. This has no critical notes or critical introductions, but provides a wealth of historical and bibliographical information for each of the novels: the chronology of composition, the history of publication, textual variants, explanatory notes. And through the edition there are appendices treating such matters as Jane Austen's English, the manners of the age, modes of address, and other historical matters important to our understanding of the novels and their period. Volume vi of the Oxford edition is entitled the *Minor Works*. This collects the remainder of Jane Austen's literary material: the three notebooks of childhood writing; the two unfinished novels, *The Watsons* and *Sanditon*; the short epistolary novel *Lady Susan*; the parody *Plan of a Novel*; together with charades, verses, and prayers; and non-literary documents relating to the sales and reception of the novels. The six novels are also included in a more recent Oxford Edition, the Oxford English Novels series. These are without Chapman's elaborate apparatus of indices and appendices; instead, there is a small range of explanatory notes and practical Introductions (part-critical, part-historical).

A good standard reading edition is Dent's Everyman series (bound and paperback). These are plain, unannotated texts, excellently edited and introduced by Mary Lascelles, with a biographical note and reading list. Another good reading edition (U.S. only, paperback) is the Riverside series, in which the volumes have outstanding critical introductions. For individual titles, some students may prefer those novels presently available in the Penguin English Library. These are newly edited texts, with historical and explanatory notes, and considerable critical introductions. The most elaborate student volumes are in the Norton Critical Editions. The annotation is slight but the texts are accompanied by a great deal of valuable ancillary material: details of composition and publication, a section of 'Backgrounds' (including extracts from Jane Austen's letters and minor works), a section of 'Reviews and Essays in Criticism' (including contemporary reviews and a selection of later criticism) and a select bibliography.

CRITICAL STUDIES AND COMMENTARY

This section opens with a rapid glance at Jane Austen's early reception and at the development of critical attitudes later in the century and onwards to the present day. This perspective has a certain historical interest. But there is an altogether better reason for beginning in this way: it is that many of the most important issues of Jane Austen criticism have occupied critics and reviewers from the time that the novels first appeared, and it is useful to remind ourselves how these issues first arose in their simplest and most direct form. Moreover, some of the later nineteenth-century criticism, for all its air of informality and unsophistication, is as perceptive and stimulating as anything written since. A further reason for taking this historical approach is that it helps us to see the novels in their immediate literary setting.

In her own lifetime Jane Austen was a fashionable rather than a popular novelist. She was never a best-seller like Sir Walter Scott, but enjoyed what we would call a highbrow readership, which included a number of her fellow-writers, among them the dramatist Sheridan, the novelists Maria Edgeworth, Mary Russell Mitford, and Sir Walter Scott himself. Her novels were admired for three main qualities—their wit, the force and variety of their characterization, and their realism. These were the qualities most glaringly absent from the fiction of the period, much of which (to use Jane Austen's own blunt term) was 'trash', in the form of Gothic melodrama, sentimental romance, and the moralizing tale meant to educate and improve. Jane Austen made fun of this rubbish. Her childhood pieces, written when she was only eleven or twelve, are firm and accurate parodies, showing up the absurdity and unreality of their extravagant characters and action, and the emptiness of their values. This element of literary satire, much subdued, continues throughout the later works.

Her novels are also critical in another way. In the very fact of her own technical skill, Jane Austen set a standard of writing which finely showed up the amateurism and incompetence of the trash novelists. Her mastery begins at the most fundamental level—in the choice of words, in sentence structure, paragraph construction, the handling of dialogue, the control of narrative; and it scarcely needs saying that in its more developed aspects her writing—in its dramatic reality, its irony, its thematic and moral organization—bears the stamp of a unique and powerful creative imagination.

Jane Austen's contemporary readers were not in a position to appreciate the full range of this achievement. At that time fiction was hardly thought of as a branch of literature, and no one looked for genius in a novelist. Yet something of Jane Austen's art was glimpsed, partially and intermittently, as we can seen in the few contemporary reviews and in the informal remarks that have come down to us in letters, diaries, and memoirs. Her readers found the novels enjoyable and refreshing. It was something new for them to meet an accurate and convincing picture of contemporary society, to encounter realistic characters, to find good sense so entertainingly, so wittily delivered.

The most important contemporary statement is Scott's review of *Emma*. Written in 1815, this is one of the classic essays on Jane Austen, a rich quarry for later critics. Scott recognized that Jane Austen was writing a new kind of fiction; that she had discovered how to create a work of art out of the familiar material of everyday life, the subject-matter spurned by novelists of the Gothic and senti-mental schools. In *Emma* he saw 'the modern novel', faithful to the situations and events of 'ordinary life', impressive and entertaining for its wit and realism, and displaying a developed technique in the prose style and the drawing of character.

Scott's recognition of 'the modern novel' was further developed in a second classic essay, the 1821 review of *Northanger Abbey* and *Persuasion* by Archbishop Whately. This is written as if in continua-tion of Scott, for both reviews appeared anonymously in the *Quarterly Review* and employed the conventional editorial 'we'. As its point of departure it takes Scott's central concept, 'the modern novel', and moves on to a highly Aristotelian discussion of the capacity of the novel to concentrate 'wide experience' into 'small compass' and to provide us with a serious and instructive view of life. Had this part of his review been read more intelligently, some later nineteenth-century critics would not have been so quick to dismiss Jane Austen's novels as trivial and commonplace merely because their social circumstances and events are so unremarkable, so unmomentous. Whately saw Jane Austen as a fundamentally serious writer, whose values are communicated dramatically, within the fiction, rather than stated didactically (and here he offered a contrast in the undramatized moralizing of Maria Edgeworth). Again, this view of Jane Austen was virtually ignored by later critics. What they did appropriate was Whately's closely argued analysis of the novelist's technique, these few pages which we meet again and again in later essays, elaborated and re-worded, often taken over almost unchanged, particularly the sections treating her *economy* in the handling of plot and action, and her capacity to effect minute yet significant discriminations across a range of similar characters.

At this point, Jane Austen criticism foundered. Scott and Whately had recognized a great writer. But Victorian England, with a strong and heady diet of Lytton, Disraeli, Dickens, Trollope, Thackeray, and George Eliot, was in no mood to discriminate the subtleties of Jane Austen's irony and form. Beside these giants, her quiet domestic stories seemed dowdy and old-fashioned; beside a strong and engaged literature, which was concerned with the social and spiritual problems of the age, her novels appeared to be nothing more than period comedies, utterly irrelevant to the harsh realities of material and spiritual suffering. By the public at large, she was forgotten. Her name was kept alive, in essays and reviews, only by the efforts of a line of devoted critics, notably G. H. Lewes who, with Macaulay, ranked Jane Austen with Shakespeare as a creator of character. But this was praise and admiration, not criticism. Not until 1870, in the essay by Richard Simpson, was there any systematic discussion of Jane Austen's work. (This period's understanding and misunderstanding of comedy, in particular the special comedy of Jane Austen, is analysed in the essay by Rachel Trickett.)

Simpson's is perhaps the most important single essay on Jane Austen that we have. It is the work of a critic responding to the powerful and original intellect that he found in the novels. He named irony as the condition of her art. Earlier critics had spoken of Jane Austen's satire and irony, but had singled them out as if they were separable ingredients in the 'mix' of the novel, and had made no attempt to inquire into their method and scope. By contrast, Simpson found irony to be an essential element in the novelist's vision, ever-present as a tension which Jane Austen maintains between, on the one hand, the notions of romantic love, and, on the other, the unromantic realities of love and marriage under the stress and pressure of real life.

Simpson was revolutionary in rejecting the assumption that Jane Austen's art of character-portrayal could not be analysed; he was the first critic to attempt to identify the nature of her development from novel to novel; and he is the only critic to open a profitable discussion about the limits of her scope as a novelist of society.

My account of nineteenth-century criticism ends with a reference to the chapter on Jane Austen in *English Women of Letters* (1862) by Julia Kavanagh. Mrs. Kavanagh was a literary journalist and novelist who lived by her pen; and she was simply concerned in this book to provide an unpretentious introduction for the ordinary reader. There is no obvious critical method. What she writes is a mixture of biographical and historical chit-chat, with lengthy plot résumés and character accounts, set down lightly and brightly for easy reading. This may put us off. But where Mrs. Kavangh scores over almost every other critic of Jane Austen is in challenging the reader with an interpretation of the novelist's experience of life. To quote a single sentence: 'If we look under the shrewdness and quiet satire of her stories, we shall find a much keener sense of disappointment than of joy fulfilled. Sometimes we find more than disappointment.' The force of this statement is to make us examine our own experience of the novels; and if this is a criterion of good criticism, it is a test that few critics of Jane Austen can pass.

Unfortunately, the views of Simpson and Mrs. Kavanagh had no immediate influence on the course of Jane Austen criticism. What flourished was another view entirely, a sentimental portrait of Jane Austen as a kind of Sunday writer, an amateur genius, a gentlewoman who surprised her family and herself with the success of her books. It was a protective myth. Here, it was thought, was genius of a special order, an author whose writings were so intimate, modest, and charming as to defy or elude the embrace of the critical spirit. It was also a persistent myth. With a few exceptions—notably the essays by Bradley (1911), Farrer (1917), and Garrod (1928)—much of the writing on Jane Austen from 1870 onwards remained at a level of affectionate and uncritical appreciation.

It is an interesting coincidence that another Shakespearian scholar, A. C. Bradley, should continue (quite independently) the view of Jane Austen's irony that originated with Simpson, in distinguishing her 'ironical amusement', her sense of detached superiority at the limitations of the outlook and knowledge of her characters. Farrer, too, was concerned with the writer's controlling point of view, and his essay is discussed later in this section with the more recent criticism to which it is closely related.

This period was ended by Mary Lascelles's *Jane Austen and her Art* (1939), the first systematic discussion of the novelist's achievement, which remains to this day the one indispensable introductory study. Its focus is on the word 'Art', as Henry James uses the term in his discussion of 'the art of the novel', meaning technique in its highest and fullest sense, treating such questions as the author's principles of selection and arrangement, the relationship effected between character and action, the narrative point of view. Miss Lascelles's approach has been the leading influence in the development of modern criticism, whose course, as a result, has not been a one-sided attention to technique as something on its own, as an element separable from the *meaning* of the work; in the essays of Mark Schorer, Dorothy Van Ghent, and Wayne C. Booth there is a widening discussion of the function of technique in the novelist's exploration and discovery of his subject-matter. With Jane Austen, this is a crucial point, for we are dealing with a writer whose acknowledged greatness has to be reconciled with the intrinsic 'smallness', even poverty, of her material —in the narrowness of her fictional scene and its lack of historic or tragic issues. This question faces us again in her *treatment* of the material—in, for example, her refusal to follow her characters into love-scenes, however decorous; in her arbitrary disposal of the characters and action when the story, as she sees it, is told. These are aspects of her generally dismissive and self-deprecating irony, which seems to belittle the seriousness of her creations. Yet the novels present us with an imaginative experience of density and richness, and the advance of modern criticism has been toward an explanation of these qualities, sometimes through attention to the formal organization and structure of the works, sometimes through the detailed analysis of particular passages (as in Reuben Brower's outstanding essay on *Pride and Prejudice*), or in the study of single aspects of technique (as in Booth's essay on 'Control of Distance' or Babb's book-length study of Jane Austen's dialogue); and *Emma* in particular has fascinated modern critics. It is a work of great artistic complexity and formal accomplishment, and of all Jane Austen's novels is the one most rewardingly to have answered the 'technical' approach. Some of the best recent essays on Jane Austen have been inspired by this novel (including those by Shannon, Trilling, Schorer, Hughes, Booth, Bradbury, and Harvey) and this phenomenon is interestingly discussed by David Lodge in his Introduction to the *Emma Casebook*.

The second major emphasis of modern criticism has been the discovery of a far more formidable and 'uncomfortable' writer than had been supposed by the admirers of 'Gentle Jane'. In part, this has been the re-discovery of Simpson's Jane Austen—a fundamentally serious mind, distinguished by its critical intelligence and irony. The distinctively twentieth-century emphasis has been 'Freudian' in discussing the novels in relation to the author's personal drives, among them aggression and frustration, sometimes (according to this line of analysis) creatively liberated in the force and clarity of her vision, sometimes, on the other hand, leading to failures of tone and treatment. This distinctive approach is seen in the essay 'Regulated Hatred' (1940) by D. W. Harding: the 'hatred' being the violence of emotion and attitude that is 'regulated' by the novelist's art. Harding suggests that we should not ignore, or merely discount as random, local irony, the disturbing implications that attend many of the novelist's statements; and in particular he argues that she was a subversive critic of her society, 'enjoyed by precisely the sort of people she disliked'. This is a highly controversial interpretation, challenging the traditional view, and rejected by some authorities. None the less, the evidence of her contemporary reception (which neither Harding nor his contestants have drawn upon) suggests that his contention is valid.

Harding's essay can profitably be read alongside Reginald Farrer's piece in the *Quarterly Review* (1917). This, too, is deliberately provocative and sets out to demolish the then prevalent notion of Jane Austen as a penner of flawless little comedies. Farrer saw a 'merciless', judging mind, a 'completely conscious and unerring artist' (the last phrase does not prevent him from giving a penetrating account of the shortcomings of the novels). This is one of the most packed and stimulating essays on Jane Austen; yet, like Simpson's, it fell upon deaf ears, and I mention it here, unchronologically, because together with Harding's essay it provides a helpful introduction to Marvin Mudrick's *Jane Austen* (1952), the most original and most fully developed interpretative study. Mudrick takes up one area of Farrer's discussion: Jane Austen's relation, as a writer, to the social world immediately around her, the world depicted in her fiction, toward which she was committed—to endorse its values, or to effect an ironic distancing (a non-committal), or to criticize. According to Mudrick, irony is the vital principle of Jane Austen's art—a developing individual irony, determined by her temperament, sometimes deployed by the novelist as a defence against her own personal involvement; sometimes employed as a means of exploration, divining the essential significance of a character or situation; while sometimes, in its absence, there can be artistic failure, as Mudrick judges to be the case with *Mansfield Park*. Mudrick applies this interpretative, evaluative analysis throughout Jane Austen's writing, from the juvenilia, through the six novels, to the last work, *Sanditon*. Some critics have complained that his approach is rigid, over-systematized and unhistorical. Yet it must be said that no other interpretative account so unfailingly compels the reader to define his own ideas about Jane Austen's view of life, her technique in realizing this view, and her successes and failures in the attempt.

The third major direction of modern criticism and literary scholarship has been *historical* in emphasis, 'placing' Jane Austen in the tradition of the English novel and in the literary context of her age; and, arising out of this, identifying Jane Austen's attention to certain ethical–philosophical ideas in eighteenth- and early nineteenth-century thought. This historical view has informed a number of valuable essays which suggest how, among other things, we can interpret the novels as Jane Austen's response to her social and historical situation.

The best and most succinct account of Jane Austen's relationship to the eighteenth-century novel is in the concluding section of *The Rise of the Novel* by Ian Watt. Her wider imaginative response to literature at large is treated by Mary Lascelles in chapter 2 of *Jane Austen and Her Art*; and Walton Litz, in *Jane Austen*, examines in detail the nature of her satirical exploitation of contemporary fiction, as part of a larger study of the moral and literary background to the novels. The most detailed historical study is *A Reading of Mansfield Park* by Fleishman, and this can be supplemented by chapter 3 of Robert Colby's *Fiction with a Purpose* (looking at *Mansfield Park* in the tradition of religious—didactic fiction) and the essay by Charles Murrah (with its fine analysis of the symbolic mode in *Mansfield Park*). Other useful historical approaches are to be found in the essay by Kliger on *Pride and Prejudice*, in McKillop's essays on *Sense and Sensibility* and *Northanger Abbey*, and in David Daiches's discussion of a Marxian Jane Austen, a writer bent on exposing the economic basis of social behaviour, an aspect also treated in the essay on *Sense and Sensibility* by Christopher Gillie and the essays on *Persuasion* and *Pride and Prejudice* by Schorer. None the less, in 'General Tilney's Hot-houses', Southam argues that the approach overall has been *literary*-historical in emphasis and that there is still much to be done in understanding Jane Austen as a novelist of Regency England.

Tanner's Introductions to *Sense and Sensibility* and *Mansfield Park*, Fleishman's study of *Mansfield Park*, the Introduction to Williams's *The English Novel* and the essay by Hough all take us helpfully in true historical direction.

The titles of *Sense and Sensibility*, *Pride and Prejudice*, and *Persuasion* imitate, perhaps ironically, a common style of title in moralizing fiction; but they also indicate Jane Austen's serious concern with concepts of value in human experience and behaviour, and Gilbert Ryle's essay 'Jane Austen and the Moralists' suggests how these ethical notions, and others which he finds as leading ideas in the other novels, belong to the traditions of eighteenth-century thought and how they are dramatized in the structure and characterization of the six novels. The question of moral judgement is also valuably discussed in D. W. Harding's contribution to the Pelican Guide to English Literature, in the essay by J. I. M. Stewart, and from a very different position, by Virginia Woolf.

The direction of all these studies has been to regard Jane Austen as a far more considerable, serious, and wide-ranging writer than previous generations had supposed. Yet there has also emerged a qualifying counterview. While Lord David Cecil has argued that Jane Austen is a great novelist because she acknowledged the precise limits of her art and vision, Angus Wilson has maintained that these limitations are a deforming constriction, not a creative discipline, a question which has been raised suggestively by several other recent critics: in the discussions of *Emma* by E. M. Hayes, Arnold Kettle, and Graham Hough; in the essay by Robert Garis on Jane Austen's success and failure in showing the experience of learning and change in her characters, an essay which should be read alongside C. S. Lewis's essay on the disillusionment of the heroines; and, more obliquely, in the essay by John Bayley, a fine discussion of Jane Austen's 'irresponsibility', a quality that lies at the heart of her success, but which also betrayed her.

This section concludes with a slightly more detailed and miscellaneous survey of some of the most helpful recent studies—general approaches, studies of the individual novels and of single aspects of the writer's art.

There are four critical studies at an introductory level, each with a particular emphasis. *Jane Austen's Novels* by Andrew Wright has useful sections on the varieties of narrative technique, style, and the leading characters of each of the novels (this last to be compared with W. D. Howells on the heroines). *Jane Austen* by Norman Sherry is an excellent basic introduction, covering the novelists' life and times as well as the novels. *Jane Austen: the six novels* by W. A. Craik, provides a perhaps rather over-elaborate commentary on the works, but does have some original points to make about the writer's handling of narrative. *Jane Austen* by Yasmine Gooneratne is a very careful and balanced account of the novels, paying less attention to the author's life and times.

The individual novels, except for *Northanger Abbey*, have been written about extensively and some of the best discussions are to be found in material which has already been referred to earlier in this section, and notably by Mudrick; so the listing here is confined to further outstanding essays and introductions: on *Sense and Sensibility*, the Introductions by Mrs. Q. D. Leavis and Ian Watt; on *Pride and Prejudice*, the essays by Reuben Brower, Mark Schorer, Dorothy Van Ghent, and the Introduction (a striking account of Jane Austen as a creative artist) and Notes to the edition by Brigid Brophy; on *Mansfield Park*, the Introductions by Mrs Q. D. Leavis and Tony Tanner (also revised as an essay), and the essays by Edwin Muir, Lionel Trilling, and David Lodge; on *Emma*, the book by Frank Bradbrook, and the essays by Bradbury, Lerner, Schorer, Trilling, and W. J. Harvey; on *Persuasion*, the Introduction by D. W. Harding, and the essays by Elizabeth Bowen, R. S. Crane, J. M. Duffy, and Schorer. *Northanger Abbey* is generally regarded as a less interesting 'apprentice' work, as we see in the essays of Emden and McKillop; the most important critical interpretative account is the chapter by Mudrick.

The fullest account of the so-called 'minor works' is B. C. Southam's *Jane Austen's Literary Manuscripts*, which considers the literary and historical importance of the manuscript material and relates this body of work to the writing of the six completed novels. The most valuable essays are those by McKillop (on the antecedents of *Northanger Abbey* in the juvenilia), by David Paul, and Brigid Brophy (who applies a Freudian interpretation to the 'History of England'), and the early works are also discussed by Mary Lascelles, Wright, and Litz. There are two recent studies of Jane Austen's language: *Jane Austen's English* by K. C. Phillips (which treats very detailed matters of vocabulary and sentence structure) and *The Language of Jane Austen* by Norman Page (which presents wider considerations).

BIOGRAPHIES AND LETTERS

There is no large-scale biography of Jane Austen and it is very doubtful if such a work can ever be written, so slight are the materials. She led a quiet and unadventurous life, contenting herself with the companionship of her family and a small circle of close friends. She was not known as an author and avoided literary society. There was only one contemporary memoir, a formal and rather stilted Biographical Notice written by her brother Henry in December 1817 for inclusion with the posthumous edition of *Northanger Abbey* and *Persuasion*. This revealed for the first time in print her authorship of the six novels, gave a few facts about her practice as a writer, and dutifully stressed the Christian side to her character.

The only other contemporary source is Jane Austen's own correspondence. Unfortunately, this is of limited value, partly because of her reticence, partly in consequence of the family's jealous guardianship. Their attitude was that the public might have the novels, but that the author's life was something sacred, not to be spread abroad. After Jane Austen's death, her sister Cassandra systematically destroyed all those letters which she considered to be private, a task of censorship which several generations of Austens carried on so successfully that only about 150 letters or fragments are known to survive (out of a correspondence that can be conservatively estimated at several thousands); so successfully, too, that we know virtually nothing about Jane Austen's inner life, and nothing certain about her relationships with men. Various stories of broken friendships and romance tragically ended have come down to us, but they are full of obscurities and contradictions, and it is quite impossible to say with confidence (however much we may be tempted to conjecture) to what extent Jane Austen's own experience of the joys and disappointments of love are contained in her novels. These and other biographical questions are investigated by R. W. Chapman in *Facts and Problems*.

Readers who want a brief and entertaining sketch of Jane Austen's life and times can do no better than to read and look at *Jane Austen and her World* by Marghanita Laski; superficially a picture book, it has, in fact, a text which is comprehensive, accurate, and delivered in style. For a scholarly account of the novelist's writing career, the first section of *Jane Austen and her Art* by Mary Lascelles is to be consulted. The most satisfactory book-length biography is *Jane Austen* by Elizabeth Jenkins. This presents a useful narrative account of the writer's life.

Readers who want to work from the major biographical sources should refer first to Henry Austen's Biographical Notice, then to the *Memoir* (1870), by Jane Austen's favourite nephew, James Edward Austen-Leigh. This account is short, highly appreciative, and partial, but it has the virtue of wide and direct reminiscence; its author consulted other survivors from Jane Austen's day. One of these was his sister, Caroline, who set down, in 1867, an important little memoir, 'My Aunt Jane Austen'. This was drawn upon both by Austen-Leigh and by the authors of the second and larger biography, the *Life and Letters of Jane Austen* (1913), which sets out to be the definitive family biography.

These books can be supplemented by Caroline Hill's *Jane Austen*, a deceptively charming and sentimental book, but one not to be neglected, for Miss Hill gained access to family papers and some of the details she includes are not to be found elsewhere.

The prime biographical source is Jane Austen's own correspondence, collected and fully annotated in the fine edition by R. W. Chapman. This volume is particularly valuable for its extensive, detailed indexes which treat Members of the Family; Other Persons; Places; General Topics; Authors, Books, Plays; Jane Austen's Novels; Jane Austen's English. However, the warning stands: the extant letters are woefully few; that, for example, we have none for the years 1802, 1803, 1806, 1810; that we have none of her letters to Henry, her favourite brother. So the picture is fragmentary; unlikely, at this point in time, to be composed into a satisfactory whole, since the other letters must by now be for ever lost or destroyed.

BIBLIOGRAPHY

The two principal bibliographies are by Keynes and Chapman. Keynes's book is particularly valuable for book-collectors and students of bibliography, since it treats in detail the first and early editions (including facsimiles of the title-pages); it also carries a chronological list of material on and about Jane Austen up to 1928. The Chapman bibliography is more selective in its listing of books and articles, but it is more up-to-date in continuing the list down to 1954, and is to be recommended for its coverage of historical and biographical matters.

The Jane Austen entry, prepared by B. C. Southam, in the *NCBEL* continues the selective list of Jane Austen studies down to 1968 and includes fuller information than Chapman on the early editions and translations. Chapman's account of the manuscript materials should be supplemented by Southam's study of the literary manuscripts; and Chapman's account of the contemporary reviews by Hogan's article on Jane Austen's early public.

BACKGROUND READING

Reading Jane Austen's novels does not call for extensive scholarship. What is required instead is some degree of historical sympathy for the social conventions and values of the time; and an attention to the novelist's language, an alertness which is particularly called for in that Jane Austen's tones and phrasing are so deceptively unarchaic, the vocabulary apparently so familiar, whereas, in reality, many of her words carry a special force of meaning, either from their use else-where in contemporary literature or from the traditions of eighteenth century ethical discussion (see Litz and Ryle on this last point; and the first section, Vocabulary, of Chapman's Appendix I to *Sense and Sensibility*). Any exploration beyond this point is into the tenor of eighteenth- and early nineteenth-century life as it is recorded at first-hand in the letters and memoirs of the age, not the least informatively in the letters of Jane Austen herself. The intellectual and philosophi-cal tradition is to be traced in the essays of Johnson (see Bradbrook) and in the poetry of Cowper, and finds its way, dramatized and transmuted, into the novels.

Only one kind of special knowledge is exploited by Jane Austen and therefore needs to be known by anyone seeking a full understand-ing of the novels—this is a knowledge of eighteenth-century litera-ture, especially the themes and conventions of prose fiction (see Ten Harmsel, Tompkins). This area of reference is a dimension of mean-ing for the novels; it takes us back to Richardson and Fielding (see McKillop and Watt), and then on to the later eighteenth-century fashions in Gothic fiction (see Birkhead, Sadleir, Varma), senti-mental fiction (see Utter and Needham, and W. F. Wright), conduct novels (see Colby); and to the epistolary method so widely used for all these schools of fiction (see Black). In the early works—*Northanger Abbey* and *Sense and Sensibility*—the literary satire is direct and readily identifiable; in the later novels it becomes more subdued and oblique less obviously satirical, but none the less a critique of what Jane Austen regarded as literature of the false imagination.

Summary accounts of this literary background and its relationship to the novels are provided by Litz, Southam, and A. H. Wright; and these works may be referred to as a preliminary to the specialist studies referred to above. But no one should fail to look at the 'trash' novels themselves. In such a comparison, the distinctive qualities of Jane Austen's writing, and her play upon inferior fiction, become all the more striking. It can also be instructive to glance at the novels of Fanny Burney and Maria Edgeworth, both of whom were admired by their contemporaries for practising what was considered to be a realistic treatment of familiar material—precisely what Scott found so praiseworthy in *Emma*.

The third area of background reading is concerned with modern approaches to the technique of fiction, approaches for which Jane Austen has proved so rewarding a subject. Among the discussions which have added so much to our understanding of 'technique' as the novelist's means of exploration and discovery, the criticism of Booth, Schorer, Van Ghent, and Watt are of special importance.

REFERENCES

TEXTS

(a) Collected works

R. W. Chapman (ed.), *The Oxford Illustrated Jane Austen* (5 vols., Oxford and New York, 1923; latest edn. 1967).

B. C. Southam (ed.), *Minor Works*, vol. vi, *The Oxford Illustrated Jane Austen* (Oxford and New York, 1954).

M. M. Lascelles (ed.) (5 vols., London and New York, 1961–4).

(b) Separate works

B. A. Booth (ed.), *Pride and Prejudice* (paperback, New York, 1963); includes Backgrounds and Criticism.

F. W. Bradbrook, *Pride and Prejudice* (London and New York, 1970).

B. Brophy (ed.), *Pride and Prejudice* (Pan, paperback, London, 1967).

R. A. Brower (ed.), *Mansfield Park* (Riverside, paperback, Boston, Mass., 1965).

J. Davie, *Northanger Abbey* and *Persuasion* (London and New York, 1971).

D. J. Gray (ed.), *Pride and Prejudice* (Norton Critical Editions, paperback, New York, 1966).

D. W. Harding (ed.), *Persuasion* (with *A Memoir of Jane Austen* by J. E. Austen-Leigh) (Penguin, paperback, Harmondsworth and Baltimore, Md., 1965).

C. Lamont, *Sense and Sensibility* (London and New York, 1970).

D. Lodge, *Emma* (London and New York, 1971).

J. Lucas, *Mansfield Park* (London and New York, 1970).

S. Parrish (ed.), *Emma* (Norton Critical Editions, paperback, New York, 1966).

M. Schorer (ed.), *Pride and Prejudice* (Riverside, paperback, Boston, Mass., 1956).

T. Tanner (ed.), *Mansfield Park* (Penguin, paperback, Harmondsworth and Baltimore, Md., 1966).

—— *Sense and Sensibility* (Penguin, paperback, Harmondsworth and Baltimore, Md., 1969).

L. Trilling (ed.), *Emma* (Riverside, paperback, Boston, Mass., 1957).

A. H. Wright (ed.), *Persuasion* (Riverside, paperback, Boston, Mass., 1965).

CRITICAL STUDIES AND COMMENTARY

Much of the early criticism listed here is available in the collections edited by Southam, *Jane Austen: The Critical Heritage* and Watt, *Jane Austen* (in the Twentieth Century Views series), and this availability is indicated at the end of the entry by an *S* or *W* respectively. Some of the more recent essays are available in the *Emma* 'Casebook' edited by Lodge (indicated by *C*) and in *Critical Essays on Jane Austen* edited by Southam (indicated by *CE*). All these volumes have considerable Introductions, discussing the materials they head and taking up wider critical issues.

H. S. Babb, *Jane Austen's Novels: the fabric of dialogue* (Columbus, Ohio, 1962).

J. Bayley, 'The "Irresponsibility" of Jane Austen': [*CE*].

W. C. Booth, 'Control of Distance in Jane Austen's *Emma*', in his *The Rhetoric of Fiction* (London and Chicago, 1961): [*C*].

E. Bowen, '*Persuasion*', *London Magazine* (April 1967).

F. W. Bradbrook, *Emma* (London and New York, 1961).

M. Bradbury, 'Jane Austen's *Emma*', *Critical Quarterly*, iv (1962): [*C*].

—— '*Persuasion* Again', *EIC* xviii (1968).

A. C. Bradley, 'Jane Austen', *Essays and Studies*, ii (1911); reprinted in his *A Miscellany* (London, 1929).

B. Brophy, 'Jane Austen and the Stuarts': [*CE*].

R. Brower, 'The Controlling Hand: Jane Austen and *Pride and Prejudice*', *Scrutiny*, xiii (1945); reprinted in his *Fields of Light* (New York, 1951): [*W*].

Lord D. Cecil, 'Jane Austen' (Leslie Stephen Lecture, Cambridge, 1935), reprinted in his *Poets and Story-Tellers* (London, 1949).

R. A. Colby, '*Mansfield Park*: Fanny Price and the Christian Heroine', in his *Fiction with a Purpose* (London and Bloomington, Ind., 1967).

W. A. Craik, *Jane Austen: the six novels* (London and New York, 1965).

R. S. Crane, '*Persuasion*', in his *Idea of the Humanities*, vol. ii (London and Chicago, 1967).

D. Daiches, 'Jane Austen, Karl Marx and the aristocratic dance', *American Scholar*, xvii (1948).

J. M. Duffy, '*Emma*: the awakening from innocence', *ELH* xxi (1954).

—— 'Structure and Idea in *Persuasion*', *NCF* viii (1954).

C. S. Emden, 'The Composition of *Northanger Abbey*', *RES* xix (1968).

R. Farrer, 'Jane Austen', *Quarterly Review*, ccxxviii (1917): [extracts in *C*].

A. Fleishman, *A Reading of Mansfield Park* (Minneapolis, 1967).

R. Garis, 'Learning Experience and Change': [*CE*].

H. W. Garrod, 'Jane Austen: a depreciation', *Transactions of the Royal Society of Literature*, n.s. viii (London, 1928).

C. Gillie, '*Sense and Sensibility*: an assessment', *EIC* ix (1959).

Y. Gooneratne, *Jane Austen* (paperback, Cambridge, 1970).

D. W. Harding, 'Regular Hatred: an aspect of the work of Jane Austen', *Scrutiny*, viii (1940): [*W*; extracts in *C*].

D. W. Harding, 'Jane Austen and Moral Judgement', in Part II of *From Blake to Byron*, The Pelican Guide to English Literature, vol. v (paperback, Harmondsworth and New York, 1957).

—— 'Character and Caricature in Jane Austen': [*CE*].

W. J. Harvey, 'The Plot of *Emma*', *EIC* xvii (1967): [*C*].

E. N. Hayes, '*Emma*: a dissenting opinion', *NCF* iv (1950): [*C*].

G. Hough, '*Emma* and "Moral" Criticism', in his *The Dream and the Task* (London and New York, 1964): [*C*].

—— 'Narrative and Dialogue in Jane Austen, *Critical Quarterly* (Autumn 1970).

W. D. Howells, in his *Heroines of Fiction* (New York, 1901): [extracts in *C*].

R. E. Hughes, 'The Education of Emma Woodhouse', *NCF* xvi (1962): [*C*].

J. Kavanagh, 'Miss Austen's Six Novels', ch. 18 in her *English Women of Letters* (London, 1862): [*S*].

A. Kettle, 'Jane Austen: *Emma*', in his *An Introduction to the English Novel*, vol. i (London and New York, 1953): [*W; C*].

S. Kliger, 'Jane Austen's *Pride and Prejudice* in the eighteenth-century mode', *UTQ* xvi (1947).

M. M. Lascelles, *Jane Austen and her Art* (Oxford and New York, 1939).

Q. D. Leavis, Introduction to *Mansfield Park* (Macdonald's Illustrated Classics, London, 1957).

—— Introduction to *Sense and Sensibility* (as above, 1958).

L. Lerner, *The Truthtellers: Jane Austen, George Eliot, D. H. Lawrence* (London, 1967).

C. S. Lewis, 'A Note on Jane Austen', *EIC* iv (1954): [*W*].

A. W. Litz, *Jane Austen: A Study of her Artistic Development* (London and New York, 1965).

D. Lodge, 'A Question of Judgment: the theatricals at Mansfield Park', *NCF* xvii (1963).

—— 'The Vocabulary of *Mansfield Park*', in his *Language of Fiction* (London and New York, 1966).

—— (ed.), *Jane Austen: Emma, a Casebook* (paperback, London, 1968).

A. D. McKillop, 'Critical Realism in *Northanger Abbey*', in *From Jane Austen to Joseph Conrad*, edd. R. C. Rathburn and M. Steinmann, jun. (Minneapolis, 1958).

—— 'The Context of *Sense and Sensibility*', *Rice Institute Pamphlets*, xliv (1958).

M. Mudrick, *Jane Austen: irony as defense and discovery* (Princeton, N.J., and London, 1952).

E. Muir, 'Jane Austen', in his *Essays on Literature and Society* (London and Cambridge, Mass., 1965).

C. Murrah, 'The Background of *Mansfield Park*', in *From Jane Austen to Joseph Conrad* (see first entry for McKillop).

N. Page, *The Language of Jane Austen* (Oxford, 1972).

D. Paul, 'The Gay Apprentice', *Twentieth Century*, clvi (1954).

K. C. Phillips, *Jane Austen's English* (London, 1970).

G. Ryle, 'Jane Austen and the Moralists', *Oxford Review*, i (1966): [*CE*].

M. Schorer, 'Technique as Discovery', *Hudson Review*, i (1948).

—— 'Fiction and the "matrix of analogy" ', *Kenyon Review*, xi (1949).

—— 'Pride unprejudiced', *Kenyon Review*, xviii (1956).

—— 'The Humiliation of Emma Woodhouse', *Literary Review*, ii (1959): [*C*; *W*].

Sir W. Scott, Review of *Emma*, *Quarterly Review*, xiv (1815): [*S*; extracts in *C*].

E. F. Shannon, '*Emma* Character and Construction', *PMLA* lxxi (1956): [*C*].

N. Sherry, *Jane Austen* (paperback, London, 1966).

R. Simpson, Review of the *Memoir of Jane Austen*, *North British Review*, lii (1870): [*S*; extracts in *C*].

B. C. Southam, *Jane Austen's Literary Manuscripts: a Study of the novelist's development through the surviving papers* (London and New York, 1964).

—— (ed.), *Jane Austen: The Critical Heritage* (London and New York, 1968).

—— (ed.), *Critical Essays on Jane Austen* (London and New York, 1968).

—— 'General Tilney's Hot-houses: some recent Jane Austen studies and texts', *Ariel* (October 1971).

J. I. M. Stewart, 'Tradition and Miss Austen': [*CE*].

T. Tanner, 'Jane Austen and "The Quiet Thing" ': [*CE*].

R. Trickett, 'Jane Austen's Comedy and the Nineteenth Century': [*CE*].

L. Trilling, '*Mansfield Park*', *The Partisan Review*, xxi (1954), reprinted in his *The Opposing Self* (London and New York, 1955): [*W*]; revised as 'Jane Austen and *Mansfield Park*' in *From Blake to Byron*, The Pelican Guide to English Literature, vol. v (paperback, Harmondsworth and New York, 1957).

—— 'Emma and the Legend of Jane Austen', Introduction to the Riverside Edition of *Emma* (New York), also in his *Beyond Culture* (London and New York, 1965): [*C*].

D. Van Ghent, 'On *Pride and Prejudice*', in her *The English Novel: form and function* (New York, 1953).

I. Watt (ed.), *Jane Austen: A Collection of Critical Essays* (Twentieth Century Views series); (paperback, London and Englewood Cliffs, N.J., 1963).

—— *The Rise of the Novel: studies in Defoe, Richardson and Fielding* (London and Berkeley, Calif., 1957).

—— Introduction to the edition of *Sense and Sensibility* published by Harper and Row (paperback, New York, 1961): [*W*].

R. Whately, Review of *Northanger Abbey* and *Persuasion*, *Quarterly Review*, xxiv (1821): [*S*].

R. Williams, *The English Novel from Dickens to Lawrence* (London, 1970).

A. Wilson, 'The Neighbourhood of Tombuctoo': (CE).

V. Woolf, 'Jane Austen' in her *The Common Reader* (London, 1925): [*W*].

A. H. Wright, *Jane Austen's Novels: a study in structure* (London and New York, 1953; revised 1964).

BIOGRAPHIES AND LETTERS

C. Austen, *My Aunt Jane Austen: A Memoir*, ed. R. W. Chapman from a manuscript dated March 1867 (Alton, Hants, 1952).

H. Austen, 'Biographical Notice of the Author', dated December 1817; prefaced to *Northanger Abbey* and *Persuasion* (1818); included in that volume of the Oxford edition, ed. R. W. Chapman; also in Penguin edition of *Persuasion*, ed. D. W. Harding.

J. E. Austen-Leigh, *A Memoir of Jane Austen* (London, 1870; enlarged 1871); edited, introduced, and annotated by R. W. Chapman (Oxford, 1926); also in the Penguin edition of *Persuasion*, ed. D. W. Harding.

W. and R. A. Austen-Leigh, *Jane Austen: Her Life and Letters* (London, 1913).

R. W. Chapman, *Jane Austen: Facts and Problems* (Oxford, 1948).

—— (ed.), *Jane Austen's Letters* (London and New York, 1932; 2nd edn., 1952).

—— (ed.), *Letters of Jane Austen 1796–1817* (a selection) (London and New York, 1955).

C. Hill, *Jane Austen: Her Homes and her Friends* (London, 1902).

E. Jenkins, *Jane Austen* (London, 1938).

M. M. Lascelles. See CRITICAL STUDIES AND COMMENTARY.

M. Laski, *Jane Austen and her World* (London, 1969).

BIBLIOGRAPHY

R. W. Chapman, *Jane Austen: A Critical Bibliography* (Oxford and New York, reprinted with corrections 1955).

C. B. Hogan, 'Jane Austen and her Early Public', *RES* n.s. i (1950).

G. Keynes, *Jane Austen: a bibliography* (London, 1929).

B. C. Southam. (See CRITICAL STUDIES AND COMMENTARY.)

——Jane Austen entry in *NCBEL* (Cambridge and New York, 1969).

—— 'General Tilney's Hot-houses: some recent Jane Austen studies and texts', *Ariel* (October 1971).

BACKGROUND READING

An abbreviated reference indicates that the work has been fully cited in an earlier section.

E. Birkhead, *The Tale of Terror: a study of the gothic romance* (London, 1921; reprinted New York, 1963).

F. G. Black, *The Epistolary Novel in the Late Eighteenth-Century* (Eugene, Or., 1940).

W. C. Booth, *The Rhetoric of Fiction*.

F. W. Bradbrook, 'Dr. Johnson and Jane Austen', *N & Q* ccv (1960).

R. A. Colby, *Fiction with a Purpose*.

A. W. Litz, *Jane Austen*.

A. D. McKillop, *The Early Masters of English Fiction*.

G. Ryle, 'Jane Austen and the Moralists'.

M. Sadleir, *The Northanger Novels* (Oxford, 1927).

B. C. Southam, *Jane Austen's Literary Manuscripts*.

H. Ten Harmsel, *Jane Austen: a study in fictional conventions* (The Hague, 1964).

J. M. S. Tompkins, *The Popular Novel in England, 1770–1800* (London, 1932).

R. P. Utter and G. B. Needham, *Pamela's Daughters* (New York, 1937).

D. P. Varma, *The Gothic Flame* (London, 1957).

I. Watt, *The Rise of the Novel*.

A. H. Wright, *Jane Austen's Novels*.

W. F. Wright, *Sensibility in English Prose Fiction, 1760–1814* (New York, 1937).

10 · THACKERAY[1]   1811–1863

Arthur Pollard

THACKERAY has never wanted readers, though at times it has been a matter of a 'fit audience, though few'. This may have something to do with the phenomenon that Geoffrey Tillotson remarked upon: 'No young person, however intelligent and mature, can truly appreciate *Esmond* or any of Thackeray's great novels. It is not merely a question of any individual reader's power of imagination. . . . The ripe tone of the novels speaks to more than the imagination of older readers. . . . The emotions aroused by the imaginary fact are accompanied by similar emotions aroused by actual fact.' (*Thackeray the Novelist*, 1954, p. 268.) This reaction had been noted in Thackeray's lifetime. G. H. Lewes, comparing him to Horace, had remarked upon it, and so had *The Times* in its review of *The Newcomes* (*Thackeray: the Critical Heritage*, edd. G. Tillotson and D. Hawes, pp. 106, 228—hereafter cited as *C.H.*).

TEXTS

Thackeray was a prolific literary journalist, and some of his contributions are still being identified. He wrote regularly for *Fraser's Magazine* and for *Punch*. His work in these years also includes *The Yellowplush Papers* (1837–8), *The Paris Sketch Book* (1840), *The Irish Sketch Book* (1843), *Cornhill to Cairo* (1846), and *The Book of Snobs* (1846–7). In addition, he wrote two novels, *Catherine* (1839) and *Barry Lyndon* (1844), and Dr. Gordon Ray has found and edited other work in his *Thackeray's Contributions to the Morning Chronicle* (1955). There then followed the major novels—*Vanity Fair* (1848), *Pendennis* (1850), *Esmond* (1852), *The Newcomes* (1855), *The Virginians* (1859), *Lovel the Widower* (1860), *The Adventures of Philip* (1862), and the unfinished *Dennis Duval* (1864). Other work includes his two

---

[1] The original draft of this chapter was written by Geoffrey Tillotson, whose untimely death deprived us of one of the greatest Victorian scholars of our time. Though what follows is an entire re-writing, I should like to acknowledge the help I have derived from Professor Tillotson's draft together also with my evident debt to his and Donald Hawes's collection of reviews in *Thackeray: The Critical Heritage* (1968).

series of lectures on *The English Humourists of the Eighteenth Century* (1853) and *The Four Georges* (1860).

The first attempt at a collected *Works* was in the 22-volume Library edition (1867–9; with two more volumes, 1885–6). The 26-volume De-luxe edition (1878–86) contained a memoir by Leslie Stephen, while the 13-volume Biographical edition (1898–9) had introductions by the novelist's daughter, Anne Thackeray Ritchie, and Stephen's biographical notice from the *DNB*. Probably the most reliable and even accessible edition is the Oxford in 17 volumes (1908) with introductions by George Saintsbury.

We stand in dire need of a properly edited text of Thackeray. T. L. and W. Snow provided a detailed, annotated version of *Esmond* (1915), while J. E. Wells edited from manuscript *The Roundabout Papers* (New York, 1925), the product of Thackeray's occasional writings in the first years of *The Cornhill Magazine* when he was its editor. More recently, Geoffrey and Kathleen Tillotson produced an exemplary edition of *Vanity Fair* (1963), based on detailed collations of manuscript and other editions, and provided with full notes.

CRITICAL STUDIES AND COMMENTARY

(a) Thackeray's Lifetime

Of the early work *Catherine* and *Barry Lyndon* undoubtedly stand out from the rest, though mention should also be made of such collections as *The Yellowplush Papers* and *The Book of Snobs*. In this latter work he succeeded too well. Critics thereafter were often, too often, on the look-out for the recurring condemnation; "Mr. Thackeray thought too much of social inequalities', said Bagehot (quoted, *C.H.*, p. 355). Thackeray did think of social inequalities, but in doing so his finger was on the pulse of his age. Indeed, with his sensitive awareness of his own background and with his regard for the age before his own (as illustrated in his historical novels), how could he not regard social inequalities with so much interest and concern? His subtle understanding, exploitation, and revelation of class-differences is one of the strengths of his major novels.

W. C. Roscoe, Thackeray's 'first great substantial critic', as Geoffrey Tillotson has called him (*Thackeray the Novelist* (1963 edn.), p. 19) —and an underrated one, be it said—neatly placed the novelist: 'Man is his study; but man the social animal, man considered in reference to the experiences, the aims, the affections, that find their field in his intercourse with his fellow-men. . . . He stands on the debatable land between the aristocracy and the middle classes—that is his favourite position' (*The National Review*, January 1856; quoted,

C.H., pp. 267, 272). Thackeray's concentration on snobs isolated the basic incentive in English society, namely, social climbing; it did so by contrasting the aspirant with the real gentleman. Thackeray had a proper regard for standards, a regard which, not unexpectedly, failed to commend itself to the republican *United States Review* (March 1853):

Mr. Thackeray lives in a country where Rank and Trade were formerly kept very wide apart, one looking down upon the other. The two are very rapidly coming nearer, but Mr. Thackeray does not keep pace with the friendly movement. There cannot be found in all his works a single passage in which tradesmen are mentioned with respect . . . It does not become any man, in an age of industry like our own, to endeavor to prop the falling edifice of aristocratic pride.

This—in a criticism of *Esmond*—was not, in fact, quite true.

Elsewhere, and *pace The Times*'s view of *The Newcomes*, Thackeray was the satirist as idealist *manqué*, seeing clearly enough, even if sometimes only implying, the difference between what was and what ought to have been. The same spirit imbues his brilliant parodies of contemporary novelists in 'Novels by Eminent Hands', and what he did here in little he sought to do *in extenso* in *Catherine*. That novel met the fate of many ironic performances in being interpreted as just another example rather than a criticism of the mode, in this case the Newgate novel, that it sought to expose—'The public was, in our notion, dosed and poisoned by the prevailing style of literary practice, and it was necessary to administer some medicine that would produce a wholesome nausea' (*Catherine*, 'Another Last Chapter'). The autobiographical *Barry Lyndon* is also shot through with irony, but the book is handled with such delicacy that, in Trollope's words, 'the reader is almost brought to sympathise' (*Thackeray*, 1879, p. 72). Robert Bell, in a review of *Vanity Fair*, may well have the clue to this result: 'He dissects his victims with a smile; and performs the cruellest of operations on their self-love with a pleasantry which looks provokingly very like good-nature' (*Fraser's Magazine*, September 1848; *C.H.*, p. 62). Thackeray never succumbed to *saeva indignatio*. G. H. Lewes aptly cited that other Roman satirist, Horace, in reviewing *Vanity Fair*: *Ridentem dicere verum quid vetat?*

Though *Vanity Fair* elevated Thackeray's fame to a thitherto unprecedented level, Bell found in it the same characteristics of his previous work, 'the same quality of subtle observation, penetrating rarely below the epidermis, but taking up all the small vessels with microscopic vision; the same grotesque exaggeration, with the truth at the bottom; the same constitutional instinct for seizing on the ridiculous aspect of things, for turning the "seamy side" of society outwards, and for exposing false pretensions and the genteel ambition of *parvenus*'. Indeed, Bell was one of that chorus that believed that Thackeray's vision of society was too dark. 'His scepticism is pushed too far', Lewes had complained (op. cit.; *C.H.*, p. 46), and Bell echoed him with 'This revolting reflex of society is literally true enough. But it does not show us the whole truth' (op. cit.; *C.H.*, p. 64). *Pendennis* attracted the same criticisms, though Lewes thought that there was 'a broader and more generous view of humanity, a larger admixture of goodness with what is evil, and a more loving mellowed tone throughout' (*The Leader*, 21 December 1850; *C.H.*, p. 109), while by the time of *The Newcomes* Whitwell Elwin could say that Thackeray had 'nobly redeemed' himself (*Quarterly Review*, September 1855; *C.H.*, p. 234). Roscoe, however, was not persuaded; indeed, if anything, he went further in his condemnation, asserting 'that he gives a worldly view of the world; that through sarcasm and satire there shines every where a real undue appreciation of worldly things—most, of those things which he is most bitter against— money and rank; and above all, a debasing sensitiveness to the opinion of those around us, apart from any regard for them and independently of any respect for their judgement. . . . As Swift rakes in dirt, so Thackeray in meanness' (op. cit.; *C.H.*, p. 279).

R. S. Rintoul (*Spectator*, 21 December 1850) isolated another characteristic of Thackeray's which was much commented upon. 'Mr. Thackeray cannot or will not frame a coherent story, of which all the incidents flow naturally one from another' (*C.H.*, p. 98). This was not, however, regarded as a fault. Thus, making the same remark of *Vanity Fair* and *Esmond* respectively, Bell could speak of simplicity of conduct, of the story moving like 'the progress of one's own life' (*C.H.*, p. 68) and George Brimley could write: 'Unity is given not by a consecutive and self-developing story, but by the ordinary events of life blended with those peculiar to a stirring time acting on a family group, and bringing out and ripening their qualities' (*Spectator*, 6 November 1852; *C.H.*, p. 139).

Elwin provided an important clue to the proper way to read Thackeray: 'Mr. Thackeray, beyond all other novelists, loves to comment upon his own text—to stop in his story, indulge in reflections, analyse the motives of his characters, and cross-examine his readers upon their individual propensities. His book is in many parts a discourse upon human nature' (*C.H.*, p. 236). But while there is undoubtedly much in the way of directly expressed sentiment to linger over, there were critics who found lingering over the characters only a source of dissatisfaction and complaint. This was not only because too many were vicious. In fact, in the case of a Becky Sharp, such a situation might be advanced as realism in the tradition of Fielding, while Lady Eastlake thought the characters of *Vanity Fair* 'feigned names for our own beloved friends and acquaintances, seen under such a puzzling cross-light of good in evil, and evil in good' (op. cit.; *C.H.*, p. 80) and Elwin on *The Newcomes* spoke of 'the picked passages of existence' (op. cit.; *C.H.*, p. 231) which Thackeray's characters represented. The realism was sometimes criticized when it took characters from actual life or history (as in *Esmond*) and either failed to realize them imaginatively or else produced, to use the epithet in the vicious *Times* review of *Esmond*, a 'spurious' character out of line with the impression of the historical personage. Other complaints included the dullness or weakness of the heroes and heroines (i.e. the central good characters), an insufficient detachment (Thackeray 'hangs over the fictitious people too much as their creator and judge'—Forster, *The Examiner*, 13 November 1852; *C.H.*, p. 146) and an interest 'more in the external exhibitions of character and the feelings than in character itself' (Roscoe, op. cit.; p. 268). There were no complaints about style. Critics of all shades of opinion and of novel after novel remarked on its quality—'cleanness, strength, idiomatic ease, delicacy and variety' (Lewes of *Pendennis*; *C.H.*, p. 106); 'manly, clear, terse and vigorous' (Brimley of *Esmond*; *C.H.*, p. 144); 'a rich abundance of strong, idiomatic, sterling English' (Elwin of *The Newcomes*; *C.H.*, p. 238); and in similar tones, placing him in this respect alone among the novelists of the time, Goldwin Smith of *The Virginians* (*Edinburgh Review*, October 1859; *C.H.*, p. 295).

Thackeray's career as a major novelist was shorter than that of any of the other Victorians with the exception, of course, of the Brontës. From *Vanity Fair* to *Denis Duval* was a mere fifteen years, and the really important work covered only the first half of this period. After the immense success of *Vanity Fair* (1848) the critical reception of *Pendennis* (1850), though favourable, was not so unboundedly enthusiastic, but *Esmond* (1852) brought new laurels. Some reviewers found it defective as a historical novel, but generally it was thought fully the equal of its predecessors, and Forster while regarding it as 'by no means equal to *Vanity Fair* in interest', thought it excelled even that work as 'a display of literary power' (op. cit.; *C.H.*, p. 146). *The Newcomes* (1855) took Thackeray to even greater heights. Elwin was not alone in considering it his masterpiece. *The Examiner* (1 September 1855) agreed with him and *The Times* (29 August 1855) thought that it surpassed previous novels in the variety of characters and in fertility of invention, while other journals approved of it as unusual for Thackeray, a novel in which goodness triumphed. *The Virginians* (1859) provoked criticisms of unhistorical 'historical' novels, but the predominant response was to note the recurrence of Thackeray's qualities, both good and bad—realism, kindly satire, minuteness of detail, etc., and with *Lovel the Widower* (1860) the recurrence resulted in outspoken criticism—'the same old tune with much inferior words' (*Westminster Review*, xxi n.s. (January 1862)). With *The Adventures of Philip* (1862) there were still some who were left to praise, but the chorus was much diminished. The end was near. Thackeray died on 24 December 1863 and the obituaries were duly eulogistic, but few had anything, much less anything good, to say of his work written after 1855.

(b) Since 1879

Trollope's English Men of Letters *Thackeray* appeared in 1879. In it he praises *Barry Lyndon* highly, finds the truth of *Vanity Fair* incontrovertible but unpalatable, and, laying the novelist open to charges of cynicism, sees *Pendennis* and *The Newcomes* as satiric chronicles and *The Virginians* as written in the desultory, wandering manner of an idle author. Both as biography, which it attempts, and as criticism Trollope's study bears evidence of a lack of precision and, on the whole, it did not receive very good reviews. But then Trollope's own reputation was in a trough at the time. It remains interesting as one Victorian novelist's comments on another, and thereby reveals some of the assumptions from which both of them started.

In the same year as Trollope's study there appeared the 24-volume De-luxe edition (see TEXTS above) of Thackeray's *Works*, published by Smith, Elder and carrying as an appendix Leslie Stephen's 'Writings of W. M. Thackeray' (Stephen's first wife was the younger daughter of Thackeray). He places Thackeray in the setting of his early career when Bulwer Lytton and Dickens were enjoying considerable popularity. He also examines 'Thackeray's admiration of Fielding' and asserts that 'it was his ambition to tread in the steps of Fielding, though with more refinement and greater tenderness of sentiment' (*C.H.*, pp. 362, 363). He considers that Thackeray's early studies of villainy in works such as *Catherine* and *Barry Lyndon* gave him that impartiality toward his unsympathetic characters that many authors lose (ibid., p. 366), and he devotes several paragraphs to what he believes to have been the necessary and salutary attacks on snobbery.

In 1895 George Saintsbury in *Connected Impressions* placed Thackeray's achievement centrally in his powers of characterization, while A. A. Jack (*Thackeray, A Study*) made claims for him more as a preacher than an artist. W. C. Brownell supported Saintsbury, asserting that 'character is spectacle . . . and not the illustrative incarnation of interesting traits and tendencies' (*Scribner's Magazine*, February 1899; reprinted in *Victorian Prose Masters*, 1901). The first three decades of the twentieth century were distinctly lean years for Thackeray. Charles Whibley in 1903 stated more bluntly than anyone either before or since his distaste for what he considered to be Thackeray's all too manifest exploitation of the often opposed and always extravagant expression of sentimentality and cynicism. Percy Lubbock was an admirer of James, who had characterized *The Newcomes* as a 'large, loose baggy monster'. In *The Craft of Fiction* (1921) Lubbock demonstrated his devotion to the Jamesian method, and in so doing looked at *Vanity Fair* as a 'panoramic' novel, in which 'Thackeray flings together a crowd of the people he knows so well' and where the big scene is often approached, but equally often refused.

But Saintsbury was still there, and in 1931 his introductions to the Oxford edition were collected, after revision, as *A Consideration of Thackeray*. These pieces are vintage Saintsbury, full of his characteristic forthrightness, of his prejudices and his irrelevant asides, but they are also full of his mature impressions. 'Life and Abundance—these are the two things that are to be found in him' (p. 249). Thackeray's qualities are wit and humour, command of character and style. He acutely traced 'the celebrated "cynicism" [to] the harder, and the equally celebrated "sentimentality" [to] the more melting mood of this melancholy' (p. 269). One of his few complaints against Thackeray was that he took sides against Becky, than whom 'there is no woman so great in English literature out of Shakespeare' (p. 169).

In the following year Raymond Las Vergnas published *W. M. Thackeray: l'homme, le penseur, le romancier*. The work is divided into books according to its title and each of these is categorized into sections, themselves divided into several chapters. The first book considers 'Dickens and Thackeray', 'Contradictions—the Thackerayan Dualism', 'Cynic?', and 'The True Thackeray', the second 'The Models—the Historian and the Eighteenth Century', 'Social and Personal Satire', and 'The Message of Thackeray', the third 'Realism', 'The Concept of the Novel', and 'The Art of Thackeray', In 1934 Lord David Cecil's *Early Victorian Novelists* included a chapter on Thackeray. In it he claimed that Thackeray was 'the first novelist to do what Tolstoy and Proust were to do more elaborately—use the novel to express a conscious, considered criticism of life . . . to impose an organic unity on the chaos of the large-scale English novel', achieved by his creative imagination's working to impose a moral order on experience. David Cecil, however, felt that this order rested on a narrow base of ideas, and consequently the super-structure was sometimes too heavy. His main criticism was that Thackeray and his age were not in accord, and that he yielded to his age.

J. W. Dodds (*Thackeray, A Critical Portrait*, 1941) agreed in part, saying that Thackeray 'was a Victorian with roots in the eighteenth century', but went on to add: 'That he flowered gracefully, yet with as little intellectual compromise as possible, is to the credit of both his honesty and his good sense' (p. 134). Dodds describes his book, fairly accurately, as 'criticism with some biographical infiltration' (p. vii) and, while as a whole it is a thorough and honest piece of work, it adds little new to the body of Thackerayan criticism. J. Y. T. Greig (*Thackeray, A Reconsideration*, 1950) acknowledges that 'no man since the late George Saintsbury has written on Thackeray with more understanding and sympathy than Lord David Cecil' (p. 4). He did not seek to emulate these two critics. He links the works much more closely to the life than did Dodds, and he centres his interpretation round the idea of Thackeray's uncertain and evasive approach to life. This, he says, was why a man whose views pointed in the same direction as Swift's was yet unjust to Swift (p. 45). In what is a lively, if somewhat hostile, study Greig stressed the importance of the biography, because Thackeray was a novelist of memory, indeed 'a novelist manqué' because he was 'beyond reason egocentric' (p. 6).

Greig's book was followed by the major critical work of recent years, Geoffrey Tillotson's *Thackeray the Novelist* (1954). In this latter year also Kathleen Tillotson published her *Novels of the Eighteen Forties* with its fine, and all too short, chapter on *Vanity Fair*, in which especial notice may be taken of the last section where she defends Thackeray's practice of commenting on the action so frequently. Geoffrey Tillotson's book is a bold statement of Thackeray's virtues, written out of affection and voluminous acquaintance with the novelist. In it he takes issue with such critics as Lubbock and Greig and even takes the sympathetic Dr. Ray to task. In an appendix he challenges F. R. Leavis's abrupt dismissal of Thackeray in a brief mention, designating him merely 'a greater Trollope' (*The Great Tradition*, p. 31) and cleverly traces the debt of two who figure in that great tradition, George Eliot and Henry James, to Thackeray himself

The body of the book insists on a limited number of important points—on the significance of continuity rather than of design and the ways by which this is achieved, on the centrality of commentary in the Thackerayan method, and on 'truthfulness of personage and action'. The thesis is not only convincingly argued, but also extensively and impressively illustrated. Indeed, if a criticism were to be made, it might well be that the illustrations are both too many and too long.

Though, in emphasizing continuity rather than design and in speaking of the 'lack of edged shape' Tillotson was pointing to a characteristic phenomenon in Thackeray's work, he was not suggesting the absence of intention in the form of the novels. John Loofbourow looked at *Thackeray and the Form of Fiction* in 1964. His work is mainly directed to *Vanity Fair* and *Esmond*. In relation to the former he considers parody of 'fashionable' sentimental novels and of chivalric romance, while with the latter he centres his concern upon epic relationships. The work ends with an expansion of David Cecil's suggestion of a likeness between Thackeray and Proust as well as considering possible links with James. Loofbourow looks in detail at passages, but his suggestion of parallels, especially with the *Aeneid*, seems at times to be pressed too far in the direction of deliberateness on the part of Thackeray. James H. Wheatley's *Patterns in Thackeray's Fiction* considers the work more broadly, yet within a narrower compass. Nor are his patterns simply stylistic ones. After dealing with the early parodies, he devotes two chapters to *Vanity Fair*, treating such topics as the 'ethical' argument, causality, and psychology, and then two final chapters cover *Pendennis*, *Esmond*, and *The Newcomes*, with references to realism and experience and some comparison of the heroes.

Some shorter pieces deserve mention. They include J. A. Lester's 'Thackeray's Narrative Technique' (*PMLA* lxix (June 1954)), mainly concerned with 're-doublings' or reversions in time and with 'semi-scenes' between direct narration and summary, and G. Armour Craig's 'On the Style of *Vanity Fair*' in *Style in Prose Fiction*, ed. H. C. Martin (1959). The latter makes enlightened points on Thackeray's use of detachment and silence and has also some interesting comparisons between Osborne in *Vanity Fair* and Dickens's Dombey. A. E. Dyson writes suggestively in his chapter 'Thackeray: An Irony against Heroes' (*The Crazy Fabric*, 1965). He confines himself to *Vanity Fair*, and centrally to the contrast between Becky and Amelia. He is perhaps a shade too emphatic in saying that the former's 'judgments on people are the novelist's own', but this is corrected in his awareness that the absence of a clear answer in Thackeray's over-all view is the measure of his complexity, not of any lack of aware-ness. Thackeray was never glib. Dorothy Van Ghent ('On *Vanity Fair*', *The English Novel: Form and Function*, 1953) is less sympathetic than these others, repeating the old criticisms of Thackeray's self-intrusion into the novels, but she writes intelligently of his character-images, by which an individual's appearance and behaviour has a double significance, both personal and social, thereby suggesting both the cruelty and perversity of Vanity Fair. All these last three, together with Kathleen Tillotson's chapter mentioned above, and Arnold Kettle's in *An Introduction to the English Novel* (1951), where he sees 'the artistic motive-force of *Vanity Fair* [as] Thackeray's vision of bourgeois society and of the personal relationships engendered by that society' (Kettle is another who will not always accept the novel-ist's comments in his own person), are collected in *Twentieth Century Interpretations of Vanity Fair*, edited by M. G. Sundell (1969). Another collection of critical essays is *Thackeray*, edited by Alexander Welsh (1968).

The most recent full-length study is Juliet McMaster's *Thackeray: The Major Novels* (1971), in which, though each of four chapters is devoted respectively to *Vanity Fair*, *Pendennis*, *Esmond*, and *The New-comes*, the first part of each chapter takes in a major theme and refers outside the novel which is the subject of the chapter. Thus the remarks on *The Newcomes* are preceded by consideration of familial and social relationships. The first chapter deals with Thackeray's confidential tone with the reader, and the second with the ironic potential of his *alter egos*. Indeed, Mrs. McMaster places much emphasis on 'the ironic nature of [Thackeray's] moral vision'. Barbara Hardy in *The Exposure of Luxury: Radical Themes in Thackeray* (1972) argues for the novelist's radical criticism of society. She therefore concentrates on content with chapters on rank and reversal, the power of money, nature and art, and love. Her work is especially valuable in its relation of the public and private worlds of Thackeray's characters.

BIOGRAPHY AND LETTERS

Thackeray requested that no biography should be written. His daughter, Anne, contributed what amount to largely biographical introductions to the edition (see TEXTS above) of the *Works* (1898–9). Each is concerned with the circumstances surrounding the volume to which it relates, and there were therefore notable gaps in the history of Thackeray's life. In the same year there appeared the sym-pathetic *Life of Thackeray* by 'Lewis Melville' (Lewis S. Benjamin), which was, however, more of a compilation than a sustained account, and was attacked as inaccurate and as 'the inept laudation of an incompetent judge' (*Spectator*, 18 November 1899). An earlier work was Jane T. Prime and Alicia Bayne's *Memorials of the Thackeray Family* (1870).

The decline in Thackeray's critical reputation had some parallel in biographical considerations. Thus Michael Sadleir in his *Edward and Rosina, 1803–1836* (1931) (later, *Bulwer and His Wife*) included a chapter attacking Thackeray as 'both a hypocrite and a snob'. Simon Nowell-Smith replied 'In Defence of Thackeray' (*Nineteenth Century* (July 1933)). The recovery was beginning. In the previous year, entirely without help from the Thackeray family who still opposed a 'Life', Malcolm Elwin attempted a psychological interpretation, seeking an explanation of some of the apparent contradictions in the novelist's behaviour. His theories have since been supported considerably by publication of the letters. The first really extensive and reliable biography, however, was Lionel Stevenson's *The Showman of Vanity Fair* (1947). This was followed in 1950 by Lambert Ennis's *Thackeray, The Sentimental Cynic*, which sought 'to trace [Thackeray's] conduct during the major crises of his life' in terms of his characteristic attitudes. The work is notable for its treatment of the novelist's 'preoccupation with masks', both his own and other people's disguises. The major biography, however, is that by Gordon Ray— *Thackeray: The Uses of Adversity, 1811–1846* (1955) and *Thackeray: The Age of Wisdom* (1958). In them he traces Thackeray's life in detail and places his writings in the setting of the time. Indeed, this is one of the great strengths of the work. It is not just a life of Thackeray. It begins with a long account of the Thackeray family and especially of their connection with India, and every phase of the novelist's career is richly supported with a description and examination of the background against which it took place. These volumes therefore give us an interesting account of the literary world of the time, and in this they are the more important for the perspective in which they place Thackeray. Ray had earlier published *The Buried Life* (1952), whose sub-title 'A Study of the Relations between Thackeray's Fiction and His Personal History' sufficiently indicates its subject, in which, among other things, he gives valuable guidance to possible originals for a number of the novelist's characters.

Ray had benefited from the relaxation in the attitude of Thackeray's descendant, Mrs. Fuller, and the first product of his researches was the impressive four volumes of *Letters and Private Papers of William Makepeace Thackeray* (1945–6). Despite the extent of this work, Ray knew also of many other letters which he could not obtain permission to print, and yet others have turned up since. There had been three earlier volumes, namely, Jane Octavia Brookfield's *A Collection of Letters of William Makepeace Thackeray, 1847–55* (1887), Lucy W. Baxter's *Thackeray's Letters to an American Family* (1904), and Blanche Warre Cornish's *Some Family Letters of William Makepeace Thackeray* (1911).

Specialist biographical studies include Eyre Crowe's *With Thackeray in America* (1893), W. W. Hunter's *The Thackerays in India* (1897), J. G. Wilson's exhaustive *Thackeray in the United States* (1904), and E. B. Chancellor's *The London of Thackeray* (1923). Articles worthy of mention in this connection are W. Vulpius's 'Thackeray in Weimar' (*Century Magazine*, April 1897), E. C. Strickland Gibson's 'Thackeray and Charterhouse' (*Cornhill Magazine*, June 1922), H. C. Minchin's 'Thackeray in the Temple' (*Cornhill Magazine*, September 1928), and E. W. Whitton's 'Thackeray and the Army' (*Nineteenth Century*, November 1931).

BIBLIOGRAPHY

The chief primary reference book is H. S. Van Duzer's *A Thackeray Library* (1919), which is based on the author's collection and covers first editions and manuscripts, together with portraits, water-colours, etchings, and drawings. It is arranged alphabetically without discrimination of major works from insignificant articles. There is an extensive bibliography in the second volume of Lewis Melville's *William Makepeace Thackeray* (1910), superseding that in his *Life* (1899). The second volume of Ray's edition of the *Letters* has a section on articles newly identified as Thackeray's and he also contributed 'Thackeray and Punch: 44 Newly Identified Contributions' to *TLS* (1 January 1949), while E. M. White has listed 'Thackeray's Contribution to *Fraser's Magazine*' in *SB* (vol. xix).

There is a full list of primary and secondary items in *NCBEL*, vol. iii (1969) and Lionel Stevenson has contributed a detailed and perceptive commentary on Thackeray's bibliography to the volume he edited on *Victorian Fiction: A Guide to Research* (1964). More recently, on secondary bibliography, note should be taken of D. Flamm's *Thackeray's Critics* (1966), which annotates comment on the novelist from 1836 to 1901.

BACKGROUND READING

With Trollope, Thackeray both derived more from and reflected more of his age than any other writer of the time. G. M. Young's

Victorian England: Portrait of an Age (1936) is a masterly survey, and to this should be added G. Kitson Clark's *The Making of Victorian England* (1962) and, for the years 1852 to 1867, W. L. Burn's *The Age of Equipoise* (1964). Two other books worth mentioning for the treatment of social change are T. H. S. Escott's *Social Transformations of the Victorian Age* (1897) and O. F. Christie's *The Transition from Aristocracy, 1832–1867* (1927).

REFERENCES

TEXTS

(*a*) *Collected works*

Library Edition (22 vols., London, 1867–9: with 2 more vols., 1885–6).
De-luxe Edition, with memoir by L. Stephen (26 vols., London, 1878–86).
Biographical Edition, with introductions by A. T. Ritchie (13 vols., London, 1898–9).
Oxford Edition, with introductions by G. Saintsbury (17 vols., London, 1908).

(*b*) *Separate works*

M. Anisman (ed.), *Barry Lyndon* (New York, 1971).
G. N. Ray (ed.), *Contributions to the Morning Chronicle* (London and Urbana, Ill., 1955).
G. and K. Tillotson (edd.), *Vanity Fair* (London, 1963).
J. E. Wells (ed.), *Roundabout Papers* (New York, 1925).

The *English Humourists and the Four Georges, Henry Esmond, The Newcomes, Pendennis, Vanity Fair*, and *The Virginians* are published in Everyman's Library and *Henry Esmond* and *Vanity Fair* are available also in many paperback editions.

CRITICAL STUDIES

W. C. Brownell, *Victorian Prose Masters* (New York, 1901).
Lord D. Cecil, *Early Victorian Novelists* (London, 1934).
G. A. Craig, 'On the Style of *Vanity Fair*', in *Style in Prose Fiction*, ed. H. C. Martin (New York, 1959).
J. W. Dodds, *Thackeray: A Critical Portrait* (London and New York, 1941).
A. E. Dyson, *The Crazy Fabric* (London and New York, 1965).
J. Y. T. Greig, *Thackeray: A Reconsideration* (London and Hamden, Conn., 1950).
B. Hardy, *The Exposure of Luxury: Radical Themes in Thackeray* (London, 1972).
A. A. Jack, *Thackeray: A Study* (London, 1895: reissued, 1970).
A. C. Kettle, *An Introduction to the English Novel* (London, 1951).

J. Loofbourow, *Thackeray and the Form of Fiction* (Princeton, N.J., 1964).

R. Las Vergnas, *William Makepeace Thackeray, l'homme, le penseur, le romancier* (Paris, 1932).

J. A. Lester, 'Thackeray's Narrative Technique', *PMLA* lxix (June 1954).

P. Lubbock, *The Craft of Fiction* (London, 1921; Hamden, Conn., 1957).

J. McMaster, *Thackeray: The Major Novels* (Manchester and Toronto, 1971).

G. Saintsbury, *A Consideration of Thackeray* (London, 1931).

M. G. Sundell (ed.), *Twentieth Century Interpretations of Vanity Fair* (paperback, Englewood Cliffs, N.J., 1969).

G. Tillotson, *Thackeray the Novelist* (Cambridge, 1954; New York, 1964).

—— and D. Hawes (edd.), *Thackeray: the Critical Heritage* (London and New York, 1967).

K. Tillotson, *Novels of the Eighteen-Forties* (Oxford and New York, 1954).

A. Trollope, *Thackeray* (London, 1879; Detroit, Mich., 1902).

D. Van Ghent, *The English Novel: Form and Function* (New York, 1953).

A. Welsh (ed.), *Thackeray* (paperback, Englewood Cliffs, N.J., 1968).

J. H. Wheatley, *Patterns in Thackeray's Fiction* (London and Cambridge, Mass., 1969).

C. Whibley, *William Makepeace Thackeray* (London, 1903).

BIOGRAPHY AND LETTERS

L. W. Baxter (ed.), *Thackeray's Letters to an American Family* (London, 1904).

J. O. Brookfield (ed.), *A Collection of Letters of William Makepeace Thackeray, 1847–55* (London, 1887).

E. B. Chancellor, *The London of Thackeray* (London, 1923).

B. W. Cornish (ed.), *Family Letters of William Makepeace Thackeray* (London, 1911).

E. Crowe, *With Thackeray in America* (London, 1893).

M. Elwin, *Thackeray* (London and New York, 1932).

L. Ennis, *Thackeray, the Sentimental Cynic* (Evanston, Ill., 1950).

E. C. S. Gibson, 'Thackeray and Charterhouse', *Cornhill Magazine* (June 1922).

W. W. Hunter, *The Thackerays in India* (London, 1897).

'Lewis Melville', *The Life of William Makepeace Thackeray* (2 vols., London, 1899).

H. C. Minchin, 'Thackeray in the Temple', *Cornhill Magazine* (September 1928).

S. Nowell-Smith, 'In Defence of Thackeray', *Nineteenth Century* (July 1933).

J. T. Prime and A. Bayne, *Memorials of the Thackeray Family* (London, 1870).

G. N. Ray (ed.), *The Letters and Private Papers of William Makepeace Thackeray* (London and Cambridge, Mass., vols. i–ii, 1945; vols. iii–iv, 1946).

—— *The Buried Life* (London, 1952).

—— *Thackeray: The Uses of Adversity, 1811–1846* (London and New York, 1955).

—— *Thackeray: The Age of Wisdom, 1847–1863* (London and New York, 1958).

M. Sadleir, *Edward and Rosina* (London, 1931).

L. Stevenson, *The Showman of Vanity Fair* (London, 1947).

W. Vulpius, 'Thackeray in Weimar', *Century Magazine* (April 1897).

E. W. Whitton, 'Thackeray and the Army', *Nineteenth Century* (November 1931).

BIBLIOGRAPHY

D. Flamm, *Thackeray's Critics* (Chapel Hill, N. C., 1966).

'Lewis Melville', *William Makepeace Thackeray* (vol. ii, London, 1910).

G. N. Ray, *The Letters* (vol. ii, London, and Cambridge, Mass., 1945).

—— 'Thackeray and Punch', *TLS* (1 January 1949).

L. Stevenson (ed.), *Victorian Fiction: A Guide to Research* (Cambridge, Mass., 1964).

H. S. Van Duzer, *A Thackeray Library* (New York, 1919; reissued, 1967).

G. Watson (ed.), *NCBEL* (vol. iii, Cambridge and New York, 1969).

E. M. White, 'Thackeray's Contributions to *Fraser's Magazine*', *Studies in Bibliography*, xix (1968).

BACKGROUND READING

W. L. Burn, *The Age of Equipoise* (London, 1964).

O. F. Christie, *The Transition from Aristocracy* (London, 1927).

T. H. S. Escott, *Social Transformations of the Victorian Age* (London, 1897).

G. Kitson Clark, *The Making of Victorian England* (London, 1962).

G. M. Young, *Portrait of an Age* (London and New York, 1936).

11 · DICKENS 1812–1870

Michael Slater

TEXTS

The last complete edition of Dickens's works to be published during
his lifetime, the 21-volume Charles Dickens Edition, was advertised
as having been revised and corrected throughout by the author, who
also supplied running headlines for the recto of each leaf. Until
recently, in so far as publishers and editors have troubled at all about
printing a reliable text of the novels, it has been this edition to which
they have turned. In fact, however, there has been little concern
about this and even such 'prestige' editions as the luxurious Nonesuch Dickens (1937–8) and the more easily available Oxford Illustrated Dickens (1947–59)—this being the one most commonly cited
in scholarly work on Dickens—have no textual authority. In his
important paper, 'Editing a Nineteenth Century Novelist', listed
below under CRITICAL STUDIES AND COMMENTARY, the late John Butt
pointed out faults of the Charles Dickens Edition and made the case
for treating the text of the first volume-edition of each novel as the
copy-text for a definitive edition. This policy was adopted for the
Clarendon Edition, inaugurated under the general editorship of Butt
and Kathleen Tillotson, two volumes of which (*Oliver Twist* and
Edwin Drood) have so far appeared. This edition documents the
genesis and composition of each novel but offers no critical assessment
or explanatory annotation. Meanwhile, *Hard Times*, edited by
George H. Ford and Sylvère Monod, has appeared in the Norton
Critical Editions series (available in paperback) and this gives both a
reliable text and explanatory annotation together with specimens of
notable critical comment on the novel. Duane DeVries's Cromwell
edition of *Bleak House* resembles the Norton *Hard Times* in supplying
all Dickens's working memoranda and number-plans for the novel,
as well as an authoritative text and selected criticism, though it is less
thorough in its annotation. It will shortly be rivalled by a *Bleak
House* (Norton) edited by Ford and Monod. R. D. McMaster's *Little
Dorrit* (Macmillan) is another textually authoritative edition which
also supplies Dickens's memoranda, number-plans, etc., but dis-
penses with critical extracts in favour of a substantial editorial
introduction and detailed explanatory annotation. George Ford's

Riverside edition of *David Copperfield* draws on Butt's textual work and includes in an appendix passages excised by Dickens in proof.

Apart from these editions, modern reprints of Dickens must be valued more for what they offer in the way of commentary and elucidation than for their textual authority. The pleasantly-produced Oxford Illustrated Dickens has already been mentioned as being the edition most frequently in use; but the introductions to *Oliver Twist* (Humphry House), *Barnaby Rudge* (Kathleen Tillotson), and *Little Dorrit* (Lionel Trilling) are the only important critical work to be found in it. Of the multitudinous paperback reprints those appearing in the Penguin English Library series are perhaps the most distinguished; they supply illustrations, explanatory footnotes and, in some cases, also reproduce Dickens's working-notes and number-plans; (for the novels available in this series see the REFERENCES to this chapter).

The 'non-canonical' periodical writings (i.e., those never collected in volume-form by Dickens) are extensive and not yet all collected. Many were gathered by B. W. Matz into two volumes entitled *Miscellaneous Papers* in the Gadshill Edition of Dickens's works and these appear, with additions, in the Nonesuch Edition as *Collected Papers*. A scholarly edition by Harry Stone of all Dickens's uncollected writings in *Household Words* was published in 1968 and 1969. For details of Dickens's journalism, and of separately published minor works, the bibliographies listed in the appropriate section below should be consulted.

CRITICAL STUDIES AND COMMENTARY

(a) Introduction

A great dividing line in the history of Dickens criticism may be recognized about the year 1940 when essays by Edmund Wilson, drawing on the new biographical information that became public in the 1930s, and George Orwell, followed later by Humphry House's *The Dickens World* (see section on BACKGROUND READING below), inaugurated a renaissance in Dickens studies, which have been growing apace ever since. This survey has accordingly been divided into three parts: pre-1940 criticism and 'modern' (i.e. post-1940) criticism; finally, outstanding studies of particular books are noted. An excellent guide to the history of Dickens's reputation from 1836 to 1954 exists in George H. Ford's *Dickens and his Readers* (essential reading for all Dickens students) and I have drawn freely on it in what follows. It may be supplemented by the Dickens volume in the 'Critical Heritage' series, edited by Philip Collins, which presents a thorough sampling of contemporary reviews of Dickens's works, and also by the essays by K. J. Fielding, Sylvère Monod, Michael Slater, Philip Collins, and George Ford in *Dickens and Fame 1870–1970* (the Centenary issue of *The Dickensian*). Various useful collections of Dickens criticism may be mentioned here at the outset (the REFERENCES will indicate which articles are reprinted in which collection). Ford and Lane's *The Dickens Critics*, which ranges from Edgar Allan Poe to Angus Wilson, provides the best selection, but Stephen Wall's Penguin anthology (which includes many of Dickens's own comments on his work) is also good. There is also W. Ross Clark's *Discussions of Charles Dickens* which, apart from Gissing, represents only modern critics. Martin Price's *Dickens*, appearing as it does in the 'Twentieth Century Views' series, concentrates entirely on modern criticism. A special number of *A Review of English Literature*, published in 1961, gathers together essays by distinguished scholars on various aspects of Dickens's art, some of which are mentioned separately below. The Centenary Year of 1970 called forth several symposia of this kind, notably the special issues of *Studies in the Novel*, *Nineteenth Century Fiction* (republished as *Dickens Centennial Essays*), and *Études anglaises*, and the two volumes of essays edited respectively by Robert Partlow and Michael Slater. Two other earlier collections adopt the novel-by-novel approach and will therefore find more appropriate mention under (*d*) below. Robert Partlow's *Dickens Studies Annual* offers a yearly selection, somewhat uneven in quality, of original critical essays.

(*b*) Dickens's reputation 1836–1940

From the appearance of Sam Weller in the fourth monthly number of *Pickwick Papers* (July 1836) to the death of Little Nell at the end of the weekly serialization of *The Old Curiosity Shop* (February 1841) the story of Dickens's reputation is one of general and enthusiastic acclaim. His exuberant comedy, moral purity, and vigorous social criticism—especially of the New Poor Law in *Oliver Twist*—won him thousands of devoted readers. There was indeed some murmuring against the 'lowness' of his subject-matter, and Thackeray satirized *Oliver Twist* along with other 'Newgate' novels in his *Catherine* (1839) but the unstinted praise of R. H. Horne in his *New Spirit of the Age* (1844) was more typical of the public's attitude. *Barnaby Rudge* seems to have been less popular and may well, as Ada Nisbet argues in her 'The Mystery of *Martin Chuzzlewit*', have been responsible for the comparative failure of *Chuzzlewit* (though the *succès fou* of *A Christmas Carol* in December 1843 reassured Dickens that he could still command the public's wholehearted devotion). There was a gap of two years (the first such pause in Dickens's career) before the next novel, *Dombey and Son*, appeared and, when the public apprehended that little Paul was destined for as early a grave as Little Nell, sales picked up considerably. The (again comparative) diminution of public enthusiasm for the novel after Paul's death probably affected the sales of the early numbers of *Copperfield*, but the eager response to this masterpiece, once it had established itself, ensured an enthusiastic welcome for *Bleak House*; thereafter Dickens's popularity maintained a steady level, considerably strengthened by his editorial relationship with the public as 'conductor' of the weekly journals, *Household Words* and *All the Year Round*. Ford has persuasively suggested that the 'wide-sweeping criticism of society' in Dickens's later novels tended to split his public into loyalist admirers for whom he could do no wrong, and intellectuals alienated by his destructive and (in their view) ill-informed attack on various institutions of Victorian England. Stephen's scathing review of *Little Dorrit* represents the latter attitude. Against it, however, should be set such things as Ruskin's praise of *Hard Times* and Matthew Arnold's of *Copperfield*. From the 1840s onwards Carlyle profoundly influenced Dickens's social thinking; this relationship has been explored in studies by Michael Goldberg and William Oddie.

The critical debate about Dickens's literary status in Victorian England hinged around the question of realism, and there was a tendency, as in Masson's famous essay on *Pendennis* and *Copperfield*, to contrast him with Thackeray, the latter being seen as the more 'truthful' novelist, free of grotesque distortion and fantastic exaggeration. Thackeray had himself, in his essay 'Going to see a Man Hanged', memorably attacked Dickens's depiction of Nancy in *Oliver Twist* on the grounds of untruthfulness. The most important Victorian critical assessments of Dickens are undoubtedly those by a French critic, Hippolyte Taine (1856), by Walter Bagehot (1858), and by G. H. Lewes (1872).

After his death Dickens's popularity with the general public continued unabated, as the Chapman and Hall sales figures quoted by Ford show. A Dickens Fellowship (still flourishing) was founded in 1902 and G. K. Chesterton, once its President, became the great spokesman for Dickens enthusiasts. His vivid criticism, with which all Dickens students should be familiar, shows remarkable insight into Dickens's genius and art, but it is the early 'jolly' Dickens on whom he lavishes his greatest praise, and his work should be complemented by that of the other indispensable Dickens critic of the early twentieth century, George Gissing, who praised Dickens as a great realist and social critic and emphasized the sombre power of the later novels. Shaw was another who relished the latter for their social criticism, asserting that *Little Dorrit* was 'a more seditious book than *Das Kapital*'. This attitude was carried to extreme lengths in T. A. Jackson's *Charles Dickens. The Progress of a Radical* (1937) which presented the novelist as developing into a fully-fledged Marxist. Despite its inevitable distortions, however, Jackson's work remains a significant contribution to Dickens studies.

Though many other influential voices were raised in Dickens's favour during the first forty years of this century—notably those of Swinburne, the American critic E. P. Whipple, George Santayana (who disposed in a spirited way of complaints about 'exaggeration'), Quiller-Couch and Lord David Cecil—intellectual opinion, especially in Bloomsbury, set firmly against him. Aldous Huxley jeered at Little Nell in *Vulgarity in Literature*, but most damaging, perhaps, were E. M. Forster's patronizing remarks in *Aspects of the Novel*, designating Dickens's characters as 'flat' creations (compared with the 'rounded' characters of such writers as Jane Austen). Much modern Dickens criticism may be seen as still replying to Forster.

(c) Modern Criticism (1940–1971)

Edmund Wilson's seminal essay, 'Dickens: the Two Scrooges', and George Orwell's 'Charles Dickens', published within a year or so of each other, are fundamental to any acquaintance with modern Dickens criticism. Beyond these the student should familiarize himself with K. J. Fielding's admirable *Charles Dickens: A Critical Introduction*, and Angus Wilson's penetrating and deeply interesting study, *The World of Charles Dickens*; both these books relate the life to the works and touch on all aspects of Dickens's art. Another basic book, focusing on Dickens as a serial novelist, is Butt and Tillotson's *Dickens at Work* which may be supplemented by Sylvère Monod's *Dickens the Novelist* and H. P. Sucksmith's *The Narrative Art of Charles Dickens* (these studies all offer valuable insights into Dickens's art as well as exposition of his brilliant craftsmanship). An outstanding merit of F. R. and Q. D. Leavis's *Dickens the Novelist* is the close analytical attention paid to Dickens as a master of English prose. Robert Garis's illuminating investigation of the concept of 'style as theatre' in his *The Dickens Theatre* should also be read. Randolph Quirk has explored Dickens's use of language in two important essays (see also G. L. Brook's *The Language of Dickens*), and Taylor Stoehr has written interestingly on the narrative technique (super-naturalism') developed in the later novels. William Axton's *Circle of Fire* is also concerned with stylistic and structural aspects of the novel, persuasively relating them to the idiom of popular Victorian drama (see also Earle Davies's *The Flint and the Flame* for the particular influence of Charles Matthews's comic monologues). The latest significant contribution to the discussion of form in Dickens is perhaps J. Hillis Miller's *The Form of Victorian Fiction*. Closely related to this area of Dickens studies is the exploration, inaugurated by Edmund Wilson's essay, of his use of symbolism; here the classic work is undoubtedly Miller's *Charles Dickens: the World of his Novels*, though Carl Bodelsen's 'Some Notes on Dickens's Symbolism' and John Holloway's essay, 'Dickens and the Symbol', should also be mentioned. Steven Marcus's uneven *Dickens: from Pickwick to Dombey* also extensively discusses Dickens's symbolism, considering it from a more strictly Freudian viewpoint than Miller's. Valuable studies of Dickens's characterization and treatment of the moral life are Angus Wilson's 'The Heroes and Heroines of Charles Dickens' and Barbara Hardy's *The Moral Art of Dickens*. Ross H. Dabney's study of the theme of mercenary marriage in the novels is also relevant. Dabney's book involves us with Dickens as a social critic: any investigation of this subject, or of the topicality of his novels, must begin with Orwell's essay and Humphry House's *Dickens World* (see the section on BACKGROUND READING). The most important contemporary critic in this respect is Raymond Williams; see his essays in *The Critical Quarterly* (1964), and in *Dickens 1970*. Grahame Smith's illuminating *Dickens, Money and Society* is also essential reading here.

No great modern celebrator of Dickens's humour has yet arisen in response to the growing restlessness at the post-Wilsonian emphasis on the darker side of his achievement, but few would dispute that it is for this quality above all that his works remain the most popular of all our classics. It is perhaps to Chesterton that we must turn, or to J. B. Priestley, Chesterton's successor as eulogist of Dickensian exuberance, for discussion of Dickens's comedy which really measures up to its subject; Priestley's fine essay on Dick Swiveller in *The English Comic Characters* may be particularly recommended. There have, none the less, been valuable modern contributions to the criticism of this fundamental aspect of Dickens's work, notably Sylvère Monod's essay, 'A French View of Dickens's Humour', A. O. J. Cockshut's discussion in *The Imagination of Charles Dickens*, Northrop Frye's 'Dickens and the Comedy of Humors', and various articles by James Kincaid brought together in his *Dickens and the Rhetoric of Laughter*; see also the 'Epilogue on Humour' at the end of

Ada Nisbet's chapter on Dickens in Lionel Stevenson's *Victorian Fiction*, mentioned below.

(d) Studies of individual novels

The collection of original essays on individual novels edited by John Gross and Gabriel Pearson and called *Dickens and the Twentieth Century* contains much important work and has exercised great influence on succeeding Dickens criticism. Nearly all the essays are well worth reading, as are the valuable studies of the novels from *The Old Curiosity Shop* onwards published by A. E. Dyson in his *The Inimitable Dickens*, and so, to avoid repetition, they will not be included in the following round-up. Dyson's volume in Macmillan's 'Modern Judgements' series reprints notable studies of particular novels (as well as two interesting general essays by Angus Wilson and C. B. Cox). The appendix to this chapter will indicate which of the essays about to be mentioned are included in this volume.

The two most stimulating critiques of *Pickwick Papers* known to the present writer are W. H. Auden's characteristically idiosyncratic 'Dingley Dell and the Fleet' and Barbara Hardy's 'The Triumph of Dingley Dell'. *Oliver Twist* has been the subject of many fine studies, notably Graham Greene's famous essay, 'The Young Dickens', Kathleen Tillotson's contribution to the 1959 volume of *Essays and Studies*, and Arnold Kettle's chapter on this novel in his *Introduction to the English Novel*. Three important introductory essays to editions should also be mentioned—by Humphry House (Oxford Illustrated Edition), by Angus Wilson (Penguin English Library) and by J. Hillis Miller (Rinehart Edition). *Nicholas Nickleby* has not attracted so much attention but W. W. Robson's lecture to the Manchester Scientific and Literary Society is illuminating; see also Michael Slater's introductory essay to the Scolar Press reprint of this novel. Aldous Huxley's attack on the end of *The Old Curiosity Shop* has already been mentioned and it would be difficult to find an equally spirited modern defence of the novel; J. C. Reid's discussion in *The Hidden World of Charles Dickens* seems to me among the most interesting of recent critiques. *Barnaby Rudge* has always been among the least popular of the novels but it has found distinguished modern apologists in Kathleen Tillotson (introduction to the Oxford Illustrated Edition—see above) and A. E. Dyson (in his *The Inimitable Dickens*). Dyson also writes particularly illuminatingly on *Martin Chuzzlewit*, and Dorothy Van Ghent focused on this novel in her important essay, 'The Dickens World: a View from Todgers's', which deals especially with Dickens's animism as a structural device. John

Butt and Michael Slater have both discussed the *Christmas Books* at some length and Edward Wagenknecht's introduction to *The Chimes*, reprinted in *Dickens and the Scandalmongers* (see the section on BIOGRAPHIES AND LETTERS, below), is also valuable. Three outstandingly interesting discussions of *Dombey and Son* are Kathleen Tillotson's in her *Novels of the Eighteen-Forties* (see the section on BACKGROUND READING below), F. R. Leavis's in *Dickens the Novelist* and Harry Stone's 'The Novel as Fairy Tale: Dickens's *Dombey and Son*'. Much has been written on *David Copperfield*, among the most notable essays being Gwendolyn B. Needham's 'The Undisciplined Heart of David Copperfield', Mark Spilka's '*David Copperfield* as Psychological Fiction' which interestingly compares Dickens's art with Kafka's (a comparison Spilka treats at more length in his *Dickens and Kafka*), George Ford's introduction to the Riverside *Copperfield* (see above), Philip Collins's '*David Copperfield*: "A Very Complicated Interweaving of Truth and Fiction" ' and Q. D. Leavis's chapter on the novel in *Dickens the Novelist*. *Bleak House* has also attracted much critical interest but perhaps Ann Y. Wilkinson's '*Bleak House*: from Faraday to Judgment Day' may stand as the most remarkable single study of this work. George Ford's essay, 'Self-help and the Helpless in *Bleak House*' is also important and the nature and significance of the novel's topicality has been explored by Trevor Blount in a number of fascinating essays. The most celebrated commentators on *Hard Times* have been Ruskin, Shaw, and F. R. Leavis, all already mentioned, but K. J. Fielding's admirable essay, '*Hard Times* and Common Things', should also be read, as should Patrick Brantlinger's 'The Case Against Trade Unions in Early Victorian Fiction' and D. Sonstroem's 'Fettered Fancy in *Hard Times*'. Lionel Trilling's introduction to the Oxford Illustrated Edition of *Little Dorrit* has been a most influential piece of Dickens criticism and did much to focus critical attention on this book. The most outstanding recent study has undoubtedly been F. R. Leavis's chapter in *Dickens the Novelist*, entitled 'Blake and Dickens: *Little Dorrit*'. Sir James Fitz-James Stephen's savage attack on this novel has been already mentioned; he also harshly reviewed *Tale of Two Cities* and his criticisms are still worth reading. G. Robert Stange's 'Dickens and the Fiery Past' and three essays by Sylvère Monod are among the best modern studies of Dickens's second historical novel. Philip Collins's 'A Tale of Two Novels' interestingly discusses the placement of *Tale of Two Cities* and *Great Expectations* in Dickens's career. Three other very rewarding studies of *Great Expectations* are those by Stange, Dorothy Van Ghent, and Julian Moynahan; Shaw, too, wrote a provocative introduction to the novel in 1937 when it was first published with the original ending, discarded by Dickens, restored. Henry James's severe review of *Our Mutual Friend* is really part of the great Victorian debate about truth in Dickens's fiction already mentioned, but it is perhaps salutary to bear its challenging strictures in mind as we read some of the subtle modern interpretations of this work, e.g. Robert Morse's. Ernest Boll has written a good study of the novel's craftsmanship. A vast literature concerned with detection rather than criticism has accumulated round Dickens's last novel, the unfinished *Mystery of Edwin Drood*, and Felix Aylmer's controversial book is probably the most recent significant contribution to this collection, but there does exist at least one fine critical essay on the work, to be found in V. S. Pritchett's *The Living Novel*.

BIOGRAPHIES AND LETTERS

K. J. Fielding has provided an excellent guide to this area of Dickens studies in his *Charles Dickens: A Survey*. He notes that the earliest substantial biography of Dickens, written by his close friend, John Forster, remains 'indispensable'. Forster drew largely on Dickens's letters for his book and the immediacy of the work owes much to this and to Forster's intimate personal knowledge of his subject. Against this must be set the effect of the discretion imposed on Forster (because many of those whom he wrote about were still living) and his virtual ignoring of certain of the novelist's relationships, notably those with his wife and with Wilkie Collins, a close friend and collaborator in his later years. The most frequently cited edition of Forster is J. W. T. Ley's. Ley reprinted the revised text of 1876 with copious additional notes, drawing on such sources as Robert Langton's *Childhood and Youth of Charles Dickens* and F. G. Kitton's book of first-hand anecdotes, *Charles Dickens by Pen and Pencil*, which greatly supplemented Forster's account. Recently, A. J. Hoppé has edited Forster's original text supplying further additional annotation, especially about Ellen Ternan, but Ley's work remains the 'standard' edition.

Dickensian biography was given a new lease of life by the revelations made in the 1930s (initially in the *Daily Express*) by Thomas Wright, and also by Gladys Storey, who set down the reminiscences of her friend, Kate Perugini (Dickens's elder daughter) in *Dickens and Daughter*. Since then, there has been continual and acrimonious controversy as to whether the young actress, Ellen Ternan, was or was not Dickens's mistress in his later years. Ada Nisbet's *Dickens and Ellen Ternan* and Felix Aylmer's *Dickens Incognito* (which also provided the pair with an illegitimate child though this 'discovery' was immediately discredited) argue for an illicit relationship but they are vigorously opposed by Edward Wagenknecht in his *Dickens and the Scandalmongers*.

Dame Una Pope-Hennessy's *Charles Dickens* was the first biography to make use of the new facts and it can still be recommended as readable and generally reliable, as can Hesketh Pearson's cheerful *Dickens: His Character, Comedy and Career*. K. J. Fielding's excellent *Dickens: A Critical Introduction* (see the section on CRITICAL STUDIES above) can be complemented pictorially by J. B. Priestley's straightforward account in his *Dickens. A Pictorial Biography*, or by Martin Fido's *Charles Dickens: an authentic account of his life and times* (the finest, most suggestive Dickensian picture-gallery, however, will be found in Angus Wilson's *The World of Charles Dickens* mentioned above). The writing of the definitive life of Dickens must await the completion of the Pilgrim Letters (see below) but the nearest approach to it so far is undoubtedly Edgar Johnson's *Charles Dickens: his Tragedy and Triumph*, which combines detailed scholarship and readability to a remarkable degree, though the book's main thesis—that as Dickens grew older his insight into society became sharper and more comprehensive—does not command general assent. Four other important sources of biographical information are: J. W. T. Ley's *The Dickens Circle*, which surveys the novelist's important friendships (no satisfactory biography of Forster yet exists, unfortunately); Arthur A. Adrian's *Georgina Hogarth and the Dickens Circle*, which adds greatly to our knowledge about Dickens's children; innumerable articles in *The Dickensian* on all aspects of Dickens's life, notably those by William J. Carlton; and K. J. Fielding's admirable and definitive edition of Dickens's speeches.

A heavily bowdlerized selection of Dickens's letters was published by his daughter, Mary, and sister-in-law, Georgina Hogarth, and remained the only one available until Walter Dexter published Dickens's letters to his wife in *Mr. and Mrs. Charles Dickens*. Another special collection, concerned with Dickens's philanthropic activities, was made by Edgar Johnson of some of Dickens's letters to Baroness Burdett-Coutts. Dexter also edited the three volumes of letters in the Nonesuch Edition and these, despite their great rarity and textual unreliability, will remain the standard edition until they are superseded by the much fuller and more accurate Pilgrim Edition, inaugurated by Humphry House in 1949 and now under the general editorship of his widow, Madeline House, and Graham Storey. This splendid edition supplies detailed and scholarly annotation and is an essential reference book for all students of Dickens; the first two volumes, published in 1965 and 1969, cover Dickens's life up to the end of 1841.

BIBLIOGRAPHY

F. G. Kitton's two volumes, *The Novels of Charles Dickens* and the *Minor Writings of Charles Dickens*, contain much useful and still valid information about the genesis, publication, and editions of the various works. William Miller's *The Dickens Student and Collector*, despite the faults exposed in Philo Calhoun and Howell J. Heaney's pamphlet, *Dickensiana in the Rough*, is an invaluable reference book, notable especially for its substantial lists of contemporary reviews, dramatizations, and plagiarisms of Dickens's works. An excellent modern selective bibliography with occasional comments is appended to K. J. Fielding's British Council pamphlet; this covers all aspects of Dickens studies as does Ada Nisbet's impressive and exhaustive survey of Dickens scholarship and criticism up to the end of 1962 in Lionel Stevenson's *Victorian Fiction*. Miss Nisbet's helpful and discriminating commentary is a pleasure to read and her work is particularly remarkable for its thorough coverage of foreign criticism of Dickens. It may be supplemented by J. Don Vann's 'Checklist of Dickens Criticism 1963–7' in the special Dickens issue of *Studies in the Novel*, which includes as well Lauriat Lane, jun.'s helpful survey, 'Dickens Studies 1958–68: an Overview', and by Joseph Gold's *The Stature of Dickens: a Centenary Bibliography*. There is also a most useful selective checklist of major Dickens criticism up to the end of 1960 appended to Ford and Lane's *The Dickens Critics* (see above). Current work on Dickens is listed annually in the Victorian Bibliography published in each June issue of *Victorian Studies* (three cumulated volumes of these bibliographies have been issued covering the period 1932–64) and also in each issue of the quarterly *Dickens Studies Newsletter*; it is assessed annually in the September issue of The *Dickensian* from 1968 onwards. Finally, the most comprehensive all-purpose reference work for Dickens studies is Philip Collins's entry in the third volume of the *NCBEL*.

BACKGROUND READING

(a) Social history and history of ideas

The standard reference work for the social history of Victorian England is Elie J. Halévy's *History of the English People in the Nineteenth Century* but Dickens students seeking to familiarize themselves with the novelist's setting will find the following works outstandingly helpful: G. M. Young's *Victorian England; Portrait of an Age*; John W. Dodd's *The Age of Paradox. A Biography of England 1841–1851*; Asa Briggs's *Victorian People*; J. F. C. Harrison's *The Early Victorians 1832–51*; and Geoffrey Best's *Mid-Victorian Britain 1851–75*. Of works more sharply focused on Dickens two fairly lightweight but adequate introductions may be mentioned; Cruikshank's *Charles Dickens and Early Victorian England* and Ivor Brown's *Dickens in his Time*. The great work in this field, however, is undoubtedly Humphry's House's *The Dickens World* which places the novels firmly in their historical setting and is essential reading for all concerned with studying Dickens as a social critic. Two specialized aspects of this are dealt with by Philip Collins in his suggestive and fascinating books, *Dickens and Crime* and *Dickens and Education*, which show how complex Dickens's attitude to these matters was. Alexander Welsh's *The City of Dickens* is a most intelligent and sensitive exploration both of Dickens's response to Victorian London and to the moral and religious climate of his day. Another aspect of Dickens's response to his age receives illuminating treatment in Herbert L. Sussman's *Victorians and the Machine*.

(b) Literary History

No single modern history of Victorian literature has yet appeared which can be regarded as the standard authoritative work. But a good, general—if somewhat chatty—introduction is provided by Amy Cruse's *The Victorians and Their Books*, and stimulatingly idiosyncratic surveys may be found in G. K. Chesterton's *The Victorian Age in Literature* and Mario Praz's *Hero in Eclipse in Victorian Fiction*. Kathleen Tillotson's masterly *Novels of the Eighteen-Forties* is without doubt one of the finest contributions to Victorian literary history to date, and essential reading for all Dickens students. Much first-hand information about the literary life of the period exists in Anthony Trollope's *Autobiography*, and Dickens's own relations with some of his publishers are treated in Arthur Waugh's' *A Hundred Years of Publishing* (a 'house' history of Chapman and Hall) and (more thoroughly) in Royal Gettmann's *A Victorian Publisher* (on Bentley). The important subject of Dickens's original illustrators is closely studied in John Harvey's *Victorian Novelists and their Illustrators*, by Q. D. Leavis in *Dickens the Novelist*, and by Michael Steig in a number of articles, notably one entitled 'Dickens, Hablôt Browne and the Tradition of English Caricature'. Particular genres of Victorian fiction relevant to Dickens are examined in W. C. Phillips's *Dickens, Reade and Collins: Sensation Novelists*, Cazamian's *The Social Novel in*

England and Keith Hollingsworth's *The Newgate Novel*. Patricia Thomson's *The Victorian Heroine* places Dickens's heroines firmly in their literary-historical context; Peter Coveney's *The Image of Childhood* does the same for Dickens's children; Angus Wilson's brilliant and profound essay, 'Dickens on Children and Childhood', should also be read. Dickens, it is well known, was by far the most popular of the great Victorian novelists, and he also enjoyed a very wide readership as editor of *Household Words* and *All The Year Round*. A definitive study of this mass readership exists in R. D. Altick's great work, *The English Common Reader*. This may be supplemented by Louis James's *Fiction for the Working Man* which deals extensively with the cheap imitations of Dickens produced for the mass market. Finally, no student of Dickens should ignore the theatre of his day, which fascinated him and had such an impact on his work. The standard history is that by Allardyce Nicoll and a good introductory survey is provided by George Rowell's *The Victorian Theatre*.

REFERENCES

TEXTS

(a) Collected works

Works, Nonesuch Edition (London, 1937–8).
Works, Oxford Illustrated Edition (London, 1947–59).

(b) Separate works

T. Blount (ed.), *David Copperfield* (Penguin, paperback, Harmondsworth, 1966).
A. Calder (ed.), *Great Expectations* (Penguin, paperback, Harmondsworth, 1965).
M. Cardwell (ed.), *Edwin Drood* (London, 1972).
D. Craig (ed.), *Hard Times* (Penguin, paperback, Harmondsworth, 1969).
D. DeVries (ed.), *Bleak House* (Crowell, paperback, New York, 1971).
A. Easson (ed.), *The Old Curiosity Shop*, introduction by Malcolm Andrews (Penguin, paperback, Harmondsworth, 1972).
P. Fairclough (ed.), *Oliver Twist*, introduction by Angus Wilson (Penguin, paperback, Harmondsworth, 1966).
—— (ed.), *Dombey and Son*, introduction by Raymond Williams (Penguin, paperback, Harmondsworth, 1970).
G. Ford (ed.), *David Copperfield* (Riverside, paperback, Boston, Mass., 1958).
—— and S. Monod (edd.), *Hard Times* (Norton, paperback, New York, 1966).
P. N. Furbank (ed.), *Martin Chuzzlewit* (Penguin, paperback, Harmondsworth, 1968).

J. Holloway (ed.), *Little Dorrit* (Penguin, paperback, Harmondsworth, 1967).

R. McMaster (ed.), *Little Dorrit* (Macmillan, paperback, Toronto, 1969).

B. W. Matz (ed.), *Miscellaneous Papers* (Gadshill Dickens, vols. xxxv and xxxvi, London, 1908).

N. Page (ed.), *Bleak House*, introduction by J. Hillis Miller (Penguin, paperback, Harmondsworth, 1971).

R. L. Patten (ed.), *Pickwick Papers* (Penguin, paperback, Harmondsworth, 1972).

M. Slater (ed.), *The Christmas Books* (Penguin, Harmondsworth, 1971).

H. Stone (ed.), *Uncollected Writings from 'Household Words'* (Bloomington, Ind. 1968; London, 1969).

K. Tillotson (ed.), *Oliver Twist* (London, 1966).

J. S. Whitley and A. Goldman (edd.) *American Notes* (Penguin, paperback, Harmondsworth, 1972).

G. Woodcock (ed.), *Tale of Two Cities* (Penguin, Harmondsworth, 1970).

CRITICAL STUDIES AND COMMENTARY

(a) Introduction

J. Butt, 'Editing a Nineteenth Century Novelist' in G. Barnard (ed.), *English Studies Today* (Berne, 1961).

—— (ed.), *A Review of English Literature*, vol. ii, no. 3 (London, 1961).

W. R. Clark (ed.), *Discussions of Charles Dickens* (paperback, Boston, Mass., 1961).

G. Ford, *Dickens and his Readers* (Princeton, N.J., 1955).

—— and L. Lane (edd.), *The Dickens Critics* (Ithaca, N.Y., 1961).

J. Lee (ed.), *Studies in the Novel*, vol. i, no. 2 (Denton, Texas, 1969).

S. Monod (ed.), *Études anglaises*, vol. xxiii, no. 2 (Paris, 1970).

A. Nisbet and B. Nevius (edd.), *Dickens Centennial Essays* (Berkeley and Los Angeles, 1971).

R. Partlow (ed.), *Dickens The Craftsman* (Carbondale, Ill., 1970).

—— (ed.), *Dickens Studies Annual* (Carbondale, Ill., 1970–).

M. Price (ed.), *Dickens* (Englewood Cliffs, N.J., 1967).

M. Slater (ed.), *Dickens 1970* (London and New York, 1970).

—— (ed.), *Dickens and Fame 1870–1970* (paperback, Dickens Fellowship, London, 1970).

(b) Dickens's Reputation 1836–1940

M. Arnold, 'The Incompatibles', in Arnold, *Irish Essays and Others* (London, 1882).

W. Bagehot, 'Charles Dickens', *National Review*, vii (1858); reprinted in Bagehot, *Literary Studies* (London, 1879) and Bagehot, *Collected works* (London, 1965).

Lord D. Cecil, *Early Victorian Novelists* (London, 1934).

G. K. Chesterton, *Charles Dickens* (London, 1906).

—— *Appreciations and Criticisms of the Works of Charles Dickens* (New York, 1911).

E. M. Forster, *Aspects of the Novel* (London and New York, 1927).

G. Gissing, *Charles Dickens* (London, 1898).

—— *Critical Studies of the Works of Charles Dickens* (New York, 1924).

M. Goldberg, *Carlyle and Dickens* (Athens, Georgia, 1972).

R. H. Horne, *A New Spirit of the Age* (London, 1844; reprinted, U.K., 1971).

A. Huxley, *Vulgarity in Literature* (London, 1930); passage on Little Nell printed in Ford and Lane (edd.), *The Dickens Critics*.

T. A. Jackson, *Charles Dickens: The Progress of a Radical* (London, 1937; New York, 1938).

G. H. Lewes, 'Dickens in Relation to Criticism', *Fortnightly Review* (February 1872); reprinted in Ford and Lane (edd.), *The Dickens Critics*.

D. Masson, 'Pendennis and Copperfield: Thackeray and Dickens', *North British Review* (May, 1851); reprinted in Ford and Lane (edd.), *The Dickens Critics*.

A. B. Nisbet, 'The Mystery of *Martin Chuzzlewit*' in *Essays Dedicated to Lily B. Campbell* (Los Angeles, Calif., 1950).

W. Oddie, *Dickens and Carlyle* (London, 1972).

A. T. Quiller-Couch, *Dickens and other Victorians*, (Cambridge, 1925).

J. Ruskin, 'A Note on *Hard Times*', *Cornhill Magazine*, ii (1860), and *Unto This Last* (London, 1862); reprinted in Ford and Lane (edd.), *The Dickens Critics*.

G. Santayana, 'Dickens', *The Dial*, lxxi (1921); reprinted in Santayana, *Soliloquies in England* (London, 1922) and Ford and Lane (edd.), *The Dickens Critics*.

G. B. Shaw, Introduction to Hard Times (London, 1912); reprinted in Ford and Lane (edd.), *The Dickens Critics*.

—— 'On Dickens', *The Dickensian*, x (1914).

—— Introduction to *Great Expectations* (Edinburgh, 1937); reprinted in H. Hamilton (ed.), *Majority 1931–52* (London, 1952).

Sir J. F. Stephen, '*Little Dorrit*', *Edinburgh Review*, cvi (1857).

A. Swinburne, 'Charles Dickens', *Quarterly Review* (July, 1902).

—— *Charles Dickens* (London, 1913).

H. Taine, 'Charles Dickens: Son Talent et ses oeuvres', *Revue des deux Mondes*, 1 February 1856; reprinted in *Histoire de la littérature anglaise* (Paris, 1863–4); translation into English (Edinburgh, 1871).

W. M. Thackeray, *Catherine, a Story, by Ikey Solomons, Esq., junior, Fraser's Magazine* (May 1839–February 1840); reprinted in Oxford Edition of Thackeray's Works (ed. G. Saintsbury, 1908).

—— 'Going to see a Man Hanged', *Fraser's Magazine*, (August 1840); reprinted in Oxford Edition of Thackeray's *Works* (ed. G. Saintsbury, 1908).

E. P. Whipple, *Charles Dickens* (Boston, Mass., 1878).

(c) *Modern Criticism, 1940–71*

W. Axton, *Circle of Fire: Dickens's Vision and Style and the Popular Victorian Theatre* (Lexington, Ken., 1966).

C. A. Bodelsen, 'Some Notes on Dickens' Symbolism', *English Studies*, xl (1959).

G. L. Brook, *The Language of Dickens* (London, 1970).

J. Butt and K. Tillotson, *Dickens at Work* (London, 1957).

A. O. J. Cockshut, *The Imagination of Charles Dickens* (London, 1961).

R. H. Dabney, *Love and Property in the Novels of Dickens* (London, 1967).

E. Davis, *The Flint and The Flame, The Artistry of Charles Dickens* (St. Louis, Mo., 1963; London, 1965).

K. J. Fielding, *Charles Dickens: a Critical Introduction* (London, 1965).

N. Frye, 'Dickens and the Comedy of Humors' in R. H. Pearce (ed.), *Experience in the Novel* (New York and London, 1968).

R. Garis, *The Dickens Theatre: a Reassessment of the Novels* (Cambridge, Mass., and London, 1965).

B. Hardy, *The Moral Art of Dickens* (London and New York, 1970).

J. Holloway, 'Dickens and the Symbol' in Slater (ed.), *Dickens 1970*.

J. Kincaid, *Dickens and the Rhetoric of Laughter* (Oxford and New York, 1971).

F. R. and Q. D. Leavis, *Dickens the Novelist* (London, 1970; New York, 1971).

S. Marcus, *Dickens: from Pickwick to Dombey* (New York and London, 1965).

S. Monod, 'A French View of Dickens's Humour' in J. Butt (ed.), *A Review of English Literature* (July, 1961).

—— *Dickens the Novelist* (Norman, Okla., 1968).

G. Orwell, 'Charles Dickens' in *Inside the Whale* (London, 1940); reprinted in Orwell, *Critical Essays* (London, 1954), and (in part) in Ford and Lane (edd.), *The Dickens Critics*, and Clark (ed.), *Discussions of Charles Dickens*.

J. B. Priestley, *The English Comic Characters* (London, 1925).

R. Quirk, *Charles Dickens and Appropriate Language* (Durham, N.C., 1959).

—— 'Some Observations on the Language of Dickens' in J. Butt (ed.), *A Review of English Literature* (July 1961).

G. Smith, *Dickens, Money and Society* (Berkeley and Los Angeles, Calif., 1968).

T. Stoehr, *Dickens: the Dreamer's Stance* (New York, 1965).

H. P. Sucksmith, *The Narrative Art of Charles Dickens. The Rhetoric of Sympathy and Irony in his Novels* (London, 1970).

R. Williams, 'Social Criticism in Dickens: Some Problems of Method and Approach', *Critical Quarterly*, vi (1964).

—— 'Dickens and Social Ideas' in Slater (ed.), *Dickens 1970*.

A. Wilson, 'The Heroes and Heroines of Dickens' in Butt (ed.), *A Review of English Literature* (July ,1961); reprinted in Price (ed.), *Dickens*.

—— *The World of Charles Dickens* (London, 1970).

E. Wilson, 'Dickens: the Two Scrooges' in *The Wound and the Bow* (Boston, Mass., 1941).

(d) Studies of Individual Novels

(i) Collections

A. E. Dyson (ed.), *Dickens* (London, 1968).

—— *The Inimitable Dickens. A Reading of the Novels* (New York and London, 1970).

J. Gross and G. Pearson (edd.), *Dickens and the Twentieth Century* (London, 1962).

(ii) Separate books and essays

W. H. Auden, 'Dingley Dell and the Fleet' in Auden, *The Dyer's Hand* (New York and London, 1962); reprinted in Price (ed.), *Dickens*.

Sir F. Aylmer, *The Drood Case* (London, 1964).

T. Blount, 'The Graveyard Satire of *Bleak House* in the Context of 1850' *RES* n.s. xiv (1963).

—— 'The Chadbands and Dickens's View of Dissenters', *MLQ* xxv (1964).

—— 'The Documentary Symbolism of Chancery in *Bleak House*', *The Dickensian*, lxii (1966).

—— 'Dickens and Mr. Krook's Spontaneous Combustion' in Partlow (ed.) *Dickens Studies Annual*, i (1970).

P. Brantlinger, 'The Case against Trade Unions in Early Victorian Fiction', *VS* xiii (1969).

J. Butt, 'Dickens's Christmas Books' in Butt, *Pope, Dickens and Others* (Edinburgh, 1969).

P. A. W. Collins, 'A Tale of Two Novels', in Partlow (ed.) *Dickens Studies Annual*, ii (1972).

K. J. Fielding, '*Hard Times* and Common Things' in M. Mack and I. Gregor (edd.), *Imagined Worlds* (London, 1968).

G. Ford, 'Self-help and the Helpless in *Bleak House*' in R. C. Rathburn and M. Steinmann (edd.), *From Jane Austen to Joseph Conrad* (Minneapolis, Minn., 1968).

G. Greene, 'The Young Dickens' in Greene, *The Lost Childhood and Other Essays* (London, 1951); reprinted in Ford and Lane (edd.), *The Dickens Critics*, and Dyson (ed.), *Dickens*.

B. Hardy, '*Pickwick Papers*' in Hardy, *The Moral Art of Dickens*.

H. James, 'The Limitations of Dickens' in James, *Views and Reviews* (Boston, Mass., 1908); reprinted in Ford and Lane (edd.), *The Dickens Critics*.

A. Kettle, '*Oliver Twist*' in *An Introduction to the English Novel* (London, 1951); reprinted in Ford and Lane (edd.), *The Dickens Critics*.

F. R. Leavis, '*Dombey and Son*' in Leavis, *Dickens the Novelist*.

—— 'Blake and Dickens: *Little Dorrit*' in Leavis, *Dickens the Novelist*.

J. H. Miller, Introduction to *Oliver Twist* (Rinehart, paperback, New York, 1969).

S. Monod, 'Some Stylistic Devices in *A Tale of Two Cities*' in Partlow (ed.), *Dickens the Craftsman*.

—— 'Dickens' Attitudes in a *A Tale of Two Cities*' in Nisbet (ed.), *NCF* xxiv (1970).

—— '*A Tale of Two Cities*: a French View' in Slater (ed.), *Dickens Memorial Lectures* (paperback, The Dickens Fellowship, London, 1970).

R. Morse, '*Our Mutual Friend*', *Partisan Review*, xvi (1949); reprinted in: Ford and Lane (edd.), *The Dickens Critics*; Clark (ed.), *Discussions of Charles Dickens*; Dyson (ed.), *Dickens*.

J. Moynahan, 'The Hero's Guilt: the Case of *Great Expectations*', *EIC* x (1960); reprinted in Clark (ed.), *Discussions of Charles Dickens*.

G. B. Needham, 'The Undisciplined Heart of David Copperfield', *NCF* ix (1954).

V. S. Pritchett, '*Edwin Drood*' in Pritchett, *The Living Novel* (London, 1946).

J. C. Reid, *The Hidden World of Charles Dickens* (University of Auckland Bulletin no. 61, 1962).

W. W. Robson, 'A Talk about *Nicholas Nickleby*', *Proceedings of the Manchester Scientific and Literary Society*, cx (1968).

M. Slater, 'The Christmas Books', *The Dickensian*, lxv (1969).

—— *The Composition and Monthly Publication of* '*Nicholas Nickleby*' (Scolar Press, paperback, Menston, Yorks., 1973).

D. Sonstroem, 'Fettered Fancy in *Hard Times*', *PMLA* lxxxiv (1969).

M. Spilka, '*David Copperfield* as Psychological Fiction' in Spilka, *Dickens and Kafka* (Bloomington, Ind., 1963).

G. R. Stange, 'Expectations Well Lost: Dickens's Fable for his Time', *College English*, xvi (1954); reprinted in Ford and Lane (edd.), *The Dickens Critics and Clark* (ed.), *Discussions of Charles Dickens*.

—— 'Dickens and the Fiery Past: *A Tale of Two Cities* Reconsidered', *English Journal*, xlvi (1957).

Sir J. F. Stephen, '*A Tale of Two Cities*', *Saturday Review*, 17 December 1859; reprinted in Ford and Lane (edd.), *The Dickens Critics*.

H. Stone, 'The Novel as Fairy Tale: Dickens's *Dombey and Son*', *English Studies*, xlvii (1966).

K. Tillotson, '*Dombey and Son*' in Tillotson, *Novels of the Eighteen-Forties* (London, 1954); reprinted in Dyson (ed.), *Dickens*.

—— '*Oliver Twist*', *Essays and Studies*, n.s. xii (1959).

L. Trilling, '*Little Dorrit*' in Trilling, *The Opposing Self*; reprinted in: Ford and Lane (edd.), *The Dickens Critics*; Clark (ed.), *Discussions of Charles Dickens*; Price (ed.), *Dickens*; Dyson (ed.), *Dickens*.

D. Van Ghent, 'The Dickens World: a View from Todgers's', *SR* lviii (1950); reprinted in Ford and Lane (edd.), *The Dickens Critics*, and Price (ed.), *Dickens*.

A. Y. Wilkinson, '*Bleak House*: from Faraday to Judgment Day', *ELH* xxxiv (1967).

BIOGRAPHIES AND LETTERS

A. A. Adrian, *Georgina Hogarth and the Dickens Circle* (Cambridge, Mass., and London, 1957).

Sir F. Aylmer, *Dickens Incognito* (London, 1959).

W. Dexter (ed.), *Mr. and Mrs. Charles Dickens: his Letters to her* (London, 1935).

—— (ed.), *The Nonesuch Dickens. Letters* (London, 1938).

The Dickensian (London, 1905–).

M. Fido, *Charles Dickens: an Authentic Account of his Life and Times* (London, 1970).

K. J. Fielding, *The Speeches of Charles Dickens* (London, 1960).

—— *Charles Dickens: a Survey* (British Council paperback, London, 1966).

J. Forster, *The Life of Charles Dickens* (London, 1872–4; rev. edn., London, 1876); one-volume edn., ed. by J. W. T. Ley (London, 1928); ed. by A. Hoppé (London, 1966).

M. House and G. Storey (edd.), *Letters of Charles Dickens* (The Pilgrim edition), vol. i (London, 1965); vol. ii (London, 1969); in progress.

E. Johnson, *The Heart of Charles Dickens* (New York, 1952; London [*as Letters from Charles Dickens to Angela Burdett-Coutts 1841–62*], 1953).

—— *Charles Dickens; His Tragedy and Triumph* (New York, 1965).

F. G. Kitton, *Charles Dickens by Pen and Pencil* (London, 1890).

R. Langton, *The Childhood and Youth of Charles Dickens* (Manchester, 1891).

J. W. T. Ley, *The Dickens Circle* (London, 1918).

A. B. Nisbet, *Dickens and Ellen Ternan* (Berkeley and Los Angeles, Calif., 1952).

H. Pearson, *Dickens: his Character, Comedy and Career* (London, 1949).

Dame U. Pope-Hennessy, *Charles Dickens 1812–1870* (London, 1945).

J. B. Priestley, *Charles Dickens: A Pictorial Biography* (London, 1961).

G. Storey, *Dickens and Daughter* (London, 1939).

E. Wagenknecht, *Dickens and the Scandalmongers, Essays in Criticism* (Norman, Okla. 1965).

T. Wright, *The Life of Charles Dickens* (London, 1935).

BIBLIOGRAPHY

P. Calhoun and H. J. Heaney, 'Dickensiana in the Rough', *PBSA* xli (1947).

A. Cohn and K. Denning, 'The Dickens Checklist'. Quarterly in L. Stevenson (ed.), *The Dickens Studies Newsletter* (1970–).

P. A. W. Collins, 'Charles Dickens' in G. Watson (ed.), *NCBEL* iii (1969); separately published as *A Dickens Bibliography*, by The Dickens Fellowship (London, 1970).

J. Don Vann, 'A Checklist of Dickens Criticism, 1963–7' in Lee (ed.), *Studies in the Novel*, i (1969).

J. Gold, *The Stature of Dickens: a Centenary Bibliography* (Toronto, 1971).

F. G. Kitton, *The Novels of Charles Dickens: a Bibliograph and a Sketch* (London, 1897).

—— *The Minor Writings of Charles Dickens. A Bibliography and a Sketch* (London 1900).

L. Lane, jun., 'Dickens Studies 1958–68: an Overview' in Lee (ed.), *Studies in the Novel*.

W. Miller, *The Dickens Student and Collector* (London, 1946; Supplements, Brighton, 1947 and 1953).

A. Nisbet, 'Charles Dickens' in L. Stevenson (ed.), *Victorian Fiction: a Guide to Research* (Cambridge, Mass., 1964).

Victorian Bibliography. Annually in June issue of *Victorian Studies* (Bloomington, Ind., 1958–).

'The Year's Work in Dickens Studies'. Annually in September issue of *The Dickensian* (1968–   ).

BACKGROUND READING

(a) Social history and history of ideas

G. Best, *Mid-Victorian Britain 1851–75* (paperback, London, 1971).

A. Briggs, *Victorian People: A Reassessment of Persons and Themes 1851–67* (London, 1954).

I. Brown, *Dickens in his Time* (London, 1963).

P. A. W. Collins, *Dickens and Education* (London, 1963).

—— *Dickens and Crime* (London, 1964).

R. J. Cruikshank, *Charles Dickens and Early Victorian England* (London, 1949).

J. W. Dodds, *The Age of Paradox. A Biography of England 1841–51* (New York, 1952; London, 1953).

E. J. Halévy, *A History of the English People in the Nineteenth Century* (Paris, 1912–32; English translation by E. I. Watkin and D. A. Barker, London, 1924–34: *England in 1815, The Triumph of Reform,* and *Victorian Years*).

J. F. C. Harrison, *The Early Victorians 1832–51* (paperback, London, 1971).

H. House, *The Dickens World* (London, 1960).

H. L. Sussman, *Victorians and the Machine: The Literary Response to Technology,* (Cambridge, Mass., and London, 1968).

A. Welsh, *The City of Dickens* (London, 1971).

G. M. Young, *Victorian England: Portrait of an Age* (London, 1953).

(b) Literary history

R. D. Altick, *The English Common Reader. A Social History of the Mass Reading Public 1800–1900* (Chicago, 1957).

L. Cazamian, *The Social Novel in England 1830–50,* trans. Fido (London, 1972).

G. K. Chesterton, *The Victorian Age in Literature* (London, 1913).

W. C. Phillips, *Dickens, Reade and Collins: Sensation Novelists* (London, 1919).

P. Coveney, *The Image of Childhood* (paperback, London, 1967).

A. Cruse, *The Victorians and Their Books* (London, 1935).

R. A. Gettmann, *A Victorian Publisher: a Study of the Bentley Papers* (Cambridge, Mass., 1960).

J. Harvey, *Victorian Novelists and their Illustrators* (London, 1970).

K. Hollingsworth, *The Newgate Novel 1830–47* (Detroit, Mich., 1963).

W. L. G. James, *Fiction for the Working Man* (London, 1963).

Q. D. Leavis, 'The Dickens Illustrations: their Function' in F. R. and Q. D. Leavis, *Dickens the Novelist*.

A. Nicoll, *Early Nineteenth Century Drama 1800–50* (vol. iv of *A History of English Drama,* Cambridge, 1955).

M. Praz. *The Hero in Eclipse in Victorian Fiction* (London, 1956).

G. Rowell, *The Victorian Theatre: a Survey* (London, 1956).

M. Steig, 'Dickens, Hablôt Browne and the Tradition of English Caricature', *Criticism* (Summer issue, 1969).

P. Thomson, *The Victorian Heroine: A Changing Ideal 1837–73* (London, 1956).

K. Tillotson, *Novels of the Eighteen-Forties* (London, 1954).

A. Trollope, *Autobiography* (London, 1883).

A. Waugh, *A Hundred Years of Publishing. Being the Story of Chapman and Hall, Ltd.* (London, 1930).

A. Wilson, 'Dickens on Children and Childhood' in Slater (ed.), *Dickens 1970*.

Bradford A. Booth[1]

THE vicissitudes of Anthony Trollope's reputation contribute an interesting page to literary history, but unfortunately much that has been said is in error. For example, Mr. Hugh Sykes Davies, an informed and generally perceptive critic, asserts that Trollope students owe much to Michael Sadleir's admirable biography (1927), for defending and explaining a writer 'who seemed on the very point of slipping into oblivion'. Since I myself have perhaps contributed to the confusion by comparing Trollope's reputation to that of Melville, without precise reference to dates, it might therefore be well to examine the evidence.

For twenty years following Trollope's death in 1882 his work was indeed utterly neglected. The usual explanation of this fall from critical grace is that with the obsolescence of 'Victorianism'—whatever that slippery term may mean—Trollope appeared to represent both a way of life and a literary methodology that were hopelessly *passé*. Furthermore, it is said, the revelations of his *Autobiography*, which disclosed, first, that he repudiated the theory of divine inspiration in art, contending instead that a bit of sealing-wax on one's study-chair is an indispensable element in literary success; and, second, that he was keenly interested in procuring from publishers decent contracts for his work—these stamped him as an egregious Philistine who must, of course, be repudiated by those whose views of art are more ethereal and less prudential.

But a study of publishing records demonstrates that, in point of fact, the neglect of Trollope did not extend nearly as long as has been thought. By 1902 virtually all his work was back in print, including 30 titles published in Amsterdam and a 30-volume Collectors' Edition. From 1902–6 John Lane published a very successful edition of 12 novels, and Dodd, Mead published an edition of 18 novels. In 1912 there were 23 Trollope titles available, and book-lovers could choose among 11 editions of *Barchester Towers* and 8 of *Framley Parson-*

---

[1] Professor Booth died on 1 December, 1968. He would undoubtedly have revised his essay before publication, but it is printed here substantially as he left it. A few details have been silently changed, and a few insertions made (in square brackets), to take account of work on Trollope in the last four years.—Ed.

age. Nor was there any apparent diminution of interest in Trollope during the next fifteen years. When Sadleir's biography was published 23 Trollope titles, again, were in print. For purposes of comparison, in 1968 there were 25 novels available. Clearly, then, Sadleir's study did not call attention to an unknown author or one who was 'on the point of slipping into oblivion'.

The great Trollope revival, however, came in the 1930s and was ratified during the war years when thousands of people, from soldiers at the front and ordinary citizens in bomb-shelters, on the one hand, to General Montgomery and Churchill on the other, testified to the pleasure they found in stressful times in reading the novels of this enchanting writer. By 1950 the Oxford University Press was advertising 35 Trollope titles in its World's Classics series. The history of literature does not appear to contain another novelist so many of whose works have been separately reprinted. Indeed, only five of Trollope's 47 novels have not been republished in the twentieth century (and one of these five appeared in a new edition in 1899). And the end is not in sight. Should you care today to purchase a copy of *The Warden* or *Barchester Towers*, you may choose from among 17 editions in English and a dozen more in different foreign languages. The other Barsetshire novels are available in from five to nine different editions. If some of Trollope's minor novels have been allowed quietly to go out of print in the World's Classics series, there is ample evidence that the major titles are more popular than ever, and that their author remains for thousands of readers one of the most genuinely satisfying of English writers.

There are those who will say that Trollope retains his appeal because he is a soothing writer, that since the society he depicts appears to be pleasantly ordered and structured, with honesty, prudence, and conformity always rewarded, and duplicity and chicanery always brought to book, he confirms the established virtues while turning his face away from all that is disagreeable. It is probably true that some people have responded to Trollope's world in terms of nostalgia for an age outwardly peaceful, where rebellion, still underground, only dimpled placid surfaces. But if Trollope is to endure, it cannot be on these grounds, which derive, in my opinion, from a misreading of his philosophy and of his artistic intent. I believe it can be demonstrated that Trollope *did* question many, if not all, received Victorian values, not merely in the late novels, in which a number of recent critics have seen something approaching despair, but even in the apparently peaceful Barsetshire series, in which relatively innocuous subjects, such as the immorality of clerical sinecures, offer a paradigm of uneasiness and discontent with traditional modes and values.

To turn, finally, from the reactions of general readers to those of formal critics, it is perhaps surprising to note that there is a decided tendency today to credit Trollope with higher seriousness and greater artistry than Dr. Leavis, for example, has found. Close study is revealing behind these deceptively simple novels greater subtlety of mind and more sophisticated literary techniques than had hitherto been suspected. Thus, at any rate, after nearly a century Trollope and his work continue to elicit thoughtful attention.

TEXTS

It is one of the anomalies of literary history that the work of poets and dramatists should be subjected to meticulous textual collation and scrupulous annotation while the work of novelists is reprinted through successive editions with the grossest errors uncorrected,[1] and without the kind of editorial help (the identification of obscure allusions, explanation of contemporary references, historical notes, etc.) which students and general readers need. [Recently Penguins have begun to answer this need with a series of well-annotated and textually competent editions.]

Students who read one Trollope novel will probably choose, or be assigned, *Barchester Towers*. Though recent critics are generally agreed that this is, technically, not Trollope's best work, yet it undoubtedly remains the most typical. As has been seen, the reader looking for a text will be overwhelmed with multiple choices. For reasons of economy he may wish to purchase one of the many paperbacks, yet it should be remembered that for one's permanent library the compact, carefully printed, and well bound World's Classics volumes are an excellent investment. Only a few of them, however, carry an introduction. Most students will probably welcome an edition with a sound critical essay which sets the author in the literary and cultural milieu out of which he emerged and which assesses the novel in the light of changing values.

There are two paperbacks containing both *The Warden* and *Barchester Towers* (Modern Library, edited by H. Hatcher; and Riverside Editions, edited by L. Auchincloss). Since, ideally, a reading of *The Warden* should precede *Barchester Towers*, these volumes are very useful. *The Warden* is available singly in the New American Library

---

[1] It has recently been discovered, for example, that a page and a half of important material which appeared in the serial text of *The Claverings* has been inadvertently omitted from all subsequent editions.

(edited by G. Tillotson) and from the Washington Square Press (edited by B. A. Booth). *Barchester Towers* is found in the New American Library (edited by R. Daniel), in the Washington Square Press series (edited by R. H. Singleton), and in the Rinehart series (edited by B. A. Booth). *Doctor Thorne* is available in the Riverside series (edited by Elizabeth Bowen), but *Framley Parsonage* and *The Small House at Allington*, though appearing without introduction in many editions, are not published with a critical essay. On the other hand, *The Last Chronicle of Barset* appears in three paperbacks with introductions: Penguin (P. Fairclough), Norton (G. W. Brace), and Riverside (A. Mizener). It also appears in the World's Classics with an introduction by B. A. Booth. An expensive but very handsome library set of both the Barsetshire and the Palliser novels, all with introductions, was obtainable from the Oxford University Press. [The Oxford Trollope library set is now out of print, but the Palliser novels from this edition have been reprinted in Oxford Paperbacks.] The Palliser (or Parliamentary) novels consist of *Can You Forgive Her?*, *Phineas Finn*, *The Eustace Diamonds*, *Phineas Redux*, *The Prime Minister*, and *The Duke's Children*. All of these are also available in the World's Classics.

For further reading, I would personally recommend the following novels: *The Belton Estate*, *The Claverings*, *The Vicar of Bullhampton*, *Ayala's Angel*, *Dr. Wortle's School*, *Orley Farm*, *Rachel Ray*, and *The Way We Live Now*. The fact that other critics have compiled other lists merely demonstrates that the level of Trollope's accomplishment is remarkably even.

[For a full list of available editions the reader must consult the latest catalogues of books in print. The major novels are available in many editions. The minor novels are harder to obtain except in World's Classics editions, and some of these editions now have to be bought second-hand.]

CRITICAL STUDIES AND COMMENTARY

I know nothing in literature like the chaos of Trollope criticism. Nobody has called *Martin Chuzzlewit* Dickens's best novel, or *Philip* Thackeray's best, or *Daniel Deronda* George Eliot's best, or *One of Our Conquerors* Meredith's best. Yet there is scarcely a Trollope novel which somebody has not called his best, and somebody else his worst.

How can one account for the fact that *The Bertrams*, which according to Hugh Walpole should be eternally and remorselessly forgotten, had for Harold Laski 'all the magic of the Barchester series', and is to the Stebbinses of all Trollope's novels 'the most modern in tone and the most haunting in mood'. Or why *Castle Richmond*, which to Walpole is one of Trollope's six absolute failures, is to the Stebbinses 'full of anxiety . . . poignant suspense . . . delicate restraint . . . without a misspent word'. Or why *The Belton Estate*, thought by Henry James 'a work written for children . . . a *stupid* book . . . essentially, organically stupid', should be rated by Sadleir as one of Trollope's five greatest books. Or why *The Three Clerks* should be to Walpole 'a very poor novel' and to Beatrice Curtis Brown, who in her critical study devotes more time to it than to any other Trollope novel, a 'lyrical account of innocent young love'.

I have tried to suggest elsewhere the reasons for such diversity of opinion, but basically the significance of Trollope's novels appears to differ as one reader senses and another fails to sense the meaning of his work. It is also perhaps true that some readers, having enjoyed one type of Trollope novel, cannot bring themselves to conceive of his having written another type. They are not prepared, at any rate, to be sympathetic to new perspectives and new values. Henry James, whose 1883 essay on Trollope, later published in *Partial Portraits* (1888), may be said to inaugurate the modern criticism of Trollope, found the Barsetshire series very pleasant but decided that the 'political novels are distinctly dull, and I confess that I have not been able to read them'. One feels that had so perceptive a reader persevered, he would inevitably have discovered subtleties of craftsmanship which no one could appreciate better than he. The same reluctance to meet a new challenge is seen in the response of George Saintsbury to *The Way We Live Now*. In 1920, still writing as a Victorian, Saintsbury found this novel a 'dreary book'. He was the last writer to render such a blinkered judgement.

It should be noted that though James is not infallible on Trollope, having been put off by Trollope's unfortunate penchant for playing the intrusive author, he was one of the first to grasp Trollope's happy, instinctive perception of human varieties. Trollope's apprehension of the real, James felt, makes him one of the most trustworthy of the writers 'who have helped the heart of man to know itself'.

Sadleir's *Commentary*, referred to above, demands a further word here. In praising Trollope's 'profound understanding of ordinary life' Sadleir properly identifies the nature of Trollope's genius. But in describing Trollope as 'the supreme novelist of acquiescence' Sadleir makes an assumption that most critics would now resist. As Donald Smalley has pointed out, there is little acquiescence in *The Way We Live Now*, that 'sour and pitiless picture of a sordid scene', as Sadleir himself described it. To find acquiescence even in *The Warden* is, surely, not to read that little masterpiece very perceptively. Sadleir taught people to examine Trollope thoughtfully, however, and thus his book has not lost its currency.

Hugh Walpole's *Trollope* (1928) is written with the verve and bounce for which that writer is noted, but it is carelessly thrown together and is critically disappointing. Trollope gives us 'wonderful true pictures of a section of human life', Walpole admits, but his work lacks universality and poetical mysticism. The novels do not 'challenge the whole general material and spiritual world in the conduct of a single character'. We are made vastly wiser about Barsetshire 'but only a little wiser about ourselves'. It is perhaps possible to support such arguments, but Walpole contents himself with assertions.

The next major Trollope study, that of the Stebbinses (1945), is noted below under BIOGRAPHIES AND LETTERS. Students may wish, however, to look at another publication of the same year, Elizabeth Bowen's *Anthony Trollope: A New Judgment*. This charming *jeu d'esprit* is cast in the form of two dialogues: between a sensitive soldier and his stiffish uncle, who dislikes Trollope, and between the young man and the ghost of Trollope himself. The soldier, seeking the source of Trollope's appeal to war-weary readers, finds it in Trollope's love of the ordinary.

Beatrice Curtis Brown's *Trollope* (1950), a monograph in the English Novelists Series, is slight, and rather idiosyncratic but often quite perceptive. Miss Curtis Brown regards Trollope as 'the perfect bed-book writer', and contends that the Barsetshire novels do not have 'the stature of . . . the political novels. . . . They deal with what concerns the human day; but these others with what concerns human life'. *Barchester Towers*, she shrewdly observes, is 'one of the books most entertaining to read, yet one of the less deeply interesting —it makes a shallower impact on the mind although it undoubtedly makes a lasting impact on the memory'.

A. O. J. Cockshut's *Anthony Trollope: A Critical Study* (1955) is thoughtful and informed, an important book. Though the author devotes his attention chiefly to the novels of Trollope's later years, especially *The Way We Live Now*, he develops a challenging overview of Trollope's career and accomplishment. Like the Stebbinses, he holds that Trollope's life was one long 'progress to pessimism', that the novels from 1867 reveal each 'a further stage in the steepening curve of the author's pessimism', and that as we watch Trollope we see 'the gradual darkening of his imagination and failure of his hopes'.

This interpretation of Trollope and his work is rejected in Bradford A. Booth's *Anthony Trollope: Aspects of His Life and Art* (1958). It is argued here that Trollope, like Dickens, no doubt changed with the times, but that 'progress to pessimism' is seriously misleading as an explanation of his literary life. *The New Zealander*, a general survey of Victorian England dating from the outset of Trollope's career [but not published until 1972], is a savage indictment of English political and social life. *The Two Heroines of Plumplington*, a Barsetshire novelette dating from his last years, could not be more lighthearted; and nothing could be more gloriously optimistic than the passage in the *Autobiography* which explains how the social philosophy of *The Way We Live Now* should be interpreted.

The vagaries of Trollope criticism are neatly illustrated by the fact that in his valuable little monograph *Trollope* (1960) in the Writers and Their Work series Hugh Sykes Davies asserts that, beyond the Barsetshire and Palliser groups, one of Trollope's two best novels is *The Claverings*, a title which Miss Brown does not even mention. Beyond recommending some unfamiliar novels Mr. Sykes Davies deserves our thanks for two welcome admonitions: first, that we should not mistake Trollope's realism for photography, missing the unostentatious imagination which has shaped scene and character; and secondly, that we should not allow the uniformity and directness of Trollope's style to render us insensitive to its subtleties.

In a recent full-length study, Robert J. Polhemus's *The Changing World of Anthony Trollope* (1968), it is argued that Trollope perceived of change as the dominant characteristic of his age and that he imaginatively chronicled in his novels the forms and facts of historical, social, and psychological change. This may be. Less persuasive are Mr. Polhemus's contentions that Trollope's failure to deal with the Jamesian 'fine consciousness' is part of the inherent anti-élitist, democratic thrust of his work, and that his 'commonplace use of language' is part of a 'rhetorical attempt to convince readers that he is giving them unvarnished reality'. [Trollope's stance as artist and moralist has been discussed by Ruth apRoberts (1971), and David Skilton has placed Trollope in the context of his time in *Trollope and His Contemporaries* (1972).]

Turning to briefer studies. Paul Elmer More's long essay on Trollope in *The Demon of the Absolute* (1929) rings today with deep Victorian overtones, but it is not without interest in terms of the current debate on Trollope's reading of life. Chiding Sadleir for underemphasizing Trollope's commitment to ethics, More contends that the most pervasive element in the novels is religion. Furthermore, he asserts, Trollope is a bracing antidote to the 'futilitarians', because to him pre-eminently 'life presented itself as a game worth the candles'.

Historians of the 1930s approached Trollope with a good deal of ambivalence. In his *Early Victorian Novelists* (1935) Lord David Cecil tells us that Trollope is not in the highest degree imaginative, his stories are ill-constructed, his style pedestrian—but he has the saving grace of humour. He makes us laugh. Ernest Baker in his massive history of the novel (vol. viii, 1937) finds that in Trollope's hands the art of fiction stood still, but his novels are 'a lucid, undistorting mirror for a wide span of the social life of his day'.

Enthusiasm for Trollope during the war years culminated in the publication of a new journal *The Trollopian*, subsequently continued as *Nineteenth Century Fiction*. Over the past two decades more than a score of Trollope studies, some of them of lasting interest, have appeared in this journal, which should be carefully examined by Trollope students. The enthusiasm of the 1940s is also exemplified on a level of considerable knowledge and critical sophistication in C. B. Tinker's 1947 essay in the *Yale Review*. Tinker not only accepts Trollope in his role as intrusive author but defends the chatty editorial aside as preserving a genial relationship between author and reader.

Since 1950 there has been a significant tendency to base the enthusiasm for Trollope less on his gifts for humour and for whimsical characterization than on an increased awareness of his artistry and craftsmanship. Joseph E. Baker's 1954 *College English* essay 'Trollope's Third Dimension' claims for Trollope 'great artistry' in suggesting more about a social situation than is explicit in a scene. In 'Anthony Trollope: The Palliser Novels' (published in *From Jane Austen to Joseph Conrad*, 1958) Arthur Mizener finds 'delicacy in ironic balance' (a critical conjure-phrase) at the centre of Trollope's skills. Trollope had 'little interest in the delicate cabinet-making which fascinates artificers of the well-made novel', and thus he is subject to some abuse, but his imagination was rich and varied. Jerome Thale in 'The Problem of Structure in Trollope' (*NCF*, 1960) finds considerably more organizational subtlety in the novels than most critics have suspected. The sense of form to which Trollope built involves an intricate pattern of 'parallels, contrasts, repetitions, and slight variations'. Trollope's sense of design, it would appear, involves playing variations on a theme. In the same journal (1960) Audrey L. Laski under the title 'Myths of Character: An Aspect of the Novel' examines Trollope's developing conception of the Dukes of Omnium, discovering, as Trollope himself hoped, the artfully expanding characterizations through the political novels.

One of the major issues of Trollope criticism is interestingly posed by an exchange of points of view in the pages of *PMLA*. In 'Thematic Alternation in Trollope' (1962) John E. Dustin, while admitting 'unsuspected profundities' in some of the late novels, contends that Trollope's range is cripplingly limited to two subjects: family hostilities generated by problems of inheritance, entail, and disputed wills; and the career of a bright young man of the city who commits an error of moral judgement and is made to suffer. William Cadbury replied (1963) in 'Shape and Theme: Determinants of Trollope's Forms', claiming that Dustin 'ignores the effective totality of each novel', which 'is a function of the *importance* of origins of conflict to the development of the whole action: the number, complexity, and relatedness of the various plots; and the nature, significance, and extent of the world presented'.

Noting a variety of responses to Trollope's style, David Aitken in ' "A Kind of Felicity": Some Notes about Trollope's Style' (1966) attempts to determine whether certain Trollopian subtleties are evidence of self-conscious artistry or of the instinctive finesse of a practised craftsman. He concludes that though Trollope paused to give a Macaulayan polish and balance to certain key passages, it served him normally to write *currente calamo*.

Two articles which touch, in different ways, on Trollope's relation to his age, may be highly recommended. Asa Briggs's 'Trollope, Bagehot and the English Constitution' (*Cambridge Journal*, 1952; reprinted in Briggs's *Victorian People*, 1954) provides insights both of Trollope's politics and of his understanding of Victorian England. Seymour Betsky's 'Society in Thackeray and Trollope' (in *From Dickens to Hardy*, 1958) is a very rewarding essay—an incisive and knowledgeable examination of Trollope's portrait of his age. These articles, in brief compass, are more compelling than is John Hazard Wildman's earlier monograph *Anthony Trollope's England* (1940). It is relevant here to mention John Hagan's 'The Divided Mind of Anthony Trollope' (1959), in which it is contended that despite a generally clear-eyed view of society Trollope exhibits 'unconscious, unarticulated perplexities'. These are particularly evident in his treatment of marriage and social advancement, where he is caught between his innate social conservatism and his emotional commitment to real value.

Turning to studies of individual novels, it is of significance that *The Warden*, long considered a mere antechapel before the cathedral of *Barchester Towers*, is now recognized as a structure claiming recognition on its own merits of beautiful simplicity. As such, it has provoked more recent discussion than any other Trollope novel. Maude Houston in 'Structure and Plot in *The Warden*' (1955) contends that the structural skills which went into this novel have been seriously underestimated, and she argues that plot *was* important for Trollope. In an excellent essay 'Mr. Harding's Church Music' Sherman Hawkins (1962) explores the wide variety of techniques (from personal allusions, parodies, and Augustan mock-heroics to 'the symbols, allegories, and myths so dear to contemporary novelists') which Trollope employs. Mr. Hawkins finds in Septimus Harding much of the 'tenderness, the need of affection, the shyness and melancholy which Trollope's bearish manner and aggressive practicality concealed'. M. A. Goldberg in 'Trollope's *The Warden*: A Commentary on the "Age of Equipoise" ' (1963) declares that in this first Barsetshire novel Trollope captured the spirit of the 1850s: peace, quietude, equipoise, stability, compromise. These qualities, of course, constitute the ethos of Mr. Harding. In this connection it might be remarked that B. A. Booth in his introduction to the novel rebuts Frank O'Connor, who called Mr. Harding a mere 'prototype'. Of considerable interest to recent investigators is the factual basis of ecclesiastical sinecures which suggested to Trollope his story. In 'Dickens and the Origin of *The Warden*' (1947) Lionel Stevenson traces the germ of the novel to an article on the Charterhouse in *Household Words*. Ralph Arnold surveys a relevant clerical scandal in *The Whiston Matter* (1961), G. A. Best adds significant material in 'The Road to Hiram's Hospital' (1961), R. B. Martin in *Enter Rumour* (1962) chronicles fully the story of St. Cross Hospital, and, finally, Carol Ganzel in 'The *Times* Correspondent and *The Warden*' (1967) believes that the theme of *The Warden* was suggested by a series of letters on simony in the parish of St. Ervan's, Cornwall, contributed to *The Times* by Sidney Godolphin Osborne, the newspaper correspondent whose 1849 letters to *The Times* on Ireland had been answered by Trollope in the *Examiner*. This theory squares with Trollope's own account, as related by T. H. S. Escott. The importance of the Osborne letters lies in the fact that the dilemma of Mr. Harding and much of the character of John Bold may be found in the St. Ervan's affair.

Barchester Towers, not unexpectedly, continues to provoke interest. In 'Character and the Mock Heroic in *Barchester Towers*' (1964) William Cadbury demonstrates that Trollope's usual attempt to present character in the round is subordinated to the presentation of a unified world. In this novel we see as a whole the social world which the characters form. Trollope adopts a variety of techniques to keep the reader distanced from both characters and action since the panoramic novel is fragmented by a too great illusion of reality. W. David Shaw in 'Moral Drama in *Barchester Towers*' (1964) suggests that Trollope overcomes Kirkegaard's 'Either–Or' dilemma by giving the social definition of the moral drama two different forms: metaphors of situation, and a stylistic rendering of comically mannered or theatrical speech. By his self-amused intrusions Trollope 'achieves a species of dramatic irony that is so bland and dry that we may almost miss its artistry'.

Two other novels which have generated recent discussion are *Orley Farm* and *The American Senator*. Robert M. Adams in '*Orley Farm* and Real Fiction' (1953) argues that though this novel is one of Trollope's four greatest, it fails because of the author's indecision. He did not work out his problem to a conclusion but pretended that it could be solved 'with a catchword and a betrothal'. Similarly, in '*Orley Farm*: Artistry manqué' (1958), B. A. Booth finds *Orley Farm* 'one of Trollope's richest and most satisfying books', but it fails to achieve indisputable distinction both because Trollope had no consistent view of Lady Mason and because there is no greatness in her. Her strength is exerted in support of a morally indefensible position.

For obvious reasons *The American Senator* has been of more than passing interest to critics in the United States. In 'Trollope Illustrates the Distinction' (1949) John Hazard Wildman describes how, through some of the best nineteenth-century caricatures, Trollope demonstrates the rigid differences between two seemingly similar nations. David Stryker pursues the same subject in 'The Significance of Trollope's American Senator' (1950), pointing out the relationship between the novel and Trollope's own experiences as described in *North America*. The most thoughtful treatment, however, is found in Edgar F. Harden's 'The Alien Voice: Trollope's Western Senator' (1966). Mr. Harden, placing the novel in the tradition of satire, concludes that Trollope is not writing about America or England but about the gulfs of separateness between human beings—neighbours, different classes, clergy and parish, member and constituency, army and nation, wooer and wooed, husband and wife, family and heir, host and guest, and diplomats.

Two articles on *The Way We Live Now* demand attention. Sabine Nathan in 'Anthony Trollope's Perception of the Way We Live Now' (1962) contends that *The Way We Live Now* was conceived out of Trollope's realization that his own world-outlook, corresponding to that of the early manufacturers, was no longer valid. The novel brilliantly describes the clash of two ideologies. Because Trollope was personally involved he brought to bear on his material an interested perception and was able to create a work of art. In 'Melmotte's Death: A Prism of Meaning in *The Way We Live Now*' (1967) Roger L. Slakey points out that Trollope's novels frequently turn on a misinterpretation of language. *The Way We Live Now* is Trollope's most powerful handling of a separation between meaning and language. In it language exists without reference to proper meaning, and people are at the mercy of words. Melmotte's death is, in part, a prism through which Trollope examines the meaning of a word.

Finally, in 'The Uses of the Village: Form and Theme in *The Vicar of Bullhampton*' (1963) William Cadbury argues that this novel is concerned with an analysis of right and wrong, and suspense is derived from one's perception of the emerging pattern of ethics. *The Vicar of Bullhampton* is not a completely satisfying novel, because the narrowness of its perspective reduces the effect of real life, but it does present with great insight Trollope's view of the importance of charity.

During the early decades of the twentieth century Trollope was more widely read than we have been led to believe, but it is true that his work did not stimulate much critical attention. His self-deprecating evaluation of his novels as entertainment and homily was accepted without serious question. Today the art of his major work is being closely examined, and studies exist of minor novels of which it is not possible to speak in this brief chapter. Trollope's position among major writers of English fiction would appear to be secure.

BIOGRAPHIES AND LETTERS

Trollope has never proved an attractive subject to biographers. He was no Byron. The only elements of general interest in his life story are his transformation from black sheep of the family to noted author and distinguished citizen of the realm, and the incredible capacity for work which enabled him for most of his life to carry on simultaneously two professions. 'A poor clerk', said postal officials of young Trollope, but before he died the service was proud to count him one of its most distinguished members. The difficulty for the modern biographer is that in telling this story he has been anticipated by Trollope himself, whose *Autobiography* has not been out of print in this century. When in 1913 T. H. S. Escott published the first biography, he defined his limited purpose in the title: *Anthony Trollope: His Public Services, Private Friends, and Literary Originals*. His emphasis is on those aspects of Trollope's life which the autobiographer had understandably scanted. But Escott was a journalist, not a critic, and the task of writing the first significant biography fell to Michael Sadleir.

Sadleir, a publisher, novelist, and trained bibliographer, subtitled his Trollope study 'a commentary', signifying thereby his varied biographical and critical purposes and the general rather than specific nature of his approach. Sensitive, thorough, judicious, a master of narrative, Sadleir created a sympathetic portrait of Trollope and, more importantly, persuaded critics to take seriously a novelist whose works they were accustomed to read as, in Graham Greene's nomenclature, 'entertainments'. That Trollope and Sadleir are words immediately associated is entirely understandable, for Sadleir, if he cannot be said to have rescued Trollope from oblivion, nevertheless established him critically as one of the half-dozen major Victorian novelists. One measure of the esteem in which the study is held is that it is still available in hard cover and has recently been reissued in paperback.

In *The Trollopes* (1945) Lucy P. Stebbins and her son Richard gave a lively narrative of a whole clan of novelists (including Anthony's mother, brother, and sister-in-law), but focused, quite naturally, on Anthony. Unfortunately, the Stebbinses are far more successful with the minor Trollopes, who do not call for 'in-depth' treatment, than with Anthony. Critics who know Trollope best have been in fairly common agreement that the Stebbinses' thesis is unconvincing. The Stebbinses, leaning heavily on popular Freudianism, contend that Trollope became 'champion' of his inept father, was jealous of his mother's literary success, and resented the favouritism shown his elder brother. This resulted in tensions which drove him into inordinate ambition, paroxysms of overwork, and the development of a desperate materialism. As he succeeded, he failed; the shadows deepened, and he ultimately fell victim to complete 'Disillusionment' as they title a key chapter. [The biography by James Pope Hennessy (1972), while not breaking new scholarly ground, is the most comprehensive of recent treatments and contains extensive criticism of the novels.]

Neither Trollope's *Autobiography* nor, more significantly, the large selection of *Letters* edited by B. A. Booth (1952) supports the Stebbinses' interpretation of his life and character. Whatever face a man may turn to the world in his public stance, it is in his private letters, as Newman remarked, that we may see him plainly. Most of the surviving Trollope letters are of a business nature, and the collection is therefore in many ways disappointing. But the letters to members of his family, particularly the large group to his son Henry, display none of the ennui, the cynicism, the disillusionment which the Stebbinses and one or two other recent critics find in his last years. Despite a certain brusqueness of manner, by which he attempted to cover up an essential shyness, Trollope reveals himself in his letters to have been no maladjusted victim of despair but an ardent, and even at times naïve, celebrant of the British establishment.

BIBLIOGRAPHIES

Michael Sadleir, Trollope's biographer, is also his bibliographer. In 1922 Sadleir made Trollope the centre of his *Excursions in Victorian Bibliography*, a treatment of eight novelists, and then in 1928 he expanded a section of the earlier work into *Trollope: A Bibliography*. This constitutes not only the definitive bibliography of Trollope but is one of the landmarks of the scientific description of Victorian books. As a historian of publishing practices and procedures, he established norms for the identification of states, variants, and Victorian binding styles. These he further refined for *XIX Century Fiction*, the monumental two-volume catalogue of his own incomparable collection. The Trollope *Bibliography* is currently in print both in England and in the United States.

The student will find several other books helpful in various ways. Mary Leslie Irwin's *Anthony Trollope: A Bibliography* (1926) has, of course, been superseded by Sadleir, but it still remains useful for its listing of early reviews of Trollope's work. In this connection it is appropriate to mention Donald Smalley's *Trollope* in the Critical Heritage Series (1969), a volume which reprints significant reviews and other early commentary on Trollope's work. Students will be well advised, further, to consult the *NCBEL* which lists both Trollope's writings and the most important critical commentary up to 1966. The relevant annual bibliographies, containing items not always found in the *CBEL*, are those published in *PMLA* and in *VS*.

BACKGROUND READING

It is often said of Trollope that he is the brightest of all reflectors of mid-Victorian life. Obviously, the extent to which this is true can be measured only by those who bring to the reading of his novels a sound knowledge of all aspects of a complex age. Fortunately, there are a number of excellent studies of Victorian social and intellectual history. Against these Trollope's work becomes more meaningful and our appreciation of his accomplishment better informed.

The standard social history is probably G. M. Trevelyan's *Illustrated English Social History*, (1952). Lighter and less formal are E. F.

Benson, *As We Were: A Victorian Peep Show* (1932), Esmé Wingfield-Stratford, *Those Earnest Victorians* (1935), and Peter Quennell, *Victorian Panorama* (1937). Specialized approaches to social life that will sharpen one's appreciation of Trollope are provided by Ralph Henry Nevill in *English Country House Life* (1925) and by Ralph Dutton in *The Victorian Home* (1954). Useful information on the setting of many Trollope novels is found in Joseph Henry Wade's *Cathedral Cities of England and Wales* (1924). The problems of class distinction, on which so many Trollope novels turn, are discussed in Tom Hatherley Pears's *English Social Differences* (1955). The broad view of Victorian life is provided in *Early Victorian England* (edited by G. M. Young, 1934).

A standard text in the history of ideas for this period is D. C. Somervell's *English Thought in the Nineteenth Century* (1947), and a valuable adjunct volume is that published by the BBC in 1949 under the title *Ideas and Beliefs of the Victorians*. E. L. Woodward's *The Age of Reform 1815–1870* (1938) describes the Victorian devotion to causes, and C. R. Fay's *Life and Labour in the Nineteenth Century* (4th edn, 1951) offers a useful insight into working conditions in the period. All of these are helpful in the interpretation of Trollope's social perspective.

Students interested in the religious backgrounds to Trollope's novels will find very useful Ford K. Ford's *Fathers of the Victorians: The Age of Wilberforce* (1962), a study of the Evangelicals. Of broader scope is A. O. J. Cockshut's *Anglican Attitudes: A Study of Victorian Religious Controversies* (1959), and additionally recommended is the symposium volume *1859: Entering an Age of Crisis* (1959). Though Trollope was no philosopher, his work is not unmarked by the philosophic currents of his time. Henry David Aiken's *The Age of Ideology: The Nineteenth Century Philosophers* (1957) is very helpful for an understanding of them. Virtually all aspects of this complex age are helpfully sketched in Walter Houghton's *The Victorian Frame of Mind 1830–1870* (1957).

Very little that was significant in his age escaped Trollope's keen eye and alert intelligence. Those who, by wide reading, know the period well will best appreciate his importance as social historian.

REFERENCES

TEXTS

(a) Collected works

There is no complete edition of all Trollope's novels. The following are the most extensive editions:

F. Harrison (ed.), *Barsetshire Novels* (8 vols., London, 1906, 1923, 1928).

Oxford World's Classics (36 vols., London, 1907–).

M. Sadleir (ed.), *Barchester Novels* (Shakespeare Head, 14 vols., Oxford, 1929).

—— and F. Page (edd.), *Oxford Illustrated Trollope* (15 vols., London, 1948–54; never completed).

(b) Separate works

[Each year sees new editions of Trollope's works published, and other editions going out of print. Editions which Professor Booth considered specially worthy of note are mentioned above, pp. 202–3. For a full list the reader must consult the latest catalogues of books in print.]

CRITICAL STUDIES AND COMMENTARY

R. M. Adams, 'Orley Farm and Real Fiction', *NCF* viii (1953).

D. Aitken, ' "A Kind of Felicity": Some Notes about Trollope's Style', *NCF* xx (1966).

Ruth apRoberts, *Trollope: Artist and Moralist* (London, 1971); published in the U.S. as *The Moral Trollope* (Athens, Ohio, 1971).

R. Arnold, *The Whiston Matter* (London, 1961).

E. Baker, *A History of the English Novel*, viii (London, 1937).

J. E. Baker, 'Trollope's Third Dimension', *College English* xvi (1954).

G. F. A. Best, 'The Road to Hiram's Hospital', *VS* v (1961).

S. Betsky, 'Society in Thackeray and Trollope', in Boris Ford (ed.), *From Dickens to Hardy* (Baltimore, Md., 1958).

B. A. Booth, *Anthony Trollope: Aspects of His Life and Art* (Bloomington, Ind., 1958).

—— 'Orley Farm: Artistry Manqué', in R. C. Rathburn and M. Steinmann (edd.), *From Jane Austen to Joseph Conrad* (Oxford, 1958).

E. Bowen, *Anthony Trollope: A New Judgment* (Oxford, 1945).

A. Briggs 'Trollope, Bagehot and the English Constitution', *Cambridge Journal* v (1952); reprinted in Briggs's *Victorian People* (London, 1954).

B. C. Brown, *Trollope* (London, 1950).

W. Cadbury, 'Shape and Theme: Determinants of Trollope's Forms', *PMLA* lxxviii (1963).

—— 'Form and Theme in *The Vicar of Bullhampton*', *NCF* xviii (1963).

—— 'Character and the Mock Heroic in *Barchester Towers*', *TSLL* v (1964).

Lord D. Cecil, *Early Victorian Novelists* (London, 1935).

A. O. J. Cockshut, *Anthony Trollope: A Critical Study* (London, 1955).

H. S. Davies, *Trollope* (London, 1960).

J. E. Dustin, 'Thematic Alternation in Trollope', *PMLA* lxxviii (1962).

Carol Ganzel, 'The *Times* Correspondent and *The Warden*', *NCF* xxi (1967).

M. A. Goldberg, 'Trollope's *The Warden*: A Commentary on the "Age of Equipoise" ', *NCF* xvii (1963).

J. Hagan, 'The Divided Mind of Anthony Trollope', *NCF* xiv (1959).

E. F. Harden, 'The Alien Voice: Trollope's Western Senator', *TSLL* viii (1966).

S. Hawkins, 'Mr. Harding's Church Music', *ELH* xxix (1962).

M. Houston, 'Structure and Plot in *The Warden*', *University of Texas Studies in English* xxxiv (1955).

H. James, 'Trollope', in his *Partial Portraits* (1888).

A. L. Laski, 'Myths of Character: An Aspect of the Novel', *NCF* xiv (1960).

R. B. Martin, *Enter Rumour* (New York, 1962).

A. Mizener, 'Anthony Trollope: The Palliser Novels', in R. C. Rathburn and M. Steinmann (edd.), *From Jane Austen to Joseph Conrad* (New York, 1958).

P. E. More, 'My Debt to Trollope', in *The Demon of the Absolute* (Princeton, N.J., 1928).

S. Nathan, 'Anthony Trollope's Perception of the Way We Live Now', *Zeitschrift für Anglistik* x (1962).

R. J. Polhemus, *The Changing World of Anthony Trollope* (Berkeley and Los Angeles, Calif., 1968).

J. Pope Hennessy, *Anthony Trollope* (London, 1971; New York, 1972).

M. Sadleir, *Trollope: A Commentary* (London, 1927).

G. Saintsbury, 'Trollope Revisited', in *Essays and Studies* (London, 1920).

W. D. Shaw, 'Moral Drama in *Barchester Towers*', *NCF* xix (1964).

D. Skilton, *Anthony Trollope and his Contemporaries* (London, 1972).

R. L. Slakey, 'Melmotte's Death: A Prism of Meaning in *The Way We Live Now*', *ELH* xxxiv (1967).

L. and R. Stebbins, *The Trollopes* (New York, 1945).

L. Stevenson, 'Dickens and the Origin of *The Warden*', *NCF* xvii (1947).

D. Stryker, 'The Significance of Trollope's *American Senator*', *NCF* v (1950).

J. Thale, 'The Problem of Structure in Trollope', *NCF* xv (1960).

C. B. Tinker, 'Trollope', *Yale Review* xxxvi (1947).

The Trollopian, 1945 *et seq.* Continued as *Nineteenth Century Fiction* (*NCF*).

H. Walpole, *Trollope* (London, 1928).

J. H. Wildman, *Anthony Trollope's England* (Providence, R.I., 1940).

—— 'Trollope Illustrates the Distinction', *NCF* iv (1949).

BIOGRAPHY AND LETTERS

B. A. Booth (ed.), *The Letters of Anthony Trollope* (Oxford and New York, 1952).

T. H. S. Escott, *Anthony Trollope: His Public Services, Private Friends, and Literary Originals* (London, 1913).

M. Sadleir, *Trollope: A Commentary* (London, 1927).
L. and R. Stebbins, *The Trollopes* (New York, 1945).

BIBLIOGRAPHIES

M. L. Irwin, *Anthony Trollope: A Bibliography* (New York, 1926).
M. Sadleir, *Excursions in Victorian Bibliography* (London, 1922).
—— *Trollope: A Bibliography* (London, 1928).
D. Smalley, 'Trollope', in L. Stevenson (ed.), *Victorian Fiction: A Guide to Research* (Cambridge, Mass., 1964).
—— (ed.), *Trollope: The Critical Heritage* (London, 1969).

BACKGROUND READING

H. D. Aiken, *The Age of Ideology: The Nineteenth Century Philosophers* (London, 1957).
P. Appleman, W. A. Madden, M. Wolff (edd.), *1859: Entering an Age of Crisis* (Bloomington, Ind., 1959).
E. F. Benson, *As We Were: A Victorian Peep Show* (London, 1932).
A. O. J. Cockshut, *Anglican Attitudes: A Study of Victorian Religious Controversies* (London, 1959).
R. Dutton, *The Victorian Home* (London, 1954).
C. R. Fay, *Life and Labour in the Nineteenth Century* (4th edn., London, 1951).
F. K. Ford, *Fathers of the Victorians: The Age of Wilberforce* (London, 1962).
W. Houghton, *The Victorian Frame of Mind 1830–1870* (New Haven, Conn., 1957).
Ideas and Beliefs of the Victorians (BBC, London, 1949).
R. H. Nevill, *English Country House Life* (London, 1925).
T. H. Pears, *English Social Differences* (London, 1955).
P. Quennell, *Victorian Panorama* (London, 1937).
D. C. Somervell, *English Thought in the Nineteenth Century* (London, 1947).
G. M. Trevelyan, *Illustrated English Social History*, iv (London, 1952).
J. H. Wade, *Cathedral Cities of England and Wales* (London, 1924).
E. Wingfield-Stratford, *Those Earnest Victorians* (London, 1935).
E. L. Woodward, *The Age of Reform 1815–1870* (London, 1938).
G. M. Young (ed.), *Early Victorian England* (Oxford, 1934).

13 · THE BRONTËS
Charlotte Brontë 1816–1855
Emily Brontë 1818–1848
Anne Brontë 1820–1849

Miriam Allott

THE Brontë sisters published pseudonymously between them during their lifetimes one volume of selected poems and six novels: *Poems by Currer, Ellis and Acton Bell* (1846); *Jane Eyre* (1847), *Shirley* (1849), and *Villette* (1853) by Charlotte Brontë ('Currer Bell'); *Wuthering Heights* (1847) by Emily Brontë ('Ellis Bell'); and *Agnes Grey* (1847) and *The Tenant of Wildfell Hall* (1848) by Anne Brontë ('Acton Bell'). Charlotte Brontë's *The Professor* (written *c.* 1845–6) was published posthumously in 1857, the author once more appearing pseudonymously as 'Currer Bell'. Other Brontë material to have appeared since then includes their letters and remaining poems; various juvenilia written by Charlotte and her brother Branwell, from their childhood to their early maturity, as chronicles of their imaginary realm, Angria; the handful of exercises written by Charlotte and Emily for their Brussels teacher, M. Heger; a fragment of a new novel by Charlotte; and the moving birthday 'diary-papers' in which Emily and Anne set down what they thought the future might have in store for them. The total amount of work is not large and students can readily familiarize themselves with all of it. The same cannot be said of studies of the Brontës. The list of books and commentaries in the section on the Brontës in the *CBEL* (*The Nineteenth Century*, 1969 edn.) occupies some six columns in small print; of these the first three columns cover most of the important studies written before 1940, while the remaining three represent the vast proliferation of Brontë criticism and commentary which has since taken place, one of the most noticeable features here being the weight of attention now centred on Emily at the expense of her sister Charlotte.

General interest in the Brontës on the part of the reading public was already firmly established by 1899, when Mrs. Humphry Ward —who is still one of our best guides to their work—was preparing her introductory essays for the Haworth Edition of their novels. 'Judging by the books that have been written or read in recent years,' wrote

Mrs. Ward in her preface to *Jane Eyre*, 'by the common verdict as to the Brontë sisters, their story and their work, which prevails almost without exception, in the literary criticism of the present day; by the tone of personal tenderness, even of passionate homage, in which many writers speak of Charlotte and Emily; and by the increasing recognition which their books have obtained abroad, one may say with some confidence that the name and memory of the Brontës were never more alive than now . . . and that Charlotte and Emily Brontë are no less secure . . . than Jane Austen or George Eliot or Mrs. Browning of literary recollection.' This interest, first stimulated by the immediate and dramatic success of *Jane Eyre* in October 1847 and reinvigorated by 'Currer Bell's' prefatory remarks about her dead sisters in the 1850 one-volume edition of *Wuthering Heights* and *Agnes Grey*, began to flourish more vigorously still with the appearance in 1857 of Mrs. Gaskell's remarkable *Life of Charlotte Brontë*, and from then on there is continuous evidence of the fascination which the Brontë story held for the nineteenth-century reader.

Such fascination, which of course is still felt by many people today, has in some respects done the Brontës a critical disservice. The engrossing circumstances of their lives—impoverished, shadowed with fatal disease, and restricted in almost everything except passionate imagination and intensity of feeling—and the vividness with which these circumstances throw into relief the mysterious working of creative genius have again and again in the past drawn attention away from the writings to concentrate it on the writers, and especially on the gathering together of every detail of their day-to-day experiences. In the forty years between the publication of Mrs. Gaskell's *Life* and that of Mrs. Ward's critical introductions, several notable Victorians—George Henry Lewes, William Roscoe, Swinburne, and Leslie Stephen among them—attempted in various essays to look at their work critically and to understand its nature, but the full length studies of the period, together with a great many more shorter pieces, show the strong pull of biographical interest and speculation. It is in these years that the Brontë legends begin to grow, and also that the tradition is established which makes biographical study of the Brontës preponderantly the province of the enthusiastic if not always accurate amateur.

The founding of the Brontë Society in the 1890s, the setting up of a Brontë Museum in Haworth Parsonage (the Brontës' Yorkshire home near Keighley), and the regular publications from 1895 onwards of the Brontë Society have had generally speaking the effect of fostering this kind of enthusiasm. The indebtedness of students of the Brontës to the Society cannot easily be measured (early numbers of the *Transactions* carried some of the first attempts to assemble useful biographical information, and there have been numerous valuable contributions since that time), but it must also be said that many addresses delivered to the Society over the years—some of them by distinguished scholars and critics—and subsequently published in the *Transactions*, are obviously hampered by the need to steer an uneasy course between scholarly accuracy and popular appeal. Serious students of the Brontës might now welcome a tighter editorial control over the documentation of material published in the *Transactions*.

In fact a want of systematically ordered, reliable information, especially about textual matters and source materials, still shadows Brontë studies to this day, this in spite of the emphasis on concentrated critical analysis of theme, structure, and texture in the novels, which began to be generally felt in the 1940s, and to which *Wuthering Heights* in particular has so readily lent itself. Although a steady stream of critical essays and studies continues to come from the publishers and to fill with oppressive regularity the pages of literary journals, we still have no completely reliable edition of either the letters or the novels; one of the few modern attempts so far at a scholarly edition of any work by the Brontës is C. W. Hatfield's *The Complete Poems of Emily Brontë* (1941). Some of these omissions are at last slowly being made good: a critical text of the novels is proposed in a new edition of them which is now in the process of being published by the Clarendon Press (*Jane Eyre* was the first, in 1969), and the groundwork for a new edition of the letters has been laid by Mildred Christian's bibliography of Brontë manuscripts (see under BIBLIOGRAPHIES below).

TEXTS

It is not so surprising, then, that for the best edition of the novels we must still go back to the Haworth Edition, published in seven volumes (1899–1900) as *The Life and Works of Charlotte Brontë and Her Sisters*. This includes *Poems by Currer, Ellis and Acton Bell* (1846), the selection of Emily's poems printed by her sister in the 1850 one-volume edition of *Wuthering Heights* and *Agnes Grey*, Patrick Brontë's *Cottage Poems* (1811), and also Mrs. Gaskell's *Life*, with an introduction and notes by Clement Shorter. The strength of the edition lies in Mrs. Ward's intelligent, well-informed commentaries on the novels. New facts about the Brontës have come to light since these penetrating essays were written, and this must be kept in mind when one is reading them. None the less, they remain among the surest critical guides we have, displaying a breadth and proportion which would probably have pleased their author's famous uncle, Matthew Arnold. Mrs. Ward's familiarity with English, French, German, and even Russian literature (it comes easily to her, for example, to draw a parallel between Bazarov's death scene in *Fathers and Sons* and that of Helen Burns in *Jane Eyre*), along with her natural feeling for the novelist's processes of recreating actual experience, enables her to come as close as anyone has done to understanding the quality of the Brontë sisters' artistic achievement, and the exact nature of its relationship with English and European romanticism. She discusses the effects on Charlotte's work of her hereditary Celtic strain and her Yorkshire Pennine environment, and also notes the special influence of her responsiveness to contemporary French literature: 'The dithy-rambs of *Shirley* and *Villette*, the "Vision of Eve" of *Shirley* and the description of Rachel in *Villette* would have been impossible to Emily; they come to a great extent from the reading of Victor Hugo and George Sand.' On the other hand, she probably overestimates the importance of sensational German 'Gothick' influences on Emily, who had learnt some German in Brussels in 1842 and, it is generally agreed, was familiar with tales from the German, published in *Black-wood's Magazine* in the 1830s and 1840s. Mrs Ward's style, moreover, sometimes frees itself from the clinical coolness often preferred today. But most modern readers will find themselves in sympathy with her final assessment of the relative weaknesses and strengths of the three sisters: she speaks comparatively little, though not slightingly, of Anne; she recognizes in Charlotte and Emily, in spite of the dithy-rambs and amateurish 'lack of literary reticence' of the one and the occasional crudities of the other, a 'similar *fonds* of stern and simple realism' and a 'similar faculty of observation at once shrewd and passionate'; and she finds in the end that the differences between them are 'almost wholly in Emily's favour'.

Apart from the Haworth Edition, there are some six or seven collections of the Brontës' works which should be noted briefly here. The first of these was published, without editorial comment, by Charlotte Brontë's publishers (Smith, Elder & Company) in 1872-3. The remaining collections, of which no less than three were being published in the same period as the Haworth edition, all include editorial commentary of one kind or another, but vary greatly both in the amount of Brontë material included and in the range and quality of the comment offered upon it. The most complete edition of all writings by all the Brontës (including Branwell), is the *Shakespeare*

Head Brontë, edited in twenty volumes by T. J. Wise and J. A. Symington in 1931–8. In spite of some serious editorial shortcomings, this is an essential edition for students of the Brontës as it contains, besides the novels, poems, and letters, a full representation of the Brontë juvenilia and a wealth of previously unpublished material. It will be mentioned again, later in this survey, in the account of BIOGRAPHIES AND LETTERS.

The *Shakespeare Head Brontë* carries little editorial comment that is critically illuminating. More helpful in this respect is the earlier Temple Edition, which includes the works of the three sisters with biographical comments by May Sinclair, who later produced a full-length study, *The Three Brontës* (1912, revised 1914). This collection was first published under an unidentified editorship in 1893. It was subsequently reprinted in 1901 and then reissued, with May Sinclair's commentaries, in 1905 and 1938.

These commentaries are often shrewder than their rhapsodical style might lead one to expect. This gives the Temple Edition rather more interest than its near-contemporary, the Thornton Edition (including only the novels), published in twelve volumes in 1901 with a commentary by Temple Scott which draws on biographical material already assembled in Clement Shorter's *Charlotte Brontë and her Circle* (1896, rev. edn. 1914). (This edition also includes Mrs. Gaskell's *Life*, with a useful commentary by B. W. Willett.)

The third collection to be compiled in the same period as the Haworth Edition was published for the World's Classics series in 1901–7 and is chiefly notable for its inclusion of the poems, and for the General Introduction (attached to Charlotte's *The Professor*) by Theodore Watts-Dunton, whose close associate, the Victorian poet Swinburne, had been one of the first to celebrate the peculiar poetic power of *Wuthering Heights* and to discuss its resemblances to Elizabethan and Jacobean tragedy (see under CRITICAL STUDIES AND COMMENTARY below). The re-editing by H. W. Garrod in 1930 of this novel for the World's Classics was a considerable literary event, since Garrod was the first to restore the text of the first edition. Charlotte had 'improved' Emily's style and punctuation, smoothing away some of her pungent dialect, when editing her sister's novels for Smith, Elder & Company in 1850, and the improved version had become the received text. New editions based on the text of 1847 include those printed in 1963 and 1965, the former published in New York as a Norton Critical Edition, with a textual commentary by the editor, William M. Sale jun., and the latter published by the University of London Press with a critical commentary by T. Crehan.

Garrod's World's Classics edition of *Wuthering Heights* was reprinted in 1950. In the preceding year appeared the Heather Edition of the sisters' works, in six volumes, edited by the popular Yorkshire writer and novelist Phyllis Bentley. Her biographical introduction for the first volume of the Heather Edition and her prefatory discussions for the Collins' New Classics series 1947–1954, while not critically adventurous, are informative and economical.

Editions of the individual works of the Brontës are legion and their number is continually increasing with the multiplication of paperback books. Everyman's Library (which originally published in 1907–14 all the Brontë novels, except Anne Brontë's *Agnes Grey*, with Ernest Rhys as editor of *Wuthering Heights* and May Sinclair as editor of the rest) has recently reprinted in paperback Charlotte's four novels and Emily's *Wuthering Heights*. These now carry useful introductions by Margaret Lane. The volume containing *Wuthering Heights* is particularly good value since it includes some sixty of Emily's poems (selected by Philip Henderson), and throws in for good measure the biographical and critical prefaces written by Charlotte for the 1850 edition. The Norton Critical Edition of *Wuthering Heights*, mentioned above, is another useful, though much more expensive, paperback. It includes, besides the editor's textual commentary and Charlotte's prefatory essays, a selection of brief extracts from some contemporary reviews and longer representative pieces from modern criticism.

The two novels most often reprinted singly are *Jane Eyre* and *Wuthering Heights*. These are the only two Brontë novels now listed as in print by Penguin, Signet, Pan (which includes some poems with *Wuthering Heights*), and Rinehart paperbacks. In the last series, which is more expensive than the others, J. L. Davies edits *Jane Eyre*, and Mark Schorer *Wuthering Heights*. *Wuthering Heights* is also printed in paperback for the University of London Press, Collier, and the Premier series (published by Fawcett, Oldsbourne). This contrasts with the situation toward the turn of the century, when it was *Jane Eyre* which received special editorial attention, notably in 1889 from C. K. Shorter, whose introductory material draws freely on the recollections of Charlotte's friend Ellen Nussey; and in 1902 from W. Robertson Nicoll, who prints with it 'The Moores', one of Charlotte's preliminary sketches for *The Professor*, and also includes in his introductory material a survey of selected critical views and impressions.

The least widely available Brontë novels are Charlotte's *The Professor* and Anne's *Agnes Grey* and *The Tenant of Wildfell Hall*. Of these Charlotte's, as pointed out, is still available in Everyman paperbacks, but for Anne's it is best at the moment to go back to the earlier standard editions. Neither of her novels has proved sufficiently popular to encourage publishers to keep on printing it in cheap editions, though experiments of this kind have been made from time to time. *Agnes Grey*, for example, appeared in 1966 in Cassell's paperback series, The First Novel Library, with an introduction by Fielden Hughes.

CRITICAL STUDIES AND COMMENTARY

The most comprehensive survey of Brontë criticism to have appeared is Mildred G. Christian's admirable 'The Brontës' in *Victorian Fiction: A Guide to Research*, edited by Lionel Stevenson (1964), and listed below in BIBLIOGRAPHIES. Its fourth section—the first three deal respectively with bibliographies and manuscripts, editions, and biographies —offers a compact, descriptive account of something like a hundred books, articles, and shorter notes published during the past thirty years. The survey, which is more extensive than the present one, is indispensible for those who wish to acquaint themselves in detail with recent Brontë studies. While not directly concerned with early criticism, it does list and comment upon several centennial attempts to map the growth of the literary reputation of the Brontës since the 1840s. Almost all these attempts, as Miss Christian indicates, throw into relief the extent to which Emily had by this time superseded Charlotte in popular esteem.

The best known and most detailed of these centennial celebrations is Melvin R. Watson's '*Wuthering Heights* and the Critics' (*The Trollopian*, 1948), which starts from the assumption that *Wuthering Heights* 'is now generally acknowledged to be one of the greatest English novels', though 'only after a battle with the critics and the general public which has lasted a large part of the hundred years since its publication'. The essay attempts to trace the principal stages in the battle, beginning with the almost universal attack by contemporary reviewers on the book's violence, crudity, and apparent indifference to moral values. According to Mr. Watson, even when the tide began to turn and readers no longer felt impelled to compare it unfavourably with *Jane Eyre*, praise was 'rhapsodic rather than analytical', and the book had to wait until the 1930s to be properly understood. This account is affected to some extent by the author's own reading of *Wuthering Heights*—his view of Heathcliff as in some sense sinning because sinned against renders him too severe on early critics who found Heathcliff's violence more troubling and harder to explain—

and also by a want of feeling for the better insights and appreciations of nineteenth-century criticism. Miss Christian rightly singles out his 'curious blindness to the skill of Mrs. Humphry Ward as a critic'. One could add that more credit might be given to the real attempts to understand Emily Brontë's peculiar imaginative gifts made by several earlier commentators (for example, by G. H. Lewes and Sidney Dobell in 1850, and by Swinburne in 1885). But the essay gets the broad outlines right, is faithfully documented, and incorporates substantial quotations from many of the numerous critics cited.

Recent work on the Brontës' critical reputation includes Judith O'Neill's somewhat sketchy *Critics on Charlotte and Emily Brontë* (1968), a short but helpful selection of essays, mostly represented in brief extracts, and mostly of the twentieth century. Her prefatory remarks, together with the number of essays devoted to Emily (there are fifteen pieces on Emily and six on Charlotte), once again emphasize the movement away from, as she puts it, 'Charlotte's more simple certainties to Emily's wild and puzzling questions'. She erroneously places the real beginning of this development as late as 1916, the original date of Viginia Woolf's essay on these two Brontë sisters collected in *The Common Reader* (1925). Of her twenty-two 'critics' only four or five (one of them being Charlotte herself) are Victorians, and their comments belong exclusively to the short period from 1848 to 1853. An attempt to provide a fuller picture of the movements of nineteenth-century critical response to the Brontës, by reprinting less well known or not easily accessible material, is made by the present writer in two anthologies: *The Brontës* (at present in preparation for the Critical Heritage Series), which is concerned with contemporary reactions to their work, and the Casebook, *Emily Brontë: Wuthering Heights* (*1970*), which aims to represent critical attitudes to this novel from the time of its publication to the present. The essays chosen for these collections, together with the introductory material, support in most respects accepted views concerning the immediate recognition of Charlotte's flawed but original genius, the relative popularity of her novels—*Shirley* was for many something of a disappointment after *Jane Eyre*; *Villette*, though not perhaps so highly regarded as it is by some readers today, was generally seen as finally establishing her literary reputation—and the degree to which her work originally overshadowed Emily's and Anne's in the popular mind. More emphasis than is perhaps usual is given to the fact that even the most hostile of Emily's early reviews bear witness to her book's disturbing power, and it is also shown that for more than one creative writer of the day there was no question of the strength and uniqueness of her creative imagination. Another recently published critical anthology is *The Brontës* (1970), edited by Ian Gregor as a contribution to the series, Twentieth Century Views, which reprints seven already established essays (some of them are referred to elsewhere in this section) devoted to various aspects of the work of Charlotte and Emily Brontë and written over the period 1926–67; it also includes three new essays ('The place of Love in *Jane Eyre* and *Wuthering Heights*', by Mark Kinkead-Weekes; 'Charlotte Brontë, the Imagination and *Villette*', by A. D. Hook; and 'The Other Emily' by Denis Donoghue).

Undoubtedly the most influential of the Brontës' modern critics in establishing Emily Brontë's reputation has been Lord David Cecil, whose 'Charlotte Brontë' and 'Emily Brontë and *Wuthering Heights*' form two chapters of his *Early Victorian Novelists* (1934), a book which itself represents an important landmark in the revaluation of the Victorian novel. Lord David's judgements do not differ essentially from Mrs. Ward's in her introductory essays for the Haworth Edition. Like her, he sees in Charlotte weaknesses which in any writer less passionate would have been fatally crippling. 'Formless, improbable, humourless, exaggerated, uncertain in their handling of character', her novels are nevertheless transfigured for him, as for Mrs. Ward, by her passionate intensity of feeling. Again like Mrs. Ward, he has no doubt at all that Emily is the greater writer. It is sometimes said too sweepingly that his pronouncements put an end to Charlotte's pre-eminence for the modern reader (a movement of taste is involved which is more general than this judgement allows for), but he is also the first to write at length with such freshness of detail about her work. His final verdict places her with the fascinating 'unplaceable anomalies, the freak geniuses' who elude the tidy arrangements of 'the conscientious Court Chamberlains of criticism intent to range the motley mob of English writers in their correct order of precedence'.

Lord David Cecil's inadvertently damaging effect on Charlotte's literary reputation is partly explained by the nature and quality of his subsequent chapter on Emily, which has influenced, directly or indirectly, so much that has been said or written about her since. In the first place, he establishes with a wealth of illustration and personal comment, her novel's toughness of structure, the firmness of its grip on the actual, and the vivid particularity of its descriptive detail. In discussing her careful working out and documenting of 'the concrete facts with which the action deals', he acknowledges, as many other critics have done, the remarkable analysis of this aspect of her novel by C. P. Sanger, whose monograph, *The Structure of Wuthering Heights* (1926), systematically presents for the first time the accuracy of her complex chronological scheme, the symmetrical patterning of her intricate family relationships, and her grasp of the elaborate legal processes by which Heathcliff manages to acquire the Earnshaws' property. Lord David broadens the frontiers of understanding still further by offering a coherent reading of the book's total meaning which still seems to many readers to take care of certain of its most puzzling features, especially its 'moral unorthodoxy' and its mixture of naturalistic and non-naturalistic elements. Even when they disagree—as many have done—over Lord David's final interpretation, such readers usually seem to have felt that he was right to insist on *Wuthering Heights* being in some respects a 'metaphysical' novel. This point had been foreshadowed by Swinburne in the 1880s and later by Virginia Woolf in the brief but imaginative reflections made in her essay of 1916 (referred to above) concerning Emily's 'gigantic ambition' to unite in a book a world 'cleft into gigantic disorder'. As Lord David sees it, the novel deals with a cosmos which is the expression 'of certain living spiritual principles—on the one hand the principle of storm—of the harsh, the ruthless, the wild, the dynamic; and on the other the principle of calm—of the gentle, the merciful, the passive and the tame . . .'

It is over Lord David Cecil's view of the relationship between these principles that subsequent readers and critics have differed. For him these principles are 'not conflicting' and not, in themselves, destructive. They become so in life only because 'in the cramped condition of their earthly incarnation these principles are diverted from following the course that their nature indicates. . .'. At the close of the novel an equilibrium is re-established which is an inevitable harmony following Heathcliff's posthumous union with his affinity, Catherine. The numerous subsequent studies of *Wuthering Heights* which might be said to belong to the same order of inquiry tend either to lean to Lord David's view that the novel achieves a harmonious resolution of contraries, or to suggest instead that while the book aspires toward such a resolution there remains none the less an irreducible element of conflict between them. The latter view necessarily entails taking into account Emily Brontë's possible emotional ambivalence toward her central figure, and also the further possibility that her book is not the consistent metaphysical dissertation that Lord David Cecil claims it to be.

Of the many essays following in Lord David's wake during the next twenty years, one of the earliest, Boris Ford's analysis in *Scrutiny*

(1939), perhaps comes nearest to seeing the book merely as an expression of 'simple certainties': it is 'a very precisely balanced structure of "pleasant" and "unpleasant", "normal", and "abnormal" ', everything in it making toward the tranquil closing paragraph. Martin Turnell, in a somewhat more sophisticated piece, '*Wuthering Heights*' (1940) takes up a position between Lord David and Ford. He agrees that it is 'a metaphysical novel' contrasting 'two profoundly different ways of life, one represented by the Lintons, and the other by Heathcliff', and that in the end order is re-established. But he also sees, as his predecessors do not, that the conflict of extremes produces the disorder in the novel's universe, and that the harmony is reached only by getting rid of 'all the anomalous elements'. Hence the importance of the second-generation story, where the union of the younger Catherine and Hareton is 'a *compromise* between the Lintons and the Heathcliffs of a former generation'.

Both Martin Turnell and Boris Ford find support for their arguments from close scrutiny of the book's texture, structure, and style, a method used more ambitiously by another contributor to *Scrutiny*, G. D. Klingopulos, in his '*Wuthering Heights*' (1947), an essay forming one of a series devoted to 'The Novel as Dramatic Poem'. The possibility of such an approach had been hinted at by Swinburne, who speaks of the book's 'fresh dark air of tragic passion' and refers the reader to Shakespeare and Webster. For G. D. Klingopulos, in 1947, the novel is altogether less morally and artistically coherent than some recent critics had claimed. Yet, as he rightly said, it exacts in 'some half-dozen or so speeches of Catherine's and Heathcliff's' the same kind of attention as the poetry of an Elizabethan play exacts 'at the crises of its meaning'. The 'calm' conclusion, which, as he reminds us, is spoken by the impercipient Lockwood and follows the shepherd boy's story of seeing 'Heathcliff and a woman' wandering on the moors, has 'a certain ambiguity', but Emily Brontë 'is the first writer to have used the novel for that kind of statement which is contained in the finest English poetry'. All the same, the world which Emily created 'is emptier than Shakespeare's and her view less reassuring'. What she offers in her closing paragraph is 'merely a possible hypothesis', recalling the tragic universality represented by the chorus in Greek tragedy.

In Melvin R. Watson's 'Tempest in the Soul: The Theme and Structure of *Wuthering Heights*' (1949) the dramatic analogy is probably taken too far. The novel is 'consciously organized like a five-act tragedy', with a Prologue (chapters 1–3) setting its tone and character 'like that of a Greek tragedy'. For his critic, the novel is undeniably a masterpiece, but it is not, as David Cecil contends, 'a metaphysical dissertation': Emily Brontë 'was attempting something more concrete, more closely related to human experience'. Heathcliff's villainous actions 'are produced by the distortion of his natural personality'. The second-generation story is essential since it allows time for Heathcliff's hatred to subside and for the love between Hareton and Cathy to grow, the two processes thus ensuring the 'calm and symbolic ending of the book'.

Closer to G. D. Klingopulos than to Melvin Watson in recognizing the anomalous elements in Emily Brontë's creative genius is Derek Traversi in his centennial observance, 'Wuthering Heights after a Hundred Years' (1949). Heathcliff, in one light, is a stock figure from romantic literature, 'a man of great force of character and improbable wickedness', and the plot-ingredients are 'a mixture of brutal melodrama and exaggerated sentiment'. But such elements are transformed by an intensely individual imaginative power which derives from the author's essentially religious experience of life. Behind Catherine's passionate discriminations between Linton and Heathcliff lies 'a moral problem of the utmost seriousness'. Indeed the creative impulse urging the book into being depends on the clash between such 'opposite conceptions of life'. With these two last points my own 'Wuthering Heights: The Rejection of Heathcliff' (1958) largely agrees, though the emphasis falls in different places. For Mr. Traversi, the key to the novel is 'the transformation of romantic passion into pagan feeling of a definite if peculiar religious character'. In my own reading it lies in the attempt to explore the implications of alternative commitments, first to the values of storm (the first-generation story) and then to those of calm (the second-generation story), 'and if possible to reconcile them'. My view, like that of Mr. Turnell, is that the 'calm' of the second-generation story depends on the reduction of the destructive 'storm' elements, but after examining the structure and texture of the novel, especially its use of nature imagery, I conclude that Emily Brontë cannot finally escape from her emotional commitment to Heathcliff: 'there can only be an intellectual judgment that for the purposes of ordinary life he will not do'. Her 'philosophy', then is less 'demoniac' than Cecil would have it, and her preoccupations less consistently metaphysical than many other readers have allowed. The view that Emily Brontë has 'no single vision of the world' and that her novel offers us 'one way of seeing opposed to another' is further discussed in Mr. Kinkead-Weekes's recent essay (mentioned above, p. 226).

The most exhaustive and exhausting discussion of *Wuthering Heights* as a metaphysical—indeed (at the time of its appearance) a smartly up-to-the-minute theological—statement is J. Hillis Miller's lengthy chapter on Emily Brontë in his *The Disappearance of God* (1963). His interesting but eccentric analysis of the novel is necessarily affected by his general thesis about an absentee Deity. Emily's characters, suffering the 'anguish of complete separation', are required to 'die into life', and only through the purgatorial suffering of Cathy and Heathcliff can the new generation reach happiness and God be 'transformed from the transcendent deity of extreme Protestantism, enforcing in wrath his irrevocable laws', to an immanent amiable deity who can be possessed 'here and now'. What this perhaps comes down to in the end is merely a modish restatement of David Cecil's reading of the novel.

So far as essays devoted to the moral or metaphysical aspects of the novel are concerned, the wheel may be said to come full circle with Philip Drew's level-headed essay on 'Charlotte Brontë as a critic of *Wuthering Heights*' (1964), in which Charlotte's 1850 preface—emphasizing that 'Heathcliff ... stands unredeemed, never once swerving in his arrow-straight course to perdition'—is defended as a corrective to those who minimize the destructive elements in Heathcliff in order to see him exclusively as a splendidly heroic figure. A totally 'non-metaphysical' example of this attitude is Arnold Kettle's Marxist defence of Heathcliff—included in his *An Introduction to the English Novel* (vol. 1, 1951)—as a man rightfully revenging himself on the bourgeois property-owners who surround him.

John Hagan's 'The Control of Sympathy in *Wuthering Heights*' (1967) usefully complements Philip Drew's essay by drawing attention to the methods used by Emily Brontë in order to arouse sympathy for the violent and destructive yet wretchedly tormented characters at the centre of her first-generation story. This approach helps to counter the exaggerations of certain modern studies which dwell on the perverse or neurotic tendencies in the novel with a sophistication and critical ingenuity undreamed of by its first readers and reviewers. Such studies include Richard Chase's 'The Brontës: or Myth Domesticated' (1947) and Dorothy Van Ghent's '*Wuthering Heights*' (in her *The English Novel: Form and Function*, 1953). The latter contains an arresting interpretation of 'the window image' in the novel, but Dorothy Van Ghent's confusions in determining where in Catherine's and Heathcliff's 'otherness' really resides are effectively pointed out by John Hagan. This kind of confusion, which he also finds in David Cecil's essay, he believes to be the result 'of trying to discover in the novel more metaphysical concreteness than it can yield'.

Most of the essays mentioned incorporate references to previous commentaries, some of which are omitted from this survey, either because they break little new ground, or because their concentrated examination of particular details tends to draw their entire critical perspective out of true. Among these are Freudian studies of Emily Brontë's imagery (surprising things have been said, for example, about her use of door-keys, locks, and entrances), an argument dedicated to the proposition that the true villain of the piece is Nellie Dean, and various exegeses of James Branderham's intolerably lengthy sermon on 'Seventy times seven' (*Matthew* 18: 22) in Lockwood's dream in Chapter three. By entirely disregarding the sardonically humorous flavour of this sequence, heavy weather indeed has been made of Lockwood's accusing Branderham in this dream of 'the sin that no Christian need pardon' (the 'sin', of course, is that of boring his listener to death).

Among studies which do concentrate usefully on particular aspects of the novel, especially its style and narrative technique, reference should be made to Mark Schorer's 'Fiction and the Matrix of Analogy' (1949), a short piece which illustrates the recurrence and urgency of Emily Brontë's use of imagery drawn from 'the fierce life of animals and the relentless life of the elements' (the critical conclusions derived from this analysis are less convincing). An earlier discussion of the vigour and directness of Emily Brontë's style is Iris Cooper-Willis's *The Authorship of Wuthering Heights* (1936), which refutes, on the basis of the book's literary qualities, the now long-exploded theory that Branwell was the true author of his sister's novel. On Emily Brontë's intricate story-within-a-story method of telling her tale, as indeed on her style and on the symbolic function of the natural setting and the two principal houses, Thrushcross Grange and Wuthering Heights, almost every commentator has had something to say, as these elements of her art obviously contribute vitally to the book's meaning and effect. Her narrative technique, with its 'multiple perspectives', was at one time thought to be a sign of faulty organization (this view is taken for granted by H. W. Garrod in his preface to the 1930 World's Classics edition), but it is now usually seen to be entirely in keeping with the author's firm control over her material. A description of the method is included in J. F. Goodridge's *Emily Brontë: Wuthering Heights* (1964), a short primer devised for students and sixth-formers which also recapitulates other major points concerning the book's structure and technique.

Four studies which do break new ground must certainly be mentioned before closing this part of the present survey; two of these are of the 1950s and the others appeared in 1969. The earliest is Mary Visick's short monograph, *The Genesis of Wuthering Heights* (1955), which deserves credit for demonstrating with commendable brevity that Emily Brontë's novel is closely related to her poems. In the characters of Edgar, Heathcliff, and Catherine, in the themes of passion, loss, and reclamation, 'we find ourselves watching the creative imagination in the act . . . of totally reforming the material' on which it had worked when creating the figures of her romantic Gondal fantasy (known to us only through her poems), especially its passionate heroine 'A.G.A.' and her two principal lovers, the mild Lord Alfred Aspinall and his powerful rival Julian. As Mary Visick points out, earlier writers had attempted to trace this connection, for example Mary Robinson in *Emily Brontë* (1883) and Mabel Hope Dodds in various essays in *MLR* written between 1923 and 1944. But neither of these writers had been able to draw on Fannie Ratchford's *Gondal's Queen* (1955), which attempts to reconstruct Emily's and Anne's Gondal saga exclusively as the basis of Emily's Gondal poems, thus expanding the author's earlier work on the Brontës' juvenile fantasies in *The Brontës' Web of Childhood* (1941). Other explorations in the same field include Laura Hinkley's *The Brontës: Charlotte and Emily* (1945) and W. D. Paden's *An Investigation of Gondal* (1958). A summary of the manner in which the manuscripts of Emily's 'Gondal' and 'non-Gondal' poems came to be known, collected, and so discussed in relation to the novel is given in my own review of Mrs. Visick's book (*EIC*, 1959).

Mary Visick points to Emily Brontë's conscious attempt to move away from the wishful indulgence of romantic fantasy, a process which many Brontë students feel that Charlotte may have had more difficulty in mastering. The whole question of Emily's artistic development, indeed the entire nature of her achievement both as a poet and as a novelist, are all explored in close detail by Jacques Blondel in his *Emily Brontë: Expérience spirituelle et création poétique* (1955), the most substantial scholarly study of Emily Brontë's life and work yet published. M. Blondel has made himself an authority on everything to do with his subject. His book includes a lengthy bibliography, the first serious, sustained, critical analysis of Emily's poems to have appeared in print, and a full exploration of every aspect of *Wuthering Heights* itself. His book draws throughout on many familiar and some less known critical and biographical studies, including a number from abroad. Of special interest are his comments on Emily Brontë's use of her natural setting to establish a vital continuity between character and environment; his views on her art as a highly individual blend of realism and romanticism, in which her '*amour de soi*' prompts her to create a powerful myth at the same time as it prevents her from achieving anything approaching a genuinely 'Shakespearian' detachment; and his able treatment of the probable literary influences upon her work (Scott, Byron, Shakespeare, and various English and German Gothic tales), in which he modifies earlier studies of her possible source materials, for example by Mrs. Ward in the Haworth Edition, Florence Dry in *The Sources of Wuthering Heights* (1937) and Leicester Bradner in 'The Growth of Wuthering Heights' (1933). M. Blondel's book could have done with a touch of Gallic wit to enliven the solemn thoroughness of its appraisal, but it is an essential contribution to Brontë studies and there is a strong case for its translation into English (the Abbé Dimnet's much shorter and now out-dated *Les Soeurs Brontë* (1910), was translated into English in 1927).

On a somewhat smaller scale are the two studies published in 1969, namely John Hewish's *Emily Brontë, A Critical and Biographical Study*, and Mrs. Q. D. Leavis's 'A Fresh Approach to *Wuthering Heights*' (included in her own and Dr. F. R. Leavis's *Lectures in America*, 1969). Both studies attempt in different ways to distinguish, as Mrs. Leavis puts it, 'what is genuine from what is merely confusion'. Mr. Hewish's book is a level-headed and succinct résumé of the salient facts—as opposed to conjecture and fanciful speculation—concerning Emily Brontë's life, literary affinities, publishing history, and critical reputation since 1847. He also offers his own critical reading of her novel as a 'remarkably dramatised' work which 'answers few questions and asks many'. Mrs. Leavis's essay is, as one might expect, much more emphatically a critical reappraisal, which seeks above all to reaffirm the novel's 'truly human centrality'. The tendency of her argument is in keeping with certain recent movements of opinion (noticeable, for example, in commentaries by John Hagan, Philip Drew, Mark Kinkead-Weekes, and myself) which have the effect of drawing attention to the fresh, even sunny, 'normality' of Emily Brontë's treatment of the younger Catherine in her childhood days, her feeling for the ordinary human emotions of affection and grief (in Edgar and Frances, for instance), and the progress of one part of her story toward renewal, consolidation, and commitment to the central currents of life. Mrs. Leavis's essay gives the fullest contemporary expression so far to the recognition of these qualities, and although it deals rather too simplistically for some readers with the darker side of Emily Brontë's imagination, her re-appraisal goes a long way toward countering the exaggerations found in some modern essays of the kind mentioned earlier. Mrs. Leavis also provides, for good measure, four Appendices on, respectively, 'The Northern Farmer, Old Style', 'Violence', 'Superstition and Folklore', and '*Wuthering Heights* and *The Bride of Lammermoor*'.

Critical studies of Charlotte Brontë since David Cecil's essay of 1934 are not only fewer in number than those devoted to Emily but, generally speaking, also less interesting, largely because Charlotte, although capable of a comparable intensity of feeling, possesses a less arrestingly original, and therefore intellectually less stimulating, quality of mind and vision. There has been no continuous, absorbing debate about the 'correct' reading of any of her four novels as there has been about *Wuthering Heights*. The issue most canvassed concerns the relative merits of her two most successful novels, *Jane Eyre* and *Villette*, and many recent studies, even if ostensibly devoted to a single novel, seem to be prompted by the impulse to reassess her whole development from *The Professor* to *Villette*, and to discover wherever possible the same kind of structural complexity—including the use of poetic symbolism—which readers had already found in *Wuthering Heights*. (The latter preoccupation is particularly noticeable in two of the essays—by David Lodge and Mark Kinkead-Weekes—devoted to Charlotte Brontë in the recent volume of Twentieth Century Views, referred to above.)

Attempts to reassess her work began to accumulate noticeably in the 1950s. The methods adopted during this period by certain critics anxious to redress the balance in her favour are indicated by D. W. Crompton in his 'The New Criticism: A Caveat' (1960), which alludes specifically to *Jane Eyre* in warning us against 'the assumption that . . . the presence of an underlying unifying theme is by itself sufficient guarantee of a book's quality . . . many books can be found to be better than they are by by-passing the main issues and concentrating on playing hunt-the-slipper with theme and symbol'. The richness of *Jane Eyre*'s 'structural unity' can readily be demonstrated, but 'having made the point . . . one is left with the fact . . . that *Wuthering Heights* is a great book and that *Jane Eyre* . . . is relatively immature in conception and execution and yields little more from sustained consideration than it does from a single reading'.

The path to this 'new criticism' of Charlotte Brontë had been sign-posted a decade earlier in M. H. Scargill's influential 'All Passion Spent: A Revaluation of *Jane Eyre*' (1950). This article argues that Charlotte had in this novel broken completely with naturalistic tradition: 'The conventions have become symbols: the fictional lover has become The Lover; the mad woman of the Gothic novel has been put to allegorical use.' The novel is 'the record of an intense spiritual experience', which is comparable with the 'ordeal of purgation' in *King Lear* and is similarly expressed in poetic symbolism. However, Mr. Scargill is fairly succinct in this essay and, once engaged with the vivid particularity of individual episodes, is more intelligent about the novel than might be expected from his misleading general thesis.

The most perceptive investigations of the interplay of reason and feeling in Charlotte Brontë's work are made by R. B. Heilman in his survey, 'Charlotte Brontë's "New" Gothic', included in *From Jane Austen to Joseph Conrad*, edited by R. C. Rathburn and M. Steinmann (1958) and supplemented later by his 'Charlotte Brontë, Reason and the Moon' (1960). As he sees it, Charlotte, by her tart humour and dry factuality, deliberately reduces what he calls the 'primitive Gothic' elements in her work, namely those which seek 'a relatively simple thrill or momentary intensity of feeling'. At the same time, she finds her own ways of achieving the ends served by this 'primitive' Gothicism, for example by the use of frightening symbolic dreams, surrealistic descriptive effects and the exploration of new regions of feeling in the relations between men and women. Mr. Heilman traces these qualities from *The Professor* to *Villette*, which of all the novels is the most richly 'saturated' with both the 'old' Gothic and the 'new'. In his second essay, the interplay between reason and intuition in Charlotte's work is further explored through her use of moon imagery in *Jane Eyre*; according to Charles Burkhart's supplementary 'Another Key Word for *Jane Eyre*' (1961), her use of the word 'nature' acts as an additional guide to this interplay.

More traditional in method is Kathleen Tillotson's '*Jane Eyre*' in her *Novels of the Eighteen-Forties* (1954). Mrs. Tillotson situates the book firmly in its decade, where circumstances were right for it to get off to a flying start. It would have been too 'low' for 1837, too outspoken for 1857 and, though fresh, had no more novelty than was welcome at the time. Its perennial appeal is ensured by its universality, and immediacy, and by the intimacy with which the reader knows its heroine. The novel's success in these respects is partly due to Charlotte's technical skill—one example is her handling of the present tense in the childhood scenes, a point expanded by Edgar P. Shannon in his 'The Present Tense in *Jane Eyre*' (1955). Success is also, and more importantly, due to Charlotte's at last learning to discipline her indulgence of romantic fantasy. The conscientious down-to-earth truthfulness and greyness of *The Professor* is seen here as a necessary first stage in her journey from 'the burning clime' of Angria toward a more ordered and complex achievement. How carefully Charlotte did in fact work over the text of this novel is discussed in detail in M. M. Brammer's 'The Manuscript of *The Professor*' (1960).

Mrs. Tillotson's argument concerning Charlotte's subordination of her feeling for romantic fantasy is taken up and amplified in R. A. Colby's '*Villette* and the Life of the Mind' (1960), an informed, well-documented and readable discussion which presents Charlotte as a writer in whom the romantic imagination at last 'reconciles itself to real life'. *Villette* is thus highly regarded; the various elements making for its success, including the mingling of the strains of English and French romanticism with mid-Victorian realism, are discussed in a manner which sheds light on Charlotte's artistic development and on this book's place in the general evolution of the English novel.

Villette is also chosen by Roy Pascal (along with Lawrence's *Sons and Lovers*, and Joyce's *A Portrait of the Artist as a Young Man*) to illustrate his arguments about the fictionalizing of personal experience in 'The Autobiographical Novel' (1959). The author, he feels, is now using her heroine 'to get nearer to the truth about her own character' whereas in *The Professor* she had 'sidled away' from the personal problem facing her in the emotional experience associated with her Brussels teacher, M. Heger. Another aspect of Charlotte's recreation of experience in this novel is discussed by Georgia S. Dunbar in 'Proper Names in *Villette*' (1960).

Shirley, with its uncharacteristic mingling of public and private themes and its loose structure, has always presented problems for Charlotte's admirers and does not fit tidily into their accounts of her development. It is, however, defended by Jacob Korg in 'The Problem of Unity in *Shirley*' (1957), where it is described as a philosophical novel possessing considerable thematic unity. A different view is taken by J. M. S. Tomkins in 'Caroline Helstone's Eyes' (*Brontë Society Transactions*, 1961), which argues that the author's inadvertent alteration of Caroline's eyes from blue to brown in the course of the story is a clue to the author's re-direction of purpose after the death of her sister Anne. Earl A. Knies in 'Art, Death and the Composition of Shirley' (1965) shows from a study of the manuscripts of Charlotte's letters at the time that the novel was destined from the beginning to achieve only moderate success (the same critic also contributed a piece on 'The use of the "I" in *Jane Eyre*' to *College English*, 1960).

The culmination of this renewed critical interest in Charlotte

Brontë's novels is marked by R. B. Martin's full-length study, *Accents of Persuasion* (1966)—the title is taken from one of Charlotte's early letters to her publisher's concerning her own and her sisters' artistic intentions. Deliberately omitting all biographical material, this is a steady examination of each novel in turn in order to distinguish the writer's major themes and her success in giving them 'artistic life'. The principal conclusions stress the strong feeling throughout of 'the self-reliant Protestant ethic that so dominated her life'; the gradual maturing in each novel of the central character, who finally reaches the point where reason and passion can be reconciled; and the technical importance for this novelist of sustaining a consistent 'point of view' which largely ensures the special success of *Villette*, an 'autumnal', resigned, clear-eyed novel of acceptance. The latter is perhaps the most controversial judgement in what is otherwise an unsurprising, competently handled, and usually observant study.

It seems appropriate that this commentary on commentaries should be brought to a close with the first full-length studies of the Brontë sisters as a group to have appeared for some years. Each is of the late 1960s, comparatively short (none is as elaborate as M. Blondel's study of Emily), and produced by a University teacher of English Literature. They include Inga-Stina Ewbank's *Their Proper Sphere* (1966), Wendy Craik's *The Brontë Novels* (1968), and Norman Sherry's *The Brontë Sisters: Charlotte and Emily* (1969). The first is an agreeably written discussion which subordinates critical assessment to the examination of the three sisters as women writers of their day. The book's subtitle is 'A Study of the Brontë Sisters as Early-Victorian Female Novelists' and, in keeping with this brief, the author points to thematic parallels in novels by early nineteenth-century English women writers, especially those concerned with governesses. The book also contains a detailed descriptive analysis, with plenty of quotation, of each of the novels in turn. An undertaking of a more consciously revaluative and exploratory kind is offered by Mrs. Craik, who shares with R. B. Martin the determination to investigate her subject as far as possible without biographical assistance. While admiring Emily's achievement in *Wuthering Heights*, this critic has no doubts about Charlotte's equal artistic importance; indeed she sees her as a major novelist in her own right. Her views on Anne are also warmer than those of many of her predecessors. She compares *Agnes Grey* with *Mansfield Park*, and *The Tenant of Wildfell Hall* with the fictionalized treatises of Harriet Martineau.

Mrs. Craik's and Mrs. Ewbank's commentaries on Anne's novels follow in the wake of the first substantial critical reassessment of her work, namely *Anne Brontë: Her Life and Work* (1959), in which the biographical material is contributed by Ada Harrison and the critical analysis of her poems and novels by Derek Stanford. The latter singles out in particular her quietly ironical narrative style and her deft powers of characterization. Apart from Winifred Gérin's *Anne Brontë*, also of 1959 (see under BIOGRAPHIES AND LETTERS below), the only other real attempt to save Anne from being totally over-shadowed by her sisters is W. T. Hale's sensible monograph, *Anne Brontë: Her Life and Writings* (1929).

From the most recent of the three studies of the Brontë sisters, Norman Sherry's introductory primer on Charlotte and Emily, Anne is severely excluded as insufficiently important. This book, nevertheless, is remarkable for condensing a great deal of material into a very short space. It includes most of the essential biographical facts about the Brontë family; a summary of the principal themes and methods in Charlotte's and Emily's work (including a sensitive if brief account of Emily's poetry); and succinct assessments of their individual achievements. For this critic, Emily certainly possesses the greater originality and her novel is ultimately 'Shakespearian' in vision, since it shows a good natural order re-establishing itself after a temporary disturbance by the forces of evil. Charlotte's strength lies in the intensity with which she dramatizes individual passion; *The Professor* and *Shirley* illustrate her weaknesses when this concern is deliberately subdued to share the honours with public or social themes.

BIOGRAPHIES AND LETTERS

All biographies of the Brontë family stem from Mrs. Gaskell's masterly *The Life of Charlotte Brontë* (1857), which was based on letters by Charlotte, many of them written to Mrs. Gaskell herself, and on other material derived from Charlotte's father Patrick Brontë, her husband Arthur Nicholls, and her close friend Ellen Nussey. This biography is still required reading in spite of some inevitable omissions: Mrs. Gaskell could only write about Emily from hearsay; she was understandably reticent about Charlotte's feelings for M. Heger; and she was obliged to suppress in the third edition, under the threat of legal proceedings, her remarks about Branwell Brontë's love affair with his employer's wife, Mrs. Robinson, and her angry criticism of the conditions at the Cowan Bridge School, which had led to the early deaths of the two eldest Brontë children, Maria and Elizabeth.

Since Mrs. Gaskell's day, numerous biographical studies have helped to make her omissions good, but for all ordinary purposes the best supplement to her work is Margaret Lane's *The Brontë Story* (1953). This was designed specifically as a companion to Mrs. Gaskell's book. It re-tells her story, supplying material to which she did not have access or did not use. Many passages incorporate Mrs. Gaskell's own words.

The third essential biographical tool for students of the Brontës is the four-volume collection, *The Brontës: Their Lives, Friendships and Correspondence*, edited by T. J. Wise and J. A. Symington for the *Shakespeare Head Brontë* (1932–8; see under TEXTS above). This contains, besides the few letters written by Emily and Anne, the bulk of Charlotte's correspondence, notably with her school-friends, Ellen Nussey and Mary Taylor; her publisher and his reader, George Smith and W. S. Williams; her fellow-novelist and biographer, Elizabeth Gaskell; her reviewer, George Lewes; and M. Constantin Heger of the Pensionnat Heger in Brussels, where she studied French in 1842–4. Her letters to M. Heger, written in French and expressing an intense emotional attachment whose precise nature is hard to define have been the subject of controversy ever since their first publication and translation by M. H. Spielmann in *The Times* in July 1913.

Recent investigations by Mildred Christian and others cast some doubt on the comprehensiveness of the Wise–Symington collection and on the reliability of its text. Its editorial commentary is certainly inadequate. But it usefully extends the initial work put in by Clement Shorter in his three volumes, *Charlotte Brontë and her Circle* (1896), *Charlotte Brontë and her Sisters* (1905), and *The Brontës: Life and Letters* (1908). Shorter had been placed in a fortunate position by Ellen Nussey. She had wished him to correct what she regarded—in some cases rightly—as misleading accounts of the Brontës in books by T. Wemyss Reid (*Charlotte Brontë: A Monograph*, 1877), Mary Robinson (*Emily Brontë*, 1883), and J. B. Leyland (*The Brontë Family, with Special Reference to Patrick Branwell Brontë*, 1886), and had accordingly supplied him with a great deal of new biographical information and manuscript material. With her help and that of T. J. Wise, who had secured still more manuscript material from her and from Arthur Nicholls, Shorter produced his own studies and also edited Mrs. Gaskell's *Life* for the Haworth Edition (see TEXTS above).

Most modern biographies re-work the materials assembled in the books I have mentioned. Since they are numerous, vary greatly in quality and emphasis, and are usually written with a popular audience in mind, the problem of selection is particularly difficult. After

Margaret Lane's *The Brontë Story*, probably the most useful general accounts are Phyllis Bentley's *The Brontës* (1947) and Laurence and E. M. Hanson's more comprehensive *The Four Brontës* (1949). E. M. Delafield's *The Brontës: Their Lives Recorded by their Contemporaries* (1935) is also a useful compilation. A full, detailed biography of Charlotte was published in 1967 by Winifred Gérin, *Charlotte Brontë: The Evolution of Genius*, which followed the same author's *Anne Brontë* (1959) and *Branwell Brontë* (1961). Other records of Anne apart from Winifred Gérin's, are by Ada Harrison and W. T. Hale (see under CRITICAL STUDIES AND COMMENTARY (above)). Biographies of Emily, about whom so little is known, are frequently given to sensational conjecture. A sensible early account is Charles Simpson's *Emily Brontë* (1929), which is particularly interesting on the probable influence on *Wuthering Heights* of Emily's familiarity with Law Hill, where she worked as a governess during 1837–8; and Winifred Gérin completed her studies of the Brontë family with the publication in 1971 of *Emily Brontë: A Biography*.

Perhaps one should also add here Phyllis Bentley's attractive picture-book, *The Brontës and their World* (1969), which, along with other studies published from late 1969 onwards, appeared after this chapter was first prepared. Dr. Bentley includes a narrative of the sisters' lives and background, but her book is above all to be recommended as a collection of illustrations which will illuminate with some vividness—especially for those unfamiliar with the Brontë country—the kind of landscape and setting which stimulated so remarkably the Brontës' creative imagination.

BIBLIOGRAPHIES

There is still no really reliable bibliographical guide to the writings of the Brontës. Although incomplete and sometimes inaccurate, the fullest surveys are T. J. Wise's *A Bibliography of the Writings in Prose and Verse of the Members of the Brontë Family* (1917) and his *A Brontë Library. A Catalogue of Printed Books, Manuscripts and Autograph Letters by the Members of the Brontë Family* (1929); Butler Wood's 'A Bibliography of the Works of the Brontë Family' and his 'Supplement' (*Brontë Society Transactions*, 1895 and 1898), and J. P. Anderson's bibliography in Augustine Birrell's *Charlotte Brontë* (1887). Other catalogues, including her own census of Brontë (1887). Other catalogues, including her own census of Brontë manuscripts in the United States, are listed by Mildred Christian in her discussion of bibliographies and manuscript material in 'The Brontës' (*Victorian Fiction: A Guide to Research*, 1964). Apart from the sections on the Brontës in

CBEL, other general guides to work on and by the Brontës include Jacques Blondel's bibliography in his study of Emily Brontë's poetry and novel (see under CRITICAL STUDIES AND COMMENTARY) and his supplementary account, 'Emily Brontë: Récentes explorations' (*Études anglaises*, 1958). W. Ruff records the first American editions of Brontë novels in *Brontë Society Transactions* (1934).

BACKGROUND READING

For the literary background of the novel helpful guides are Kathleen Tillotson's *The Novels of the Eighteen-Forties* (1954) mentioned above; Richard Stang's *The Theory of the Novel in England, 1850–1870* (1958); and Patricia Thomson's *The Victorian Heroine: A Changing Ideal* (1960) The religious background of the Brontës is discussed in G. Elsie Harrison's lively, if biased, *The Clue to the Brontës* (1948), which discusses the Wesleyan Methodism to which their father was attracted. This should be read in conjunction with A. B. Hopkins's balanced *The Father of the Brontës* (1958). For Victorian ideas and attitudes reference should be made to Walter E. Houghton's *The Victorian Frame of Mind, 1830–1870* (1957) and the earlier *Ideas and Beliefs of the Victorians* (1949), edited by H. Grisewood. A standard reference work is *Early Victorian England, 1830–65*, edited by G. M. Young in two volumes (1934).

REFERENCES

TEXTS

(a) Collected works

Mrs. H. Ward and C. K. Shorter (edd.), *The Life and Works of Charlotte Bronte and her Sisters* (Haworth Edition, 7 vols., London, 1899–1900).

T. Scott (ed.), *The Novels of the Sisters Brontë* (Thornton Edition, 12 vols., London, 1901).

T. Watts-Dunton (ed.), *The Novels and Poems of Charlotte, Emily and Anne Brontë* (World's Classics, 7 vols., London, 1901–7).

M. Sinclair (ed.), *The Novels of Charlotte, Emily and Anne Brontë* (Temple Edition, 12 vols., London, 1905, 1938).

T. J. Wise and J. A. Symington (edd.), *The Shakespeare Head Brontë* (20 vols., Oxford, 1931–8); novels, 11 vols., life and letters, 4 vols.; miscellaneous and unpublished writings, 2 vols.; poems, 2 vols.; bibliography, 1 vol.

C. W. Hatfield (ed.), *The Complete Poems of Emily Brontë* (New York and London, 1941).

P. Bentley (ed.), *The Works of the Brontë Sisters* (Heather Edition, London, 1949).

M. Lane (ed.), *Novels by Charlotte and Emily Brontë* (Everyman, London, 1964).

(b) Separate works

(*i*) *Charlotte*

J. L. Davies (ed.), *Jane Eyre* (Rinehart, 1950).
J. Jack and M. Smith (edd.), *Jane Eyre* (Oxford 1969).
W. R. Nicoll (ed.), *Jane Eyre* (London, 1902).
C. K. Shorter (ed.), *Jane Eyre* (London, 1889).

Also in Penguin, Signet, and Pan editions.

(*ii*) *Emily*

T. Crehan (ed.), *Wuthering Heights* (London, 1965).
W. M. Sale, jun. (ed.), *Wuthering Heights* (Norton, New York, 1963).
M. Schorer (ed.), *Wuthering Heights* (Rinehart, 1950).

Also in Penguin, Signet, and Pan editions.

(*iii*) *Anne*

F. Hughes (ed.), *Agnes Grey* (London, 1966).

CRITICAL STUDIES AND COMMENTARY

M. Allott, '*Wuthering Heights*: The Rejection of Heathcliff?', viii (1958).
—— 'Gondal and *Wuthering Heights* again', *EIC* ix (1959).
—— (ed.), *Emily Brontë: Wuthering Heights*. A Casebook (London, 1970).
—— (ed.), *Charlotte Brontë: Jane Eyre and Villette*. A Casebook (London, 1973).
—— (ed.) *The Brontës: The Critical Heritage* (in press).
J. Blondel, *Emily Brontë: Expérience spirituelle et création poétique* (Presses Universitaires de France, Paris, 1955).
L. Bradner, 'The Growth of Wuthering Heights', *PMLA* xlviii (1933).
M. M. Brammer, 'The Manuscript of *The Professor*', *RES* n.s. 11 (1960).
C. Burkhart, 'Another Key Word for *Jane Eyre*, *NCF* xv (1961).
Lord D. Cecil, 'Charlotte Brontë' and 'Emily Brontë and *Wuthering Heights*', *Early Victorian Novelists* (London 1934).
R. Chase, 'The Brontës: or Myth Domesticated', *Kenyon Review*, ix (1947).
R. A. Colby, '*Villette* and the Life of the Mind', *PMLA* lxxv (1960).
I. Cooper-Willis, *The Authorship of Wuthering Heights* (London, 1936).
W. Craik, *The Brontë Novels* (London, 1968).
D. W. Crompton, 'The New Criticism: A Caveat', *EIC* x (1960).
E. Dimnet, *Les Soeurs Brontë* (Paris, 1910; English translation, London, 1927).
M. H. Dodds, 'Gondaliand', *MLR* xviii (1923).
—— 'A Second Visit to Gondaliand', *MLR* xxi–xxii (1926–7).
—— 'Heathcliff's Country', *MLR* xxxix (1944).
P. Drew, 'Charlotte Brontë as a Critic of *Wuthering Heights*', *NCF* xviii (1964).
F. S. Dry, *The Sources of Wuthering Heights* (Cambridge, 1937).

G. S. Dunbar, Proper Names in *Villette*', *NCF* xiv (1960).

I.-S. Ewbank, *Their Proper Sphere: A Study of the Brontë Sisters as Early-Victorian Female Novelists* (London, 1966).

B. Ford, '*Wuthering Heights*', *Scrutiny*, vii (1939).

J. F. Goodridge, *Emily Brontë: Wuthering Heights* (London, 1964).

I. Gregor (ed.), *The Brontës: A Collection of Critical Essays* (paperback, Engle-wood Cliffs, N.J., 1970).

J. Hagan, 'The Control of Sympathy in Wuthering Heights', *NCF* xxi (1967).

W. T. Hale, *Anne Brontë: Her Life and Writings* (Bloomington, Ind., 1929).

A. Harrison and D. Stanford, *Anne Brontë: Her Life and Work* (London, 1959).

R. B. Heilman, 'Charlotte Brontë's "New" Gothic' in R. C. Rathburn and M. Steinmann (edd.), *From Jane Austen to Joseph Conrad* (Minneapolis, Minn., 1958; reprinted 1967).

—— 'Charlotte Brontë, Reason and the Moon', *NCF* xv (1961).

J. Hewish, *Emily Brontë, A Critical and Biographical Study* (London, 1969).

L. Hinkley, *The Brontës: Charlotte and Emily* (New York, 1945).

A. Kettle, 'Emily Brontë: *Wuthering Heights*', *An Introduction to the English Novel*, vol. ii (London, 1953).

G. D. Klingopulos, '*Wuthering Heights*', *Scrutiny*, xiv (1947).

E. A. Knies, 'The use of the "I" in *Jane Eyre*', *College English* (April 1960).

—— 'Art, Death and the Composition of *Shirley*', *Victorian Newsletter*, xxviii (1965).

J. Korg, 'The Problem of Unity in *Shirley*', *NCF* xii (1957).

Q. D. Leavis, 'A Fresh Approach to *Wuthering Heights*', included in Q. D. and F. R. Leavis, *Lectures in America* (London, 1969).

R. B. Martin, *The Accents of Persuasion: Charlotte Brontë's Novels* (London, 1966).

J. H. Miller, 'Emily Brontë', in his *The Disappearance of God* (Cambridge, Mass., London, 1963).

J. O'Neill (ed.), *Critics on Charlotte and Emily Brontë* (London, 1968).

W. D. Paden, *An Investigation of Gondal* (New York, 1958).

R. Pascal, 'The Autobiographical Novel', *EIC* ix (1959).

F. E. Ratchford, *The Brontës' Web of Childhood* (New York, 1941).

—— *Gondal's Queen: a novel in Verse by Emily Jane Brontë* (Austin, Texas, 1955).

A. M. F. Robinson, *Emily Brontë* (London, 1883).

C. P. Sanger, *The Structure of Wuthering Heights* (London, 1926).

M. H. Scargill, 'All Passion Spent: A Revaluation of *Jane Eyre*', *UTQ* xix (1950).

M. Schorer, 'Fiction and the Matrix of Analogy', *Kenyon Review*, xi (1949).

E. P. Shannon, 'The Present Tense in *Jane Eyre*', *NCF* x (1956).

N. Sherry, *The Brontë Sisters: Charlotte and Emily* (London, 1969).

K. Tillotson, '*Jane Eyre*' in her *Novels of the Eighteen-Forties* (Oxford, 1954).

J. M. S. Tomkins, 'Caroline Helstone's Eyes', *Brontë Society Transactions*, xiv (1961).

D. Traversi, '*Wuthering Heights* after a Hundred Years', *Dublin Review*, ccxxii

M. Turnell, '*Wuthering Heights*', *Dublin Review*, ccvi (1940).

D. Van Ghent, 'The window figure and the two-children figure', in her *The English Novel: Form and Function* (New York, 1953).

M. Visick, *The Genesis of Wuthering Heights* (Hong Kong and Oxford, 1958; reprinted 1965).

Melvin R. Watson, '*Wuthering Heights* and the Critics', *The Trollopian*, iii (1948).

—— 'Tempest in the Soul: The Theme and Structure of *Wuthering Heights*', *NCF* iv (1950).

V. Woolf, '*Jane Eyre*' and '*Wuthering Heights*', in her *The Common Reader* (London, 1925).

BIOGRAPHIES AND LETTERS

P. Bentley, *The Brontës* (London, 1947).

—— *The Brontës and their World* (London, 1967).

E. M. Delafield (ed.), *The Brontës: Their Lives Recorded by their Contemporaries* (London, 1935).

E. Gaskell, *The Life of Charlotte Brontë* (London, 1957).

W. Gérin, *Anne Brontë* (London, 1959).

—— *Branwell Brontë* (London, 1961).

—— *Charlotte Brontë: The Evolution of Genius* (Oxford, 1967).

—— *Emily Brontë: A Biography* (Oxford, 1971).

M. Lane, *The Brontë Story: A Reconsideration of Mrs Gaskell's Life of Charlotte Brontë* (London, 1953).

J. B. Leyland, *The Brontë Family, With Special Reference to Patrick Branwell Brontë* (2 vols., London, 1886).

T. W. Reid, *Charlotte Brontë: A Monograph* (London, 1877).

A. M. Robinson, *Emily Brontë* (London, 1883).

C. K. Shorter, *Charlotte Brontë and her Circle* (London, 1896; rev. edn., 1914).

—— *Charlotte Brontë and her Sisters* (London, 1905).

—— *The Brontës: Life and Letters* (2 vols., London, 1908).

C. Simpson, *Emily Brontë* (London, 1929).

M. H. Spielmann (ed.), 'The Love Letters of Charlotte Brontë to Constantin Heger', *The Times*, 29 July 1913 (privately printed 1914).

T. J. Wise and J. A. Symington (edd.), *The Brontës: Their Lives, Friendships and Correspondence*, 4 vols., in their *The Shakespeare Head Brontë* (see under TEXTS: (a) *Collected works* above).

BIBLIOGRAPHIES

J. P. Anderson, 'Bibliography', in A. Birrell's *Charlotte Brontë* (London, 1887).

M. G. Christian, 'The Brontës: Bibliographies and Manuscripts', in L. Stevenson (ed.), *Victorian Fiction, A Guide to Research* (Oxford, and Cambridge, Mass., 1964).

—— 'A Census of Brontë Manuscripts in the United States, *The Trollopian*, ii–iii (1947–8).

W. Ruff, 'First American Editions of Brontë Novels', *Brontë Society Transactions*, viii (1934).

T. J. Wise, *A Bibliography of the Writings in Prose and Verse of the Brontë Family* (London, 1917).

—— *A Brontë Library: a Catalogue of Printed Books, Manuscripts and Autograph Letters by Members of the Brontë Family* (London, 1929).

B. Wood, 'A Bibliography of the Works of the Brontë family', *Brontë Society Transactions*, i (1895).

—— 'A Supplement to the Bibliography of the Works of the Brontë Family', *Brontë Society Transactions*, vi (1897).

BACKGROUND READING

H. Grisewood (ed.), *Ideas and Beliefs of the Victorians* (London, 1949).

G. E. Harrison, *The Clue to the Brontës* (London, 1948).

A. B. Hopkins, *The Father of the Brontës* (Baltimore, Md., 1958).

W. E. Houghton, *The Victorian Frame of Mind, 1830–1870* (Oxford and New Haven, Conn., 1957).

R. Stang, *The Theory of the Novel in England, 1850–1870* (London, 1959).

P. Thomson, *The Victorian Heroine: A Changing Ideal* (London, 1956).

G. M. Young (ed.), *Early Victorian England, 1830–1865* (2 vols., Oxford, 1934).

Jerome Beaty

TEXTS

There is no complete, standard, or critical edition of George Eliot's work. Most critical and scholarly references are to the Cabinet Edition (21 vols., 1877–80), the last edition published during the author's lifetime by her publisher, Blackwood. It contains all the novels, 'Brother Jacob' and 'The Lifted Veil', *The Spanish Gypsy*, '*Jubal*' *and Other Poems*, *The Impressions of Theophrastus Such*, and a volume added later called *Essays and Leaves from a Note-Book*. The three-volume *Life* by J. W. Cross was added in 1885 (see BIO-GRAPHIES AND LETTERS). This edition does not include the translations of Strauss's *The Life of Jesus, Critically Examined* (3 vols., 1846) or of Ludwig Feuerbach's *The Essence of Christianity* (1854); the latter, with a foreword by H. Richard Niebuhr and an introduction by Karl Barth, is available in paperback (1957). Neither *The Complete Poetical Works* (1888) nor the limited edition of *Complete Poems of George Eliot*, ed. M. Browne (1889) is in fact complete; see, for example, Bernard J. Paris, 'George Eliot's Unpublished Poetry'. Thomas Pinney's edition of *Essays of George Eliot* (1963) brings together all the usually collected essays and some other non-fiction, such as 'Leaves from a Note-Book', and adds newly published or collected material such as 'Notes on Form in Art'. For previously collected works it indicates variants. It has useful appendices: 'George Eliot's Essays and Reviews' and 'Articles Wrongly or Doubtfully Attributed to George Eliot'. It is acknowledgedly far from a complete edition of the non-fiction prose, however. Haight's biography (see BIOGRAPHIES AND LETTERS) in an appendix prints a very early essay and the beginning of a story ['Edward Neville']; other notebook materials published include Anna Theresa Kitchel, *George Eliot's Quarry for 'Middlemarch'* (1950), and Jerome Beaty, 'George Eliot's Notebook for an Unwritten Novel'; a good deal of similar material appears in scattered, as yet unpublished, dissertations.

Many of the best texts of individual novels in terms of careful editing, annotation, and, to a lesser extent, indications of variants, have appeared in paperback editions in the past quarter-century; in general, the editing of such texts has become increasingly sophisticated and scholarly over the years. Thus Gordon S. Haight's edition of *Adam Bede* (1948) is very sparsely annotated—chiefly explaining dialect terms, identifying hymns, etc.—and has little textual information, while his edition of *Middlemarch* (1956) has useful publishing information and details about the selection of the copy text; it is more heavily annotated, clarifying allusions and references in the text, and it indicates many of the more interesting variants between manuscript, first, and later editions. The third Haight edition, *The Mill on the Floss* (1961), includes an internal chronology of the novel, a biographical chart, a full-page textual note including manuscript information as well as a selected bibliography. It disclaims any attempt at giving all variants, admitting that it offers only 'some of the interesting passages that can be deciphered'. It indicates volume-endings of the first edition, includes many more variants than the edition of *Middlemarch*, and is more painstakingly annotated. The first paperback *Daniel Deronda* (1961) is merely a cheap reprint but is notable because of the introduction by F. R. Leavis in which he 'recants' his earlier position regarding the separability of the two 'halves' of the novel (see *The Great Tradition* in CRITICAL STUDIES AND COMMENTARY). Most fully benefiting from the growth of George Eliot studies and the increasing sophistication of the editing of Victorian novels in general is the Penguin English Library. *Middlemarch* (1965) is edited by W. J. Harvey; though it does not indicate variants as does Haight it is more fully annotated though not a 'fully annotated edition of *Middlemarch* [which] would be an immense and probably tedious affair'. It has an excellent introduction. Barbara Hardy's introduction to *Daniel Deronda* (1967) in the same series heralds a new approach to that novel; the text is based on the Cabinet Edition with collation of the first book-edition though only a few variants are recorded; the notes do not claim to be 'exhaustive' though they are necessarily rather full, the best available so far but no doubt soon to be outdistanced as the flood of scholarly paperbacks continues. Q. D. Leavis's *Silas Marner* (1968) is the most recent of the Penguins.

CRITICAL STUDIES AND COMMENTARY

There are several collections of various kinds of previously published commentaries on George Eliot's work. The broadest in scope and most suitable for one who wants just a glance at the range and nature of critical comment is Gordon S. Haight (ed.), *A Century of George Eliot Criticism* (1965), which includes slightly more than fifty items, not, however, reprinted in their entirety. More than twenty date from George Eliot's lifetime (at least one review of each of the novels, of

The Spanish Gypsy, of *The Legend of Jubal,* and of 'The Lifted Veil' and 'Brother Jacob'), and sixteen from the years 1947–62. Most of the important critics or critical positions of the period are represented (Henry James, with seven items, may be over-represented). David Carroll (ed.), *George Eliot: The Critical Heritage* (1971), offers the fullest view of George Eliot as seen in her time: sixty-nine items, most of them British or American reviews of the novels published soon after the first appearance of each novel, a few reviews of Cross's *Life* (see BIOGRAPHY AND LETTERS) and obituary notices, and some of George Eliot's reactions to criticism. Almost all the reviews are published in full except for long extracts from the novels. The introduction presents a judicious analysis of the critical and extra-critical concerns represented, and a brief statement about George Eliot's reputation after 1885. There are headnotes identifying the reviewers (when known). A similar but smaller and on the whole less satisfactory sampling of contemporary response appears in John Holstrom and Laurence Lerner (edd.), *George Eliot and Her Readers* (1966). The items are not always presented in full and the 'linking paragraphs', though informative and intelligent, seem by their very nature less useful than Carroll's sustained introduction. All but one of the ten items in George R. Creeger (ed.), *George Eliot: A Collection of Critical Essays* (1970), are from 1954–66. Two of the ten items appear in the Haight volume. The Haight and Creeger volumes render Richard Stang (ed.), *Discussions of George Eliot,* more or less obsolete. Barbara Hardy (ed.), *Critical Essays on George Eliot* (1970), differs from these collections in containing ten essays written expressly for the volume, one on each of the longer works of fiction plus W. J. Harvey, 'Idea and Image in the Novels of George Eliot' and John Bayley, 'The Pastoral of Intellect'. The recurring emphasis here, as in so much George Eliot criticism of the last decade, is the conflict between what Mrs. Hardy describes as 'her stated meliorism . . . and her bleakly dramatized conclusions'. J. P. Couch, *George Eliot in France,* details the general neglect of the novelist in France, despite a few favourable reviews and a conscientious translator, until she was championed by Brunetière in 1881; there is a somewhat cursory appendix on the influence of France on George Eliot.

Modern criticism of George Eliot may have been said to begin with Lord David Cecil, *Early Victorian Novelists* (1934 and 1935), though the seminal work is surely F. R. Leavis, *The Great Tradition* (1948), the George Eliot section of which appeared in *Scrutiny* in 1945–6. Leavis vehemently maintains that only five novelists—Jane Austen, George Eliot, Henry James, Joseph Conrad, and D. H.

Lawrence—belong to the great English tradition. These authors offer unique moral vision embodied in original and appropriate forms or modes of fiction. Jane Austen he left to his wife, Lawrence he reserved for later; to the middle three he devoted this book. He succeeded in offending almost everyone, yet his views on these three novelists (and to some extent on the novel itself) have prevailed for a generation. Though he was not the first he was the most influential of critics to reverse the Victorian preference for the early Eliot novels, to place *Middlemarch* at the apex of her achievement, and to give serious attention to *Felix Holt* (especially the Mrs. Transome portions) and *Daniel Deronda* (especially the Gwendolen Harleth portions). That *Daniel Deronda* should be halved—a fat novel with a thin masterpiece struggling to get out—everyone denied, and years later, in a 1960 essay reprinted as the introduction to the Harper Torchbooks edition (1961), Leavis himself admitted that such surgery would be impossible; but most critics wound up agreeing about the superb, perhaps unparalleled achievement of 'Gwendolen Harleth'. Most also agreed (and Leavis was neither the first nor only critic so to claim) that *Silas Marner* is a 'minor masterpiece' (the emphasis on *minor* also regretted later). It was a critical commonplace at the time (Henry James having set the fashion earlier) to hold the 'two George Eliots' theory, and the prevailing version of that theory was to attribute all that was good in her work to her emotional depths, her unconscious, her childhood memories, and all that was bad to her intellect, her conscious intent, her cosmopolitan later life. Two excellent books of the late 1940s, Gerald Bullett, *George Eliot: Her Life and Her Books* (1947) and Joan Bennett, *George Eliot: Her Mind and Her Art* (1948) were, despite their many virtues (and Mrs. Bennett's excellent chapter, 'Vision and Design'), limited in impact by this kind of dichotomizing. Leavis, too, was aware of this 'truism' but characteristically turned it on its head: the 'good' George Eliot, he said, was the intellectual, and the 'bad' the nostalgic, wish-fulfilling girlish dreamer. It is not this thesis, however, that has made his study the new orthodoxy, but his critical judgements of the novels and of portions of the novels, supported by an unerring eye for the telling passage and a passionate commitment to the importance of fiction and the craft of fiction as a form of moral and cultural knowledge and value. This is an essential critical work.

Three 'great tradition' figures are dealt with as 'writers who compel us to reconsider our view of man' in Laurence Lerner, *The Truthtellers: Jane Austen, George Eliot, D. H. Lawrence* (1967). The first half, which 'deals mainly with what they have in common', though rich in insights and tantalizingly brief suggestions—such as the possibilities of a behaviourist criticism of fictional characters—is somewhat fragmentary and unsatisfying; the fuller treatment (40–60 pages each) of the three authors in the second half gives the author more scope to exercise his originality and discrimination. It is in resisting the commonplaces and making distinctions that he shines. On *The Mill on the Floss*, for example: Maggie's giving up Stephen is not a case of principle over-riding impulse but one kind of impulse countering another; we do not share Maggie's yearning for Stephen but we sympathize with her yearning; her application of 'duty' is not unacceptable in itself but because she has an unacceptable standard of duty; her rescue of Tom is not a moral decision but, again, an impulse. Lerner says from the beginning that his thesis (which we discover on the last page is that the three writers define-by-example the pre-Romantic, the positive Romantic, and the subversive Romantic) was not imposed but emerged; this lack of focus and sustained argument is the weakness of the study—and the absence of a reductive, systematic thesis is also its strength, permitting the free play of sensitivity and intelligence unshackled by the need to prove a point. In direct contrast is another three-novelist study: Calvin Bedient, *Architects of Self: George Eliot, D. H. Lawrence, E. M. Forster* (1972), which argues that George Eliot, except in *Middlemarch*, is constantly urging the total sacrifice of the passional self to the social self. Ignoring all those attempts (admittedly not always successful) in George Eliot's fiction to structure a synthesis of duty and desire (Stonyshire–Loamshire, Hebraism–Hellenism), he then accuses the novelist of being an 'either/or' moralist. The critical evaluations, though not the criteria, are almost precisely those of Leavis and the post-Leavis consensus.

George Eliot is linked with four other novelists in C. B. Cox, *The Free Spirit: A Study of Liberal Humanism in the Novels of George Eliot, Henry James, E. M. Forster, Virginia Woolf, Angus Wilson* (1963). The 'free spirit' (the term is Henry James's) is essentially that of the nineteenth-century liberal with 'faith in historical progress, individual freedom, tolerance, and the power of reason', and Cox undertakes 'to examine the attempts of certain important novelists to deal with the moral problems of these free spirits, and with the difficulties they confront when trying to put these ideals into practice'. Like Willey (see BACKGROUND READING) he calls George Eliot 'The Conservative-Reformer', and divides her characters accordingly into two types: conservatives like Mrs. Poyser and Caleb Garth, who are not seekers, do not change but fulfil themselves 'through acceptance of traditional ideas of good and evil', and who live a vital, good, and dignified life in their communities; and reformers, like Maggie and Dorothea, who 'separate themselves from established routines of the community' in a quest for intellectual and moral growth. These 'free-spirits', cut off from community, confronted with a knowledge of evil, approach a view of reality as moral chaos which George Eliot cannot bear. 'All her novels have major flaws because she was afraid to face the realities of a world without God.' But Cox resists the temptation to suggest that George Eliot is merely 'a pessimistic writer who betrays her vision by providing sentimental conclusions for her stories', and he traces her development in part through increasingly 'strenuous efforts to understand the ways in which moral awareness could progress', though admitting finally that 'In the end she has nothing practical to offer except simple Christian truisms. Instead of new horizons, we have the traditional service of family and community.' A similar theme, pursued at greater length and detail and in a somewhat different, more historically limited context, is offered by U. C. Knoepflmacher in *Religious Humanism and the Victorian Novel: George Eliot, Walter Pater, and Samuel Butler* (1965). He summarizes its thesis in a later work, *George Eliot's Early Novels: The Limits of Realism* (1968), the first of a proposed two-volume study: 'Just as her "religion of humanity" represented an attempt to counter, as well as to conserve, the elements of Christian belief, so does her fiction involve both a reversal and a continuation of the modes and attitudes of the English Romantics.' Like many others, at least since Bourl'honne (see BACKGROUND READING), he sees in George Eliot's work 'two conflicting impulses. She wanted to unfold before her readers the temporal actuality she believed in; yet she also wanted to assure them—and herself—that man's inescapable subjection to the flux of time did not invalidate a trust in justice, perfectibility, and order.' It was this very inconsistency, Knoepflmacher maintains, that made her seek 'new theoretic forms' and that resulted in at least two masterpieces—*Silas Marner* and *Middlemarch*: 'Paradoxically enough the very imperfection of her philosophy led to the perfection of her art.' He gives serious attention to 'The Lifted Veil' (though he may make too much of it) and is at his best in making a case for *Silas Marner* as more than a 'minor masterpiece'. (*Silas Marner* has been fortunate in the last few years; the best single essay on the novel is David Carroll, '*Silas Marner*: Reversing the Oracles of Religion', in *Literary Monographs*, edd. Eric Rothstein and Thomas K. Dunseath (1967).) Knoepflmacher is the best of the 'George Eliot's not one of us' critics.

The best books since *The Great Tradition*, however, are Barbara Hardy, *The Novels of George Eliot: A Study in Form* (1959), and W. J. Harvey, *The Art of George Eliot* (1961). Both attack successfully the then conventional view of George Eliot as the deep thinker and ponderous moralist whose force of mind overcame the inadequacy of form and lack of unity in the 'loose baggy monsters' that are her novels. In order to do so both critics had to counter the prevailing Jamesian criteria for the art of the novel, and both books are important for students of the novel as a genre as well as for students of George Eliot. Mrs. Hardy, rather than imposing a pre-conceived 'form' upon the novel which all novels 'must' have, first defines the kind of 'unheroic tragedy' that George Eliot herself describes and traces the tragic process through the novels from several different angles. She explores the relationship of character and plot to form, and analyses the various tones that the omniscient narrator's voice may take (rather than assuming all 'intrusions' of the narrator are aesthetic sins). She is equally discriminating in dealing with imagery, distinguishing the pathetic from the ironic image in function and effect and showing how a dramatic scene may itself be an image. The best chapters in this excellent book are those on imagery and the chapter called 'Possibilities'—wherein she shows that for many of George Eliot's characters there is not only the life as it unfolds in the fiction but 'a strong and deliberate suggestion of the possible lives her characters might have lived'; the result of this alternative shadow is a significant increase in the realism and a more convincing presentation of moral values. Harvey is even stronger on novel theory, on the 'omniscient author' convention, and on matters of over-all structure, both the temporal structure and the 'architecture'. It is difficult to choose between these books, and indeed one should not: they are both essential.

Mark Schorer's 1949 essay, 'Fiction and the Matrix of Analogy'—the frame and *Middlemarch* portions of which are reprinted in Haight (ed.), *A Century of George Eliot Criticism*—is the seminal work on the study of imagery in fiction. The approach—essentially revealing the thematic structure or meaning of a work through the 'matrix' of implications in overt and submerged metaphor—has contributed a great deal to our understanding of fiction and the art of fiction, but it can be and has been (to some degree by Schorer himself) applied too systematically and reductively, in isolation from other elements, including direct statement. Reva Stump, *Movement and Vision in George Eliot's Novels* (1959), intelligently applies this technique to *Adam Bede*, *The Mill on the Floss*, and *Middlemarch*, illuminating many elements and passages in the novels but not always avoiding the tendency in such studies to find metaphorical implications everywhere and avoiding explicit elements that do not 'fit'; the piling up of instances, italicizing words for emphasis, etc., make the reading rather heavy going. Karl Kroeber, *Styles in Fictional Structure: The Art of Jane Austen, Charlotte Brontë, George Eliot* (1971), somewhat wistfully regrets that literary study, especially in matters of style, is not, like scientific research, cumulative, and by use of computers he tabulates parts of speech, 'nouns—concrete and abstract, in narrative and dialogue', 'verbs—modals and progressives', 'ratio of subordinating conjunctions to connecting conjunctions', in all twenty-two tables. On the whole, these tables seem more useful for the triggering of Kroeber's own excellent perceptions than as data banks for further deposits. He sees this as clearly as the reader does and insists the computer is a tool for the critic whose insights or hunches may be confirmed or modified by quantification. 'More useful stylistic judgments begin with assessments of the central purpose of the style in question . . .'; students of imagery and metaphor, please note. John Holloway, *The Victorian Sage* (1953), does define the purpose of George Eliot's style: like Carlyle, Disraeli, Newman, Arnold, and Hardy she is a 'Victorian sage'—that is, one who wishes to make you *see* what is there but what you have not seen consciously before—and this 'quickening' of the reader is done through language, words, and cannot be represented adequately by summary or argument. Without benefit of computer, he shows how this purpose controls and defines such elements as character, scene, incident, metaphor, and even the ethics of the novels. Though the details selected reinforce his argument rather than representing fully and adequately the novels, the over-all argument is sound, and this is an important study.

Jerome Thale, *The Novels of George Eliot* (1959), is a lucid introduction to the novels, one chapter devoted to each (none to *Scenes*) in order of publication. This sensible study has perhaps been outstripped by subsequent criticism, though it is still a good place to begin; the chapter on *Romola*—'The Uses of Failure'—in which he treats that much-maligned novel as an unsuccessful experiment, but one essential for George Eliot's growth toward the more ambitious later novels, is particularly worthwhile. Ian Milner, *The Structure of Values in George Eliot* (1968) is a useful, if somewhat low-keyed, antidote to the recent emphasis on the 'dark' side of George Eliot and her 'evasion' of the sombre implications of her vision of the real world. Admitting that the idealized figures are sometimes unconvincing, he insists on their function as 'the touchstone by which good and evil, within the human soul and in society, are revealed . . . In the age of the anti-hero the "heroic" good man seems out of place. Yet he is the central focus of George Eliot's vision. Imperfectly realized, he voices her constant and most characteristic faith. . .'

Almost without exception, critics since the Second World War have agreed that *Middlemarch* is the summit of George Eliot's achievement, that it may be the best English novel in the nineteenth (or any other) century, that it belongs in the company of the best Continental novels. David Daiches, *Middlemarch* (1963), is the best independent study of that masterly novel: subtle but sensible, he sees the novel whole without reducing it to a formula or ignoring its complexities, even its contradictions. He tries to define 'the moral ideas around which the action is constructed and the interweaving fates of the characters developed', but admits that 'the novel is richer than any moral formula.' Its contradictions, he concludes, 'suggest the richness and many-sidedness of life . . . *Middlemarch* illuminates experience as much today as it ever did.' This may not be the last word on *Middlemarch*, nor does it make 'obsolete' other studies of that novel in the works already mentioned, but it is certainly the place to begin and the standard against which other studies are to be measured or the framework within which they are to be placed. Barbara Hardy (ed.), '*Middlemarch*': *Critical Approaches to the Novel*, (1967), contains an introduction by the editor and eight original essays by seven authors looking at such diverse aspects of the novel as its structure, intellectual background, language, critical reception, the revisions George Eliot made in proof, and the details within the novel (objects, events, images). Jerome Beaty, '*Middlemarch*' *from Notebook to Novel* (1960) examines the composition of the novel from its origin in the beginnings of two separate works through the recorded research and plans in those notebooks published by Anna Theresa Kitchel, *George Eliot's Quarry for* '*Middlemarch*' (1950) (see TEXTS); the effect of its publication in half-volume parts, and analyses in detail the composition of a single chapter. There is also, somewhat surprisingly, a book-length study of George Eliot's earliest fiction, T. A. Noble, *George Eliot's* '*Scenes of Clerical Life*' (1965), which is very useful in its description of the theory behind the work, the critical reception, and the 'experiments in narrative' these tales represent, though critically the study is somewhat disappointing.

BIOGRAPHY AND LETTERS

Unquestionably the standard biography is Gordon S. Haight, *George Eliot: A Biography* (1968), which supersedes all others, except for historical interest or for incidental remarks or interpretations. It is not, however, a life-and-works volume. There is virtually no interpretation of the novels and little use of the novels to illuminate the biography; such scholarly scrupulosity is welcome, but it is difficult at times to see in the biography the woman who wrote the novels. It eschews not only criticism but intellectual history and psychological analysis. The 'key' to the biography—that George Eliot was a woman who needed a man to lean on—is neither novel nor ultimately satisfactory. There are no doubt many interpretative biographies to come, but for the facts of the life, including the correction of many traditional errors and rumours, this is the indispensable, exhaustive, and virtually self-sufficient history of George Eliot's life.

Leslie Stephen, *George Eliot* (1902), is understandably 'old-fashioned' both as biography and criticism, but he is a perceptive reader and even when 'wrong' is worth reading; this English Men of Letters volume is useful too as a barometer of George Eliot's reputation between the time of her death in 1880 and the revival and revaluation of her work in the 1930s and 1940s. A recent equivalent, Walter Allen, *George Eliot* (1964), in the Master of World Literature Series, is disappointing; the biographical contribution is nil and the criticism rather conventional and tired, especially from so good a critic. Allen does open a new window, however: George Eliot, he maintains, is one of the few Victorians that we are prepared to judge in the context of her European contemporaries rather than merely in relation to her English ones, and, though in that wider context she is 'second-rate', that she can be put in such company at all is high praise.

More strictly biographical, Anna T. Kitchel, *George Lewes and George Eliot* (1933), is an original and perceptive work on this key relationship, and, if it needs correction at times, it has not been and probably will not be soon superseded. Haight's *George Eliot and John Chapman* (1940) which makes extensive use of and incorporates Chapman's diaries, tells us all we can know about that somewhat ambiguous relationship: Chapman's censoring of his diaries ironically permits the speculation that George Eliot was Chapman's mistress, a contention that Haight himself rebuts. K. A. McKenzie's *Edith Simcox and George Eliot* (1961), based on sections of Miss Simcox's manuscript 'Autobiography of a Shirt Maker', recounts the passionate, almost hysterical adoration of the novelist by the 'shirt maker' in the late 1870s.

The monumental and indispensable edition of the letters is Gordon S. Haight (ed.) '*The George Eliot Letters* (7 vols., 1954–5). Meticulously edited, fully annotated, indexed (though somewhat fallibly), with brief but full biographies of the main correspondents, this is without question a necessary item for the student, critic, and scholar who has the time to go beyond the biography, though, it must be admitted, George Eliot is not one of the world's great letter-writers.

Neither the Haight biography nor his edition of the letters wholly supplants *George Eliot's Life as Related in Her Letters and Journals*, arranged and edited by J. W. Cross (3 vols., 1885), which contains not only some additional material and comment but also projects the image of the author the world apparently accepted for some seventy years. A loving and pious monument to the memory of his wife of seven-and-a-half months, it presents her as a monumental bore. Here is the George Eliot icon fractured by the iconoclasts of the anti-Victorian late Victorians, Edwardians, and Georgians.

BIBLIOGRAPHY

There is no definitive bibliography of George Eliot or of writings about her. M. L. Parrish, *Victorian Lady Novelists* (1933), and P. H. Muir, 'Bibliography of First Editions of the Books of George Eliot', *Bookman's Journal* (1927–8, supplement) describe the separately published works. Thomas Pinney's edition of the essays (see TEXTS) lists the periodical writings and other non-fiction.

J. P. Anderson, 'Bibliography', appended to Oscar Browning, *Life of George Eliot* (1890), lists the works and a number of subsequent early editions as well as indicating, for shorter items, whether they were collected and where, and it is an excellent checklist of early criticism, including reviews. Within its defined limitations this has been extended and updated by J. D. Barry, 'The Literary Reputation of George Eliot's Fiction', *Bulletin of Bibliography*, iv (1959). The most recent and fullest checklist, though admittedly incomplete and excluding the works themselves, is William H. Marshall, 'A Selective Bibliography of Writings About George Eliot', *Bulletin of Bibliography*, xxv (May and September 1967). The best description and evaluation of selected materials through 1962 is W. J. Harvey, 'George Eliot', in *Victorian Fiction: A Guide to Research*, ed. Lionel Stevenson (1964).

There are three descriptions of the important holdings, chiefly manuscripts, at Yale, all published in the *Yale University Library Gazette*: R. L. Purdy, 'Journals and Letters of George Eliot', vii (1932); G. S. Haight, 'The Tinker Collection of George Eliot Manuscripts', xxix (1955), and 'The George Eliot and George Henry Lewes Collection', xxxv (1961). Haight's general description of manuscript locations, 'George Eliot', *Victorian Newsletter*, xiii (1958) was followed a few years later by revelation in the same journal of the location of two new notebooks: B. R. Jerman, 'Nineteenth-Century Holdings at the Folger', xxii (1962).

BACKGROUND READING

The two best—and brief—works in English applying intellectual background to the fiction of George Eliot as a whole, are Basil Willey *Nineteenth-Century Studies: Coleridge to Matthew Arnold* (1949), and George Levine, 'Determinism and Responsibility in the Works of George Eliot', *PMLA* lxxvii (1962), both reprinted (with omissions) in Haight (ed.), *A Century of George Eliot Criticism* (see CRITICAL STUDIES AND COMMENTARY). Both deal with the continuingly influential 'two George Eliots' notion defined by P. Bourl'honne, *George Eliot: Essai de biographie intellectuelle et morale, 1819–1854* (1933), a study which sees a conflict between George Eliot the optimist who feels man may progress toward the good and George Eliot the pessimistic thinker who reasons that man is wholly determined. (Bourl'-honne's study is still valuable for its detailed accounts of the influence of Feuerbach and Spinoza, as well as that of Comte, Lewes, and Spencer, on George Eliot's thought.) Willey emphasizes the conservative–reformer split (see Cox, *The Free Spirit*, CRITICAL STUDIES AND COMMENTARY)—the nostalgia for the ordered past and the belief in and hope for progress—which makes George Eliot so much a part of her time. George Levine convincingly attacks the assumption that she could not be both a consistent determinist and a believer in moral responsibility, finding these views reconciled in the philosophical tradition of Hume that runs through Mill 'forward to one of the most powerful contemporary schools of academic philosophy—that of linguistic analysis'. N. N. Feltes, 'George Eliot and the United Sensibility', *PMLA* lxxix (1964), though somewhat lighter in background material than the Levine essay, makes a welcome, judicious, and convincing attempt to synthesize the alleged head–heart, thought–feeling split in George Eliot, showing in her appreciation of Newman, in Lewes, and extensively in her own novels, especially *Middlemarch*, that the concept of 'felt thought' bridges the chasm. Bernard J. Paris, *Experiments in Life: George Eliot's Quest for Values* (1965) rephrases the conflict as that of 'realism' versus 'moralism'; traces George Eliot's intellectual history *before* she started writing fiction, with emphasis on the empiricism and positivism of Comte, Mill, Spencer, Lewes, and, especially, Feuerbach, from all of whom 'she derived the premises upon which her aesthetic theory, her representation of life, and her understanding of moral and religious phenomena are based. The principles of the positivistic cosmology and epistemology constitute the most general laws of her fictional worlds; they are the presuppositions which govern every phase of her thought.' His application of intellectual background to the fiction, though provocative, is somewhat Procrustean. An earlier and more general book—M. L. Cazamian, *Le Roman et les idées en Angleterre* (1923)—also applies intellectual background rather mechanically to the novels in its George Eliot chapter, though it is still useful for the background material. Miriam Allott, 'George Eliot in the 1860s', avoids the dubious assumption that George Eliot's thought was fixed by the time she began writing fiction, and takes into account elements of feeling and mood, ill-health and middle age, as George Eliot, in this decade, approached and passed her fiftieth birthday. Having always seen potential tragedy in the clash between the individual and the general (the world), since the individual is doomed to defeat, the novelist could earlier celebrate the Promethean striving, but now was faced with the 'sombre implications of her own doctrine', and bordered on despair, a despair she was able to shake off finally in *Middlemarch*. The most intelligent, subtle, and convincing relating of intellectual background to the fiction is W. J. Harvey, 'Intellectual Backgrounds of the Novel: Casaubon and Lydgate', in *'Middlematch' : Critical Approaches to the Novel*, ed. Barbara Hardy (see CRITICAL STUDIES AND COMMENTARY). Harvey praises Bourl'honne but warns of the tendency of such general studies to become maps that are 'too neat or precise to delineate the twists and turns, the labyrinths and metamorphoses of something so protean as the thought of an individual'. By showing that Casaubon was engaged in the pseudo-science of mythography (and not just lagging behind Strauss and other German Higher Critics) and that Lydgate in his search for the primitive tissue 'was mistaken in the direction of his research' because he was a little too early for cell theory, Harvey illuminates a basic relationship in the novel and reinforces the 'sense of amplitude, solidity or density that we derive from the actual novel'.

It is difficult to draw a firm line between criticism and background. J. M. Prest, *The Industrial Revolution in Coventry* (1960) clearly offers background information; C. T. Bissell, 'Social Analysis in the Novels of George Eliot', and Jerome Beaty, 'History by Indirection: The Era of Reform in *Middlemarch*', primarily seek to demonstrate the use of sociology and history in the novels or a novel. William Myers, 'George Eliot: Politics and Personality', in *Literature and Politics in the Nineteenth Century*, ed. John Lucas (1971), describes the explicit and implicit political attitudes in the novels, relates them to those of other Victorian novelists, especially Trollope, discriminates shrewdly and, though he judges the attitudes on the whole adversely, praises her insistence on keeping her characters in and of society: he finds 'potent and significant', for example, 'the image of Gwendolen Harleth at the end of [*Daniel Deronda*] . . . solitary and helpless in the midst of a larger world'. Similarly, the essays dealing with George Eliot and religion may place her in a tradition, such as rationalism, as does Humphry House, 'Qualities of George Eliot's Unbelief', in *All in Due Time* (1955); or in historical context, as does H. R. Murphy, 'The Ethical Revolt against Christian Orthodoxy in Early Victorian England'; may infer the religious position largely from the novels themselves, as does Martin Svaglic, 'Religion in the Novels of George Eliot', or, like Donald C. Masters, 'George Eliot and the Evangelicals', deal with one element in her treatment of religion.

Richard Stang, *The Theory of the Novel in England, 1850–1870* (1959), describes the wider context of novel theory and criticism within which George Eliot's position, as described in the following articles, may be viewed: W. Casey, 'George Eliot's Theory of Fiction; J. D. Rust, 'The Art of Fiction in George Eliot's Reviews'; G. S. Haight, 'George Eliot's Theory of Fiction'; W. J. Hyde, 'George Eliot and the Climate of Realism'; Richard Stang, 'The Literary Criticism of George Eliot'.

REFERENCES

TEXTS

(*a*) *Collected works*

The Works of George Eliot (20 vols., Cabinet Edition, Edinburgh and London, 1877–80).

The Complete Poetical Works (New York, 1888).

Complete Poems of George Eliot (Boston, Mass., 1889).

C. L. Lewes (ed.), *Essays and Leaves from a Note-Book* (21st vol. of Cabinet Edition, Edinburgh and London, 1884).

T. Pinney (ed.), *Essays of George Eliot* (New York and London, 1963).

(*b*) *Novels*

G. S. Haight (ed.), *Adam Bede* (paperback, Boston, Mass., 1948).

—— (ed.), *Middlemarch* (paperback, Boston, Mass., 1956).

—— (ed.), *The Mill on the Floss* (paperback, Boston, Mass., 1961).

B. Hardy (ed.), *Daniel Deronda* (paperback, Harmondsworth and Baltimore, Md., 1967).

W. J. Harvey (ed.), *Middlemarch* (paperback, Harmondsworth and Baltimore, Md., 1965).

Q. D. Leavis (ed.), *Silas Marner* (paperback, Harmondsworth and Baltimore, Md., 1968).

(c) Other works

J. Beaty, 'George Eliot's Notebook for an Unwritten Novel', *Princeton University Library Chronicle*, xviii (1957).

['Edward Neville'] in Haight, *Biography*.

L. Feuerbach, *The Essence of Christianity*, trans. [George Eliot] (London, 1854; paperback, U.S., 1957).

A. T. Kitchel, *George Eliot's Quarry for 'Middlemarch'* (Berkeley and Los Angeles, Calif., and London, 1950).

B. J. Paris, 'George Eliot's Unpublished Poetry', *SP* lvi (1959).

D. F. Strauss, *The Life of Jesus, Critically Examined*, trans. [George Eliot] (London, 1846).

CRITICAL STUDIES AND COMMENTARY

J. Bayley, 'The Pastoral of Intellect', in Hardy (ed.), *Critical Essays*.

J. Beaty, *'Middlemarch' from Notebook to Novel: A Study of George Eliot's Creative Method* (Urbana, Ill., 1960).

C. Bedient, *Architects of Self: George Eliot, D. H. Lawrence, E. M. Forster* (Berkeley and Los Angeles, Calif., and London, 1972).

J. Bennett, *George Eliot: Her Mind and Her Art* (Cambridge, 1948).

G. W. Bullett, *George Eliot: Her Life and Her Books* (London, 1947).

D. R. Carroll (ed.), *George Eliot: The Critical Heritage* (London, 1971).

—— 'Silas Marner: Reversing the Oracles of Religion', in *Literary Monographs*, E. Rothstein and T. K. Dunseath (edd.) 1 (Madison and Milwaukee, Wis.; London, 1967).

Lord D. Cecil, *Early Victorian Novelists* (London, 1934; Chicago, 1935).

J. P. Couch, *George Eliot in France: A French Appraisal of George Eliot's Writings, 1858–1960.* (University of North Carolina Studies in Comparative Literature, 41, Chapel Hill, N.C., 1967).

C. B. Cox, *The Free Spirit: A Study of Liberal Humanism in the Novels of George Eliot, Henry James, E. M. Forster, Virginia Woolf, and Angus Wilson* (London, 1963).

G. R. Creeger (ed.), *George Eliot: A Collection of Critical Essays* (paperback, Englewood Cliffs, N.J., 1970).

D. Daiches, *Middlemarch* (Studies in English Literature, London and Great Neck, N.Y., 1963).

G. S. Haight (ed.), *A Century of George Eliot Criticism* (paperback, London and N.Y., 1965).

B. Hardy, (ed.), *Critical Essays on George Eliot* (London, 1970).

—— (ed.), *'Middlemarch': Critical Approaches to the Novel* (London, 1967).

—— *The Novels of George Eliot: A Study in Form* (London, 1959).

W. J. Harvey, *The Art of George Eliot* (London, 1961).

—— 'Idea and Image in the Novels of George Eliot', in Hardy (ed.), *Critical Essays*.

J. Holloway, *The Victorian Sage: Studies in Argument* (London and New York, 1953).

J. Holstrom and L. Lerner (edd.), *George Eliot and Her Readers* (London, 1966).

U. C. Knoepflmacher, *George Eliot's Early Novels* (Berkeley and Los Angeles, Calif., 1968).

—— *Religious Humanism and the Victorian Novel: George Eliot, Walter Pater, and Samuel Butler* (Princeton, N.J., 1965).

K. Kroeber, *Styles in Fictional Structures: The Art of Jane Austen, Charlotte Brontë, George Eliot* (Princeton, N.J., 1971).

F. R. Leavis, 'George Eliot's Zionist Novel', *Commentary*, xxx (1960); re-printed as introduction to *Daniel Deronda* (paperback, Harper Torchbooks, New York, 1961).

—— *The Great Tradition: George Eliot, Henry James, Joseph Conrad* (London and New York, 1948).

L. Lerner, *The Truthtellers: Jane Austen, George Eliot, D. H. Lawrence* (London, 1967).

I. Milner, *The Structure of Values in George Eliot* (paperback, Acta Universitatis Carolinae Philologica, Monographia 23, Prague, 1968).

T. A. Noble, *George Eliot's 'Scenes of Clerical Life'* (Yale Studies in English, 159, New Haven, Conn., and London, 1965).

M. Schorer, 'Fiction and the Matrix of Analogy' *Kenyon Review*, xi (1959); reprinted in part in Haight (ed.), *A Century.* . . .

R. Stang (ed.), *Discussions of George Eliot* (paperback, Boston, Mass., 1960).

R. Stump, *Movement and Vision in George Eliot's Novels* (Seattle, Wash., 1959).

J. Thale, *The Novels of George Eliot* (New York, 1959).

BIOGRAPHIES AND LETTERS

W. Allen, *George Eliot* (Masters of World Literature, London, 1964).

O. Browning, *Life of George Eliot* (London, 1890).

J. W. Cross, *George Eliot's Life as Related in Her Letters and Journals* (3 vols., added to Cabinet Edition of *Works*, London, Edinburgh, and New York, 1885).

G. S. Haight, *George Eliot: A Biography* (Oxford and New York, 1968).

—— *George Eliot and John Chapman: With Chapman's Diaries* (New Haven, Conn., and London, 1940).

—— (ed.), *The George Eliot Letters* (7 vols., New Haven, Conn., and London, 1954–5).

A. T. Kitchel, *George Lewes and George Eliot* (New York, 1933).

K. A. McKenzie, *Edith Simcox and George Eliot* (Oxford, 1961).

Sir L. Stephen, *George Eliot* (English Men of Letters, London, 1902).

BIBLIOGRAPHIES

J. P. Anderson, 'Bibliography', in Browning, *Life*.

J. D. Barry, 'The Literary Reputation of George Eliot's Fiction', *Bulletin of Bibliography*, iv (1959).

G. S. Haight, 'George Eliot', *Victorian Newsletter*, xiii (1958).

—— 'The George Eliot and George Henry Lewes Collection', *Yale University Library Gazette*, xxxv (1961).

—— 'The Tinker Collection of George Eliot Manuscripts', *Yale University Library Gazette*, xxxv (1955).

W. J. Harvey, 'George Eliot', in Lionel Stevenson (ed.). *Victorian Fiction: A Guide to Research*, (Cambridge, Mass., 1964).

B. R. Jerman, 'Nineteenth-Century Holdings at the Folger', *Victorian Newsletter*, xxii (1962).

W. H. Marshall, 'A Selective Bibliography of Writings About George Eliot, to 1965', in 2 parts, *Bulletin of Bibliography*, xxv (1967).

P. H. Muir, 'A Bibliography of the First Editions of Books by George Eliot', *Bookman's Journal*, iv, supplement (1927–8).

M. L. Parrish, *Victorian Lady Novelists: George Eliot, Mrs. Gaskell, The Brontë Sisters, First Editions in the Library at Dormy House, New Jersey* (London, 1933).

R. L. Purdy, 'Journals and Letters of George Eliot', *Yale University Library Gazette*, vii (1932).

BACKGROUND READING

M. Allott, 'George Eliot in the 1860's', *VS* v (1961).

J. Beaty, 'History by Indirection: The Era of Reform in *Middlemarch*', *VS* i (1957), reprinted with omissions in Haight (ed.), *A Century*. . . .

C. T. Bissell, 'Social Analysis in the Novels of George Eliot', *ELH* xviii (1951).

P. Bourl'honne, *George Eliot: Essai de biographie intellectuelle et morale, 1819–1854* (Paris, 1933).

W. Casey, 'George Eliot's Theory of Fiction', *West Virginia University Bulletin, Philological Papers*, ix (1953).

M. L. Cazamian, *Le Roman et les idées en Angleterre: L'Influence de la science* (Strasbourg and New York, 1923).

N. N. Feltes, 'George Eliot and the Unified Sensibility', *PMLA* lxxix (1964).

G. S. Haight, 'George Eliot's Theory of Fiction', *Victorian Newsletter*, x (1956).

W. J. Harvey, 'Intellectual Backgrounds of the Novel: Casaubon and Lydgate', in Hardy (ed.), '*Middlemarch*': *Critical Approaches*.

H. House, 'Qualities of George Eliot's Unbelief', in *All in Due Time* (London, 1955).

W. J. Hyde, 'George Eliot and the Climate of Realism', *PMLA* lxxii (1957), reprinted with omissions in Haight (ed.), *A Century*. . . .

G. R. Levine, 'Determinism and Responsibility in the Works of George Eliot', *PMLA* lxxvii (1962), reprinted with omissions in Haight (ed.), *A Century*. . . .

D. C. Masters, 'George Eliot and the Evangelicals', *Dalhousie Review*, xli (1962).

H. R. Murphy, 'The Ethical Revolt against Christian Orthodoxy in Early Victorian England', *American Historical Review*, lx (1955).

W. Myers, 'George Eliot: Politics and Personality', in John Lucas (ed.), *Literature and Politics in the Nineteenth Century* (London, 1971).

B. J. Paris, *Experiments in Life: George Eliot's Quest for Value* (Detroit, Mich., 1965).

J. M. Prest, *The Industrial Revolution in Coventry* (London, 1960).

J. D. Rust, 'The Art of Fiction in George Eliot's Reviews', *RES* vii (1956).

R. Stang, 'The Literary Criticism of George Eliot', *PMLA* lxxii (1957).

—— *The Theory of the Novel in England, 1850–1870* (New York, 1961).

M. J. Svaglic, 'Religion in the Novels of George Eliot', *JEGP* liii (1954), reprinted with omissions in Haight (ed.), *A Century*. . . .

B. Willey, *Nineteenth Century Studies: Coleridge to Matthew Arnold* (London and New York, 1949); chapter on G. Eliot reprinted with omissions in Haight (ed.), *A Century*. . . .

F. B. Pinion

TEXTS

As criticism proliferates, a sound knowledge of the texts is the surest prerequisite for discrimination. The only up-to-date and authoritative texts of Hardy are those of editions published by Macmillan (London) and St. Martin's Press (New York), and certain American paperbacks.

Hardy's recension of the main part of his first (unpublished) novel is edited by Carl Weber. Among the many items in H. Orel's valuable collection of Hardy's miscellaneous prose are the prefaces (including the General Preface), three essays on the novel, and 'The Dorsetshire Labourer'.

There are selections of Hardy's poetry by G. M. Young, John Crowe Ransom, P. N. Furbank, John Wain, and (with stories) D. Morrison. The first contains an introduction which tends toward important larger truths rather than to precision, and has an astonishing appraisal of one of Hardy's best poems; Wain's is a slim volume which includes all Hardy's prefaces to his poems. The Furbank selection is edited for schools and colleges. Irving Howe's selection of Hardy's poetry and prose gives good value, and has a useful introduction.

Scholarly criticism must take account of successive revisions of the texts. (See the works listed under CRITICAL STUDIES.) Valuable work was done on this subject by Mary Chase in *Thomas Hardy, from Serial to Novel*, but closer study is rewarding, as articles by R. C. Slack on *Jude*, O. B. Wheeler on *The Return of the Native*, J. Laird on *Tess*, and Dale Kramer's thorough study of *The Woodlanders* amply illustrate. An article by F. B. Pinion in *The Thomas Hardy Year Book* discusses, with reference to textual variations, why Hardy chose to change the geographical background of that novel. John Paterson's examination of the opening of *Jude* concludes somewhat doubtfully (is it necessary to assume that Hardy *began* the novel with the educational theme which had occurred to him as the subject for a short story in April 1888?). His analysis of *The Return of the Native* is based on textual changes, and is impressive, but some of his conclusions have been questioned. Such differences in interpretation underline the need for

an edition of the most important of Hardy's novels giving all significant variants.

CRITICAL STUDIES AND COMMENTARY

Earlier criticism undoubtedly had a spaciousness, and an occasional
grandeur, with reference to the Wessex background, to character,
nature and Fate. Few will have time for the leisurely approach of
Lionel Johnson; the rhetoric of Lascelles Abercrombie should not
blind us to his misleading critical simplifications. He sees Oak, Venn,
and Winterbourne as brothers more identical than could ever be
found in life. Such facile impressions haunted Hardy criticism for a
long period (long after S. C. Chew found all Hardy's women to be of
one type). The greater our familiarity with the novels, the more we
shall recognize that variety and continual change were consistently
characteristic of their author.

D. H. Lawrence's essay is unique. Anyone unacquainted with its
author will find it 'queer stuff' and too often 'about anything but
Thomas Hardy' (to quote his own words). Moreover, close study of
his categorizations will illustrate how inconsistently he has re-created
Hardy's characters. Yet the reader who can see his way through a
welter of irrelevance will find rare insights, particularly in the analysis of Sue Bridehead.

J. W. Beach is readable, and, despite occasional inaccuracies and
a failure to reveal much about Hardy's technique as a novelist, is
worth reading. Chew makes the traditional surveys, but should be
read critically. H. C. Duffin's early work was expanded into a
volume of considerable size and complexity. It has both gained and
suffered from accretiveness, and needs careful sifting; nevertheless, it
contains much perceptive detail with reference to the novels, the
poems, and *The Dynasts*.

No Hardy critic is more scholarly than W. R. Rutland. His researches on Hardy's first novel (*The Poor Man and the Lady*), on
Hardy's reading—particularly for *The Dynasts*—and his account of
Victorian thought and opinion are more valuable than his criticism;
his analyses of *Tess* and *Jude* prove him to be reactionary. Despite
occasional critical lapses, especially towards the end, Lord David
Cecil's work shows more vision and penetration than any previous
study; it is unfortunate that he tends to see the Will in the guise of an
Aeschylean fury.

The Thomas Hardy centennial number of *The Southern Review* is
very uneven. Some articles, particularly on the poetry, are slight and
unimportant (those by F. R. Leavis, R. P. Blackmur, and Delmore

Schwartz will be referred to later). Bonamy Dobrée shows good judgement on *The Dynasts*. Donald Davidson enlarges on the ballad qualities of Hardy's fiction; but his conclusion, 'Perhaps these are dangerous simplifications', seems to have done little to diminish the fascination of this subsequently overworked theme. Katherine Anne Porter makes a reasoned reply—to be followed by J. I. M. Stewart in *English Studies* (1948)—to T. S. Eliot's facile generalizations and inquisitorial alarm in *After Strange Gods*. Besides Schwartz's essay, the most valuable contributions are those by M. D. Zabel and Jacques Barzun. Both are concerned with Hardy's central dilemma in an age of scientific beliefs conflicting with tradition when intellect and heart were at odds. Hardy, in an intrepid search for truth at the cost of happiness and cherished beliefs, forged not only an 'aesthetic' out of the discords of experience but an 'art'. 'Truth and Poetry do not fight a manichean fight which will leave Science or Ignorance master of the field; they merge into each other by degrees and constitute together the sum total of mind-measured reality.' H. J. Muller sees dangers to our understanding of Hardy from trends in contemporary criticism; he recognizes Hardy's weaknesses but restores the main perspectives.

Hardy was never a facile or over-confident rationalist; any 'meliorism' he subscribed to was a remote abstraction, which was often overclouded by the 'seemings' of experience. His intellectual integrity and artistic achievement still await their true assessment. After a period of acclaim, he has suffered unduly from critical prejudice and neglect. He was an intellectual much in advance of his age, and grew tired of compromising his genius to placate magazine editors. When he could afford it, he abandoned novel-writing to express himself, as he had always wished, in poetry. This did not save him from being described in 1934 as 'really a good Victorian'. Despite being a student all his life, exceptionally well-read, scholarly, and discerning, he has been condescendingly referred to as a literary Hodge.

A re-assessment was evidently desirable. A. J. Guerard's study (1949) marked an important advance in this direction. The trend of modern criticism has been to move away from panoramic surveys to studies of the idiosyncratic and close-up, of the 'grotesque', the symbolical, and the interplay of imagery. Guerard rejected the view that Hardy cast wistful backward glances at the old agricultural order (a view which nevertheless continued to characterize Hardy criticism for at least twelve more years), and that his mature philosophy is reflected widely in the novels. He insisted on Hardy's genius, and particularly his anti-realism; but the work is astonishingly uneven.

Douglas Brown found it impossible to deal with considerable areas of Hardy in a book of moderate length. His sensitivity to tone and texture in Hardy's poetry and prose produces his best work; the presence of the agricultural bias (reasserting itself in D. Daiches, *Some Late Victorian Attitudes*) and an almost reflex response in ballad terms are the weaker elements. Among the general surveys of a more recent date, those by George Wing and J. I. M. Stewart are strongly recommended; R. C. Carpenter is more inclusive and rather myth-biased, but provides a very useful introduction for the student; Irving Howe writes particularly well on the novels, less notably on the poetry, and inadequately on *The Dynasts*. Roy Morrell strongly challenges some common conclusions or assumptions, especially John Holloway's view that Hardy's characters are puppets of the Will, a view even more uncompromisingly held by Edwin Muir in *Essays on Literature and Society*.

The latest publications include a fascinating study by J. Hillis Miller which raises a number of debatable issues, a scholarly work on the novels by Michael Millgate, a study by F. R. Southerington which is critically valuable when Tryphena Sparks is forgotten, a concentrated survey by Jean Brooks, a readable but rather disproportionate 'critical biography' by J. I. M. Stewart, and an interesting, somewhat contrived, schematic analysis of Hardy's major novels by Perry Meisel.

J. O. Bailey's essay on Hardy's 'Mephistophelian visitants' is worth attention despite its over-inclusiveness. J. F. Scott introduces the 'Gothic' influence, but uses the term in a very wide anti-realist sense. C. R. Anderson illustrates Hardy's 'unique genius' in the 'metaphorical' use of changing perspectives, including landscape, to comment on situation or life.

The two novels which have received the most important critical attention are *The Mayor of Casterbridge* and, more recently, *Jude the Obscure*. Next come *The Return of the Native* and *Tess of the d'Urbervilles*. It is pleasing to find some worthwhile essays on other novels: L. O. Jones on *Desperate Remedies* and J. F. Danby on *Under the Greenwood Tree*, for example, though the view that Hardy's later pessimism may be discerned in this second novel is very questionable. Howard Babb discusses the metaphorical significance of natural settings for several scenes in *Far from the Madding Crowd*. Clarice Short assesses the comic in *The Hand of Ethelberta*, and shows how its ethos differs from that of the more serious novels. For *The Return of the Native*, Paterson must not be overlooked; J. Hagan throws new light on the role of Diggory Venn, but leaves us with the question whether this uncanny romantic agent was really intended as a comment on the irony of circumstance or was simply a convenient tool in a plot the outcome of which was ill-starred from the start; R. C. Schweik shows how the three principal characters present different phases of civilization, all being inadequate to the situation, greater than their associates, and victims of their own errors; Hardy's ambivalent conception of Eustacia is discussed by David Eggenschwiler.

The Mayor of Casterbridge has elicited more substantial criticism than any other novel. D. A. Dike, on the parallels with the *Oedipus Rex* of Sophocles, and John Moynahan, on the influence of Saul and David on the Henchard–Farfrae conflict, are important. F. R. Karl discusses the part played by chance, showing how it reflects the bleakness of the Darwinian cosmos, how Farfrae and Elizabeth-Jane, unlike Henchard, can adapt themselves, and how the 'external determinism' of Greek tragedy is now 'internalized and seen as of man's own making'. R. C. Schweik's clear-cut argument that Henchard's early downfall is due to character and his final tragedy to Fate, and that Hardy in the latter part of the novel asserts his intellectual Darwinian outlook, appears to overlook the fact that the network of circumstance in which Henchard is caught includes his character. J. C. Maxwell challenges the agricultural bias as exemplified in a study of the novel by Brown.

Not nearly as much criticism has been evoked by *The Woodlanders*. W. M. Matchett's essay shows that man is a small part in the web of circumstance, and is a reminder that Hardy's mature views of nature were not nearly so simple or 'pastoral' as critics have been prone to think. The Unfulfilled Intention is apparent in the story as well as in the setting of *The Woodlanders*. Hardy's views on nature (including human nature) are uncompromising in *Jude*. In *Tess of the d'Urbervilles* they are ambivalent as a result of Hardy's intrusive comments, which conflict with his imagined experience. Most of the best criticism of this novel is concerned with its imagery. Dorothy Van Ghent (in Guerard's *Collection of Critical Essays*) deals with the main presentations including landscape, but tends to mythologize unnecessarily and overstress folk instinctivism, folk fatalism, and folk magic. Ian Gregor (*The Moral and the Story*), after an interesting account of Hardy's accommodation of the serial form of the novel for magazine readers, presents examples of 'the interlocking pattern of symbol and image', before stressing unduly the resistance of the agricultural community to the machine, and claiming that the ballad world and its disintegration are the basic elements of Hardy's fiction. Tony Tanner's essay, one of the most illuminating and extensive on the imagery of the novel, succeeds in conveying a sense of Hardy's style, 'the incomparable clarity of his eyes' through which he makes us see. David Lodge's subject is Hardy's various 'voices', his shifting linguistic clues or viewpoints. His analysis of Hardy's style should not be overlooked, though the interpretation of the central illustrative passage is based upon a questionable reading of the novel.

Many writers have discussed Hardy's style, concentrating on its infelicities and solecisms, and failing to give its variations and development adequate consideration. The qualities which still make so much of his prose live and hold the attention are yet to be assessed.

An essay on *The Well-Beloved* by Helmut Gerber reflects the contrast between the attitudes of Pierston and Somers on women and art. By not being hard to please and by giving the public what it wants, Somers prospers. In this and the bitter ending of the novel, the author of *Tess* and *Jude* may have disguised a wry comment on his reading public. *Jude the Obscure* is Hardy's most complex work, and few of its critics are wholly convincing. Arthur Mizener (in the centennial issue of *The Southern Review*) identifies Hardy with *Jude* too much (the original title was *The Simpletons*), and proves by false premisses and simple logic that *Jude* cannot be a tragedy. Norman Holland, Jr. goes too far in pursuit of the Jewish–Jerusalem–Crucifixion theme in a brilliantly illuminating essay, the title of which is misleading; Hardy did not indict Christianity (without it he saw little hope for mankind) so much as the 'Christianity' of Victorian Churches and society. F. P. W. McDowell illustrates how patterns of imagery and contrast create a kind of kaleidoscope with 'changing vistas of meaning'. A. Alvarez (in Guerard's *Collection*) is so sensible that one regrets the suddenness of his conclusion (his statement that the power of the novel is poetic rather than fictional requires definition; to some *Jude* appears less poetic than earlier novels); the *sequitur* that after *Jude* there was no other way for Hardy to go but poetry is debatable. W. J. Hyde analyses the novel in terms of four levels of existence: the natural (ignoring the conventions), Arnold's Hebraism, his Hellenism, and Mill's fusion of the Greek ideal of self-development and the Platonic and Greek idea of self-government. The analysis of Sue by R. B. Heilman is brilliantly done (if not overdone); to this Lawrence's study may be regarded as complementary. Ian Gregor (in *Imagined Worlds*, edd. M. Mack and I. Gregor), maintains that, without the Wessex background to present his multiple views of life, Hardy found his 'extra-temporal' or 'cosmic' dimension in the 'choric' figure of Father Time. It will seem to some readers that Hardy's allegorical aims were here beyond his reach, that the new dimension is an interpolation, incidental rather than coextensive with the novel as a whole, and that Little Father Time was asked to carry too great a burden of doom and significance.

On Hardy's fiction in general, G. D. Klingopulos (*Pelican Guide to English Literature*, ed. B. Ford, vol. vi) and Walter Allen are well worth reading. The latter, despite rather too much emphasis on Hardy's provincialism and naïveté, and the malignity of his universe, shows a clarity and strength all too rarely combined in Hardy criticism. His remarks on the texture of the writing in *Jude* may not seem to support Alvarez. Allen prefers the more poetic scenes in *The Return of the Native*; Hardy's verse, none the less, is more ascetic, and, generally speaking, nearer the style of *Jude*.

Of the shorter surveys of *The Dynasts*, those in the works by Abercrombie, Evelyn Hardy, Hynes (in Guerard's *Collection*), Southerington, and Weber (*Hardy of Wessex*) may be recommended. Hynes's criticism is close to the text, though he misjudges, I think, when he concludes that the flatness in speech of the principal human characters reflects the mechanical part played by the puppets of the Will and the antinomial, ironic view in which man believes he is free. This conclusion, and the collateral view that metaphor is restricted to the Overworld because the Spirits alone see the relationships of things, seems to disregard the inequalities of opportunity for Hardy as a writer in the different kinds of scenes, and it particularly overlooks the restrictive effect of a general adherence to historical records. The principal Spirits, after all, reflect Hardy's views in a way which was impossible through the speech of his human *dramatis personae*.

There are three larger works on *The Dynasts*: Bailey deals with Hardy's philosophy, with particular reference to the question of how far it was influenced by Hartmann; H. Orel provides a series of essays. W. F. Wright discusses Hardy's indebtedness to the historians very fully, and adds a valuable chapter on successive revisions of the text. On Hardy's sources Rutland gives considerable guidance, and an essay on the subject by Emma Clifford is of great interest. Sherman shows how reflections on London contributed to the shaping thought of this epic drama.

Hardy's poetry presents a formidable critical problem. Anything approaching thoroughness may lead to pedestrianism, and this undoubtedly afflicts one major study. Many poems are discussed by Duffin, but a larger typological survey is necessary. The most accomplished is that of Hynes; it does not minimize Hardy's weaknesses; it contains some stimulating criticism of individual poems; but the view that the criterion of the 'antinomial pattern' is a trustworthy guide to the best must be qualified. Satires of circumstance had such an appeal for Hardy that (when prose fiction was abandoned) they automatically seemed to qualify for verse; the result is that they often present unrealized experience, mere sketches, or mechanical responses. This is the major complaint of Blackmur in the centennial number of *The Southern Review*, though he insists that Hardy's sensibility was violated by ideas. In the same issue, Schwartz rightly argues that, though Hardy's beliefs (when merely intellectualized) had an ill effect on his poetry, they created the feelings or conflict of feelings from which much of his best poetry sprang. Leavis (even more unrelenting than in *New Bearings in English Poetry*) animadverts on Hardy's stylistic gaucherie and dullness, finds many fresh and original perceptions, but can admit no more than six poems to 'major status'. His influence has been so dominant that it is not surprising that other critics express similar views. Among other articles on Hardy's poetry, the most important are those by C. Day-Lewis, J. Middleton Murry in *Aspects of Literature*, F. L. Lucas in *Eight Victorian Poets*, and C. M. Bowra in *Inspiration and Poetry*. A recent study by K. Marsden deserves attention. Bailey's work shows massive research, and provides valuable background information on the poems individually. Its surmises and alternatives may, however, lead to surprising interpretations by less expert scholars.

Guerard's collection of critical essays contains two of the best from the centennial issue of *The Southern Review*, those by Zabel on 'the aesthetic of incongruity' and by Schwartz on Hardy's poetry and beliefs. From the same source come W. H. Auden's autobiographical reactions to the poetry, and Davidson's essay on the ballad qualities in Hardy's fiction. David Perkins writes thoughtfully and illuminatingly on 'the poetry of isolation', but it is doubtful whether, beneath the surface, *The Mayor of Casterbridge* can be seen to belong to an anachronistic form of tragedy, as Paterson claims. Dorothy Van Ghent on *Tess*, Alvarez on *Jude*, extracts from Lawrence (that on Sue is broken off too early), Holloway on Hardy's major fiction (biased toward the conclusion that Hardy's interest in the novel declined as he lost confidence in the rural order), Guerard's classification of the women in the novels (not his most inspired work), and Hynes on *The Dynasts* complete this selection.

BIOGRAPHIES AND LETTERS

The Life of Thomas Hardy (first published as *The Early Life* and *The Later Years*) was prepared by Hardy himself, the last four chapters being added by his second wife, who edited the whole. Hardy late in life was provoked to take this action by inaccuracies in studies by E. Brennecke and F. A. Hedgcock. The form the work takes often gives the impression of a hasty compilation; yet its main value derives from the fact that the greater part of it is based on, or presents, contemporary notes. It has been a commonplace to criticize it for its omissions (for some of which Florence Hardy was responsible). Certainly it tells us little of Hardy's private life: he had divulged that to an exceptional degree in his poetry before he set to work on his autobiography. Altogether few writers have told us so much about themselves. Students will continually find something new in this record, and it will remain the most indispensable guide to his life and thought. Evelyn Hardy's edition of two of Hardy's notebooks contains some interesting entries and comments; much of the second is included in F. E. Hardy's *Life*.

Emma Hardy's *Some Recollections* describes her early life in Plymouth and Cornwall up to the time of her marriage. The opening of the 'St. Juliot' chapter in F. E. Hardy's *Life* (pp. 67–73) is quoted from it. For Hardy, later developments—her incurable disorder, their differences, his neglect, and the memory of her loyalty and their early romance—imparted a poignancy to some of these recollections which resulted in some of his finest poems.

Numerous poems written by Hardy after her death reveal the 'sweets' and 'division' of their life as he recalled it. The subject is discussed in two important studies of Hardy's life and works, by Evelyn Hardy and Carl Weber, and more completely in the latter's edition of *Hardy's Love Poems*. Another important critical biography is Edmund Blunden's; he has the scholarship to evoke, by apt quotation and reference, not only the man and his work but also the age. F. E. Halliday's recent work provides an attractive introduction to Hardy.

Further impressions of Hardy may be gained from recorded conversations—those with William Archer and V. H. Collins being the most informative and reliable; from recollections by Newman Flower, and from a judicious selection of the short monographs published by the Toucan Press. Although it draws too credulously on some of these, D. F. Barber's *Concerning Thomas Hardy* contains interesting local recollections of Hardy in his old age.

How much the publication of Hardy's numerous letters would contribute further to our knowledge of his life remains to be seen. On the whole they are so circumspect and impersonal that one cannot expect new light to be shed in many places. Florence Hardy's letters are more revelatory, but sometimes, one suspects, not wholly reliable or sound in judgement. Two small collections of Hardy's letters have been edited by Weber, the one rather miscellaneous, the other containing all the letters from Hardy to his first wife that are known to survive. The most important of the published letters (especially for their bearing on *Jude the Obscure*) are those to Mrs. Henniker, in *One Rare Fair Woman*, edited by Evelyn Hardy and F. B. Pinion. Of the unpublished letters in England and Scotland, the principal are to (Sir) George Douglas (see W. M. Parker, *English*, xiv, Autumn 1963, and Sir George Douglas, *The Hibbert Journal*, April 1928), Edward Clodd (banker, rationalist, and popular writer on evolution and folklore), and (Sir) Edmund Gosse. Many more are in libraries and private collections in the U.S.A. A descriptive checklist of *Thomas Hardy's Max Gate Correspondence* by Carl and Clara Weber provides useful biographical detail, especially for the later years.

BIBLIOGRAPHIES

The standard work on Hardy's publications is by R. L. Purdy. There are some important appendices, e.g. on the Hardy–Tinsley correspondence, Hardy's friendship with Mrs. Henniker, and the Hardy Players and their productions. As Purdy wrote in his preface, 'The book has become, one might say, a biography of Hardy in bibliographical form.'

Works and articles on Hardy up to 1840 are listed alphabetically, under the names of authors, periodicals, and newspapers, in Weber's centenary bibliography of Hardiana. It is an invaluable reference book for the scholar who knows what he wants; otherwise, its amazing inclusiveness tends to defeat its main purpose.

The first post-1940 checklist is to be found in *Modern Fiction Studies* (Autumn 1960), a Hardy number containing various articles, some of which have already been mentioned. The latest bibliographies, from 1955 to 1964, are those edited by R. C. Slack.

G. S. Fayen's bibliographical chapter presents a lengthy and valuable selective summary and analysis. Select bibliographies will be found in Wing (*Hardy*), and both studies by Stewart. More restricted but descriptive bibliographies are included in Carpenter's *Thomas Hardy* and Pinion's *A Hardy Companion*.

BACKGROUND READING

Denys Kay-Robinson's topographical guide to Hardy's Wessex, though more complete and up-to-date than Hermann Lea's, has the initial disadvantage of being arranged on a regional basis. Ruth Firor's scholarly and comprehensive study deals not only with many aspects of folklore but also with Hardy's interest in local prehistoric remains and Napoleonana. The plight of the agricultural labourer never assumes large proportions in Hardy and is generally incidental, but his article, 'The Dorsetshire Labourer', should be read in conjunction with *The Mayor of Casterbridge* and *Tess of the d'Urbervilles*. Douglas Brown presents the subject more historically in his *Thomas Hardy*, as does W. C. Hyde in an essay on the non-sociological presentation of Hardy's rustics. The socio-economic background is a major feature of a recent work by Merryn Williams.

The interest of the Hardy family in music throughout three generations and its impact on Hardy's works receive special attention in *Music and Letters* (April 1940). The influence of paintings on Hardy's visualizations and description is the subject of an essay by Alastair Smart.

So extensive was Hardy's reading in fiction, classical works and anthologies, the Bible, Shakespeare, poetry, history (local and Napoleonic especially), scientific literature, and philosophy that no adequate assessment of it has been made. Hardy states that he was one of the 'earliest acclaimers of *The Origin of Species*'. The effect of Darwinism was to give modern significance to chance and irony in Greek drama. Encouraged by the writings of Mill and Spencer, and the influence of Leslie Stephen, Hardy sought the truth in advanced contemporary thought; yet, though he had lost his Christian faith, he continued to affirm that its essential spirit of brotherhood or 'loving-kindness', 'operating through scientific knowledge', constituted the only hope for humanity. The key to Hardy as a thinker and poet lies in his adjustments to a modern scientific view of life. In *Darwin Among the Poets*, Lionel Stevenson traces Hardy's newly fashioned philosophy in his poems. Webster's scholarly work presents the background, though, as he admits, too much of Hardy's philosophy is seen in the fiction. Bailey traces Hardy's scientific interests as seen in his works.

The Victorian reading public is best reflected in 'Candour in English Fiction' (*Thomas Hardy's Personal Writings*, ed. Orel) and in contemporary reviews (L. Lerner and J. Holmstrom (edd.), *Thomas Hardy and His Readers*, and R. G. Cox, *Thomas Hardy, The Critical Heritage*).

G. W. Sherman in 'The Wheel and the Beast' shows the link between Hardy's impressions of London and his conception of the Will. D. J. De Laura breaks new ground in a fascinating but not wholly conclusive essay on Hardy's reaction to Arnold's secular humanism. Perhaps more needs to be said on whether the 'beautiful and ineffectual' Angel Clare embodies a comment on Arnold's doctrine rather than on Shelleyanism, and whether Hardy at heart could have been in greater sympathy with Frederic Harrison's optimistic evolutionary positivism than with the practical Christianity of *Robert Elsmere*. On such questions, Hardy's thoughts must have been complex and subject to change; even so, his 'Apology' to *Late Lyrics and Earlier* has a relevance which is fundamental.

Rutland (mentioned above under CRITICAL STUDIES AND COMMENTARY) provides one of the best guides to the Victorian intellectual crisis and Hardy's reading. More extensive in some directions is Pinion's *A Hardy Companion*, which presents not only the Wessex background but a great deal on the wider intellectual and cultural influences which affected Hardy, and illustrates the complexity of his concept of 'Nature'.

REFERENCES

TEXTS

The works published by Macmillan (London) and St. Martin's Press (New York) include the Wessex Library edition (complete), *The Collected Poems*, and the following paperbacks: *Under the Greenwood Tree, Far from the Madding Crowd, The Return of the Native, The Trumpet-Major, The Mayor of Casterbridge, The Woodlanders, Tess of the d'Urbervilles, Jude the Obscure*; also (with introductions by John Wain) *The Dynasts, Selected Shorter Poems*, and *Selected Stories*.

In addition to *Selected Poems* (ed. J. C. Ransom), American paperback editions of the following novels (all with introductions) are recommended: (Rinehart and Riverside) *Far from the Madding Crowd, The Return of the Native, The Mayor of Casterbridge*; (Riverside) *Tess of the d'Urbervilles, Jude the Obscure*; (Norton) *The Return of the Native, Tess of the d'Urbervilles*.

P. N. Furbank (ed.), *Selected Poems of Thomas Hardy* (London, 1964).
I. Howe (ed.), *Selected Writings of Thomas Hardy* (paperback, New York, 1966).
S. Hynes (ed.), *Great Short Works of Thomas Hardy* (paperback, New York, 1967).
D. Morrison (ed.), *Thomas Hardy, Stories and Poems* (London, 1970).
H. Orel (ed.), *Thomas Hardy's Personal Writings* (Lawrence, Kans., 1966; and London, 1967).
J. C. Ransom (ed.), *Hardy: Selected Poems* (New York, 1961).
J. Wain (ed.), *The Dynasts* (paperback, London and New York, 1965).
—— (ed.), *Selected Shorter Poems of Thomas Hardy* (paperback, London, 1966).
—— (ed.), *Selected Stories of Thomas Hardy* (paperback, London, 1966).
C. J. Weber (ed.), *An Indiscretion in the Life of an Heiress* (New York, 1965).
G. M. Young (ed.), *Selected Poems of Thomas Hardy* (London, 1940).

CRITICAL STUDIES AND COMMENTARY

L. Abercrombie, *Thomas Hardy* (London, 1912).

W. Allen, *The English Novel* (London, 1954).

C. R. Anderson, 'Time, Space, and Perspective in Thomas Hardy', *NCF* ix (1954).

H. Babb, 'Setting and Theme in *Far from the Madding Crowd*', *ELH* xxx (1963)

J. O. Bailey, 'Hardy's "Mephistophelian Visitants" ', *PMLA* xli (1946).

—— *Thomas Hardy and the Cosmic Mind: A New Reading of 'The Dynasts'* (Chapel Hill, N.C., 1956).

—— *The Poetry of Thomas Hardy* (Chapel Hill, N.C., 1970).

J. W. Beach, *The Technique of Thomas Hardy* (Chicago, 1922; reprinted New York, 1962).

C. M. Bowra, *Inspiration and Poetry* (London, 1955).

Jean R. Brooks, *Thomas Hardy, The Poetic Structure* (London, 1971).

D. Brown, *Thomas Hardy* (London, 1954).

R. C. Carpenter, *Thomas Hardy* (New York, 1964).

Lord D. Cecil, *Hardy the Novelist* (London, 1943).

M. Chase, *Thomas Hardy, from Serial to Novel* (Minneapolis, Minn., 1927; reprinted New York, 1964).

S. C. Chew, *Thomas Hardy, Poet and Novelist* (New York, 1928; reprinted 1964).

E. Clifford, 'Thomas Hardy and the Historians', *SP* lvi (1959).

D. Daiches, *Some Late Victorian Attitudes* (London, 1969).

J. F. Danby, '*Under the Greenwood Tree*', *Critical Quarterly*, i (1959).

C. Day-Lewis, 'The Lyrical Poetry of Thomas Hardy', *British Academy Warton Lecture* (London, 1951).

D. A. Dike, 'A Modern Oedipus, *The Mayor of Casterbridge*', *EIC* ii (1952).

H. C. Duffin, *Thomas Hardy* (3rd edn., Manchester, 1937).

D. Eggenschwiler, 'Eustacia Vye, Queen of Night and Courtly Pretender', *NCF* xxv (1971).

B. Ford (ed.), *Pelican Guide to English Literature*, vol. vi, Dickens to Hardy (paperback, Harmondsworth, 1958).

H. E. Gerber, 'Hardy's *The Well-Beloved* as a Comment on the Well-Despised', *English Language Notes* (September 1963).

I. Gregor and B. Nicholas, *The Moral and the Story* (London, 1962).

A. J. Guerard, *Thomas Hardy, The Novels and the Stories* (Cambridge, Mass., 1949).

—— (ed.), *Hardy: A Collection of Critical Essays* (paperback, Englewood Cliffs, N.J., 1963).

J. Hagan, 'A Note on the Significance of Diggory Venn', *NCF* xvi (1961).

R. B. Heilman, 'Hardy's Sue Bridehead', *NCF* xx (1966).

N. Holland, '*Jude the Obscure*: Hardy's Symbolic Indictment of Christianity', *NCF* ix (1954).

J. Holloway, *The Victorian Sage* (London, 1953).

I. Howe, *Thomas Hardy* (New York, 1967; London, 1968).

W. J. Hyde, 'Theoretic and Practical Unconventionality in *Jude the Obscure*', *NCF* xx (1965).

S. Hynes, *The Pattern of Hardy's Poetry* (Chapel Hill, N.C., and Oxford, 1961).

L. Johnson, *The Art of Thomas Hardy* (London, 1894).

L. O. Jones, '*Desperate Remedies* and the Victorian Sensation Novel', *NCF* xx (1965).

F. R. Karl, '*The Mayor of Casterbridge*: A New Fiction Defined', *Modern Fiction Studies*, vi (1960).

D. Kramer, 'Revisions and Vision: Thomas Hardy's *The Woodlanders*', *Bulletin of the New York Public Library* (April–May 1971).

J. Laird, 'The Manuscript of Hardy's *Tess of the d'Urbervilles*, and What it Tells us', *AUMLA* xxv (1966).

D. H. Lawrence, 'Study of Thomas Hardy' (1914) in *Phoenix* (London, 1961), and in A. Beal (ed.), *D. H. Lawrence: Selected Literary Criticism* (London, 1961).

D. Lodge, *Language of Fiction* (London, 1966).

F. L. Lucas, *Eight Victorian Poets* (London, 1930).

F. P. W. McDowell, 'Hardy's "Seemings or Personal Impressions" ', *Modern Fiction Studies*, vi (1960).

M. Mack and I. Gregor (edd.), *Imagined Worlds* (London, 1968).

K. Marsden, *The Poems of Thomas Hardy* (London, 1969).

W. M. Matchett, '*The Woodlanders*, or Realism in Sheep's Clothing', *NCF* ix (1955).

J. C. Maxwell, 'The "Sociological" Approach to *The Mayor of Casterbridge*' in Mack and Gregor (edd.), *Imagined Worlds*.

Perry Meisel, *Thomas Hardy, The Return of the Repressed* (New Haven, Conn., and London, 1972).

J. H. Miller, *Thomas Hardy, Distance and Desire* (Cambridge, Mass., 1970).

M. Millgate, *Thomas Hardy, His Career as a Novelist* (London, 1971).

R. Morrell, *Thomas Hardy: The Will and the Way* (Oxford, 1965).

J. Moynahan, '*The Mayor of Casterbridge* and the Old Testament's First Book of Samuel', *PMLA* lxxi (1956).

E. Muir, *Essays on Literature and Society* (London, 1949; rev. edn., 1965).

J. M. Murry, *Aspects of Literature* (London, 1920).

H. Orel, *Thomas Hardy's Epic Drama: A Study of the 'The Dynasts'* (Lawrence, Kans., 1963).

J. Paterson, *The Making of 'The Return of the Native'* (Berkeley, Calif., and London, 1960).

—— 'The Genesis of *Jude the Obscure*', *SP* lvii (1960).

F. B. Pinion, 'The Country and Period of *The Woodlanders*', *The Thomas Hardy Year Book* (Mt. Durand, Guernsey, 1971).

W. R. Rutland, *Thomas Hardy, A Study of His Writings and Their Background* (Oxford, 1938; reprinted New York, 1962).

R. C. Schweik, 'Theme, Character, and Perspective in Hardy's *The Return of the Native*', *PQ* xli (1962).

R. C. Schweik, 'Character and Fate in Hardy's *The Mayor of Casterbridge*', *NCF* xxi (1966).

J. F. Scott, 'Thomas Hardy's Use of the Gothic', *NCF* xvii (1963).

G. W. Sherman, 'The Influence of London on *The Dynasts*', *PMLA* lxiii (1948).

C. Short, 'In Defence of *Ethelberta*', *NCF* xiii (1958).

R. C. Slack, 'The Text of Hardy's *Jude the Obscure*', *NCF* xi (1957).

F. R. Southerington, *Hardy's Vision of Man* (London, 1971).

The Southern Review, vi (Summer 1940).

J. I. M. Stewart, *Eight Modern Writers* (*OHEL*, vol. xii, Oxford, 1963).

—— *Thomas Hardy, A Critical Biography* (London, 1971).

T. Tanner, 'Colour and Movement in Hardy's *Tess of the d'Urbervilles*', *Critical Quarterly* x (1968).

O. B. Wheeler, 'Four Versions of *The Return of the Native*', *NCF* xiv (1959).

G. Wing, *Hardy* (Edinburgh, London, and New York, 1963).

W. F. Wright, *The Shaping of 'The Dynasts'* (Lincoln, Nebr., 1967).

BIOGRAPHIES AND LETTERS

W. Archer, *Real Conversations* (London, 1904).

D. F. Barber, *Concerning Thomas Hardy* (London, 1968).

E. Blunden, *Thomas Hardy* (London, 1941).

V. H. Collins, *Talks with Thomas Hardy at Max Gate, 1920–22* (London, 1928).

N. Flower, *Just As It Happened* (London, 1950).

F. E. Halliday, *Thomas Hardy, His Life and Work* (Bath, 1972).

Emma Hardy, *Some Recollections* (Oxford, 1961).

Evelyn Hardy, *Thomas Hardy, A Critical Biography* (London, 1954; New York, 1970).

—— (ed.), *Thomas Hardy's Notebooks* (London, 1955).

Evelyn Hardy and F. B. Pinion, *One Rare Fair Woman* (London and Coral Gables, Fla., 1972).

F. E. Hardy, *The Life of Thomas Hardy* (London and New York, 1962).

C. J. Weber, *Hardy of Wessex* (2nd edn., New York and London, 1965).

—— (ed.), *Letters of Thomas Hardy* (Waterville, Me., 1954).

—— (ed.), '*Dearest Emmie*': *Thomas Hardy's Letters to His First Wife* (London, 1963).

—— (ed.), *Hardy's Love Poems* (London, 1963).

C. J. and C. Weber (edd.), *Thomas Hardy's Max Gate Correspondence* (Waterville, Me., 1968).

BIBLIOGRAPHIES

M. Beebe, B. Culotta, and E. Marcus, 'Criticism of Thomas Hardy: A Selected Checklist', *Modern Fiction Studies*, vi (1960).

G. S. Fayen, 'Thomas Hardy' in L. Stevenson (ed.), *Victorian Fiction* (Cambridge, Mass., 1964).

R. L. Purdy, *Thomas Hardy, A Bibliographical Study* (Oxford, 1954).

R. C. Slack (ed.), *Bibliographies of Studies in Victorian Literature* (Chicago and London, 1967).
C. J. Weber, *The First Hundred Years of Thomas Hardy* (New York, 1942; reprinted 1965).

BACKGROUND READING

J. O. Bailey, 'Hardy's "Imbedded Fossil" ', *SP* xlii (1945).
R. G. Cox (ed.), *Thomas Hardy, The Critical Heritage* (London and New York, 1970).
R. Firor, *Folkways in Thomas Hardy* (Philadelphia, Pa., 1931; reprinted New York, 1962).
D. J. De Laura, ' "The Ache of Modernism" in Hardy's Later Novels', *ELH* xxxiv (1967).
W. C. Hyde, 'Hardy's View of Realism', *VS* ii (1958–9).
D. Kay-Robinson, *Hardy's Wessex Reappraised* (Newton Abbot, 1972).
H. Lea, *Thomas Hardy's Wessex* (London, 1913).
L. Lerner and J. Holmstrom (edd.), *Thomas Hardy and His Readers* (London, 1968).
F. B. Pinion, *A Hardy Companion* (London and New York, 1968).
G. W. Sherman, 'The Wheel and the Beast', *NCF* iv (1949).
A. Smart, 'Pictorial Imagery in the Novels of Thomas Hardy', *RES* xii (1961).
L. Stevenson, *Darwin among the Poets* (Chicago, 1932; reprinted New York, 1963).
H. C. Webster, *On a Darkling Plain* (2nd edn., Chicago, 1964).
Merryn Williams, *Thomas Hardy and Rural England* (London and New York, 1972).

S. Gorley Putt

TEXTS

Henry James wrote twenty-two novels (two unfinished) and 112 tales. Some of the novels were twice the length of ordinary novels; some of the tales were as long as a short novel. In his early sixties, James revised the main bulk of this immense output of novels and tales for the handsome New York edition published by Scribner in 1907–9, in twenty-four volumes. The English issue of this edition was published by Macmillan. The two novels left unfinished at James's death in 1916, *The Ivory Tower* and *The Sense of the Past*, were seen through the press by Percy Lubbock the following year, and then added as volumes xxv and xxvi of the New York edition. It is from these revised texts that the majority of later reprints of James's fiction derive: a point very well worth noting in so far as the revisions and augmentations made by James in his sixties have given many readers an altogether distorted view of his early style. It was for this New York edition, too, that James wrote the famous eighteen Prefaces, later reprinted in one volume as *The Art of the Novel*, with an influential introduction by Richard P. Blackmur. These leisurely commentaries on his own work enshrine James's 'garnered wisdom' as a consistently serious and self-aware writer of fiction. They constituted a series of much-quoted essays which, like the New York edition revisions themselves, have greatly affected readers' views of James and his intentions. It is fair to suggest that while the impressions thus conveyed are faithfully borne out by James's later practice as a novelist, they may not always offer an accurate historical account of the mind of the young James. Just as his autobiographies recreate a marvellous picture of childhood in words and concepts no child could have entertained, so the Prefaces to, and revisions of, James's early work must always be read with some degree of reservation.

In England, the New York edition was the basis for a 'New and Complete Edition' in thirty-five volumes, issued by Macmillan. Percy Lubbock, the editor, added James's first novel, *Watch and Ward* and also *Confidence*, *The Europeans*, and *The Bostonians*, all of which the author himself had excluded from the New York edition, together with several tales which James had discarded in preparing his collected edition. These Lubbock reprints, in both ordinary and pocket editions, formed the mainstay for British readers of James between the two World Wars, together with a useful Martin Secker 'Uniform Edition of the Tales' presenting in cheap pocket-form, and again from the revised New York edition texts, fourteen of the longer *nouvelles*. It was not until Dr. Leon Edel's splendid Hart-Davis edition of *The Complete Tales of Henry James* that it was possible to read the impressive corpus of James's short stories in their earliest form—or, rather, the first appearance in book-form, containing merely the author's minor corrections after their début in periodicals on both sides of the Atlantic. Since collections in book-form normally followed soon after magazine appearances, the changes were usually quite small, and in any case made at roughly the identical stage of the writer's artistic development. To complete the main story of the noble New York edition, it is a pleasure to add that Scribners (New York) have published a reprint of the entire series. At the time of writing, there has been no complementary English reprint.

A glance at the tabular arrangement of the first appearance of James's novels and tales, as listed for convenience on pp. 293–5, should give a reader some rough indication of the probable degree of 'improvement' enjoyed (or suffered, according to one's view of the development of James's style) when the relevant texts were revised for the 1907–9 republication.

Between the muted wartime centenary of his birth in 1943 and the fiftieth anniversary of his death in 1966, the revival of interest in Henry James's fiction led not only to an immense output of critical books and essays, but also to a welcome if haphazard reprinting of odd volumes by various publishers, as volumes of the collected editions already noted disappeared steadily from the second-hand bookshops. Thus, the novels *Watch and Ward*, *Roderick Hudson*, *The Tragic Muse*, *The Reverberator*, *The Other House*, *The Sacred Fount*, were reprinted in uniform format by Hart-Davis; while *Roderick Hudson*, *Washington Square*, *What Maisie Knew*, *The Princess Casamassima*, and *The Spoils of Poynton* were included in John Lehmann's Chiltern Library. More recently, a uniform Bodley Head edition has been making its appearance, of which the following have so far been issued: *The Europeans* and *Washington Square* (in one volume), *The Awkward Age*, *The Bostonians*, *The Spoils of Poynton*, *The Portrait of a Lady*, *What Maisie Knew*, *The Wings of the Dove*, *The Ambassadors*, *The Golden Bowl*, *The Princess Casamassima*. These well-produced volumes carry introductions by Leon Edel.

The fate of the short stories, before the thrice-blessed Leon Edel edition, has been haphazard in the extreme: there have been a be-wildering number of collections, overlapping in many places and still leaving yawning gaps in others. They have become far too numerous for useful collation, but a glance at some of them will illustrate the problem for new readers who have been stirred by the increasing hubbub about James to sample him first in short doses. In the Hart-Davis series already noted, fourteen stories were selected by David Garnett; in the Chiltern Library, ten by Michael Swan; for the World's Classics, sixteen were selected by Gerard Hopkins, and another four, again selected by Michael Swan, for Penguin. A representative sample of very many similar American collections is the selection of fifteen stories by Morton D. Zabel for Bantam Books. If one adds the fourteen-volume Secker edition of *Uniform Tales* already listed, it is of interest that over these six sample collections, only 45 of the 112 tales are scattered. Of these, 26 appear in one collection only; 13 are duplicated in two versions; four appear three times, and two stories are included in four of the six selections. Curiously enough, the two stories most popular with these editors are the 'difficult' *nouvelles*, 'The Pupil' and 'The Jolly Corner'; the four runners-up being also rather advanced fare for the uninitiated, namely 'The Real Thing', 'The Private Life', 'The Middle Years', and 'The Beast in the Jungle'. It should, of course, be added that the three best known of James's tales—'Daisy Miller', 'The Aspern Papers', and 'The Turn of the Screw'—are all rather lengthy for printing in collections, and that the two last named were bracketed together in an Everyman's Library edition which has been reprinted innumerable times and must have introduced countless thousands of new readers to James's work.

This haphazard scattering of seed has had, during the last decade, a splendid harvest. James's has become a name as inevitable as Shakespeare's in academic reading-lists. The handbook *Books in Print, U.S.A.* shows well over a hundred entries under his name—and even this figure does not take account of the occasions when hard-back and paperback versions are issued by the same publishing firm. So 'difficult' a novel as *The Ambassadors* for instance, may be obtained in a dozen different versions in America, most of which are in paper-back form. There are as many editions of *The Portrait of a Lady*. Less popular items like *The Ivory Tower*, *The Sense of the Past*, or *The Sacred Fount* are at least available in the Scribner reprint of the New York edition already noted. In between come such titles as *The Princess Casamassima* and *Roderick Hudson* with several versions apiece. It is an extraordinary thing, worthy of wry treatment in one of James's later

stories of artistic frustration, that an American nowadays may drop
into his neighbourhood drugstore with a reasonable hope of finding,
propped up in revolving racks cheek by jowl with murder mysteries
and 'girlie' magazines, James items from Signet, Dell, Riverside
editions, Airmont, Modern Library, and similar publishers of paperbacks. And the list grows apace, too speedily for accurate listing, and
too amply to make such listing necessary. Only the rich, or those
without a trace of serendipity, need hunt for James any longer in
specialist bookshops, at least for the more popular titles. In England,
too, the sporadic and overlapping waves of reprints are evening out
into a steady tide. Penguin Books are steadily reprinting novels and
stories: at the time of writing, the available list includes *Roderick
Hudson*, *The Bostonians*, *The Europeans*, *Washington Square*, *The Spoils of
Poynton*, *The Awkward Age*, *What Maisie Knew*, *The Golden Bowl*, *The
Wings of the Dove*, *The Turn of the Screw and other stories*, *Selected Short
Stories*—and more are on the way, to be headed by *Within The Cage
and other stories*, and *The Ambassadors*.

Even if James's entire output of fiction had been destroyed, he
would still remain an inescapable literary figure. Throughout his
working life he disburdened himself, sometimes in routine reviewing
and sometimes in major essays, of a great volume of critical comment
and conjecture. His ill-starred plunge into the living theatre produced a total of fifteen plays. The travel books of this highly mobile
cultural and sociological recorder are still wonderfully readable. He
wrote copiously about painting and drama—though never, curiously
enough, about poetry. He is one of the great letter-writers of the
language. And to previous examples in the English language of the
difficult art of self-revelation, his autobiographies added an entirely
new depth and range of sensibility.

The quality of James as a critic may be sampled in the selection
from his *Literary Criticism* edited by Morris Shapira. The Prefaces
from the New York edition, constituting a theory of creative writing
with an application far beyond that of his own works, may be most
conveniently studied in their collected form in *The Art of the Novel*
(noted above). *The Notebooks of Henry James*, edited by F. O. Mathiessen and Kenneth B. Murdock, though disappointing as a source for
James's private musings on his personal life, are crammed with
preliminary sketches for his fiction, ranging from lengthy projects to
odd records of ideas and passing fancies, sometimes elaborated and
sometimes discarded. They are, and will long remain, a happy hunt-
ing-ground for critical, biographical, and psychological speculation.
The current availability of some of James's most influential criticism

may be illustrated, with the aid of the Edel–Laurence *Bibliography* (see below), by the forms in which i t is now possible to turn up his essay 'The Art of Fiction'. Originally printed in *Longman's Magazine* in 1884, it was bound up the same year by a New York publisher together with Walter Besant's essay with the same title. Four years later, it was revised for inclusion in James's *Partial Portraits* (New York and London, 1888). It was included with other critical essays by James in *The Future of the Novel*, edited by Leon Edel, and in the same editor's rearranged and expanded version of James's essays and reviews under the title *The House of Fiction*. In addition, it had already appeared in Janet Adam Smith's collection of the correspondence between James and R. L. Stevenson (see below), and in the same year had been included in a collection (not listed in the Edel–Laurence *Bibliography*), *The Art of Fiction and Other Essays*, edited by Morris Roberts. It has also been reprinted in the Morris Shapira selection noted above. Not a bad range of exposure, for an essay written before *The Bostonians* or *The Princess Casamassima*!

Toward the end of his life, James himself collected eighteen essays under the title *Notes on Novelists*. Other recent collections of his critical journalism include *Literary Reviews and Essays*, edited by Albert Mordell, and four collections (uniform, in their English publication by Hart-Davis, with *The House of Fiction* noted above): covering dramatic criticism in *The Scenic Art*, edited by Allan Wade; essays on the pictorial arts in *The Painter's Eye*, edited by John L. Sweeney; *The American Essays*, edited by Leon Edel; and a collection of his letters from Paris to the *New York Tribune*, also edited by Leon Edel as *Parisian Sketches*.

James's autobiographies and letters will be noted in a later section. His plays—nowadays, ironically, so much more successful in recent revivals than those produced in his lifetime—have been edited by Leon Edel in *The Complete Plays of Henry James*. It may be noted that several of James's stories have been adapted for the stage in recent years, including 'The Turn of the Screw' (as *The Innocents*), 'The Aspern Papers', *The Wings of the Dove*, *The Spoils of Poynton* (as *The Spoils*) and *Watch and Ward* (as *A Boston Story*); and film and television versions have brought some of the stories to audiences who may never have opened James's books.

CRITICAL STUDIES AND COMMENTARY

T. S. Eliot's celebrated remark that Henry James had a mind too fine to be violated by an idea, is—and was intended to be—a rare compliment from one creative writer to another. One could almost say the same of Shakespeare, in the sense that he rarely felt obliged to *originate* ideas, but as a dramatist could rather endow received opinions with vivid, often contrasting, liveliness. With James the novelist, as with Shakespeare the dramatic poet, this vivid presentation, based as it is on a superlative fidelity to observed phenomena plus a strictly literate skill of the very highest order, often masks the fact that at the centre of both these immensely productive and highly organized human intelligences there is, so to say, a large neutral area. One might hazard a reverent guess that this neutral area was occupied, on the part of the poet, by nothing more provocative than a resigned tendency to accept life's full range of pleasing or painful experiences; and, on the part of the novelist, by an uncommon discrimination in the assessment of human decency. To lovers of creeds and attitudes, however, such apparently thinly occupied central areas in the consciousness of a great creative artist must quite naturally represent all the mesmeric magnetism of a genuine vacuum. In they rush!

Already, barely more than half a century after his death, one can guess from the evidence that James will accumulate, over the years, the same kind of desperate tributes which have decorated the bland mask of Shakespeare with the attributes of a devout Roman Catholic, a prophet of Marxism, a military or pacifist protagonist, an Englishman or universalist, a fraudulent political tool or an inspired lawgiver. Almost from James's first fictional efforts, his readers and critics seem to have felt impelled in much the same sort of way to 'pick sides'; when it should, I think, have been fairly obvious that the novelist's sympathies were expansive enough to be engaged on more than one front at a time.[1] Sometimes, the over-partisan protagonists had plenty of excuse for their fervour. For example, when James himself so often turned to international confrontations as a method of exposing his intelligence to stimuli from both sides of the Atlantic, it was natural that hasty readers should adopt nationalistic gestures of assent or disapproval. Sometimes, more ambitious critics have pumped into the deceptive vacancy a full do-it-yourself kit of systematic symbolism, Christian redemption, or whatever. Most easily explained of all are the labours of those critics who, following James's own essentially modest view that his natural genius for moral sensibility could be exhibited only after a vast expenditure of patterns, shapes, antitheses, balances, and halls-of-mirrors, have extended still

[1] There is, fortunately, one point at which the Shakespearian analogy breaks down: it has not yet been suggested that James's novels must have been written by some more exalted personage—Mr. Asquith, perhaps, or Theodore Roosevelt?

further their author's own self-congratulatory rationalizations (in the Prefaces, Notebooks, and in scores of his most fascinating letters). As if admitting, this last group of critics, that their hero *has* no tidy general principles for them to echo, they enshrine his own professional interest in technical skills as though this, in itself, were his central belief. It is almost as if physicists should strive to find ways of colouring air and water, in order to convince themselves that these basic elements were really there at all.

In recent years, the production of books and articles about James has reached such proportions that it begins to rival what has rather gloomily been termed 'the Shakespeare industry'. Nor is the flood confined to America and Britain. As more and more countries have included the study of American Literature in their university syllabuses, so James has provided a seemingly bottomless reservoir for dissertations. Much of the work is wearisomely repetitive; this is especially true of the rash of studies of James's 'form'. As if in an effort to avoid this kind of numbing echo, other recent researchers have chosen to cling to one small topic and drag it, like a fine-tooth comb, through the whole James canon. The appearance, for example, of such published theses as Jorg Hasler's *Switzerland in the Life and Work of Henry James*, or Cristina Giorcelli's *Henry James e l'Italia*, and Alberta Fabris's *Henry James e la Francia* makes one wonder how many more of these chauvinistic exercises the serious student of James will have to confront—even though they may be presented with the disarming modesty of Dr. Hasler who took 'due note of the real proportions and relative unimportance of Switzerland for James'.

Fortunately for students faced by so wide a range of commentary, there exist three anthologies which present a very fair sample of the range of commentary available. The first, Roger Gard's ample volume in the Critical Heritage series, covers critical reactions in James's own lifetime. The second, F. W. Dupee's *The Question of Henry James*, is a very useful selection of essays tracing the growth of the novelist's reputation as he was gradually revealed, latterly perhaps in the wake of the attention paid to Marcel Proust, as a major literary figure and not merely an American who fell injudiciously in love with the glamour of Europe. The third, Tony Tanner's *Henry James* in the Modern Judgements series, presents samples of the serious work in the form of individual contributions to learned and critical journals, usually in America, during the past twenty years or so.

The Roger Gard volume covers the early recognition (or rejection) of James in such admirably well-documented detail that it is hard to imagine a reader who will require to stray further in this particular field. Especially interesting are his pairings of reviews of individual novels: one splendid sample being the reprint of a wonderfully generous and perceptive essay by W. D. Howells on *The Portrait of a Lady*, followed by a dismally obtuse notice in the *Quarterly Review* which asserts, of James's first unqualified masterpiece, that 'no one can possible care, for a single moment, what becomes of any of the characters'. The editor also very sensibly includes extracts from James's own letters, plus other biographical matter with some immediate bearing on the literary productions, such as the tribute by James's faithful amanuensis, Theodora Bosanquet (see below). The Dupee anthology contains, among other valuable texts, a couple of items from the special number of the American quarterly *Hound and Horn*, which may be selected as a turning point in James's posthumous reputation: it is difficult to think of a parallel case of any one issue of a critical magazine exerting so timely an influence on critical fashion. One of the two reprinted essays, Edmund Wilson's 'The Ambiguity of Henry James', sparked off a debate on the interpretation of the story 'The Turn of the Screw' which is still going on: a collection of some fourteen papers on this one story, edited by Gerald Willen as *A Casebook on Henry James's 'The Turn of the Screw'*, already needs a supplement to take note of still later views. The Dupee collection also includes a sample of one of the more influential anti-James critical documents, *The Pilgrimage of Henry James* by Van Wyck Brooks—a reasoned antagonistic commentary which can rise to such sweeping condemnations as this sentence about the later novels: 'Magnificent pretensions, petty performances!—the fruits of an irresponsible imagination, of a deranged sense of values, of a mind working in the void, uncorrected by any clear consciousness of human cause and effect.' To set this sentence alongside two sentences from T. S. Eliot's essay in the *Little Review*, also reprinted in the Dupee anthology, is to note the astonishing range of response stimulated by our novelist: 'James's critical genius comes out most tellingly in his mastery over, his baffling escape from, Ideas; a mastery and an escape which are perhaps the last test of a superior intelligence. He had a mind so fine that no idea could violate it.'

If the student should require a supplement to the Dupee selection from early views on James, he may be recommended to hunt up two lively appreciative works published before the novelist's death: Rebecca West's *Henry James*, and Ford Madox Ford's *Henry James: A Critical Study*. Both are short, vivid, perceptive.

The Tanner ingathering of representative critical essays scattered over literary periodicals (mostly American) during the past twenty years or so, bears witness to the now steady stream of sound academic work, usually in the form of careful analyses of a single novel, the best of which (like the editor's own introduction and contribution on *The Portrait of a Lady*) open out into wider considerations. Another useful checklist of books and articles, including a selection from journals of the past decade, is found in the bibliography (more generous than her book itself strictly required) appended to Ora Segal's *The Lucid Reflector: The Observer in Henry James's Fiction*.

As an instance of how such work, often modestly labelled, may include insights into major themes, one may select as a sample a valuable article (too recent to be included in the Tanner survey) by Nina Baym on 'Fleda Vetch and the Plot of *The Spoils of Poynton*'. The writer shows that James 'wrote about his works in the notebooks only when he did not feel ready to work on the manuscripts; they thus represent a kind of creative tuning-up'. Equally, the later Preface to the novel 'is recasting *The Spoils of Poynton* in line with the author's changed interests, rather than analysing the novel written only a decade before'. This one article, notionally devoted to a single novel, is completely persuasive in its disentanglement of James's actual performance from the trial-shots of notebook entries to the backward musings of elderly theorizing. It should warn readers not to give equal credence to every word written by The Master. The finished novels and tales are what really matter.

Of the many attempts to introduce James the novelist in one all-embracing volume, Oscar Cargill's *The Novels of Henry James* is by far the most comprehensive. This valuable handbook collects in separate chapters, dealing with each of the novels (except *Washington Square*), a whole mass of critical commentary up to about 1960, re-examined and assessed by the author with amplitude and scrupulous fairness, and held together by his own suggestive and helpful interpretations. It is a cross between the three critical anthologies noted above, and the one-man efforts now to be listed. Such a volume justifies the heavy annotation, as Dr. Cargill works patiently through his card-index and adds a wise final summary of his own. Mention may also be made here of the present writer's *Henry James: A Reader's Guide* (reprinted under the title *The Fiction of Henry James*), which deals with the tales as well as the novels.

F. W. Dupee's *Henry James* volume in the American Men of Letters Series is a beautifully balanced essay, compressing into small space and with a minimum of documentation a sensitive and sensible survey of the whole *oeuvre*, with the serene detachment of a police helicopter observing a traffic jam. Michael Swan's brief volume in the English Novelists Series was matched by a similar survey in the Writers and Critics Series by D. W. Jefferson, whose longer volume *Henry James and the Modern Reader* may be recommended particularly for the infectiousness of its communication of the sheer enjoyment (rather than the moral duty, implied by other critics) of the reading of James's fiction. Of two handbooks by Robert L. Gale, *The Caught Image* categorizes Jamesian imagery, while the second, *Plots and Characters in the Fiction of Henry James*, will assist nervous readers and offer *sub rosa* guidance to thesis-writers who grow bemused by plots or names as they chase some special aspect through the Jamesian thickets. Among other studies may be mentioned *The Comic Sense of Henry James* by Richard Poirier, which treats of the early novels up to and including *The Portrait of a Lady*; a survey of *The Early Tales* by James Kraft; *The Themes of Henry James* by Edwin T. Bowden, which pays close attention to what the subtitle calls 'A System of Observation through the Visual Arts'; *The Houses that James Built*, by Robert W. Stallman, which includes the hilarious history of a misplaced chapter in *The Ambassadors*; *The Battle and the Books*, by Edward Stone; and a burgeoning of books on individual novels which includes, in addition to the Casebook on 'The Turn of the Screw' already noted, *Jamesian Ambiguity and 'The Sacred Fount'*, by Jean F. Blackall, and *Perspectives on James's 'Portrait of a Lady'*, edited by W. T. Stafford, which promises to be the precursor of doubtless dozens of useful garnerings on single works.

More ambitious studies have tended to concentrate on James as a moralist or as a formal aesthetic theorist. In the first category comes Dorothea Krook's *The Ordeal of Consciousness in Henry James*, which brings to the study of the later novels an intensive and impressive seriousness of analysis, and supplements the more elegant and certainly more readable *Henry James: The Major Phase*, by F. O. Mathiessen, which in effect inaugurated the postwar elevation of James to a settled placed in the literary establishment, and is a book well worth rediscovery by a generation of students perhaps overwhelmed by more solemn exercises. In the second category, Laurence Holland's massive *The Expense of Vision: Essays on the Craft of Henry James* has been followed by such formal analytic studies, all full of excellent things for the patient reader only, as J. A. Ward's *The Search for Form: Studies in the Structure of James's Fiction*, *Experiments in Form: Henry James's Novels, 1896–1901* by Walter Isle, and *Strange Alloy: The Relation of Comedy to Tragedy in the Fiction of Henry James*, by Ellen D. Leyburn.

Perhaps a more rewarding approach than that of the 'form and norm' school (which does sometimes seem to be inspired less by James's novels than by his Prefaces) is represented by several recent studies which overtly tackle James's 'imagination', such as *The Imagination of Loving*, by Naomi Lebowitz, *The Negative Imagination: Form and Perspective in the Novels of Henry James*, by Sallie Sears, *The Grasping Imagination*, by Peter Buitenhuis, *Henry James and the Requirements of the Imagination*, by Philip Weinstein, and *The Ambiguity of Henry James* by Charles Samuels. Most of these critics set out with a specific limited aim (e.g. Dr. Buitenhuis placed his emphasis on the works concerned with American themes; Miss Sears concentrated on form and perspective in the three great novels of 'the major phase'; Dr. Lebowitz sought to prove that 'commitment to human relationships . . . is James's supreme ethical concern'; Dr. Weinstein was impressed by the 'exploitative' nature of the imaginative forays of James himself and some of his major characters; and Dr. Samuels graded certain representative novels as 'confusions', 'ambiguities', or 'complexities'), yet all are seduced by the whole *oeuvre* into ranging far beyond their original theses. All, too, acknowledge the close relationship between Henry James's own life and the psychological elaboration of his characters: it is probable that the appearance over the last twenty years of the five-volume Edel biography has profoundly influenced even would-be technical monographs.

A perceptive study of James's linguistic features in *The Later Style of Henry James*, by Seymour Chatman, demonstrates how the revision of his works for the New York edition rendered his characters more oblique, so that they become 'recipients rather than actors'. The austere scholarly approach of this study lends special force to its confirmation of psychological speculations.

Finally, to slake the indignation of readers who have come to feel that the adulation of James is just too much of a good thing, there is the angry rejoinder of Maxwell Geismar's *Henry James and his Cult*, which is suitably dedicated to Van Wyck Brooks who had delivered the negative response in more urbane and, in the end, more persuasive language, some thirty-six years earlier. As for the brilliantly sustained quality of F. R. Leavis's demonstration of James's qualities, it will be found not only in essays reprinted in the collections *The Great Tradition* and *The Common Pursuit*, but also in other contributions to the complete set of the journal *Scrutiny*, which also includes valuable reviews by Dr. Q. D. Leavis as well as the work of her husband.

BIOGRAPHIES AND LETTERS

There is as yet no complete edition of James's letters; but a two-volume selection edited by Percy Lubbock with a wonderfully sympathetic introduction provides an ample view of the personal and social involvements of this most considerate of men. A further selection by Leon Edel is also a happy sidelight on the concerns of a warmhearted if unpassionate correspondent. In *Theatre and Friendship*, Elizabeth Robins reprinted with a commentary several of James's letters written at the time when he was writing for, and mesmerized by, the London stage. One of the more congenial of James's personal and literary relationships is presented in Millicent Bell's *Edith Wharton and Henry James: The Story of a Friendship*. The correspondence between James and his friend R. L. Stevenson was edited by Janet Adam Smith. A similar study of James's relationships with H. G. Wells was edited by Leon Edel and Gordon Ray, including the wounding parody of James which the curious may still find in Wells's facetious book *Boon*. Other groupings of letters to individuals, on the model of George Monteiro's *Henry James and John Hay: The Record of a Friendship* will no doubt continue to appear, pending the inevitable—and much desired—umpteen-volume complete edition.

James's own autobiographical volumes—*A Small Boy and Others*, *Notes of a Son and Brother*, and the unfinished *The Middle Years*—have been reissued in one volume with an introduction by F. W. Dupee. Leon Edel's masterly biography was so generously conceived and executed that five large volumes have appeared over a period of twenty years: *The Untried Years: 1843–1870*, *The Conquest of London: 1870–1883*, *The Middle Years: 1884–1894*, *The Treacherous Years: 1895–1901*, and *The Master, 1901–1916*. This critic's deep understanding of James has enabled him to balance psychological speculation and known fact, day-to-day fidelity and a wide-ranging critical interpretation. The Edel life must inevitably overshadow such earlier work as Robert C. Le Clair's *Young Henry James: 1843–1870*; but there will always be room for special 'close-up' studies such as the amusing episode of the ageing Master retold in *Henry James in Cambridge* by Geoffrey Keynes, or the years at Lamb House, Rye, as lovingly recreated in *Henry James at Home* by the author's kinsman, H. Montgomery Hyde, who had the advantage of living for some time in the same house. Material for the growing interest in James's intellectual indebtedness to his father and his brother William, the philosopher and psychologist, was gathered as long ago as 1932 by C. Hartley Grattan in *The Three Jameses, A Family of Minds.*

BIBLIOGRAPHY

In the distinguished series of Soho Bibliographies, the volume devoted to James, which appeared in 1957, is the work of Leon Edel and Dan H. Laurence. A second edition, revised, of this indispensable work for all James scholars was called for by 1961. Professor Edel has referred to himself as 'the literary historian in this otherwise technical book'. His part in it certainly helps to cap, together with the biography and his many editions of James texts, the labours of this prince of James scholars.

BACKGROUND READING

Henry James's later style, largely affected by his habit of dictating to his highly intelligent amanuensis Theodora Bosanquet—whose little Hogarth Essay, *Henry James at Work*, provides a moving and intimate account of his bottomless concern for exactitude of phrase and feeling —very naturally led his friends to collect, if not invent, examples of his elaborate conversation. The picture of the man built up by these elaborations is often quite seriously harmful to his reputation: in laughing at improvised pomposities one is in danger of forgetting just how brutally disillusioned a moral and social critic the novelist could be. In *The Legend of the Master*, Simon Nowell-Smith has brought together a most entertaining collection, from memoirs and letters and anecdotes by James's friends, of such material; the 'background' it sketches is itself subjected, at times, to salutary scepticism. As a noted diner-out, James was of course much recorded by fanciers of wit and periphrasis: he crops up in dozens of places. But as a man and novelist he is so much *sui generis* that 'background reading' is virtually useless. The study of other late Victorian novelists, for example, will merely teach the literary historian how much James differs from them; the study of his native America may add verisimilitude to *The American Scene* (1907; reprinted 1968), without necessarily underlining how acute a social critic he could be; a knowledge of the English politics of his later years will not teach one very much about James's sensitivity to the interplay of private and public consciousness.

Recent biographical and critical studies have paid increasing attention to James's varying relationship with his elder brother William; an acquaintance with William's philosophical and psychological theories and his own relations with Henry's friends provides a 'background' which to some scholars comes perilously near to being a 'foreground'. William's *Letters* were edited by his son, Henry, in two volumes. His most famous work was *The Varieties of Religious Experience*. A useful selection from his writings was edited by C. M. Bakewell under the title *Selected Papers on Philosophy*.

James seems to have had little feeling for poetry and less for music; his 'background' arts were painting and sculpture and, of course, the theatre. Viola Hopkins Winner has produced a thorough study of *Henry James and the Visual Arts*. His long infatuation with the theatre had an effect (repeatedly acknowledged by himself) on his work extending far beyond his own plays, as may be studied in some depth in Michael Egan's *Henry James: The Ibsen Years*.

James's many travels may be followed in his own collections, such as *A Little Tour in France* (1884), *Italian Hours* (1909), and *English Hours* (1905). As 'background' to the fiction, the Prefaces and Notebooks have already been noted. But as with all truly major novelists, the relevant background of James is incorporated in the novels themselves.

Chronological checklist of the novels and tales

Now that the Edel edition of The Complete Tales is available (from which source the first appearance of the tales in the following list is derived), students may soon discover that there is no very significant difference between James the novelist and James the writer of *nouvelles*. Yet it is not always easy to recall, when reading works of one genre, what James was producing at approximately the same time in the other. The list below contains titles of tales, but not of the original volumes (sometimes bearing generalized titles such as *Terminations*, *Embarrassments*, *The Better Sort*, *The Finer Grain*) in which they appeared.

NOVELS	YEAR	TALES
	1864	'A Tragedy of Error'
	1865	'The Story of a Year'
	1866	'A Landscape-Painter', 'A Day of Days',
	1867	'My Friend Bingham', 'Poor Richard'
	1868	'The Story of a Masterpiece', 'The Romance of Certain Old Clothes', 'A Most Extraordinary Case', 'A Problem', 'De Grey: A Romance', 'Osborne's Revenge'
	1869	'A Light Man', 'Gabrielle de Bergerac'
	1870	'Travelling Companions'

Watch and Ward	1871	'A Passionate Pilgrim', 'At Isella', 'Master Eustace'
	1872	'Guest's Confession'
	1873	'The Madonna of the Future', 'The Sweetheart of M. Briseux'
	1874	'The Last of the Valerii', 'Madame de Mauves', 'Adina', 'Professor Fargo', 'Eugene Pickering'
Roderick Hudson	1875	'Benvolio'
The American	1876	'Crawford's Consistency', 'The Ghostly Rental'
	1877	'Four Meetings'
The Europeans	1878	'Rose-Agathe', 'Daisy Miller', 'Longstaff's Marriage', 'An International Episode'
Confidence	1879	'The Pension Beaurepas', 'The Diary of a Man of Fifty', 'A Bundle of Letters'
The Portrait of a Lady *Washington Square*	1880	
	1882	'The Point of View'
	1883	'The Siege of London', 'The Impressions of a Cousin'
	1884	'Lady Barberina', 'The Author of "Beltraffio" ', 'Pandora', 'Georgina's Reasons', 'A New England Winter', 'The Path of Duty'
The Bostonians *The Princess Casamassima*	1886	
	1887	'Mrs Temperly'
The Reverberator	1888	'Louisa Pallant', 'The Aspern Papers', 'The Liar', 'A Modern Warning', 'A London Life', 'The Lesson of the Master', 'The Patagonia'
The Tragic Muse	1889	'The Solution'
	1891	'The Pupil', 'Brooksmith', 'The Marriages' 'The Chaperon', 'Sir Edmund Orme'
	1892	'Nona Vincent', 'The Private Life', 'The Real Thing', 'Lord Beaupré', 'The Visits', 'Sir Dominick Ferrand', 'Collaboration', 'Greville Fane', 'The Wheel of Time', 'Owen Wingrave'
	1893	'The Middle Years'
	1894	'The Death of the Lion', 'The Coxon Fund'
	1895	'The Next Time', 'The Altar of the Dead'
The Other House	1896	'The Figure in the Carpet', 'Glasses', 'The Way it Came'
The Spoils of Poynton	1897	

What Maisie Knew	1898	'John Delavoy', 'The Turn of the Screw', 'In the Cage', 'Covering End', 'The Given Case'
The Awkward Age	1899	'The Great Condition', ' "Europe" ', 'Paste', 'The Real Right Thing'
	1900	'The Great Good Place', 'Maud-Evelyn', 'Miss Gunton of Poughkeepsie', 'The Tree of Knowledge', 'The Abasement of the Northmores', 'The Third Person', 'The Special Type', 'The Tone of Time', 'Broken Wings', 'The Two Faces'
The Sacred Fount	1901	'Mrs Medwin', 'The Beldonald Holbein',
The Wings of the Dove	1902	'The Story in it', 'Flickerbridge'
The Ambassadors	1903	'The Beast in the Jungle', 'The Birthplace', 'The Papers'
The Golden Bowl	1904	'Fordham Castle'
	1908	'Julia Bride'
	1909	'The Velvet Glove', 'Mora Montravers', 'Crapy Cornelia', 'The Bench of Desolation'
	1910	'A Round of Visits'
The Outcry	1911	
The Ivory Tower	1917	
The Sense of the Past		

REFERENCES

TEXTS

Collected Editions of Novels

New York Edition (24 vols., New York, 1907–9; London, 1908–9. Two further vols. added, New York, 1918; reissued, 26 vols., New York, 1968).

New and Complete Edition, ed. P. Lubbock (35 vols., London, 1921–3).

Other Editions of Novels

Hart-Davis edition (London): *Watch and Ward* (1959), *Roderick Hudson* (1961) *The Reverberator* (1949), *The Tragic Muse* (1948), *The Other House* (1948), *The Sacred Fount* (1959).

John Lehmann, Chiltern Library (London): *Roderick Hudson* (1947), *The American* (1949), *Washington Square* (1949), *The Princess Casamassima* (1947), *What Maisie Knew* (1947), *The Spoils of Poynton* (1947).

Bodley Head edition (London): *The Europeans* and *Washington Square* (in 1 vol., 1966), *The Portrait of a Lady* (1968), *The Bostonians* (1967), *The Princess Casamassima* (1972), *The Spoils of Poynton* (1967), *What Maisie Knew* (1969), *The Awkward Age* (1966), *The Wings of a Dove* (1969), *The Ambassadors* (1970), *The Golden Bowl* (1971).

Short Stories

The Uniform Tales of Henry James (14 vols., London, 1915–20).

The Complete Tales of Henry James, ed. L. Edel (12 vols., London, 1962–4).

Fourteen Stories by Henry James, sel. D. Garnett (Hart-Davis edn., London, 1946).

Ten Short Stories of Henry James, sel. M. Swan (Chiltern Library, London, 1948).

Selected Stories, sel. G. Hopkins (World's Classics, London, 1957).

Fifteen Short Stories, sel. M. D. Zabel (paperback, New York, 1961).

Selected Short Stories, sel. M. Swan (paperback, Harmondsworth, 1963).

The Turn of the Screw and *The Aspern Papers* (Everyman's Library, London, 1935).

Criticism

Notes on Novelists (London and New York, 1914).

R. B. Blackmur (ed.), *The Art of the Novel* (New York, 1934; London, 1935).

L. Edel (ed.), *The American Essays* (paperback, New York, 1956).

—— *The Future of the Novel* (New York, 1956).

—— *The House of Fiction* (London, 1957).

—— (ed.), *Parisian Sketches* (New York, 1957; London, 1958).

F. O. Matthiessen and K. B. Murdock (ed.), *The Notebooks of Henry James* (New York, 1947; London, 1948).

A. Mordell (ed.), *Literary Reviews and Essays* (New York, 1957).

M. Roberts (ed.), *The Art of Fiction and Other Essays* (New York, 1948).

M. Shapira (ed.), *Literary Criticism* (London, 1963).

J. L. Sweeney (ed.), *The Painter's Eye* (London and Cambridge, Mass., 1956).

A. Wade (ed.), *The Scenic Art* (New Brunswick, N.J., 1948; London, 1949).

Plays

L. Edel (ed.), *The Complete Plays of Henry James* (Philadelphia, Pa., New York and London, 1949).

CRITICAL STUDIES AND COMMENTARY

N. Baym, 'Fleda Vetch and the Plot of *The Spoils of Poynton*', *PMLA* lxxxiv (1969).

J. F. Blackall, *Jamesian Ambiguity and 'The Sacred Fount'* (Ithaca, N.Y., 1965).

E. T. Bowden, *The Themes of Henry James* (New Haven, Conn., 1956).

V. W. Brooks, *The Pilgrimage of Henry James* (London and New York, 1925).

P. Buitenhuis, *The Grasping Imagination: The American Writings of Henry James* (Toronto, 1970).

O. Cargill, *The Novels of Henry James* (New York, 1961).

S. Chatman, *The Later Style of Henry James* (Oxford, 1972).

F. W. Dupee (ed.), *The Question of Henry James* (New York, 1945; London, 1947).

—— *Henry James*, American Men of Letters Series (New York and London, 1951).

T. S. Eliot, 'On Henry James', *The Little Review* (August 1918); repr. in F. W. Dupee (ed.).

A. Fabris, *Henry James e la Francia* (Rome, 1969).

F. M. Ford, *Henry James* (London, 1913; New York, 1916).

R. L. Gale, *The Caught Image* (Chapel Hill, N.C., 1964).

—— *Plots and Characters in the Fiction of Henry James* (Hamden, Conn., 1965).

R. Gard (ed.), *Henry James: the Critical Heritage* (London, 1968).

M. Geismar, *Henry James and his Cult* (Boston, Mass., 1963; London, 1964).

C. Giorcelli, *Henry James e l'Italia* (Rome, 1968).

J. Hasler, *Switzerland in the Life and Work of Henry James* (Basle, 1966).

L. Holland, *The Expense of Vision: Essays on the Craft of Henry James* (Princeton, N.J., 1964).

W. D. Howells, 'Henry James Jr.', *Century Magazine*, Nov., 1882; and see R. Gard (ed.).

W. Isle, *Experiments in Form: Henry James's Novels, 1896–1901* (Cambridge, Mass., 1968).

D. W. Jefferson, *Henry James*, Writers and Critics Series (Edinburgh, 1960).

—— *Henry James and the Modern Reader* (Edinburgh and New York, 1964).

J. Kraft, *The Early Tales of Henry James* (Carbondale, Ill., 1969).

D. Krook, *The Ordeal of Consciousness in Henry James* (Cambridge, 1962).

F. R. Leavis, *The Great Tradition* (London, 1948; paperback 1962).

—— *The Common Pursuit* (London, 1952; paperback 1962).

—— and Q. D. Leavis, *passim* in *Scrutiny* (repr. Cambridge, 1963).

N. Lebowitz, *The Imagination of Loving* (Detroit, Mich., 1965).

E. D. Leyburn, *Strange Alloy: The Relation of Comedy to Tragedy in the Fiction of Henry James* (Chapel Hill, N.C., 1968).

F. O. Matthiessen, *Henry James: The Major Phase* (New York and Oxford, 1946).

R. Poirier, *The Comic Sense of Henry James* (London and New York, 1960).

S. G. Putt, *Henry James: A Reader's Guide* (London and Ithaca, N.Y., 1966; repr. in paperback as *The Fiction of Henry James*, London, 1968).

C. T. Samuels, *The Ambiguity of Henry James* (Urbana, Ill., 1971).

S. Sears, *The Negative Imagination: Form and Perspective in the Novels of Henry James* (Ithaca, N.Y., 1968).

O. Segal, *The Lucid Reflector: The Observer in Henry James's Fiction* (New Haven, Conn., 1969).

W. T. Stafford (ed.), *Perspectives on James's 'Portrait of a Lady'* (New York and London, 1967).

R. W. Stallman, *The Houses that James Built* (East Lansing, Mich., 1961).

E. Stone, *The Battle and the Books* (Athens, Ohio, 1964).

M. Swan, *Henry James*, The English Novelists Series (London, 1952).

T. Tanner (ed.), *Henry James: Modern Judgements* (cloth and paperback, London, 1968).

J. A. Ward, *The Search for Form: Studies in the Structure of James's Fiction* (Chapel Hill, N.C., 1967).

P. M. Weinstein, *Henry James and the Requirements of the Imagination* (Cambridge, Mass., 1972).

R. West, *Henry James* (London and New York, 1916).

G. Willen (ed.), *A Casebook on Henry James's 'The Turn of the Screw'* (paperback, New York, 1959).

E. Wilson, 'The Ambiguity of Henry James', *Hound and Horn* vii (April–June 1934); repr. in F. W. Dupee (ed.).

BIOGRAPHIES AND LETTERS

M. Bell (ed.), *Edith Wharton and Henry James: The Story of a Friendship* (New York and London, 1965).

F. W. Dupee (ed.), *Henry James: Autobiography* (New York and London, 1956), reprints James's *A Small Boy and Others* (1913), *Notes of a Son and Brother* (1914), *The Middle Years* (1917).

L. Edel, *Henry James* vol. I *The Untried Years: 1843–1870* (London, Philadelphia, Pa., and New York, 1953); vol. II *The Conquest of London: 1870–1883* (London, Philadelphia, Pa., and New York, 1962); vol. III *The Middle Years: 1884–1894* (London, Philadelphia, Pa., and New York, 1963); vol. IV *The Treacherous Years: 1895–1901* (London, Philadelphia, Pa., and New York, 1969); vol. V *The Master: 1901–1916* (London, Philadelphia, Pa., and New York, 1972).

—— (ed.), *Selected Letters of Henry James* (New York, 1955; London, 1956).

—— and G. Ray (edd.), *Henry James and H. G. Wells* (London, 1958).

C. H. Grattan, *The Three Jameses, A Family of Minds* (New York, 1932).

H. Hyde, *Henry James at Home* (London, 1969).

G. Keynes, *Henry James in Cambridge* (Cambridge, 1967).

R. C. Le Clair, *Young Henry James: 1843–1870* (New York, 1955).

P. Lubbock (ed.), *Letters of Henry James* (2 vols., London and New York, 1920).

G. Monteiro (ed.), *Henry James and John Hay: The Record of a Friendship* (Providence, R.I., 1965).

E. Robins, *Theatre and Friendship* (London and New York, 1932).

J. Adam Smith (ed.), *Henry James and Robert Louis Stevenson* (London, 1948).

H. G. Wells, *Boon* (London, 1915); see L. Edel and G. Ray (edd.).

BIBLIOGRAPHY

L. Edel and D. H. Laurence, *Henry James: Bibliography* (2nd edn., London, 1961).

BACKGROUND READING

T. Bosanquet, *Henry James at Work* (London, 1924).

M. Egan, *Henry James: The Ibsen Years* (London, 1972).

H. James, *A Little Tour in France* (Boston, Mass., 1884).

—— *English Hours* (London and Boston, Mass., 1905).

—— *The American Scene* (London and New York, 1907; repr. 1968).

—— *Italian Hours* (London and Boston, Mass., 1909).

H. James (son of William James) (ed.), *The Letters of William James* (2 vols., Boston, Mass., and London, 1920).

W. James, *The Varieties of Religious Experience* (London and New York, 1902).

—— *Selected Papers on Philosophy*, ed. C. M. Bakewell (London and New York, 1917).

S. Nowell-Smith, *The Legend of the Master* (London, 1947; New York, 1948).

V. H. Winner, *Henry James and the Visual Arts* (Charlottesville, Va., 1970).

17 · CONRAD 1857–1924

J. A. V. Chapple

TEXTS

Most of Conrad's writings were published in his lifetime, many with his own prefatory notes. There have been several editions of his works, in England, Poland, and America. The Uniform Edition, or its reprint, the Collected Edition, is often used for standard reference purposes. His plays and two minor pieces of fiction (*The Sisters* and *The Nature of a Crime*) have been separately published. Curle collected a number of dispersed essays in 1926.

There have been a great number of editions of individual works, some with introductions by first-class critics. A selection of these is given in the REFERENCES below. Zabel has been very active in this way and has also published a large selection of Conrad's writings in a single volume. A similar selection was introduced by McFee, and Conrad's critical prose has been brought together by Wright.

CRITICAL STUDIES AND COMMENTARY

Conrad's earliest works won critical praise. H. G. Wells wrote in the *Saturday Review* that *An Outcast of the Islands* was 'perhaps the finest piece of fiction that has been published this year, as *Almayer's Folly* was one of the finest that was published in 1895'. Baines (whose standard biography, listed under BIOGRAPHIES AND LETTERS, is the source for this paragraph) tells us that appreciation of this kind reached a peak of approval with *The Nigger of the 'Narcissus'* and *Lord Jim*; it only began to be seriously qualified when Conrad attempted more ambitious works of a very different nature, *Nostromo* and *The Secret Agent*, in the first decade of the twentieth century. Professional critics were then forced to recognize the reactions of ordinary readers, who had never been particularly enthusiastic: 'The subtlety of his mental processes, the keenness of his artistic senses, have placed him further away from the great reading public—if infinitely nearer to the select few who have trained faculties of literary appreciation—than many a writer of far less worth' (*Athenaeum*, 28 September 1907). *Under Western Eyes* (1910) received good reviews, but it was the 1912 serialization of *Chance* in the *New York Herald* that marked the beginning of an absolute change in Conrad's literary career: not only were the reviews lengthy and favourable, he even became a best-seller. Popularity of this kind continued to the end of his life, though it was not extended to his dramatic version of *The Secret Agent* in 1922. The early criticism is now conveniently selected and introduced by Sherry.

Curle published a book on his works as early as 1914. For Curle Conrad was a phenomenon, a volcanic (though not, of course, anarchic) genius, whose writing 'actually does mark a new epoch', when England enters the tradition of Continental literature for the first time. Curle proclaims his own heterodoxy in preferring 'the marvellous *Nostromo*' for 'an imaginative maturity quite beyond the scope of *Lord Jim*' and for being 'representative of a much subtler, more moving, and more truly creative side'. He opens rich seams for future miners, witness his brief comment on *Heart of Darkness* and 'those dangerous things—adjectives'. There is a surprising amount in this early study, but its tone and content are often embarrassingly partial and it is well worth comparing Curle's criticism with that of Henry James in *Notes on Novelists* (1914).

Fellow-novelists, in fact, often gave damagingly qualified praise. In 1920 E. M. Forster wrote positively of 'half-a-dozen great books', but went on to say that they were centrally obscure. To quote his most striking sentence, 'the secret casket of [Conrad's] genius contains a vapour rather than a jewel'. Virginia Woolf wrote in *The Common Reader* (1925) that she thought the early sea-stories like *Typhoon* and *Lord Jim* were his finest. She condemned the later works for inconclusiveness and uncertainty. Galsworthy, too, regarded the stories after *Chance* as a falling-off, and noticed the tendency of the younger generation, who had missed what he thought of as Conrad's great period, 'to tilt the nose sky-ward and talk of his "parade" '. The chill had set in.

It was not a complete frost—Morf's *Polish Heritage* (1931), Mégroz's *Mind and Method* (1931), and Crankshaw's analysis of technique (1936) come to mind—yet in 1941 M. C. Bradbrook, in a brief, pertinent study, felt impelled to call for a revival of Conrad. She placed him with Yeats as one of the greatest writers of his own time. She also found him relevant for wartime. Nobody could call him a facile optimist but he is 'strengthening', she maintained. Fortunately, she was not alone in her estimation of Conrad's worth. Zabel, whose essays have been collected in a revised form, has been most perceptive on such matters as his 'imposition of the processes of psychological experience, notably the experience of recognition, on the structure of the plot' and the reversal of egoism out towards external standards of value. Leavis, in a major section of his in-fluential *The Great Tradition* (1948), ranged from close practical criticism to an appreciation of the 'pattern of moral significances' in *Nostromo*, ending with a claim that Conrad is among the greatest novelists in any language.

Postwar criticism is extremely various. Moser, convinced of a marked decline in Conrad's work after 1912, searches for possible causes. The 'inhibiting effect of sexual subject-matter on [his] crea-tive processes' is one; a new and simpler view of the world leading to loss of genuine artistic complexity is another. He argues strongly and supports his theses with detailed analysis, though he can give a very reduced account of a novel like *The Secret Agent*. But while Moser is prepared to say that Conrad was unconscious of a 'characteristic voyeur gesture' by one of his own characters, Kirschner's primary assumption is that Conrad was a great psychologist who knew very well what he wanted to say about human nature. In his *Conrad: The Psychologist as Artist* he is sometimes obvious or commonplace in his criticism of individual works; his comparisons, however, are often enlightening.

It seems significant that more has been written on *Heart of Darkness* than on anything else by Conrad. Whole books, in fact, have been devoted to a work that is not even a full-length novel (see those edited by Dean and by Harkness). A slim volume brought out by Arthur Symons back in 1925 established, admittedly in an extreme manner, the almost Gothic orientation of much subsequent criticism of one side of Conrad—to read him, for Symons, 'is to shudder on the edge of a gulf, in silent darkness'! Poe, Beddoes, Baudelaire, Tour-neur, and others are evoked by Symons. The fashionable names may change but still for many later critics Conrad is a dark and disturbing writer. On the second page of Guerard's *Conrad* (1958) we are told that he was, like Gide, 'a much divided man'. We read on to find that *The Nigger of the 'Narcissus'* is 'a version of our dark human pil-grimage, a vision of disaster illumined by grace'; in the central scene of Wait's rescue, cannot we say 'very generally' that it 'powerfully dramatises the compulsive psychic descent of *Heart of Darkness* and "The Secret Sharer"?'

Even so, it is really very unfair to give the impression that this par-ticular critic deals darkly with only the inner, subjective aspects of Conrad's writings, since Guerard is careful to note the importance and excellence of their presentation of external realities. The adven-tures of some critics' souls among masterpieces has undoubtedly led to a degree of extravagance and improbability, and above all to a slighting of the literal level of the tales, 'the passing phase of life'. But when, as is undoubtedly the case with Guerard, a critic makes his interests clear, argues intelligently from his premisses and pays close, sensitive attention to the structure and texture of the works he is criticizing—then we will do well to run away to sea like Captain MacWhirr in *Typhoon* and just go through any dirty weather we may find knocking about. It is, for me, the best book written on Conrad to date.

In some critical oceans the song the Sirens sing is of images, myths, and symbols. So many studies of this kind have been published in the last twenty years that Hewitt has been impelled to write a forceful new preface for his brief but useful *Conrad: A Reassessment*, first published in 1952. Then it seemed necessary to proclaim that Conrad was rather more than a 'spinner of yarns about adventures in exotic latitudes', but now he has strong qualms about 'the process of relentless symbolisation' and rightly refers it to the movement that extends methods developed in criticism of poetry and poetic drama to the analysis of prose fiction.

Looking at some recent examples, we find that Wiley's *Measure of Man* sets out to examine recurrent strains of imagery (Expulsion from Eden, Deluge, etc.) and 'concrete thematic figures' (hermit, knight). Boyle, who believes that Wiley was too interested in philosophic attitudes, engages in a rather bald charting of mythic patterns in his own book, *Symbol and Meaning*. Yelton's *Mimesis and Metaphor* has more preparatory discussion and ends with special studies of 'The Secret Sharer' and *The Shadow-Line*; apart from this not much attention is given to any other particular work. Guetti's *The Limits of Metaphor*, in which Conrad is studied along with Melville and Faulkner, provides Hewitt with a quotation to help illustrate the prevailing orthodoxy—*Heart of Darkness* is 'the account of a journey into the centre of things—of Africa, of Kurtz, of Marlow, and of human existence . . .' At the same time, we might notice that Guetti argues a subtle case, itself part of a larger one, in relation to *Heart of Darkness* and 'the intimation that there is something beyond the verbal and, indeed, the imaginative capacities'. At the very least he provides a stimulating counter-statement to Leavis's famous criticism that Conrad was in one respect 'intent on making a virtue out of not knowing what he means'. Hewitt's assessment of the present critical bias is very just, but I do not think he would wish to impose an orthodoxy of an opposite kind (the plain-as-a-pikestaff school?). It is rather a matter of redressing the balance. Actually, a recent book by Said is intended to 'balance the current view of [Conrad] as a writer of "mythic" or "unconscious" fiction' by reading the letters and the shorter works together, thus providing 'the outline for an integral reading of Conrad's total *oeuvre*'. Said's performance, however, does not really measure up to his plan.

Ford asserted in his personal remembrance of 1924 that Conrad was above all else a politician. A number of recent books indicate that due regard is being paid to Conrad's political fiction, which many would now consider his finest artistic achievement. In *Politics and the Novel* Howe examined the pressures that politics and ideology exert upon literature. The scope of such a book is, of course, very wide and Howe's judgements tend to be lively, but it seems doubtful that Conrad 'cut himself off' from society to the extent claimed. Once more Zabel should be mentioned, since his long preface to *Under Western Eyes* is now more widely available in Mudrick's collection of critical essays. Zabel firmly places this novel in the context of Conrad's life and the history of his time. E. K. Hay's *Political Novels* is also the work of a very thorough writer; her resort to manuscripts and other primary sources is in great contrast to the superficiality of more instant critics, and the occasional doubtful statement does not seriously detract from the impression of thoughtful consideration given by her book as a whole. *Conrad's Politics* by Fleishman is an even more recent work of this kind, an extensive analysis of Conrad's organicist ideas, with special attention given to their intellectual background, and a study of their complex fictional embodiment.

In Rosenfield's *Paradise of Snakes* the political and mythical streams of criticism converge, in the belief that the novel form adapts myths to common experience. This examination of recurrent images and archetypal patterns in three books (*Nostromo*, *The Secret Agent*, and *Under Western Eyes*) can be fascinating, but sometimes a swallow-dip at the actual text seems to be followed by prolonged soaring in other regions. The work itself is left darkling.

Gordan's scholarly work on the sources of early Conrad stories (*Almayer's Folly*, *An Outcast*, and *Lord Jim*) has been carried further by Sherry, who provides detailed information about the sources of the Eastern novels. In addition he considers the processes of transforming them into fiction, for example the use made of different aspects of the same source-material in 'The Secret Sharer', *Lord Jim*, and *The Shadow-Line*, varieties of ordinary truth to historical fact, and that special truth which Conrad called 'the highest kind of justice to the visible universe' in the famous Author's Note to *The Nigger of the 'Narcissus'*. Sherry's recently published sequel, *Conrad's Western World*, deals with the sources of *Nostromo*, *The Secret Agent*, *Heart of Darkness*, and various stories. A brief article by Halverson and Watt deserves mention here because of its content (the discovery of a book alluded to by Conrad for its story of the original Nostromo) and the neat conclusion that refers to 'two of the most characteristic features of Conrad's imagination: parsimony of invention, prodigality of discovery'.

Stewart's *Joseph Conrad* is more expansive than his section on Conrad in the Oxford History of English Literature volume, *Eight Modern Writers*, and incorporates discoveries of the 1960s. He underlines, however, the dangers of prejudicing the case if we approach works of literature with external information. For some kinds of problem, such as the consistency or inconsistency of Jim's character, the novel *Lord Jim* 'forms the only evidence upon which it is legitimate to draw'. Stewart's book contains both biography and literary criticism, and it is therefore an up-to-date general introduction. Ryf has also provided a concise work of this kind recently. Other books of an introductory nature are Karl's *A Reader's Guide* and Gurko's *Joseph Conrad*. The former is carefully explanatory, while the latter is more freely written in an attempt to bring the life and works together at 'strategic points of intersection'.

What has been written so far by no means exhausts the subject. Graver has devoted a book to Conrad's short fiction and Lee a book to his views on colonial policy. Krzyzanowski edited *Centennial Essays* 1960 and in the same year Stallman brought out *A Critical Symposium*. Harkness has edited *Conrad's 'Secret Sharer' and the Critics*; *Chance* has been studied by Hough and *Lord Jim* by Van Ghent. Articles abound. Beebe's checklist in the special Joseph Conrad number of *Modern Fiction Studies* (see under BIBLIOGRAPHIES below) is itself accompanied by eight articles. Elsewhere, an interesting piece like Stallman's 'Conrad Criticism Today' (an extended review of Moser and Guerard) rapidly becomes an outdated survey of the state of Conrad criticism way back in 1959; it has already been replaced by Hewitt's preface of 1968. Even this selective account of lines of approach, psychological, moral, biographical, mythic, and so on, has its daunting aspects. The critical thaw, one might say, has become a flood that drowns poor Conrad's primary writings. And yet in practice readers must and probably will follow the lines of their special interests with, one hopes, at least an occasional attempt to come to grips with criticism of an uncongenial kind. Smug certitude is as unrewarding as baffled pique. Samuel Johnson, speaking of Gray's *Elegy*, rejoiced to concur with the common reader. As the years pass, Conrad seems to win the allegiance of the common and uncommon reader alike; we may never realize the full breadth of his appeal as an author unless we sometimes make the effort to stir our mental stumps.

BIOGRAPHIES AND LETTERS

Conrad's own writings are an important source. He published two extended autobiographical pieces, *The Mirror of the Sea* and *A Personal Record*, both splendid reading—though their evident artistry is a clear warning that we should not expect mere factual accuracy. Much of his fictional writing, too, springs from and illuminates his own experience. The impressive *Heart of Darkness*, for instance, is infinitely more revealing than the plain annotation of his 'Congo Diary' (in *Last Essays*). 'A writer of imaginative prose . . . stands confessed in his works', he wrote in *A Personal Record*, and in cases like *The Nigger of the 'Narcissus'* or *The Arrow of Gold* fiction might be said to contain more essential truth than the direct accounts.

The next source is Conrad's correspondence. Here the position is a little complicated. Letters to William Blackwood and D. S. Meldrum (of the publishing house of Blackwood), to R. Curle, to E. Garnett (Conrad's first literary guide), to M. Poradowska (a relative), to the American writer Warrington Dawson, and to R. B. Cunninghame Graham have been published in separate volumes. A very large number of letters are in G. J. Aubry's 'official' *Joseph Conrad: Life and Letters*; Aubry also edited Conrad's *Lettres françaises*. Other letters have been published here and there (see Symons, above, for example), but it appears that not all printed texts are reliable. (Baines notes this all too common defect in connection with *Life and Letters*.) We might also remember that even a definitive, complete edition would necessarily have vital gaps. Najder's *Conrad's Polish Background*, an excellent book which provides much of the evidence for Conrad's early life and, in particular, prints translations of the many fascinating letters to Conrad from his uncle Thaddeus, contains none from Conrad in reply. They were lost in 1917. We see the *young* Conrad, in fact, mostly through the eyes of a man of decided personality and strong opinions, intensely engaged with his nephew's concerns but only along certain narrow lines.

It is easier to find Conrad in his later life. Many more letters are extant and there are the accounts by his wife (he married at 39), his son, and others who knew him. Jessie and Borys Conrad provide domestic glimpses of a Conrad who had given up the sea. A friend like Curle contributes a much younger man's view of a great author, shrewdly sometimes, but also haphazardly—'Conrad's Ideas on Art' rubs shoulders with 'Conrad at Home' among the chapter-titles of

The Last Twelve Years. Several writings by famous contemporaries need careful assessment and, taken as a whole, underline Conrad's complexity; on the face of it at least, H. G. Wells's attitude of superiority is not easily reconciled with Bertrand Russell's deep admiration. Ford Madox Ford's collaboration with Conrad in several works means that his biographical pieces cannot possibly be ignored, though in them eccentric liveliness rides roughshod over precise detail. Part 3 of Ford's *Joseph Conrad*, incidentally, is literary criticism of a technical kind. Galsworthy, who met Conrad when he was a first mate with 'a fund of yarns', also wrote reminiscences.

In 1960 Baines's scholarly and authoritative *Joseph Conrad* superseded all previous biographies. Sensible, detailed, and meticulously researched, it is a near-definitive book on an elusive subject, who pointed out himself that he was 'the man behind' works as 'fundamentally dissimilar as . . . *Almayer's Folly* and *The Secret Agent*'. Subsequent printings incorporate corrections. It is a valuable work in most ways, though its literary criticism, sane and clear on the whole, is not of the same high quality as the rest of the book.

Conrad's extraordinary career, his precariously balanced temperament, his *Weltanschauung* with its incompatibilities—many features invite the insights of psychoanalysis. Meyer, in a recent study, has examined Conrad's life, letters, and works in this way. Rightly or wrongly, I do not think that literary critics will ever really be comfortable with a study of this nature and will often be disconcerted at the unusual look given by it to novels they thought they knew.

BIBLIOGRAPHIES

Lohf and Sheehy have compiled a full bibliography of editions, serializations, 'significant translations', and works about Conrad up to 1955. They tried to be as complete as possible, even listing unpublished theses and reviews of both primary and secondary studies. In Spring 1964 a special Joseph Conrad number of *Modern Fiction Studies* included a checklist of Conrad criticism. Its compiler, M. Beebe, deliberately stressed studies of individual works and capitalized the titles of more important studies for ease of reference. This is very helpful, but it is as well to bear in mind that Conrad criticism in works of broader scope (books by Leavis and Zabel, for instance) will not be distinguished in this way despite their interest. Subsequent numbers of *Modern Fiction Studies* list more recent books and articles on Conrad; major items are in addition reviewed. From 1968 the journal *Conradiana* has been published by the University of Maryland.

Useful selective bibliographies of Conrad are included in Hay's *Political Novels*, Najder's *Polish Background*, Rosenfield's *Paradise of Snakes*, and Fleishman's *Conrad's Politics*; all have been mentioned above. Naturally, these tend to differ according to the direction of their interest. A much fuller, general but still selective bibliography is to be found in Stewart's *Eight Modern Writers*. More recently, Ehrsam's *A Bibliography of Joseph Conrad* is a comprehensive list of primary and secondary works and even includes photographs, caricatures, and motion pictures based on Conrad's works. The Joseph Conrad Collection of the Polish Library in London has now published its Catalogue, which includes some rare items. Teets and Gerber list nearly two thousand writings about Conrad up to 1966 and manage to provide summaries of a great many of them. A supplementary volume is also promised for this already remarkable compilation.

BACKGROUND READING

Several works already mentioned are valuable as background reading. The title of Najder's *Conrad's Polish Background* indicates its scope; it also has a very useful introduction. Similarly, the full title (see REFERENCES below) of a recent book by Busza indicates its relevance. For background to Conrad's career once he had left his native Poland one should again refer to *Conrad's Eastern World*. For Sherry, it was not enough to trace '*one man* or *one incident*' and he therefore attempted to 'recreate the world Conrad knew as a seaman in the East of the 1880's'. His *Conrad's Western World* now fills in the picture. There is also a book of wide scope, Allen's *The Sea-Years*. This is based on extensive research and is a full, engrossing survey of Conrad's experiences and their larger context. Conrad's *The Mirror of the Sea*, one might add here, is often as much a description of, say, London Docks as straight autobiography. The observer merges with his background.

Although Conrad only emerges briefly in a footnote of Porter's *Critics of Empire*, this is none the less a very useful study with a good bibliography. Hay, who often treats of general political–historical matters, made use of Langer's *The Diplomacy of Imperialism* and Sir Robert Anderson's *Sidelights on the Home Rule Movement*. She and other critics refer to books describing Russian revolutionary activities by authors like Herzen; Zabel found E. H. Carr's *The Romantic Exiles* and *Michael Bakunin*, Edmund Wilson's *To the Finland Station*, and a biography (by Woodcock and Avacumavik) of Prince Kropotkin, *The Anarchist Prince*, 'especially relevant'. A number of essays in Conrad's *Notes on Life and Letters* (in Uniform Edition) are worth looking at; Stepniak's *The Career of a Nihilist* and James's *The Princess Casamassima* also claim attention.

Daiches's *The Novel and the Modern World*, which devotes a section to Conrad, finds him significantly modern when he grapples with situations in which public codes or traditional values are inapplicable. An article by Watt in *The English Mind* provides a wider intellectual background to this rejection of outer systems and distinguishes Conrad from other great modern writers, who tended 'to equate the achievement of individuality with the process of alienation'. Curle's placing of Conrad in the Continental tradition is amplified by Kirschner, who in Section iii of his *Conrad* (mentioned above) compares him with Flaubert, Maupassant, France, Turgenev, and Dostoyevsky. A final chapter, entitled 'Conrad and His Tradition', maintains the relevance of other books, including Schopenhauer's *The World as Will and Idea*, Adler's *The Neurotic Constitution*, and Freud's *The Interpretation of Dreams*. Ruthven would certainly add Freud's *Civilisation and Its Discontents*, together with *The Benin Massacre* by Boisragon; in an article Ruthven describes the general European interest in savage primitivism in relation to Conrad's *Heart of Darkness* and novels by Lawrence. Jung's *Archetypes* and Frazer's *The Golden Bough* are important in view of the myth studies of recent years, but at this point, perhaps, the *fore*ground has become quite invisible. Another book by the indefatigable Sherry, *Conrad and His World*, is exceptionally well illustrated and therefore provides a pleasant way of re-focusing upon the author seen against his background.

REFERENCES

TEXTS

(*a*) *Collected works*

The Works of Joseph Conrad (Uniform Edition, 22 vols., London and Toronto, 1923–8).
The Complete Short Stories of Joseph Conrad (London, 1933).
The Collected Edition of the Works of Joseph Conrad (22 vols., London, 1946–54).

(*b*) *Separate works*

J. Conrad and F. M. Hueffer [Ford], *The Nature of a Crime* (London and Garden City, N.Y., 1924).
J. Conrad, *Three Plays: Laughing Anne; One Day More; and The Secret Agent* (London, 1934).
R. Curle (intro.), *Last Essays* (London, Toronto, and Garden City, N.Y., 1926).

F. M. Ford (intro.), *The Sisters* (New York, 1928); U. Mursia (ed.), *The Sisters* (2nd edn., Milan, 1968).

D. Grant (ed.), *The Nigger of the 'Narcissus'* (London, 1965).

R. Kimbrough (ed.), *Heart of Darkness: An Authoritative Text* (New York, 1963); with backgrounds and criticism.

F. R. Leavis (intro.), *Nostromo* (paperback, New York, 1960).

W. McFee (intro.), *Tales of Land and Sea* (Garden City, N.Y., 1953).

T. Moser (ed.), *Lord Jim: An Authoritative Text* (New York, 1968); with backgrounds and criticism.

D. Van Ghent (intro.), *Nostromo* (paperback, New York, 1961).

R. P. Warren (intro.), *Nostromo* (New York, 1951); textually interesting.

W. F. Wright (ed.), *Joseph Conrad on Fiction* (Lincoln, Neb., 1964).

M. D. Zabel (intro.), *The Mirror of the Sea, and A Personal Record* (1960).

—— *The Shadow-Line* [*with*] *Typhoon, The Secret Sharer* (1959).

—— *Tales of Heroes and History* (1960).

—— *Tales of the East* (1961).

—— *Tales of the East and West* (1958).

—— *Under Western Eyes* (paperback, 1963).

—— *Youth* [*with*] *Heart of Darkness, The End of the Tether* (1959).

(all, Garden City, N.Y.).

—— *The Portable Conrad* (New York, 1947).

CRITICAL STUDIES AND COMMENTARY

T. E. Boyle, *Symbol and Meaning in the Fiction of Joseph Conrad* (The Hague, 1965).

M. C. Bradbrook, *Joseph Conrad: Poland's English Genius* (Cambridge and New York, 1941).

E. Crankshaw, *Joseph Conrad: Some Aspects of the Art of the Novel* (London, 1936).

R. Curle, *Joseph Conrad: A Study* (London and New York, 1914).

L. F. Dean (ed.), *Joseph Conrad's 'Heart of Darkness': Backgrounds and Criticisms* (paperback, Englewood Cliffs, N.J., 1960).

A. Fleishman, *Conrad's Politics: Community and Anarchy in the Fiction of Joseph Conrad* (Baltimore, Md., 1967).

F. M. Ford. See under BIOGRAPHIES AND LETTERS below.

E. M. Forster, 'Joseph Conrad: A Note', in his *Abinger Harvest* (London and New York, 1936).

J. Galsworthy. See under BIOGRAPHIES AND LETTERS below.

J. D. Gordan, *Joseph Conrad: The Making of a Novelist* (Cambridge, Mass., 1940).

L. S. Graver, *Conrad's Short Fiction* (Berkeley and Los Angeles, Calif., 1969).

A. J. Guerard, *Conrad the Novelist* (Cambridge, Mass., 1958).

J. L. Guetti, *The Limits of Metaphor: A Study of Melville, Conrad, and Faulkner* (Ithaca, N.Y., 1967).

L. Gurko, *Joseph Conrad: Giant in Exile* (New York, 1962; London, 1965).

J. Halverson and I. Watt, 'The Original Nostromo: Conrad's Source', *RES* x (1959).

B. Harkness (ed.), *Conrad's 'Heart of Darkness' and the Critics* (San Francisco, 1960); textually interesting.

—— (ed.), *Conrad's 'Secret Sharer' and the Critics* (Belmont, Calif., 1962).

E. K. Hay, *The Political Novels of Joseph Conrad* (Chicago, 1963).

D. Hewitt, *Conrad: A Reassessment* (new edn., London, 1969).

G. Hough, *Image and Experience: Reflections on a Literary Revolution* (London, 1960).

I. Howe, 'Conrad: Order and Anarchy', in his *Politics and the Novel* (New York, 1957; London, 1961).

H. James, 'Joseph Conrad' [from *Notes on Novelists*, 1914], in his *The Future of the Novel: Essays on the Art of Fiction*, ed. L. Edel (New York, 1956).

F. R. Karl, *A Reader's Guide to Joseph Conrad* (New York, 1960).

P. Kirschner, *Conrad: The Psychologist as Artist* (Edinburgh, 1968).

L. Krzyzanowski (ed.), *Joseph Conrad: Centennial Essays* (New York, 1960).

F. R. Leavis, *The Great Tradition: George Eliot, Henry James, Joseph Conrad* (London and New York, 1948).

R. F. Lee, *Conrad's Colonialism* (The Hague, 1969).

R. L. Mégroz, *Joseph Conrad's Mind and Method: a Study of Personality in Art* (London, 1931; New York 1964).

G. Morf, *The Polish Heritage of Joseph Conrad* (London, 1931).

T. Moser, *Joseph Conrad: Achievement and Decline* (Cambridge, Mass., 1957).

M. Mudrick (ed.), *Joseph Conrad: A Collection of Critical Essays* (paperback, Englewood Cliffs, N.J., 1966).

C. Rosenfield, *Paradise of Snakes: An Archetypal Analysis of Conrad's Political Novels* (Chicago and London, 1967).

R. S. Ryf, *Joseph Conrad* (New York, 1970).

E. W. Said, *Joseph Conrad and the Fiction of Autobiography* (Cambridge, Mass., 1966).

N. Sherry, *Conrad's Eastern World* (Cambridge, 1966).

—— *Conrad's Western World* (Cambridge, 1971).

—— *Conrad: the Critical Heritage* (London, 1973).

R. W. Stallman, 'Conrad Criticism Today', *SR* lxvii (1959).

—— (ed.), *Joseph Conrad: A Critical Symposium* (East Lansing, Mich., 1960).

J. I. M. Stewart, 'Joseph Conrad', in his *Eight Modern Writers* (*OHEL*, Oxford, 1963).

—— *Joseph Conrad* (London, 1968).

A. Symons, *Notes on Joseph Conrad, with Some Unpublished Letters* (London, 1925).

D. Van Ghent, 'On *Lord Jim*', in her *The English Novel: Form and Function* (New York, 1961).

P. L. Wiley, *Conrad's Measure of Man* (Madison, Wis., and Toronto, 1954).

V. Woolf, 'Joseph Conrad', in her *The Common Reader* (London and New York, 1925).

D. C. Yelton, *Mimesis and Metaphor: An Inquiry into the Genesis and Scope of Conrad's Symbolic Imagery* (The Hague, 1967).

M. D. Zabel, 'Conrad', in his *Craft and Character in Modern Fiction: Texts, Method, and Vocation* (New York, 1957).

BIOGRAPHIES AND LETTERS

G. J. Aubry, *Joseph Conrad: Life and Letters*, 2 vols., (London and Garden City, N.Y., 1927); [condensed as *The Sea-Dreamer: A Definitive Biography of Joseph Conrad* (Garden City, N.Y., 1957)].

—— (ed.), *Lettres françaises* (Paris, 1930).

J. Baines, *Joseph Conrad: A Critical Biography* (New York, 1960; London, 1967).

W. Blackburn (ed.), *Joseph Conrad: Letters to William Blackwood and David S. Meldrum* (Cambridge, 1966).

Borys Conrad, *My Father: Joseph Conrad* (London, 1970).

Jessie Conrad, *Joseph Conrad As I Knew Him* (London and Garden City, N.Y., 1926).

—— *Joseph Conrad and His Circle* (London and New York, 1967).

Joseph Conrad, *The Mirror of the Sea* and *A Personal Record* [in Uniform Edition, etc.].

R. Curle (ed.), *Conrad to a Friend: 150 Selected Letters from Joseph Conrad to Richard Curle* (London and New York, 1928).

—— *The Last Twelve Years of Joseph Conrad* (London and Garden City, N.Y., 1928).

F. M. Ford, *Joseph Conrad: A Personal Remembrance* (London and Boston, 1924).

—— 'Working with Conrad', in his *Return to Yesterday* (London, 1931; New York, 1932).

J. Galsworthy, 'Reminiscences of Conrad', in his *Castles in Spain and other Screeds* (London and New York, 1927), etc. [See Lohf and Sheehy, below].

E. Garnett (ed.), *Letters from Joseph Conrad, 1895–1924* (Indianapolis, Ind., 1962).

J. A. Gee and P. J. Sturm (edd.), *Letters of Joseph Conrad to Marguerite Poradowska, 1890–1920* (New Haven, Conn., and London, 1940).

B. C. Meyer, *Joseph Conrad: A Psychoanalytic Biography* (Princeton, N.J., 1967)

Z. Najder (ed.), H. Carroll (trans.), *Conrad's Polish Background: Letters to and from Polish Friends* (London, 1964).

D. B. J. Randall, *Joseph Conrad and Warrington Dawson: the Record of a Friendship* (Durham, N.C., 1968).

B. Russell, 'Joseph Conrad', in his *Portraits from Memory and Other Essays* (London and New York, 1956).

C. T. Watts (ed.), *Joseph Conrad's Letters to R. B. Cunninghame Graham* (Cambridge, 1969).

H. G. Wells, *Experiment in Autobiography: Discoveries and Conclusions of a Very Ordinary Brain (since 1866)* (2 vols., London and New York, 1934).

BIBLIOGRAPHIES

M. Beebe, 'Criticism of Joseph Conrad: A Selected Checklist', *Modern Fiction Studies*, x (1964–5).

—— *Conradiana* (1968–   ).

T. G. Ehrsam, *A Bibliography of Joseph Conrad* (Metuchen, N.J., 1969).

K. A. Lohf and E. P. Sheehy, *Joseph Conrad at Mid-Century: Editions and Studies, 1895–1955* (Minneapolis, Minn., 1957).

J. Nowak, *The Joseph Conrad Collection in the Polish Library in London* (London, 1970).

B. E. Teets and H. E. Gerber (edd.), *Joseph Conrad: an Annotated Bibliography of Writings About Him* (De Kalb, Ill., 1971).

BACKGROUND READING

A. Adler, *The Neurotic Constitution: Outlines of a Comparative Individualistic Psychology and Psychotherapy* (London, 1921).

J. Allen, *The Sea-Years of Joseph Conrad* (New York, 1965; London, 1967).

R. Anderson, *Sidelights on the Home Rule Movement* (London, 1906).

A. Boisragon, *The Benin Massacre* (London, 1897).

A. Busza, *Conrad's Polish Literary Background and Some Illustrations of the Influence of Polish Literature on His Work* (Rome, 1965–6).

E. H. Carr, *Michael Bakunin* (London, 1937; New York, 1961).

—— *The Romantic Exiles: A Nineteenth-Century Portrait Gallery* (London, 1968).

D. Daiches, *The Novel and the Modern World* (rev. edn., Chicago and Cambridge, 1960).

Sir J. G. Frazer, *The Golden Bough* (abridged edn., London, 1932).

S. Freud, *The Interpretation of Dreams* (London, 1955).

—— *Civilisation and Its Discontents* (London, 1963).

A. Herzen, *My Past and Thoughts* (New York, 1968).

H. James, *The Princess Casamassima* (2 vols., London and New York, 1948).

K. Jung, *Archetypes of the Collective Unconscious*, in *Collected Works*, vol. ix, pt. 1 (London, 1959; Princeton, N.J., 1968).

W. L. Langer, *The Diplomacy of Imperialism 1890–1902* (New York, 1951).

B. Porter, *Critics of Empire: British Radical Attitudes to Colonialism in Africa, 1895–1914* (London, 1968).

K. Ruthven, 'The Savage God: Conrad and Lawrence', in C. B. Cox and A. E. Dyson (edd.), *Word in the Desert* (London, New York, and Toronto, 1968).

A. Schopenhauer, *The World as Will and Idea* (3 vols., London, 1883–6; New York, 1964).

N. Sherry, *Conrad and His World* (London, 1973).

Stepniak [S. M. Kravchinsky], *The Career of a Nihilist: A Novel* (2nd edn., London, 1890).

I. Watt, 'Joseph Conrad: Alienation and Commitment', in H. S. Davies and G. Watson (edd.), *The English Mind: Studies in the English Moralists Presented to Basil Willey* (Cambridge, 1964).

E. Wilson, *To the Finland Station: A Study in the Writing and Acting of History* (London, 1960).

G. Woodcock and I. Avakumovic, *The Anarchist Prince* (London, 1950).

Malcolm Bradbury

I think one of the reasons why I stopped writing novels is that the social
aspect of the world changed so much. I had been accustomed to writing
about the old-fashioned world with its homes and its family life and its comparative peace. All that went, and though I can think about the new world
I cannot put it into fiction.

E. M. FORSTER in a television interview.

E. M. Forster died in 1970 at the age of 91. During his long lifetime,
he saw not only a great change in the character of English life but
also in the character of literature itself—the change, in effect, from
the spirit of Victorian to that of modern letters. His own writing
career, which included the production not only of novels but of
travel-books, essays, criticism, memoirs, and journalism, spanned
more than fifty years from the turn of the century onward. But his
career as a novelist in fact falls into a shorter period, the period from
around the century's turn until 1924, the year in which *A Passage to
India* appeared. Of the fiction he wrote over that time, five novels
went into print; more lately, the story has been complicated by the
publication of a sixth novel, *Maurice*, which appeared posthumously
in 1971, and it is likely to be complicated further by other publications. *Maurice*, however, though it went through a revision in 1960,
was written just before *A Passage to India* was first attempted, in
1913–14; it is, for all its outspoken, homosexual theme, decidedly an
Edwardian or Georgian novel, and the reviewer in the *TLS* was
hardly unfair is saying that it 'does not transcend its historical limit'.
The book's outspokenness, the basis of its appeal outside the limitations of its time, is bound none the less to affect our judgement of the
other novels; even so, the fact remains that Forster's work as a novelist belongs to a particular phase in his life and in the evolution of
modern fiction. In personal terms, the phase meant a growth away
from certain late Victorian liberal ideals and artistic forms into a
more emancipated world of manners and of aesthetic presumptions,
a world we associate with Bloomsbury; in general terms, his evolution as a novelist coincides with the great period of fictional change
and experiment that occurred in the first quarter of the century and
has since powerfully dominated it, the period of the main work of

James, Conrad, Wells, Lawrence, Virginia Woolf, and Joyce. Forster is clearly of this body, and—as with most of the other major figures of those turning, experimental years in fiction—his reputation has developed and increased slowly and steadily through the century and has come to the peak of importance in the period since the Second World War, when the scale of the development in the novel at the beginning of the century has become more apparent and the matter more theoretically discussed.

But though Forster has acquired high reputation, his reputation has not been of quite the same kind as that of Lawrence, James, Conrad, or Joyce. This is because of the kind of writer Forster is: because of the nature of the novel which he was writing, and about which, in his critical book *Aspects of the Novel*, he theorized. The publication of *Maurice* is bound to remind us vigorously of the basis in his personal life and passions from which his writing arose; it gives a local justification for his liberalism and his attitude toward human feeling, toward emancipating personal relationships, the growth of the heart. None the less Forster is a writer who embodies many of the characteristics of the traditional novel, including its capacity to generalize and make public the experience with which it deals. He is in fact a writer much of whose interest lies in the way in which he writes from a centre—in intellectual, cultural, and emotional experience—that is, while personal, neither private nor eccentric. His writing embodies shared feelings which are also vigorous mental attitudes and ideas rooted in the life of his own age and the age before his, the Victorian age. Forster thus differs from many of his contemporaries precisely in his reasonableness and his moral, social, and intellectual centrality, his lack of extremism, his quality of virtue; he engages by embodying something of the main-line evolution of English literary-intellectual life, carrying his culture as few of his contemporaries and successors have seemed able to. There are writers whom we associate with the illuminating, humane, moderating powers of art and the imagination, its power to relate feeling with moral and intellectual force. In many respects, Forster has been, for his readers and for the many writers he has influenced, such a figure: 'I believe your work to be as powerful an influence on the moral outlook of a number of my generation as Shaw's on an earlier one', Angus Wilson reported himself as saying to Forster in 'A Conversation with E. M. Forster', *Encounter* (November 1957).

But today criticism seems to have lost some of its confidence in this sort of writer, particularly if he is modern. It has tended to believe that these cultured and humanist assumptions can no longer serve the modern artist well; that the pressures upon literary language and the artist's role are now so great that authorial confidence or a cultured repose is no longer possible; that the modern aesthetic—for writers as well as critics—should be inward-looking, neo-symbolist, 'autotelic'. Hence, perhaps, a sense of Forster's historical 'limitation' as an artist—the sort of limitation he himself expresses in the quotation which heads this essay. In fact, however, Forster, who has always been humane but also ambiguous, is ambiguous even in this. On the one hand the humanist, he has also been in certain ways very much the modernist. He is not only a performer in the 'open' nineteenth-century novel but an expert technician in the modes of the twentieth. He wrote one of the most interesting modern books on the novel—*Aspects of the Novel* (1927)—all the more interesting for not being Jamesian. And we must recognize him—if we are to see him fully—not only as a novelist of morals, manners, and values, or of homes, family life, and peace, nor, indeed, as a novelist of deep personal feeling, but also, as a novelist of symbols, and metaphysical metaphors, and aesthetic complexities. His work may indeed contain many reminders of the intimate narrative contact of the nineteenth-century novelist. But he has also spoken of art as 'the one orderly product' which survives, not because it spurs us to wisdom or criticism (which is the humanist view), but because it becomes an object of harmonious contemplation (which is the symbolist view). In fact, Forster is actually both a humanist and a symbolist; not an easy combination. He has been spokesman both for the view that art can change and redeem us, can show us love and truth; and for the power of art to be its own universe of value, an object of self-sustaining integrity.

This may well explain why it is that his status has been somewhat uncertain; and also why the criticism written about him has tended to follow two different tacks. There are critics who recognize him primarily as a social and moral novelist, or a comedy-of-manners novelist, and the inheritor of a tradition that reaches back certainly to Jane Austen; and there are critics who see him primarily as a romance or symbolist novelist, and who link him rather with writers like Hawthorne and Melville, or with Proust and Virginia Woolf. There are also, of course, many critics who believe him to be divided as an artist between the two modes; Virginia Woolf, for instance, presents him as a novelist split between a desire to give us social history and a novelist concerned with the soul. Forster himself spoke of the need of the novel to give us both 'life by time' and 'life by values' (*Aspects of the Novel*), obviously tempted by, yet resisting, the extreme represented by Virginia Woolf—who, he wrote, 'is always stretching out from her enchanted tree and snatching bits from the flux of daily life as they float past, and out of these bits she builds novels' ('Virginia Woolf' in *Two Cheers for Democracy*). A good deal of Forster criticism has sensed a distinction between two contrary artistic ends here, and worried about it—some critics finding in the distinction the heart of his strength, others finding in it the centre of his weakness. What it is important to recognize is that Forster very seriously sought to reconcile a double claim made upon the novelist in the twentieth-century climate; and most of his work in various ways manifests the struggle.

TEXTS

Forster's six published novels (a novel named *Arctic Summer* was begun before *Howards End* and never finished; and one, possibly two, other unfinished novels have been referred to) consist of four which appeared fairly close to one another in the Edwardian period—*Where Angels Fear to Tread* (1905), *The Longest Journey* (1907), *A Room With a View* (1908), and *Howards End* (1910); one book that was started before the First World War but was interrupted by it and not completed until well after it, *A Passage to India* (1924), and a sixth, *Maurice*, completed in 1914, revised in 1959–60, and published posthumously in 1971. In addition to the novels, there are two collections of stories, *The Celestial Omnibus* (1911) and *The Eternal Moment* (1928): both consist of stories written before the First World War. The first five novels have all been reissued in a Uniform edition (5 vols., 1924–6) and a Pocket Edition (8 vols., 1947–62) by their original publishers, Edward Arnold, as well as in Penguin paperback. In addition, Sidgwick and Jackson, and Penguin, reissued the stories in one volume as *Collected Short Stories* (1947). *A Passage to India* also appeared in Everyman Library (no. 972) in 1942, with some important notes by Forster, revised for the reprint in 1957. *Aspects of the Novel*, his important statement about the novel-form which appeared in 1927, has also been reissued. In England, at least, there is no difficulty in obtaining Forster's work. In the United States his books are fairly accessible, though it is perhaps characteristic of the critical emphasis prevailing in the States that it is *A Passage to India* and *Aspects of the Novel* that are most easily available (for instance, the former is in Harbrace Classics and in Modern Library, cheap editions).

The manuscript of *Where Angels Fear to Tread* is in the British Museum, and that of *A Passage to India* is at the University of Texas;

the latter has been the object of several studies. For fragments of his unfinished fiction, see Rose Macaulay, *The Writings of E. M. Forster*, A. Gishford (ed.), *A Tribute to Benjamin Britten on His Fiftieth Birthday* (1963), and 'Entrance to an Unwritten Novel,' *Listener*, December 23, 1948.

Forster of course also wrote many essays, reviews, travel-books, and memoirs, valuable in themselves and also illuminating in connection with the novels. Many of the essays are collected in *Abinger Harvest* (1936) and *Two Cheers for Democracy* (1951). Of the travel-books, *The Hill of Devi* (1953) is particularly relevant for *A Passage to India*. His two biographies, of his friend *Goldsworthy Lowes Dickinson* (1934) and his great-aunt *Marianne Thornton* (1956), are both highly illuminating about his intellectual roots in Cambridge and in Victorian intellectual reform. Other works include *Alexandria: A History and a Guide* (1922) and *Pharos and Pharillon* (1923).

Forster's works are now being edited (by Oliver Stallybrass) and published by Edward Arnold in the Abinger Edition. *The Life to Come and Other Stories* (1972), *Two Cheers for Democracy* (1973), *Howards End* (1973, with description of manuscripts) and *Goldsworthy Lowes Dickinson* have appeared; future volumes will include *Arctic Summer and Other Fiction* and extracts from Forster's notebooks.

CRITICAL STUDIES AND COMMENTARY

(a) General studies

Like most of the English novelists of the early twentieth century who are now accepted classics, taught in schools and university courses, Forster has come in for extensive critical discussion and commentary only since the war. In the 1920s and 1930s he was highly admired as an interesting and important novelist—though perhaps not quite a major one, but then this applied to most other figures who now have acquired greater prestige. Time and expanding universities, probably, were the main reasons why after the war the modern novel suddenly gained much more serious attention; and it has really only been over the last twenty years that we have begun to see the size and scale of the early twentieth-century effort in fiction, and that a perspective has emerged. As I have remarked though, when postwar critical attention turned to the novel it tended to turn to modernism, and here Forster's particular manner—'his irritating refusal to be great', as Lionel Trilling puts it in one of the best books on him—sometimes told against him. As Trilling says, the danger is in misinterpreting the manner, in taking it too literally. Even so, Forster's reputation has indeed grown vastly, particularly in more recent years, and particularly for *Howards End* and *A Passage to India*. The number of books and articles has vastly accelerated and is now becoming a deluge.

As I have already suggested, it is in Forster's complicated response both to modernism and traditionalism that he seems most important; that is perhaps the hardest problem for his critics to define and to understand, and those who have responded to it have usually written best about him. Forster is not a very difficult novelist on the surface; the difficulties are subtleties; and hence books on Forster often seem rather alike. The basis of a view of him seems in fact to have been sought most profitably in three areas: in the debt that comes to him from romanticism, from the supreme value that he awards to the virtues of the developed heart, and what he makes of that emotional imperative in the twentieth-century environment: in the debt that comes to him from liberal–romantic social and cultural criticism by nineteenth-century writers like Ruskin and Carlyle, from the supreme value he awards to the connected and vitally organic society, and what in the modern world he makes of that; and in the debt that comes to him from the broad tradition of genial social comedy and social exploration in the nineteenth-century novel, and what he makes of that. All of these matters raise questions simultaneously about the form and substance of his work and about his intellectual and artistic environment and context—one which is indeed in part derived from a body of inheritance coming through from the Victorian period. 'I belong to the fag-end of Victorian liberalism', he said himself in an essay in *Two Cheers for Democracy*. But the traditionalist view of Forster that is sometimes deduced from this is surely too simple; there is a profound element of revolt as well as of inheritance, and what he does inherit he takes up with a profound sense of difficulty and struggle. He may be a markedly public author, though he speaks against the public life. But, if so, any criticism which fails to recognize that his writing questioned his intellectual and artistic environment severely and persistently is likely to be blind to some of his most considerable virtues.

Indeed, then, he was committed to a body of values and attitudes, about personal life and about the culture generally, which can be defined as liberal–romantic; but he also recognized that these values can involve many delusions, that they are also the values of a threatened intelligentsia, and that they belong to a phase of cultural confidence and power whose economic base has been thrown into question; so they must be questioned from the standpoint of a precise moral realism and discarded where they fail. *Howards End*, a 'State of England' novel that demands that society be romantically organic and connected, sees also the historical forces of unprecedented change that threaten any such hope; while *A Passage to India* contains one of the bleakest evocations of anarchy and historical disorder we have had in its dark discovery in the caves: 'Everything exists; nothing has value.' Forster's famous scepticism turns a profound irony against the kind of liberal he is often thought to be. And this has its profound technical and artistic consequences. His novels are created inter-mediately between two voices; that of the man in search of social, spiritual, and aesthetic wholeness, and that of the ironist who can persistently question that first voice, through an analytical intelli-gence illuminated by a profound sense of the 'panic and emptiness' that must threaten all such hopes. His novels are therefore founded on a severe sense of contradiction and paradox, and it is this, rather than any overt complexity of technique, that makes them hard to read. Their difficulty lies less in the structure itself than in the way tone is shaded, balance created; and hence modern criticism has not been so concerned with establishing the methods and aesthetics of a selfconscious experimentalism as with adjusting to a complex autho-rial tone. There is, in fact, a delicate experimentalism in Forster's work, a symbolist desire for a musical composition, for a rhythmic 'opening out' of the novel toward an harmonious resonance; but that is not the complete or final end, rather another part of the formal matter to be balanced by the effective critic.

Forster criticism has been chiefly concerned, then, with under-standing Forster as a liberal humanist; with recognizing his symbolist bias; and with trying to judge him in relation to the development of the modern novel. The following comments emphasize the central and essential work done on him. (A more general survey of the range of opinion can be found in my introduction to *Forster: A Collection of Critical Essays* (1966), which collects together some of the main essays on his work.) The broad themes were, indeed, well laid down in the 1930s by one book and three articles, all by British critics. The book is Rose Macaulay's *The Writings of E. M. Forster* (1938), an intellec-tual analysis of Forster's humanism with a biographical base. It still remains useful, both because it contains much valuable biographical information, and also because it sets him clearly in his cultural and intellectual environment. Miss Macaulay, in a spirit of friendly questioning, presents the basis of Forster's liberal assumptions, locat-ing it in two main contexts: that of Cambridge, his university, which gives him, she says, his concern with Reality ('. . . it is this vision of Reality, this passionate antithesis between the real and the unreal, the true and the false, being and not-being, that gives the whole body of E. M. Forster's work, in whatever *genre*, its unity. The importance he attaches to this antithesis has the urgency of a religion. There is a Way, a Truth, a Life . . .'); and that of liberal agnosticism, which gives him his faith in personal relationships and his central stress on 'Beauty, civilization, culture' as the core of his liberal view of society. The book is not strongly critical, and takes the novels largely as expressions of ideas—a point made in the review by F. R. Leavis, E. M. Forster, *Scrutiny* (September 1938); reprinted in his *The Common Pursuit* (1952), who felt it missed the essential question: the problem of the 'oddly limited and uncertain quality of his distinction —his real and very fine distinction'.

Leavis's own case in his essay, a generous and illuminating one, is that Forster's work is concerned with bringing alive the moral obligation to live 'truly and freshly from a centre', and that it is in the successes and failures of doing that that Forster must be judged. The failures, in Leavis's view, come from the way in which the comedy of his writing periodically turns toward whimsy, and the poetic disclosure he has to make turns to formalism and unreality—so that his social and moral critique often loses its force. Forster is, he says, a novelist of civilization who has a radical dissatisfaction with that civilization, which his comedy, at best, enforces. But he fails, often, to get far enough away from Bloomsbury and its delicately uncritical view of civilization to succeed fully. Leavis does look carefully at the novels, and comes out strongly in favour of the last of them, *A Passage to India*, which is, he says, 'all criticisms made,' a 'classic of the liberal spirit'. There is, interestingly, a certain consonance between Leavis's critique and that of Virginia Woolf in her 'The Novels of E. M. Forster', reprinted in *The Death of the Moth and Other Essays* (1942), though of course the two critics are working from radically different premises. She stresses that Forster is both a novelist of the material world, which is bounded by time, and a novelist of the soul: 'Beneath bicycles and dusters, Sawston and Italy . . . there always lies for him . . . a burning core. It is the soul; it is reality; it is love . . .' But his two emphases are hard to reconcile: 'It seems, then, that if he is to succeed in his mission his reality must at certain points become irradiated; his brick must be lit up; we must see the whole building saturated with light;' but this involves a change from realism to symbolism, and the conjunction of the two different realities casts doubt on both. In her approach, Virginia Woolf's own preferences are fairly apparent and, unlike Leavis, she sees him as granting too much to the world of time, and so risking the luminous transparence of which he is capable. But her emphasis on the symbolist element in Forster links interestingly with the third important pre-war essay, Peter Burra's 'The Novels of E. M. Forster', *The Nineteenth Century and After* (November, 1934,) a piece which Forster himself approved and used for the introduction to the Everyman edition of *A Passage to India*. Burra's point is that Forster has an aspiration to abstractness, but at the same time possesses a serious concern with the political and economic questions of the outer world; and the essay is particularly notable for its case that Forster pays close attention to rhythm and pattern, to the pursuit of something 'aesthetically compact'. So he exploits leitmotiv (Burra was the first critic to note, to Forster's pleasure, the way in which the wasp is used as a recurrent motif in *A Passage to India*) and also a certain number of 'elemental' characters, like Gino, Mrs. Wilcox, and Mrs. Moore, who are 'utterly percipient of the reality behind appearances'. These elements rise up out of the contradictory elements of the novel and stamp the books with a quality of prophecy or vision, while at the same time producing an aesthetic consonance. Burra is in fact the first critic to use the assumptions of *Aspects of the Novel* to illuminate Forster's own work: an approach to which several later critics were to return.

But it was in 1943 that there appeared the book that was to do most to establish Forster's critical reputation; it still probably remains the best book on his work. This was Lionel Trilling's *E. M. Forster* (1943), a brilliant analysis of Forster's 'liberal imagination' which also provides excellent criticism of the novels. More than any critic before or since, Trilling establishes the intricate relation between Forster's liberalism as a view of life and a view of art; and he centres his case in an evocation of Forster's sceptical integrity, his uncompromising honesty of vision, his refusal to indulge in a taste for the unconditioned. Forster is, he says, a liberal whose most devastating power is to criticize the liberal mind at its most vulnerable point: 'The liberal mind is sure that the order of human affairs owes it a simple logic: good is good and bad is bad. . . . Before the idea of good-and-evil its imagination fails; it cannot accept this improbable paradox.' It is this knowledge of good-and-evil, this moral realism, that controls Forster's novels and provides a spirit of pervasive scepticism and irony that questions the grander flights of the artistic imagination. Trilling's definition of irony, comedy, and scepticism as the agent of Forster's moral intention seems to me a crucial way of seeing him. His Forster is 'One of the best representatives of the intellectual tradition of Europe', one who 'reminds us of a world where will is not everything, of a world of true order, of the necessary connection of passion and prose, and of the strange paradoxes of being human. He is one of those who raise the shield of Achilles, which is the moral intelligence of art, against the panic and emptiness which make their onset when the will is tired from its own excesses.'

After the war, a considerable number of books and articles on Forster began to appear; and it became apparent that Trilling's high estimate was fairly widely accepted, particularly by the 1960s. By then the questions tended to turn to the kinds of technique that Forster uses to resolve the paradoxes and uncertainties of an artistic intelligence committed variously by his liberalism in many directions, yet seeking to produce 'something aesthetically compact, something which might have been shown by the novelist straight away, only if he had shown it straight away it would never have become beautiful'—as Forster puts the matter himself in *Aspects of the Novel*. Most of this criticism has tended either to elaborate, in one direction or another, Trilling's view of Forster as a moral realist; or else to stress his character as a romantic symbolist, or visionary novelist with a prophetic affirmation to make. The liberal and moral aspect of Forster has perhaps been most stressed in H. J. Oliver's short book, *The Art of E. M. Forster* (1960), which argues that Forster's work is 'the most interesting product of a cultured mind in modern literature'; in K. W. Gransden's brief but useful survey *E. M. Forster* (1962); and especially in Frederick C. Crews's excellent *E. M. Forster: The Perils of Humanism* (1962), which recognizes that Forster's novels are persistently dialectical and seek a mean or balance rather than a vision. Crews has an excellent chapter on the balance of Apollonian and Dionysian elements in Forster which shows how the visionary extreme is set in a world governed by comedy and irony. He also carefully examines Forster's technique of comedy, more so than Trilling, showing that the early novels are concerned with thwarting false egotism and moral self-delusion, while the last two make the comic vision into a total attitude toward life, which involves a sense of man's isolation from meaning, and therefore a sense of the human universe as one of predicament and muddle. He also examines in detail the intellectual tradition of Victorian liberalism to which Forster can be linked, giving an excellent discussion of turn-of-the-century Cambridge philosophy and, in particular, the intellectual problems of those committed to liberal values when their way to political action was limited by the decline of the Liberal Party.

But the more general tendency of postwar Forster criticism has been to emphasize not Forster's irony and comedy but his romanticism or religiosity. A brilliant and delicate example is E. K. Brown's book, *Rhythm in the Novel* (1950). About the novel-form in general, it draws very much on Forster's own discussion of this subject (*Aspects of the Novel*) and concludes with an excellent discussion of the rhythmical structure of *A Passage to India*, vastly extending Burra's earlier argument. A modification of this kind of argument, stressing that these very devices can be 'ironic symbols', is to be found in R. A. Brower's chapter 'The Twilight of the Double Vision: Symbol and Irony in *A Passage to India*' in his *The Fields of Light: An Experiment in Critical Reading* (1951). Similarly, James McConkey, in his sharp, useful *The Novels of E. M. Forster* (1957), which also reads the novels in the light of Forster's own critical terminology (People; Fantasy and Prophecy; Rhythm, etc.), recognizes this. Forster is not a mystic but a mediator between God and man; his desire for an integration between man and his universe, a man and the unseen, must remain to a great extent in the realm of mystery rather than of revelation; he suggests the presence of a transcendent reality in the world without, himself, being able to penetrate the veil. In following out these assumptions McConkey offers some delicate readings, and his stress on the prophetic voice was, at the time, a valuable one (though more recent critics have, I think, taken it much too far). Another very illuminating book which emphasizes Forster's visionary technique less than his visionary *ideas* is John Beer's *The Achievement of E. M. Forster* (1962). This stresses the degree to which Forster's inheritance lies in romanticism, in belief in the imagination, which confirms the validity of passion and links the pursuit of moral seriousness with the pursuit of the right state of being. Forster has, he suggests, the romantic existential commitment to the visionary moment—'. . . in the moment of exaltation, reality is revealed', the reality by which other states of human existence sink into various modes of unreality. He perceives that Forster's realism or scepticism is 'always vigilant, curbing his inward vision'; and he is particularly good in exploring the way that Forster handles emotions by indirect means that amount almost to diffidence. The world of Love and the unseen function as almost a philosophical contest for emotion, and Forster repeatedly draws on classical mythology or traditional romantic symbolism for expressing it. He thus creates a powerful referential apparatus, a world of visionary insight that is not simply associated with particular characters but is conveyed by symbol and tone throughout the texture of his novels. What the book perhaps underestimates, however, is the way in which this tone is interlinked with a tone of comic scepticism, which does not completely deny the romantic theme and indeed often supports it, but with all kinds of ironic complexities. A further very good illumination of Forster's debt to romanticism both as a view of the developed heart and as a vision of the developed and organic society is to be found in H. A. Smith, 'Forster's Humanism and the Nineteenth Century', in *Forster: A Collection of Critical Essays*, ed. M. Bradbury (1966).

But perhaps the most significant development in this general direction of Forster studies occurs in a brief, concentrated essay by Frank Kermode, 'The One Orderly Product (E. M. Forster)', in his *Puzzles and Epiphanies: Essays and Reviews, 1958–1961* (1962); which points out that Forster's expressed aesthetic, with its emphasis on art as the 'one orderly product' where form and meaning co-exist, is symbolist. As he points out, this case obviously best fits *A Passage to India*, where both the novelist and certain of his characters seek a notion of entire wholeness: 'completeness, not reconstruction'. The problem is that the order must lie outside the world of time, and Forster evidently believes *in* the world of time. However, the effect of this is to give vast extensiveness to the range of material that has to be included if meaning is to subsist. This recognition of the modern symbolist element in Forster has been taken further in Alan Wilde's *Art and Order: A Study of E. M. Forster* (1964), which looks at Forster primarily in the light of his development from his early rejection of an orderly aesthetic view of life in favour of a more spontaneous one to his growing awareness that the universe is chaotic, and therefore that the problem of order, in life and art, had to be reintroduced again. A 'symbolist' assumption also lies behind Wilfred Stone's *The Cave and the Mountain: A Study of E. M. Forster* (1966), a large and scholarly study with a good deal of thoroughly acquired biographical and contextual information (and good illustrations) which draws on Forster's assistance. Stone is concerned with a developing myth that he sees running through Forster's life and work, a view of the human predicament and of the vision of unity that might redeem it. The study has a Jungian or Freudian bias and emerges with a highly positivistic view of Forster's 'meanings' in his novels; he hence takes the symbolist in Forster as a kind of humane positivist.

On the whole, the tendency to play down the ironical Forster, the scrupulous moralist, the man distrustful of solutions and ambiguous in his fictive structures, seems fairly marked in recent critical study— leaving, in my view, the more accurate perspective with earlier studies like Trilling's. Latterly, several more studies of Forster have appeared: David Shusterman's useful and sensible *The Quest for*

Certitude in E. M. Forster's Fiction (1965), which does touch on Forster's scepticism and the way in which he makes this a public voice; Norman Kelvin's *E. M. Forster* (1967); George H. Thomson's *The Fiction of E. M. Forster* (1967); and Laurence Brander's *E. M. Forster: A Critical Study* (1968). Most do tend to see Forster rather positivistically, though of course the discussion is in many respects becoming more finely turned and Thomson, for instance, profitably brings in the manuscript of *A Passage to India* to help illuminate the book. No doubt the flood of Forster criticism will continue, though already the signs are that the newer work is tending to become repetitious. The recent publication of *Maurice* should, none the less, lead to a shift in emphasis and valuation, and there is more work by Forster yet to appear. In addition, the biography on which P. N. Furbank is now engaged is likely to add much fresh illumination, and may well encourage a much more personal and psychological view of a writer who has frequently been seen as primarily a socio-moral novelist.

Several important *challenges* have, we should note, been made to Forster's reputation: both from a literary-critical viewpoint, and a religious or political one. C. B. Cox, for instance, ably argues in *The Free Spirit* (1963) that Forster disturbingly tends in his novels to overstate the claims of individuals, to withdraw into secure and limited areas of experience as a viewpoint on the world, and to retire into an idealized past. A more violent assault is D. S. Savage's essay 'E. M. Forster', in *Writers of To-day*, ed. Denys Val Baker (1946), reprinted in D. S. Savage, *The Withered Branch* (1950). His standpoint is Marxist and he attacks Forster for his half-hearted liberal creed, which must necessarily depict unsatisfactory spiritual struggles because he and his characters are never able to objectify their situation and see the 'unreality' inherent in it. In 1934 Montgomery Belgion had produced a brilliant attack, 'The Diabolism of E. M. Forster', *Criterion*, xiv (October 1934), pointing out that Forster's characters are divided between the saved and the damned, that there was a sharp moral elect in his universe, and that his view of society was diabolic. Three well-argued Catholic critiques have drawn conclusions somewhat similar to Savage and Belgion. Alexander Boyle, in 'The Novels of E. M. Forster', *The Irish Monthly*, lxxviii (September 1950), claims that the artist needs intellectual certainty and that intelligent scepticism does not, in Forster's case, produce coherent art. Ernest Beaumont's article 'Mr. E. M. Forster's Strange Mystics', *Dublin Review*, ccccliii (Third Quarter 1951), is a sharp analysis showing how Forster exploits a pervasive extra-human quality in certain of his characters—like Mrs. Wilcox and Mrs. Moore—so that they have, in fact, characteristics usually associated with saint-hood. And he finds disconcerting the mixture of a kind of classical pantheism coupled with these suggestions of religious transcendence. Dennis Hickley, in 'Ou-Boum and Verbum', *Downside Review*, lxxii (Spring 1954), claims that the only Christianity Forster's characters seem to know is one of comfort; and that in fact their states of despair are really their first true religious experiences, even though they are not presented in conventional Christian terms.

(b) Studies of particular novels

With the rise of critical interest in Forster, the number of articles on his work both by English and American critics has grown very con-siderably. It is no longer possible to summarize, but only to select and point a few general tendencies. Obviously, much of the commentary develops from or is related to the work in the general studies already discussed. But what is even more marked in the critical articles on individual works is, first of all, the strongly neo-symbolist stress that has come out in modern Forster criticism, particularly in America; and secondly the emergence of a general view that *A Passage to India* is either the best of the novels, or at least the one that most deserves critical attention. (It is worth remembering here that Forster felt on finishing *A Passage to India* that it was a failure, and preferred *The Longest Journey*; while much of the earlier criticism often tended to set other novels above it—Trilling, for instance, calls *Howards End* 'Undoubtedly Forster's masterpiece'.) On the whole, here as in the general studies, there has been a broad assumption that Forster is a religious or symbolist novelist, and that the most interesting ques-tions about him have to do, therefore, with his 'vision' or else with his technique. Occasionally an essay will provide a useful corrective; for instance, John Harvey's 'Imagination and Moral Theme in E. M. Forster's *The Longest Journey*,' not only picks a less commonly dis-cussed novel but takes a nicely humane approach. Otherwise not much has been done on the earlier novels of remarkable note: *Howards End* has drawn more attention, and here three articles are particularly worth noting—Frederick P. W. McDowell, ' "The Mild, Intellectual Light": Idea and Theme in *Howards End*', *PMLA* lxxiv (September 1959); Cyrus Hoy, 'Forster's Metaphysical Novel', *PMLA* lxxv (March 1960); and Thomas Churchill, 'Place and Personality in *Howards End*', *Critique*, vi (Spring–Summer 1962). Most of these are rather abstract and theoretical pieces, a charge that can be levelled against much of the considerable amount of work that now exists on *A Passage to India*. Arnold Kettle, in his *An Introduction to the English Novel*, vol. i (1953) offers a delicate critical reading of the book that looks at the text without stepping off into deep waters. For the theoretical deep waters, see Gertude M. White's '*A Passage to India*: Analysis and Revaluation', *PMLA* lxviii (September 1953), which usefully summarizes the debate so far and then presents a Hegelian, dialectical view of the novel; and Glen O. Allen, 'Structure, Symbol, and Theme in E. M. Forster's *A Passage to India*', *PMLA* lxx (December 1955), which attempts a refusation and a less positivistic reading. More recently, as in the books already considered, the debate seems to have grown even more symbolist and positivist; and John Dixon Hunt's 'Muddle and Mystery in *A Passage to India*', *ELH*, vol. xxxiii, no. 4 (December 1966), offers some useful correctives.

The reader is perhaps best recommended to various anthologies, which collect articles, or to special numbers of periodicals. My own collection, already cited, contains many of the pieces already referred to, both in this section and the last. Oliver Stallybrass (ed.), *Aspects of E. M. Forster* (1969) contains some good new essays; there is also K. Natwar-Singh (ed.), *E. M. Forster: A Tribute* (1964). A special E. M. Forster number of *Modern Fiction Studies* appeared in 1961.

(c) Introductory studies

There are three useful introductions to Forster; Rex Warner, *E. M. Forster* (London, 1950); K. W. Gransden, *E. M. Forster* (1962); and Harry T. Moore, *E. M. Forster* (1965). Gransden's is the best. In addition, there is an excellent introductory study of Forster's best-known novel—John Colmer's *E. M. Forster's 'A Passage to India'* (1967).

BIOGRAPHIES AND LETTERS

There is no one book that is solely a biography of E. M. Forster, though an authorized biography by P. N. Furbank is in preparation. However, several of the books mentioned above (notably Macaulay, Trilling, Crews, Gransden, and in particular Stone) do contain extensive biographical information. So do several of Forster's own works mentioned above; for instance, *The Hill of Devi* (1953) contains correspondence from his two visits to India, and *Marianne Thornton* (1956)—a biography of his great aunt, who provided him with money to enable him to become a writer; this is a rich study of his intellectual heritage. The question of the degree to which Forster 'imbibed' ideas from various sources—Victorian evangelic reform,

turn-of-the-century Cambridge, political liberalism, and Bloomsbury—is constantly raised by these studies; so that most of these
works also should reappear in the final section, where Forster's intellectual and social background is considered.

BIBLIOGRAPHIES

The reader seeking a full bibliographical listing of writings *by* Forster
will find this in B. J. Kirkpatrick, *E. M. Forster* (1965); this is volume
xix of the Soho Bibliographies. For a briefer but useful listing, see the
bibliography of K. W. Gransden's good introductory book, *E. M.
Forster* (1962), mentioned under CRITICAL STUDIES AND COMMENTARY.

For lists of writings *about* Forster, the reader is referred to Helmut
E. Gerber's very thorough annotated checklist of writings on E. M.
Forster in *English Fiction in Transition (1880–1920)* ii (Spring 1959).
For a more selective listing, see the bibliography to my own *Forster:
A Collection of Critical Essays*, and the bibliography to Stone, *The Cave
and the Mountain* (both mentioned above). Also see the bibliography
of J. K. Johnstone's *The Bloomsbury Group: A Study of E. M. Forster,
Lytton Strachey, Virginia Woolf, and Their Circle* (1954), mentioned
below under BACKGROUND READING.

BACKGROUND READING

First, there is the immediate background: Forster's environment and
ideas. In addition to Forster's own works and those studies already
referred to in the section on BIOGRAPHIES AND LETTERS, the important
texts here are Johnstone's *The Bloomsbury Group* (1954), Virginia
Woolf's *A Writer's Diary* (1953), and memoirs, by Leonard Woolf,
John Lehmann, Clive Bell, and others, of his London environment.
(See Johnstone for references.) Another most illuminating and valuable book is Noel Annan's *Leslie Stephen* (1951), a superb piece of
intellectual history tracing the way in which the late Victorian
literary intelligentsia achieved the transition into the twentieth
century, with the families associated with 'Bloomsbury' as a particular example.

Two important and revealing interviews also provide 'background' in another sense, indicating the nature of Forster's creative
process and his way of life. In 1952 P. N. Furbank and F. J. Haskell
interviewed him for the *Paris Review*; the piece is reprinted in Malcolm Cowley (ed.), *Writers at Work* (1958), And in *Encounter*, ix, 5
(November 1957), Angus Wilson reports 'A Conversation with E. M.
Forster'—in this case a little less technical and a little more personal.

Finally, for an indication of Forster's influence upon other writers, see Christopher Isherwood in *Lions and Shadows* (1938), pp. 173–5, and the prefatory sonnet to W. H. Auden and Christopher Isherwood, *Journey to a War* (1939), as well as the Angus Wilson 'conversation' already mentioned.

REFERENCES

TEXTS

(*a*) *Novels*

Where Angels Fear to Tread (Edinburgh, 1905; New York, 1920).
The Longest Journey (Edinburgh, 1907; New York, 1922).
A Room With a View (London, 1908; New York, 1911).
Howards End (London and New York, 1910).
A Passage to India (London and New York, 1924).
Maurice (London and New York, 1971).

(*b*) *Stories*

The Celestial Omnibus (London, 1911; New York, 1923).
The Eternal Moment (London and New York, 1928).
Collected Stories (London, 1947).
Albergo Empedocle and Other Writings (ed. G. H. Thomson) (New York, 1971).
The Life to Come, And Other Stories (ed. O. Stallybrass) (London, Abinger Edition, 1972).

(*c*) *Selected other works*

Alexandria: A History and a Guide (Alexandria, 1922; New York, 1961).
Pharos and Pharillon (Richmond and New York, 1923).
Aspects of the Novel (London and New York, 1927).
Goldsworthy Lowes Dickinson (London and New York, 1934).
Abinger Harvest (London and New York, 1936).
Two Cheers for Democracy (London and New York, 1951) (Abinger edition, 1972).
The Hill of Devi (London and New York, 1953).
Marianne Thornton (London and New York, 1956).

CRITICAL STUDIES AND COMMENTARY

G. O. Allen, 'Structure, Symbol, and Theme in E. M. Forster's *A Passage to India*', *PMLA* lxx (December 1955).
Anon., 'A Chalice for Youth', *TLS* (8 October 1971).
E. Beaumont, 'Mr Forster's Strange Mystics', *Dublin Review*, ccccliii (Third Quarter 1951).
J. Beer, *The Achievement of E. M. Forster* (London, 1962).
M. Belgion, 'The Diabolism of E. M. Forster', *Criterion*, xiv (October 1934).
Alfred Borrello, *An E. M. Forster Dictionary* (Metuchen, N.J., 1971).

A. Boyle, 'The Novels of E. M. Forster', *The Irish Monthly*, lxxviii (September 1950).

M. Bradbury (ed.), *E. M. Forster: A Collection of Critical Essays* (Englewood Cliffs., N.J., 1966).

—— 'E. M. Forster's *Howards End*', *Critical Quarterly*, iv (Autumn 1962).

L. Brander, *E. M. Forster: A Critical Study* (London, 1968).

R. A. Brower, 'The Twilight of the Double Vision: Symbol and Irony in *A Passage to India*', in *The Fields of Light: An Experiment in Critical Reading* (New York, 1951).

E. K. Brown, *Rhythm in the Novel* (Toronto, 1950).

P. Burra, 'The Novels of E. M. Forster', *The Nineteenth Century and After*, cxvi (November 1934); reprinted as intro. to *A Passage to India* (Everyman, London, 1942).

T. Churchill, 'Place and Personality in *Howards End*', *Critique*, vi (Spring and Summer 1962).

J. Colmer, *E. M. Forster's 'A Passage to India'* (London, 1967).

C. B. Cox, *The Free Spirit: A Study of Liberal Humanism in the Novels of George Eliot, Henry James, E. M. Forster, Virginia Woolf, Angus Wilson* (London, 1963).

F. C. Crews, *E. M. Forster: The Perils of Humanism* (Princeton, N.J., and London, 1962).

H. M. Daleski, 'Rhythmic and Symbolic Patterns in *A Passage to India*', in *Studies in English Language and Literature*, edd. A. Shalvi and A. A. Mendilow (Jerusalem, 1966).

G. Dangerfield, 'E. M. Forster: A Man With a View', *Saturday Review of Literature* (27 August 1938).

J. Delbaere-Garant, ' "Who Shall Inherit England?" A Comparison Between *Howards End, Parade's End* and *Unconditional Surrender*', *English Studies*, l (1969).

E. Ellem, 'E. M. Forster: The Lucy and New Lucy Novels; Fragments of Early Versions of *A Room With a View*', *TLS* (28 May 1971).

A. Friedman, *The Turn of the Novel* (New York and London, 1966).

K. W. Grandsden, *E. M. Forster* (Edinburgh and New York, 1962; rev. edn., 1970).

H. H. A. Gowda (ed.), *A Garland for E. M. Forster* (Mysore, 1969).

R. L. Harrison, *The Manuscripts of 'A Passage to India'* (Ann Arbor, Mich., 1968).

J. Harvey, 'Imagination and Moral Theme in E. M. Forster's *The Longest Journey*', *EIC* vi (1956).

D. Hickley, 'Ou-Boum and Verbum', *The Downside Review*, lxxii (Spring 1954).

C. Hoy, 'Forster's Metaphysical Novel', *PMLA* lxxv (March 1960).

J. D. Hunt, 'Muddle and Mystery in *A Passage to India*', *ELH* xxxiii, no. 4 (December 1966).

N. Kelvin, *E. M. Forster* (Carbondale, Ill., 1967).

F. Kermode, 'The One Orderly Product (E. M. Forster)', in *Puzzles and Epiphanies: Essays and Reviews: 1958–1961* (London and New York, 1962).

A. Kettle, *An Introduction to the English Novel* (2 vols., London, 1953).

R. Langbaum, 'A New Look at E. M. Forster,' *Southern Review*, iv (Winter 1968).

F. R. Leavis, 'E. M. Forster', *Scrutiny*, vii (September 1938); reprinted in *The Common Pursuit* (London, 1952).

J. P. Levine, 'An Analysis of the Manuscripts of *A Passage to India*', *PMLA* lxxv (March 1970).

R. Macaulay, *The Writings of E. M. Forster* (London and New York, 1938).

J. McConkey, *The Novels of E. M. Forster* (Ithaca, N.Y., 1957).

F. P. W. McDowell, ' "The Mild, Intellectual Light": Idea and Theme in *Howards End*' *PMLA* lxxiv (September 1959).

—— *E. M. Forster* (New York, 1969).

H. T. Moore, *E. M. Forster* (New York, 1965).

K. Natwar-Singh (ed.), *E. M. Forster: A Tribute* (New York, 1964).

H. J. Oliver, *The Art of E. M. Forster* (Melbourne and London, 1960).

V. S. Pritchett, 'The Upholstered Prison', *New Statesman* (8 October 1971).

D. S. Savage, 'E. M. Forster', in *The Withered Branch: Six Studies in the Modern Novel* (London, 1950).

D. Shusterman, *The Quest for Certitude in E. M. Forster's Fiction* (Bloomington, Ind., 1965).

H. A. Smith, 'Forster's Humanism and the Nineteenth Century', in M. Bradbury (ed.), *E. M. Forster: A Collection of Critical Essays* (Englewood Cliffs, N.J., 1966).

O. Stallybrass (ed.), *Aspects of E. M. Forster* (London, 1969).

W. Stone, *The Cave and the Mountain: A Study of E. M. Forster* (Stanford, Calif., and London, 1966).

G. H. Thomson, *The Fiction of E. M. Forster* (Detroit, Mich., 1967).

L. Trilling, *E. M. Forster* (Norfolk, Conn., 1943; London, 1944).

R. Warner, *E. M. Forster* (London, 1950; rev. edn., 1954 and 1960).

G. M. White, '*A Passage to India*: Analysis and Revaluation', *PMLA* lxviii (September 1953).

A. Wilde, *Art and Order: A Study of E. M. Forster* (New York, 1964; London, 1965).

V. Woolf, 'The Novels of E. M. Forster', in *The Death of the Moth and Other Essays* (London and New York, 1942; also in *Collected Essays*).

BIOGRAPHIES AND LETTERS

E. M. Forster, *The Hill of Devi* (London and New York, 1953); contains letters.

BIBLIOGRAPHIES

B. J. Kirkpatrick, *E. M. Forster* (London, 1965; rev. edn., 1968).

H. E. Gerber, 'E. M. Forster: An Annotated Checklist of Writings about Him', *English Fiction in Transition (1880–1920)*, ii (Spring 1959).

F. P. W. McDowell, 'The Newest Elucidations of E. M. Forster', *English Fiction in Transition*, iv (1962).

BACKGROUND READING

J. R. Ackersley, *E. M. Forster: A Portrait* (London, 1970).

N. Annan, *Leslie Stephen: His Thought and Character in Relation to His Time* (London, and Cambridge, Mass., 1952).

W. H. Auden and C. Isherwood, *Journey to a War* (London, 1939).

C. Connolly, *Enemies of Promise* (London, 1938; 2nd edn., 1961).

G. Dangerfield, *The Strange Death of Liberal England* (London, 1935).

P. N. Furbank and F. J. Haskell (interviewers), 'E. M. Forster', in Malcolm Cowley (ed.), *Writers at Work* (London and New York, 1958).

C. Isherwood, *Lions and Shadows* (London, 1938).

J. K. Johnstone, *The Bloomsbury Group: A Study of E. M. Forster, Lytton Strachey, Virginia Woolf, and Their Circle* (London, 1954).

A. Wilson, 'A Conversation with E. M. Forster', *Encounter*, ix, 5 (November 1957).

V. Woolf. *A Writer's Diary* (London, 1953).

Mark Spilka

TEXTS

The only reasonably complete hardbound set of D. H. Lawrence's fiction was published between 1954 and 1957 by William Heinemann Ltd. as part of its Phoenix series. It includes ten long novels, two volumes of short novels, and the collected short stories in three volumes. The only reasonably complete paperback edition, covering roughly the same works, is published by Penguin. There is no complete edition—hard or soft—in America, but three publishers cover most of the fiction between them. Compass offers a paperback selection of six major novels, four short novels in one volume, and the collected tales in three volumes. The Modern Library offers hard and soft editions of four famous novels. Three others appear as Vintage paperbacks.

The unexpurgated version of *Lady Chatterley's Lover* appeared in England and America in the early 1960s in several editions. 'Expurgation' may be the word, however, for all editions of the fiction. With two exceptions (*The White Peacock*, 1966; *The Boy in the Bush*, 1970). Lawrence's works are wholly unedited, and there is no indication in them of the changes made to satisfy squeamish publishers. Lawrence's vulnerability to censorship makes the case for responsible editing especially strong. Textual discrepancies are abundant, and there is much work ahead for future bibliographers.

CRITICAL STUDIES AND COMMENTARY

Serious criticism of Lawrence's fiction did not begin until the 1950s. Though he was widely recognized during his lifetime, his achievement was obscured by its controversial and unorthodox nature, and by his own public legend. After his death in 1930 his work was almost obliterated by squabbling memorialists. Influential critics continued to attack it on moral, political, and aesthetic grounds, and by 1940 Lawrence could be justly called 'The Great Unread' in a leading journal. There were of course discerning admirers—E. M. Forster, Edmund Wilson, Richard Aldington—who wrote brief appreciations while he lived; there were fine comprehensive pieces after his death by F. R. Leavis, Aldous Huxley, and Francis Fergusson; and there were useful books, chapters, and bibliographies. But not until the 1950s was there anything like the sustained attention, healthy dialogue, and widespread interest, from which serious criticism proceeds.

Causes for the Lawrence revival are varied. By 1950 the memorial squabbles had subsided, the public legend had faded, and the work itself seemed less controversial. The battle against censorship—which Lawrence himself had launched—was almost over. His prediction of the deathward drift of industrial society had been confirmed by the holocausts of the Second World War; his radical commitment to 'full, spontaneous being' had been sanctioned by the same events. The world had finally caught up with him, and it was possible to see his life and work in something like their proper context.

The accommodations of William York Tindall may prove instructive here. In 1939 Tindall had mocked Lawrence's irrationalism in *D. H. Lawrence and Susan His Cow*; but in *Forces in Modern British Literature* (1947) he began to change his mind:

The crusade against science that Lawrence preached by allegory and symbol seems less absurd today than it used to seem. And Aldous Huxley's contention that science has gone far enough is proved by atomic fission and the irresponsibility of scientist, capitalist, and politician. About to be decomposed, we can return with understanding to these prophets.

In his Introduction to *The Later D. H. Lawrence* (1952) Tindall further decided that Lawrence was 'more artist than prophet', placed him in the symbolist tradition along with Joyce, Mann, and Kafka, and celebrated the myths and rituals of his final tales. The prophet's irrationalism had now acquired 'the radiance of great art'.

Meanwhile Frederick Hoffman had already explored another side of Lawrence's irrationalism: his quarrel with Freudian psychology. In *Freudianism and the Literary Mind* (1945) Hoffman concluded that Lawrence was right to retain his artistic view of the unconscious, that Lawrence and Freud, artist and scientist, were 'patrolling the same grounds' in different ways. In *D. H. Lawrence and Human Existence* (1951) Father William Tiverton examined still another kind of irrationalism: Lawrence's pagan sense of the ISNESS (rather than the OUGHTNESS) of religion, by which he could 'teach Christians lessons they should have known but have forgotten'. Thus, twenty years after his death, Lawrence's quarrels with the world had become occasions for critical affirmation. However controversial they had seemed, the deep seriousness of his views and their importance for contemporary life were now quite evident. As the poet Charles Olson said in 1952: 'the man who more and more stands up as the one man of this century to be put with Melville, Dostoyevsky, and Rimbaud (men who engaged themselves with modern reality in such fierceness and pity as to be of real use to any of us who want to take on the post-modern) is D. H. Lawrence'.

Within this receptive climate the Lawrence revival began to gather momentum. In 1951 an industrious American scholar, Harry T. Moore, published the first truly comprehensive biography and 'the fullest survey yet ... of Lawrence's writings'. In the 1940s Moore had been urging, simply but eloquently, that Lawrence should be read. Now, in *The Life and Works of D. H. Lawrence*, he placed the whole sweep of his work in perspective for other critics, read it sanely and perceptively himself, and used biography to illuminate (rather than darken) its nature. Moore's services of this kind have been indefatigable. In 1948 he had edited *D. H. Lawrence's Letters to Bertrand Russell* (see REFERENCES: BIOGRAPHIES AND LETTERS); in 1953 he edited a group of Lawrence's essays, *Sex, Literature, and Censorship* (see REFERENCES: TEXTS), and with Frederick Hoffman he collected the first critical anthology, *The Achievement of D. H. Lawrence* (see REFERENCES: BIBLIOGRAPHIES); in 1954 he produced a second biography, *The Intelligent Heart*, with new material on Lawrence's youth, and in 1956 came *Poste Restante: A Lawrence Travel Calendar* (for both see REFERENCES: BIOGRAPHIES AND LETTERS); in 1959, another anthology of critical essays, *A D. H. Lawrence Miscellany* (see REFERENCES: BIBLIOGRAPHIES); and finally in 1962, *The Collected Letters* in two volumes (see BIOGRAPHIES AND LETTERS section) This amazing output of useful texts was Moore's way of ensuring, almost single-handedly, that Lawrence would indeed be read.

The chief proselytizer for Lawrence's fiction, however, was the distinguished British critic, F. R. Leavis, editor of the influential journal *Scrutiny*, and polemicist *par excellence*. In *The Great Tradition* (1948) Leavis had led the New Critical shift from poetry to fiction which his own career epitomized. Through the 1930s he had extended T. S. Eliot's views on poetry in books like *New Bearings in English Poetry* and *Revaluation*. But he had always quarrelled with Eliot's views on Lawrence, and as he moved to fiction the terms of the quarrel broadened. Thus, if his title—*The Great Tradition*— comes from Eliot, his 'tradition' consists of a line of novelists—Jane Austen, George Eliot, James, Conrad—which ends in Lawrence and which is even distinguished by Lawrencean values: 'a vital capacity for experience, a kind of reverent openness before life, and a marked moral intensity'. Within the next few years Leavis began to write those *Scrutiny* essays, collected in 1955 in *D. H. Lawrence: Novelist*, which largely induced the Lawrence revival.

Leavis championed Lawrence through New Critical tactics learned in part from Eliot. First he attacked Eliot himself for dismissing Lawrence as a writer crippled by lack 'of a living and central tradition'. Leavis showed that Lawrence had led 'an extraordinarily active intellectual life' among youthful friends, had made the most of later training at Nottingham University, and had transposed his Congregational heritage of strenuous inquiry and moral seriousness to his work. Clearly Lawrence belonged to Leavis's 'great tradition', if not to Eliot's; but Leavis had to attack Eliot's, in its cultural narrowness and exclusiveness, to put him there.

Next Leavis discussed Lawrence's novels in his *Scrutiny* series, 'The Novel as Dramatic Poem'. The New Critical habit of seeing all literature as poetry—often at the expense of genre-characteristics—had immediate advantages for him. It allowed him to examine novels with the same 'scrutiny' he brought to poems: to quote and analyse long passages, to demonstrate the operative function of ideas, and to develop symbolic and dramatic patterns. Indeed, by calling the 'poem' dramatic, he could keep fidelity with rendered life and temporal progression, and avoid excessive symbol-hunting. This proved invaluable with Lawrence, whose symbols work less as implicative networks in the *symboliste* tradition (where Tindall and Moore had placed them) than as integrative and focal aids to dramatic progress. Guided then by his apter simile—the novel as dramatic (not symbolic) poem—Leavis was able to 'read' Lawrence with exemplary skill and discrimination. Through New Critical exclusions and inclusions, he was also able to create new hierarchies of accepted works. Largely through his definitive readings, *Women in Love* and *The Rainbow* are now recognized as Lawrence's greatest novels, with *Sons and Lovers*, *Lady Chatterley's Lover*, and *The Plumed Serpent* falling behind; then come longer tales and stories like *The Captain's Doll*, *St. Mawr*, and 'Daughters of the Vicar', in what constitutes an impressive body of major fiction.

Another New Critical tactic—the contextual approach to ideas—has also proved invaluable for Lawrence. In *Women in Love*, for instance, Leavis demonstrates an integrative intelligence in Lawrence, and a place for intelligence *per se*, which few critics had allowed. This novel's critique of the mind which tries to dominate and exploit emotional life, as opposed to the mind used instrumentally to define and abet it, was first explained by Leavis. It was Leavis too who established 'full spontaneous being' as Lawrence's chief concern. But beyond clarifying such concepts, he also demonstrated their dramatic integration into a complex whole by a novelist once dismissed as hopelessly abstruse and foggy. In doing so he revealed the power and force of a major creative intelligence.

Finally, Leavis's insistence on the normative value of Lawrence's work has proven oddly exemplary. If New Critics were against moral abstractions *from* literature, they were always strongly drawn to morality *in* literature. In moving from poetry to fiction, moreover, they encountered a medium which has often given moral orientation to its readers. With a prophetic novelist like Lawrence, in whom this function is pronounced, the tendency toward moral involvement with his work has also been pronounced—and not only for Leavis and his followers, but for most of the formal critics drawn to Lawrence.

Mark Schorer, for instance, had attacked Lawrence in 1948 for failing to allow technique to fathom meaning in *Sons and Lovers*. By 1953 he had come to see Lawrence's techniques as attempts to en-compass new material of enormous moral consequence—attempts which must be made, whatever the formal cost, since 'No novelist speaks more directly to us than Lawrence [in *Women in Love*], and if we can't hear him we are, I quite believe, lost.' By 1959 he could even argue that in *Lady Chatterley's Lover* Lawrence had reached that 'point in imaginative being where the preacher and the poet coincide, since the poem is the sermon'.

In *The English Novel: Form and Function* (1953) Dorothy Van Ghent was also troubled by Lawrence's apparent neglect of technique 'in the direction laid out, for instance, by James and Conrad'. She decided, however, that Lawrence takes his own direction and finds his own techniques for exploring vital problems. In *Sons and Lovers* he uses imagery in an innovative way, to express 'his vision of life as infinitely creative of individual identities, each whole and separate and to be reverenced as such'. That vision illuminates all major relations and events in the novel, and exposes such modern betrayals of wholeness as 'possessorship' and death-worship. Here Lawrence meets her own formula for morality in art, by which 'the principle of form in the work' reveals a similar principle 'in the self'.

Younger critics have moved more directly to moral affirmations. Martin Green (*A Mirror for Anglo-Saxons*, 1960) and Raymond Williams (*Culture and Society*, 1958) oppose genteel sterility and indus-trial pressures in England with Lawrencean virtues such as 'decency' and 'close spontaneous living', which they trace to his working-class origins. In America Marvin Mudrick finds *The Rainbow* original, not on formal grounds, but as 'the first English novel to record the nor-mality and significance of physical passion' and 'the only English novel to record . . . the social revolution whereby Western man had lost his sense of community' (1959); Julian Moynahan, in the best critical book of the 1960s, acclaims *The Deed of Life* in Lawrence, his exploration of vital possibilities as opposed to cerebral and abstract perspectives; and in my own book, *The Love Ethic of D. H. Lawrence* (1955), I hold that Lawrence develops a concrete vision o f experience with normative value for his readers; that he sets forth conditions for individual and, to some extent, for social regeneration; and that his vision is decidedly artistic, but in the vein of prophetic art which enables us to grasp new moral possibilities. In Israel H. M. Daleski (*The Forked Flame*, 1965) explores the theme of dualism in Lawrence, his attempt to balance male and female principles in his characters and in himself. Daleski seems as sensitive as any dedicated moralist to those times when the 'forked flame' burns brightest, or when it flickers falsely.

Still other critics affirm Lawrence's negative morality, his fiercely honest critique of modern life. In *The Art of Perversity* (1962), the only book on the shorter fiction, Kingsley Widmer presents a nihilistic Lawrence, an advocate of 'ancient demonic traditions' which seek out 'death, rebellion, and forbidden desires'. For Widmer, Lawrence's vision is amoral and asocial; his characters become vital only when they embrace 'the reality of nothingness'; even his birds, beasts, and flowers are nihilists, in their harsh aliveness, and Lawrence himself is the complete modern rebel—anarchic, demonic, vitally perverse. In *The Utopian Vision of D. H. Lawrence* (1963), Eugene Goodheart similarly places Lawrence with modern 'tablet-breakers', prophetic visionaries like Rousseau, Blake, Dostoevsky, Nietzsche, and Rilke, who break with the past and force tradition 'into new and hitherto unknown channels'. Like Widmer, he favours the tales over the novels as more suited to Lawrence's 'mythic imagination'. In *D. H. Lawrence: The Failure and the Triumph of Art* (1960), the aesthetician Eliseo Vivas makes a more guarded case for Lawrence's novels as 'constitutive symbols' through which we grasp the modern waste-land. Systematically discounting positive values like 'star-equilibrium' and *Blutbruderschaft*, he values Lawrence for symbolic presentations of 'the specific process of disintegration of which we are the victims'. Other critics who prefer an apocalyptic Lawrence include Mary Freeman (*D. H. Lawrence: A Basic Study of his Ideas*, 1955); Angelo Bertocci ('Symbolism in *Women in Love*', 1959); and Frank Kermode (*Continuities*, 1968). Barbara Hardy, in *The Appropriate Form* (1964), prefers a more sceptical Lawrence and shrewdly praises his doubts, uncertainties, oscillations. 'Lawrence is doing something very rare in art', she argues. 'He is . . . writing out of doubt and failure, expressing ideas in which he has only uncertain faith. This is the untidiness and uncertainty of incomplete and fumbling human experience. . . . To deny its power is, I suggest, to have rigid canons of art and insufficient respect for the kind of honesty which can admit despair and doubt, not just in art, but in living too.'

There is, of course, a temperate line of Lawrence critics—more appreciative than committed—which begins with Harry Moore. It includes critics like Graham Hough (*The Dark Sun*, 1956), E. W. Tedlock, jun. (*D. H. Lawrence: Artist and Rebel*, 1963), and George H. Ford (*Double Measure*, 1965). Hough deals judiciously with the major fiction and shows interestingly how Lawrence's thought culminates in *The Man Who Died*. Tedlock offers a more comprehensive reading of the fiction, and by seeing Lawrence as both vitalist *and* nihilist, helps to correct Widmer's confusion of these impulses. Ford brings a surprising amount of new information to bear on the composition of the novels, speaks sensibly to the vexed questions of *Blutbruderschaft* and 'corrosive love', and pursues Biblical and mythic themes to good effect. Of each of these critics Leavis might say, 'He has no criterion', but for many readers their general good sense and sweet-tempered eclecticism will seem refreshing.

Lawrence's adverse critics continue to thrive, but they now confine their attacks to specific novels and no longer challenge his overall importance. The uncensored version of *Lady Chatterley's Lover* has received the greatest number of such attacks. In *The Moral and the Story* (1962), Ian Gregor argues tellingly that the symbolic and realistic dimensions of that novel fail to cohere—though for another genre-critic, Mark Schorer, their coherence is the novel's triumph. In *The Quest for Love* (1964) David Holbrook conducts an all-out Freudian rant against the novel's falsification of sexual experience, convicts Lawrence of making love to himself (through Mel-*lor*-s and Const-*ance*), and of committing acts of oral aggression to allay his various anxieties. Holbrook's essay—which goes on for 150 pages—might also be called an act of oral aggression; it should be compared with that of another Freudian critic, Daniel Weiss, who argues in *Oedipus in Nottingham* (1962) that Lawrence casts off his oedipal longings in *Lady Chatterley's Lover* and perfects 'his reactive anti-Oedipal vision of life'. I reach similar conclusions in my essay 'Lawrence's Quarrel with Tenderness' (1967), but hold that Lawrence is finally not secure enough, in his belated affirmation of his father, to accept the maternal origins of masculine tenderness.

More recently the attacks on Lawrence have become more sweeping. In 'Lawrence Up-Tight' (1971) I ponder the vexed question of Lawrence's anal propensities in *Lady Chatterley's Lover* and *Women in Love*, as raised by Colin Clarke (*River of Dissolution*, 1969), and earlier critics. In *D. H. Lawrence and the New World* (1969) David Cavitch takes a provocative stand on Lawrence's psychological weaknesses—particularly his homosexual tendencies—as revealed by his complex fictional involvement with America. And in *Sexual Politics* (1970) Kate Millett makes a devastating attack on Lawrence's anti-feminism—to which Norman Mailer replies in *The Prisoner of Sex* (1971), in one of the most sympathetically insightful essays on Lawrence ever written. Alan Friedman's superb essay on Lawrence's style, 'The Other Lawrence' (1970), should serve most readers as a refreshing antidote to these renewals of old Lawrence wars.

As this survey plainly indicates, the Lawrence publications will keep coming. Over 100 books and well over a thousand articles have now appeared, and the amount and tempo are not likely to slacken in the 1970s. Lawrence has joined the modern masters—Joyce, Mann, Proust, Faulkner, Kafka—as an object of continuing study and attention. Meanwhile, thanks to the revival, all his books are back in print; some of the finest modern critics have written brilliantly about them; and the best criticism has been absorbed and transcended by succeeding critics. The 1950s and 1960s have been truly vital decades for Lawrence and his readers.

BIOGRAPHIES AND LETTERS

Of the many reminiscences of Lawrence written by his friends, only one or two are really helpful. Jessie Chambers's memoir, *D. H. Lawrence: A Personal Record* (1935), contains valuable information on Lawrence's early education and presents her version of the composition of *Sons and Lovers* (where she appears as Miriam). Richard Aldington's *Portrait of a Genius But . . .* (1950) is sensible, objective, and reasonably comprehensive. Most other memoirs are too intent on defending, destroying, or possessing Lawrence to merit serious attention. The best way to approach them is through Edward Nehls's three-volume compilation, *D. H. Lawrence: A Composite Biography* (1957, 1958, and 1959). Nehls uses selections from the memoirs along with Lawrence's letters so as to present each phase of his life from multiple points of view. The result is the most balanced and complex portrait of Lawrence extant, almost novelistic in its impact.

Harry Moore has written two of the most useful biographies for students: *The Life and Works of D. H. Lawrence* (1951) (see CRITICAL STUDIES AND COMMENTARY), and *The Intelligent Heart* (1954). These books are comprehensive, informative, reliable in scholarship, and extremely readable. The best short biography is Mark Schorer's succinct, insightful 'The Life of D. H. Lawrence' in *D. H. Lawrence* (1968).

Lawrence's letters were first collected and edited by Aldous Huxley in 1932. That volume is now out of print, but in 1962 Harry Moore published *The Collected Letters* in two volumes and included Huxley's valuable 'Introduction'. Two selected editions of the letters are also available, one edited by Richard Aldington in England (1950), the other by Diana Trilling in America (1958). Literary letters and autobiographical fragments may also be found in *Phoenix: The Posthumous Papers of D. H. Lawrence* (1936) and in *Phoenix II* (1968). Lawrence's letters to Louie Burrows, called *Lawrence in Love*, appeared in 1969, edited by J. T. Boulton.

BIBLIOGRAPHIES

The D. H. Lawrence number of *Modern Fiction Studies* (Spring 1959) contains the best checklist of criticism for Lawrence students. It includes a fine general bibliography and an invaluable list of specific readings of individual tales and novels. Keith Sagar extends these lists selectively in *The Art of D. H. Lawrence* (1966). The two critical anthologies edited by Harry Moore (1953, 1959) contain useful discussions of the critics plus helpful essays. My own paperback anthology, *D. H. Lawrence: A Collection of Critical Essays* (1963), contains a discussion of Lawrence criticism, essays on the fiction, and a selective bibliography. Warren Roberts' *A Bibliography of D. H. Lawrence* (1963) lists 88 books and pamphlets on Lawrence plus all his published works. Previous bibliographers of Lawrence's works and manuscripts include Edward D. McDonald (1925, 1931), Richard Aldington (1935), Lawrence Clark Powell (1937), E. W. Tedlock, jun. (1948), and William White (1950). For books cited with appended bibliographies, see Freeman, Goodheart, Moore, Spilka, Weiss. Other books with selective bibliographies include Anthony Beal's *D. H. Lawrence* (1961), David J. Gordon's *D. H. Lawrence as a Literary Critic* (1966), and Julian Moynahan's casebook on *Sons and Lovers* (1968). For research in progress, see the new American journal, *The D. H. Lawrence Review*, now in its sixth year of publication.

BACKGROUND READING

Lawrence's ideas about fiction were also ideas about life. The student of his fiction should therefore look to his essays on the novel, to his criticism of other novelists—especially *Studies in Classic American*

Literature and the long 'Study of Thomas Hardy' (in *Phoenix I*)—and to such philosophical works as *Fantasia of the Unconscious, Psychoanalysis and the Unconscious,* and *Twilight in Italy.* Anthony Beal's *D. H. Lawrence: Selective Literary Criticism* (1956) is a useful collection of his critical writings. Richard Foster's 'Criticism as Rage' (1959) and David Gordon's book, cited above, are the best studies of his critical theory and practice.

Since Lawrence was decidedly a poetic novelist, some attention might also be paid to the nature of his poetry. A long controversy on this subject begins with R. P. Blackmur's charge, in 1935, that Lawrence commits 'the fallacy of expressive form' in his poetry. In the 1950s critics like A. Alvarez, Harold Bloom, Graham Hough, Vivian de Sola Pinto, and Karl Shapiro began to answer Blackmur with fairer definitions of the poetry.

The following critics have written helpfully on Lawrence's controversial ideas: G. H. Bantock, on educating and rearing children; Raymond Williams, on industrial and rural society; Mary Freeman on fascism; Hoffman and Philip Rieff on psychoanalysis; Neil Myers on war; Hough and Tiverton on Christianity; C. H. Rolph and Charles Rembar on censorship; Spilka and Ford on *Blutbruderschaft*; Widmer and Tedlock on nihilism. There are no valuable discussions of Lawrence's affinities with Carlyle, Nietzsche, Blake, Hardy; but three critics—James E. Miller, jun., Karl Shapiro, and Bernice Slote —relate him to Whitman (*Start with the Sun*, 1960); George Panichas compares him with Dostoevsky; Leavis and Williams, with Tolstoy; and Emile Delavenay, U. C. Knoepflmacher and John Henry Raleigh connect him with the Victorian ethos. Finally, Tindall establishes his debts to modern anthropology (1939), and I relate the 'religious dimension' in his fiction to the 'mana' concept as defined by Ernst Cassirer in *Language and Myth* (1946).

REFERENCES

TEXTS

Heinemann, Phoenix series, London:
  Aaron's Rod (1954).
  Complete Short Stories (3 vols., 1955).
  Kangaroo (1955).
  Lady Chatterley's Lover (1963).
  The Lost Girl (1955).
  The Plumed Serpent (1955).
  The Rainbow (1954).

Short Novels (2 vols., 1956).
Sons and Lovers (1963).
The Trespasser (1935).
The White Peacock (1954).
Women in Love (1954).

Penguin paperbacks (Harmondsworth) include the above novels plus *The Boy in the Bush* (with M. L. Skinner). Most of the short fiction appears in the following Penguin collections: *England, My England; The Ladybird; Love Among the Haystacks; The Prussian Officer; The Woman Who Rode Away*.

Viking Press, Compass paperbacks, New York:
Aaron's Rod (1961).
Complete Short Stories (3 vols., 1961).
Four Short Novels (1960).
Kangaroo (1960).
The Lost Girl (1968).
The Rainbow (1961).
Sons and Lovers (1958).
Women in Love (1960).

Random House, Modern Library, New York:
Lady Chatterley's Lover (1967).
The Rainbow (n.d.).
Sons and Lovers (n.d.).
Women in Love (n.d.).

Random House, Vintage paperbacks, New York:
The Plumed Serpent (New York, 1951).
St. Mawr and *The Man Who Died* (New York, 1959).

Special editions:

Southern Illinois University Press, Carbondale, Ill., has published hardcover versions, carefully edited, of *The Boy in the Bush* (1970) and *The White Peacock* (1966). Dial Press has reissued its paperback edition of *The First Lady Chatterley* (New York, 1958), the discarded first draft of *Lady Chatterley's Lover*, and Viking has published the second draft, *John Thomas and Lady Jane* (1972). Viking has also published a critical edition called *Sons and Lovers: Text, Background and Criticism* (1968).

CRITICAL STUDIES AND COMMENTARY

R. Aldington, *D. H. Lawrence: An Indiscretion* (Seattle, Wash., 1927).
A. P. Bertocci, 'Symbolism in *Women in Love*', in H. T. Moore (ed.), *A D. H. Lawrence Miscellany* (Carbondale, Ill., 1959; London, 1961).
D. Cavitch, *D. H. Lawrence and the New World* (New York, 1969).
C. Clarke, *River of Dissolution: D. H. Lawrence & English Romanticism* (New York and London, 1969).
H. M. Daleski, *The Forked Flame* (London, 1965).
F. Fergusson, 'D. H. Lawrence's Sensibility', in W. V. O'Connor (ed.), *Forms of Modern Fiction* (Minneapolis, Minn., 1948).

G. H. Ford, *Double Measure: A Study of the Novels and Stories of D. H. Lawrence* (New York, 1965).

E. M. Forster, 'Prohecy', *Aspects of the Novel* (London and New York), 1927.

M. Freeman, *D. H. Lawrence: A Basic Study of His Ideas* (Gainesville, Fla., 1955).

A. Friedman, 'The Other Lawrence', *Partisan Review*, xxxvii (1970).

E. Goodheart, *The Utopian Vision of D. H. Lawrence* (Chicago, 1963).

M. Green, *A Mirror for Anglo-Saxons* (New York, 1960).

I. Gregor and B. Nicholas, *The Moral and the Story* (London, 1962).

B. Hardy, *The Appropriate Form* (London, 1964).

F. Hoffman, *Freudianism and the Literary Mind* (Baton Rouge, La., 1945).

D. Holbrook, *The Quest for Love* (London, 1964).

G. Hough, *The Dark Sun: A Study of D. H. Lawrence* (London, 1956; New York, 1957).

A. Huxley, (intro.), *The Letters of D. H. Lawrence* (London and New York, 1932); reprinted in H. T. Moore and F. Hoffman (edd.), *The Achievement of D. H. Lawrence* (Norman, Okla., 1953), and in H. T. Moore (ed.), *The Collected Letters of D. H. Lawrence* (2 vols., London, 1962).

F. Kermode, 'D. H. Lawrence and the Apocolyptic Types', *Continuities* (London and New York, 1968).

F. R. Leavis, *D. H. Lawrence* (Cambridge, 1930).

—— *The Great Tradition* (London, 1948).

—— *D. H. Lawrence: Novelist* (London, 1955).

N. Mailer, *The Prisoner of Sex* (Boston, Mass., and Toronto, 1971).

K. Millett, *Sexual Politics* (New York and London, 1970).

H. T. Moore, *The Life and Works of D. H. Lawrence* (New York, 1951).

—— (ed.), *Sex, Literature, and Censorship* (New York, 1953); essays by Lawrence.

J. Moynahan, *The Deed of Life: The Novels and Tales of D. H. Lawrence* (Princeton, N.J., and Oxford, 1963).

M. Mudrick, 'The Originality of *The Rainbow*', in H. T. Moore (ed.), *A D. H. Lawrence Miscellany* (Carbondale, Ill., 1959; London, 1961) and M. Spilka (ed.), *D. H. Lawrence: A Collection of Critical Essays* (Englewood Cliffs, N.J., 1963).

C. Olson, 'Materials and Weights of Herman Melville', *New Republic*, cxxvii (8 September 1952).

M. Schorer, 'Technique as Discovery', in W. Van O'Connor (ed.), *Forms of Modern Fiction* (Minneapolis, Minn., 1948).

—— '*Women in Love* and Death', in H. T. Moore and F. Hoffman (edd.), *The Achievement of D. H. Lawrence* and M. Spilka (ed.), *D. H. Lawrence: A Collection of Critical Essays*.

—— (intro.), *Lady Chatterley's Lover* (New York, 1959).

M. Spilka, *The Love Ethic of D. H. Lawrence* (Bloomington, Ind., 1955; London, 1957).

—— 'Lawrence's Quarrel with Tenderness', *Critical Quarterly*, ix (1967)

—— 'Lawrence Up-Tight, or The Anal Phase Once Over', *Novel*, iv (1971).

M. Spilka, 'Critical Exchange: On Lawrence Up-Tight: Four Tail-Pieces', *Novel*, v (1971) by Ford, Clarke, Kermode, and Spilka.

E. W. Tedlock, jun., *D. H. Lawrence: Artist and Rebel: A Study of Lawrence's Fiction* (Albuquerque, N. Mex., 1963).

W. Y. Tindall, *D. H. Lawrence and Susan His Cow* (New York, 1939).

—— *Forces in Modern British Literature* (New York, 1947).

—— (intro.), *The Later D. H. Lawrence* (New York, 1952).

Fr. Tiverton [Martin Jarrett-Kerr], *D. H. Lawrence and Human Existence* (London and New York, 1951).

D. Van Ghent, 'On *Sons and Lovers*', in *The English Novel: Form and Function* (New York, 1953).

E. Vivas, *D. H. Lawrence: The Failure and the Triumph of Art* (Evanston, Ill., 1960).

D. A. Weiss, *Oedipus in Nottingham* (Seattle, Wash., 1962).

K. Widmer, *The Art of Perversity: D. H. Lawrence's Shorter Fiction* (Seattle, Wash., 1962).

R. Williams, *Culture and Society* (London and New York, 1958).

E. Wilson, 'Signs of Life: *Lady Chatterley's Lover*', in H. T. Moore and F. Hoffman (edd.), *The Achievement of D. H. Lawrence*.

BIOGRAPHIES AND LETTERS

R. Aldington, *Portrait of a Genius But . . .* (London and New York, 1950).

—— (ed.), *Selected Letters: D. H. Lawrence* (London, 1950).

J. T. Boulton (ed.), *Lawrence in Love* (Carbondale, Ill., 1969).

Jessie Chambers [pseudonym, E.T.], *D. H. Lawrence: A Personal Record* (London, 1935; New York, 1965).

A. Huxley (ed.), *The Letters of D. H. Lawrence* (London, 1932).

E. D. McDonald (ed.), *Phoenix: The Posthumous Papers of D. H. Lawrence* (New York, 1936, 1968; London, 1961).

H. T. Moore, *The Intelligent Heart: The Story of D. H. Lawrence* (New York, 1954; London, 1955).

—— *Poste Restante: A Lawrence Travel Calendar* (Berkeley, Calif., 1956).

—— *The Collected Letters of D. H. Lawrence* (2 vols., New York and London, 1962).

E. Nehls (ed.), *D. H. Lawrence: A Composite Biography* (3 vols., Madison, Wis., 1957, 1958, 1959).

W. Roberts and H. T. Moore (edd.), *Phoenix II: Uncollected, Unpublished, and Other Prose Works* (New York and London, 1968).

M. Schorer, 'The Life of D. H. Lawrence', *D. H. Lawrence* (New York, 1968).

D. Trilling (ed.), *The Selected Letters of D. H. Lawrence* (New York, 1958).

BIBLIOGRAPHIES

(a) Comprehensive

R. Aldington, *D. H. Lawrence: A Complete List of His Works with a Critical Appreciation* (London, 1935).

D. H. Lawrence Number, *Modern Fiction Studies*, v (1959).

D. H. Lawrence Review (University of Arkansas, Fayetteville, Ark., 1968–).

E. D. McDonald, *A Bibliography of the Writings of D. H. Lawrence* (Philadelphia, Pa., 1925).

—— *The Writings of D. H. Lawrence: A Bibliographical Supplement* (Philadelphia, Pa., 1931).

L. C. Powell, *The Manuscripts of D. H. Lawrence* (Los Angeles, Calif., 1937).

W. Roberts, *A Bibliography of D. H. Lawrence* (London, 1963).

E. W. Tedlock, jun., *The Frieda Lawrence Collection of D. H. Lawrence Manuscripts* (Albuquerque, N. Mex., 1948).

W. White, *D. H. Lawrence: A Checklist* (Detroit, Mich., 1950).

(*b*) *Selective*

A. Beal, *D. H. Lawrence* (Edinburgh, 1961).

M. Freeman, *D. H. Lawrence: A Basic Study of His Ideas* (Gainesville, Fla., 1955).

E. Goodheart, *The Utopian Vision of D. H. Lawrence* (Chicago, 1963).

D. J. Gordon, *D. H. Lawrence as a Literary Critic* (New Haven, Conn., and London, 1966).

H. T. Moore, *The Life and Works of D. H. Lawrence* (New York, 1951).

—— (ed., with F. Hoffman), *The Achievement of D. H. Lawrence* (Norman, Okla., 1953).

—— *A. D. H. Lawrence Miscellany* (Carbondale, Ill., 1959; London, 1961).

J. Moynahan (ed.), *Sons and Lovers: Text, Background, and Criticism* (New York, 1968).

K. Sagar, *The Art of D. H. Lawrence* (Cambridge, 1966).

M. Spilka, *The Love Ethic of D. H. Lawrence*. (See under CRITICAL STUDIES AND COMMENTARY.)

—— (ed.), *D. H. Lawrence: A Collection of Critical Essays* (Englewood Cliffs. N.J., 1963).

D. Weiss, *Oedipus in Nottingham* (Seattle, Wash., 1962).

BACKGROUND READING

A. Alvarez, 'D. H. Lawrence: The Single State of Man', *The Shaping Spirit* (London and New York, 1958); also in H. T. Moore (ed.), *A. D. H. Lawrence Miscellany* (Carbondale, Ill., 1959).

G. H. Bantock, *Freedom and Authority in Education* (London, 1952).

A. Beal (ed.), *D. H. Lawrence: Selective Literary Criticism* (New York and London, 1956).

R. P. Blackmur, 'D. H. Lawrence and Expressive Form', *Form and Value in Modern Poetry* (New York, 1957), also in *Language as Gesture* (New York, 1952).

H. Bloom, 'Lawrence, Blackmur, Eliot, and the Tortoise', in H. T. Moore (ed.), *A. D. H. Lawrence Miscellany*.

Emile Delavenay, *D. H. Lawrence and Edward Carpenter: A Study in Edwardian Transition* (London, 1971).

G. H. Ford, *Double Measure* (New York, 1965).

R. Foster, 'Criticism as Rage: D. H. Lawrence', in H. T. Moore (ed.), *A D. H. Lawrence Miscellany*, and M. Spilka (ed.), *D. H. Lawrence: A Collection of Critical Essays*.

M. Freeman, *D. H. Lawrence: A Basic Study of His Ideas* (Gainesville, Fla., 1955).

D. J. Gordon, *D. H. Lawrence as a Literary Critic* (New Haven, Conn., and London, 1966).

F. Hoffman, *Freudianism and the Literary Mind* (Baton Rouge, La., 1945).

G. Hough, *The Dark Sun* (London, 1956; New York, 1957).

U. C. Knoepflmacher, 'The Rival Ladies: Mrs. Ward's "Lady Connie" and Lawrence's *Lady Chatterley's Lover*', iv (1960).

D. H. Lawrence, *Fantasia of the Unconscious* and *Psychoanalysis and the Unconscious* (New York, 1960; London, 1961).

—— 'Study of Thomas Hardy', *Phoenix: The Posthumous Papers of D. H. Lawrence*.

—— *Studies in Classic American Literature* (New York and London, 1964).

—— *Twilight in Italy* (London and New York, 1916).

F. R. Leavis, *Anna Karenina and Other Essays* (New York, 1969).

J. E. Miller, jun., K. Shapiro, and B. Slote, *Start with the Sun: Studies in Cosmic Poetry* (Lincoln, Neb., 1960).

N. Myers, 'Lawrence and the War', *Criticism*, iv (1962).

G. A. Panichas, 'F. M. Dostoevsky and D. H. Lawrence: Their Vision of Evil', *Renaissance and Modern Studies*, v (1961).

V. de S. Pinto, 'Poet Without a Mask', in M. Spilka (ed.), *D. H. Lawrence: A Collection of Critical Essays*.

J. H. Raleigh, 'Victorian Morals and the Modern Novel', *Partisan Review*, xxv (1958).

C. Rembar, *The End of Obscenity* (New York, 1968).

P. Rieff, (intro.), *Psychoanalysis and the Unconscious* and *Fantasia of the Unconscious* (New York, 1960).

C. H. Rolph (ed.), *The Trial of Lady Chatterley* (Harmondsworth, 1961).

K. Shapiro, 'The Unemployed Magician', in H. T. Moore (ed.), *A D. H. Lawrence Miscellany*.

E. W. Tedlock, jun., *D. H. Lawrence: Artist and Rebel* (Albuquerque, N. Mex., 1963).

W. Y. Tindall, *D. H. Lawrence and Susan His Cow* (New York, 1939).

Fr. W. Tiverton [Martin Jarrett-Kerr], *D. H. Lawrence and Human Existence* (London and New York, 1951).

K. Widmer, *The Art of Perversity* (Seattle, Wash., 1962).

R. Williams, 'Lawrence and Tolstoy', *Critical Quarterly*, ii (1960).

20 · JOYCE 1882–1941

A. Walton Litz

MORE than any other writer of his age, James Joyce was responsible
for the charges of difficulty and 'obscurity' that are often directed
against modern literature. *Ulysses* has become a symbol of the
burdens which many twentieth-century writers place upon their
readers, while *Finnegans Wake* stands in the popular mind as a hor-
rible example of the 'private' work that resists all conventional attempts at understanding. It is easy, of course, to overemphasize the
demands made by Joyce's art. He once remarked, in a tone reminis-
cent of Stephen Dedalus, that he asked of his readers nothing less than
a lifetime of study, and members of the Joyce cult lost no time in
exalting this half-serious boast into a standing order. Nothing is to be
gained from such romantic exaggerations of Joyce's obscurity.
Dubliners and *A Portrait of the Artist*, which puzzled their first readers,
are now accepted as classic works in the main tradition of English
fiction, while the once 'unreadable' *Ulysses* presents no insuperable
problems to a generation reared on the cinema and the post-Joycean
novel. Only *Finnegans Wake* seems likely to remain within the orbit of
the specialist and the enthusiast, but even this strange work has become more familiar as our mass media have assimilated the techniques of temporal dislocation and free association. Joyce's increasing
popularity and accessibility are proof of Wordsworth's famous dic-
tum that 'every author, as far as he is great and at the same time
original, has had the task of *creating* the taste by which he is to be
enjoyed'.
  Yet when the difficulties of Joyce's writing are placed in proper
perspective, they remain formidable and challenging. The puzzling
surfaces of his major works cry out for explication, and this cry has
not gone unanswered. Within his lifetime Joyce was the focus of
many critical debates, which he enjoyed and often promoted; and
since his death the production of criticism has accelerated with be-
wildering speed. Robert H. Deming's *Bibliography of James Joyce
Studies* (see BIBLIOGRAPHIES) listed over 1,400 items published before
1962, and that number had nearly doubled by 1972. During the past
decade studies of Joyce have become much more limited and detailed; the general assessments of the 1940s and early 1950s have

given way to specialized studies of sources, influences, and methods of composition. In fact, the works of Joyce are now subjected to the full range of scholarly techniques usually reserved for classical texts, and since Joyce himself was a scholiast who loved to parody scholarship it should not be surprising that many of these recent works verge on self-parody. They tend to replace Joyce's art with what one critic has called 'a textbook ideogram of his works', and it is easy—too easy—for us to dismiss them as products of the scholarly 'Joyce factory'. In spite of their pretensions, they are serious and useful attempts to illuminate the complex achievement of a great writer.

It is the aim of this essay to identify the best studies of Joyce, and to place them in the perspective of his changing reputation. Although I have tried to indicate the major critical controversies surrounding each of his works, and to do justice to all shades of critical opinion, I have placed great emphasis on those 'neutral' studies which provide the raw materials for interpretation—source studies, concordances, lexicons, guides to literary allusions and historical background. Joyce was not a profoundly learned writer, in the manner of Coleridge or even George Eliot; most often he garnered his learning from popular texts or encyclopedic surveys, and this means that his 'ideas' can be approached on the same level. Much of his knowledge of Giambattista Vico, for example, came not from Vico's dense Italian but from English translations and from Jules Michelet's introduction to his classic French version. Joyce knew a little bit about a great many things, and a little learning on the part of the reader will go a long way toward unlocking his art. Most of the so-called 'obscurities' of his works are surface difficulties, like those of Eliot's *Waste Land*; the structural patterns and leading themes are usually simple and familiar. As a result, the reading of Joyce's works must be a co-operative enterprise to which each critic adds his part and from which he always receives more than he has given.

TEXTS AND CONCORDANCES

Joyce led a nomadic, disordered life, and these circumstances are reflected in the textual histories of his major works. Of his important works only the poems and the play, *Exiles*, present few textual problems; yet it is only in the past ten years that a serious attempt has been made to provide the reader with authoritative texts. Virtually all of Joyce's significant writing is now available on both sides of the Atlantic in cheap editions, most of them paperback, but these editions vary widely in quality. The following notes are designed to help the reader in choosing the best texts available.

The various popular editions of *Chamber Music* and *Pomes Penyeach* are reasonably satisfactory, and the Viking Press *Collected Poems* is a handy volume. Those with a special interest in *Chamber Music* will wish to consult W. Y. Tindall's critical edition, based upon examination of the manuscripts. Paul A. Doyle's *Concordance to the 'Collected Poems'* may be used with any edition, since it indexes each poem by title and line-number, giving the full line in which each word appears.

Joyce's well-known difficulties in finding a publisher for *Dubliners* culminated in the production of a very unsatisfactory first edition which failed to follow his wishes in punctuation and the handling of dialogue. The failings of the first edition were compounded in subsequent editions until 1967, when Robert Scholes (with advice from Richard Ellmann) produced an authoritative text that incorporates all of Joyce's known corrections and restores Joyce's preferred method in punctuating dialogue. This text is reprinted in the Viking Critical Library, with annotations and source material, under the editorship of Robert Scholes and A. Walton Litz. Don Gifford's *Notes for Joyce* provides annotations for the individual stories. A *Word Index to James Joyce's 'Dubliners'* has recently been compiled by Gary Lane.

The fiftieth anniversary in 1964 of the publication of *A Portrait of the Artist* witnessed the appearance of two authoritative editions, both based on the Dublin holograph. James S. Atherton's edition includes an excellent introduction and informative notes. Chester G. Anderson's text (edited with the advice of Richard Ellmann) contains no apparatus, but it has recently been included in the Viking Critical Library, where it is accompanied by extensive background material, a selection of important critical essays, and elaborate explanatory notes. Don Gifford's *Notes for Joyce* also contains useful annotations. The *Word Index* compiled by Leslie Hancock is keyed to Anderson's edition.

Although *Exiles* presents no special textual problems, the serious student will wish to use Padraic Colum's edition, which includes some of Joyce's working notes for the play. He will also be interested in comparing the published text with the 'private' manuscript version discussed by Robert Adams (see CRITICAL STUDIES AND COMMENTARY).

The first edition of *Ulysses* (1922), set up by French printers and proof-read in great haste, is understandably imperfect. Furthermore, Joyce's incessant revisions of the novel during its final stages left room for omission and distortion in the final manuscript. A definitive edition of the novel will necessitate use of the complex manuscripts and proof-sheets, and several scholars have already done preliminary work on this formidable problem. Meanwhile, the standard commercial texts (The Bodley Head, 1960; Random House-Modern Library, 1961) must serve in spite of obvious imperfections. The original Random House-Modern Library edition (1934) is notoriously corrupt, having been set up from the pirated American edition of 1929 rather than the Paris first edition, but its pagination (or the pagination of the first unlimited Bodley Head edition, 1937) is the basis for references to *Ulysses* in those studies published before *c.* 1962. When the new Bodley Head edition of 1960 and the "corrected" Random House-Modern Library edition of 1961 were printed, the paginations were inexcusably altered, making it necessary for owners of the new editions to go through elaborate calculations while trying to track down references in the earlier critical studies. To compound this confusion, the Penguin paperback (1968 and after) follows still another pagination. Thus there are five different texts, with different paginations, in general use; the only solution is a conversion table. The more recent Random House reprints indicate in the margins the page numbers of the first American edition (1934). The Penguin paperback and the 1960 Bodley Head edition contain tables for converting the page numbers to those of the 1937 Bodley Head edition, while Phillip Herring's *Joyce's 'Ulysses' Notesheets in the British Museum* prints a conversion table for the 1934 Random House, the 1961 Random House, and the 1960 Bodley Head editions. Miles Hanley's *Word Index*, an indispensable guide to the novel's intricate leitmotivs, is based on the 1934 Random House-Modern Library edition.

Although difficult to obtain, the Odyssey Press edition of *Ulysses* (3rd impression, Hamburg, 1935) is the most authoritative. Its text was revised, at Joyce's request, by Stuart Gilbert.

Fortunately, the English and American editions of *Finnegans Wake* have the same pagination, which has been preserved as Joyce's 'Corrections of Misprints' (appended to early editions) have been worked into the text. The current text still contains misprints, as pointed out in the Introduction to Clive Hart's monumental *Concordance*, but on the whole it is remarkably clean. In the course of the *Wake*'s complex evolution many errors entered the text, some as the result of Joyce's carelessness or ill health, some out of his wilful desire to let the work dictate its own shape. It seems clear that the present text can be 'improved' at many points by recourse to the earlier versions, but the editorial problems this presents are ambiguous and the task of a full critical edition is overwhelming to contemplate. The present text will probably be standard for some time to come.

Hart's *Concordance* is essential for any reader of *Finnegans Wake*. It contains an index of all the 'words'; a list of the important words and syllables within compound units; and a catalogue of 'overtones', i.e. English words suggested by Joyce's portmanteau creations.

Since Joyce's death in 1941 a great deal of manuscript material has come to light, and most of it has now been published, either in scattered sources (especially Richard Ellmann's biography) or in the following editions:

Stephen Hero, the surviving portion of the early autobiographical novel which later became *A Portrait of the Artist*, was published in 1944 by Theodore Spencer, who also supplied a fine Introduction. A few additional manuscript pages turned up after 1944, and were included in the 1963 edition. Chester Anderson's *Word Index* is a help in locating connections between *Stephen Hero* and *Portrait*.

The Critical Writings of James Joyce, edited by Ellsworth Mason and Richard Ellmann, brings together the early essays and reviews, the Paris and Pola notebooks, the later political articles, and the two broadsides ('The Holy Office' and 'Gas from a Burner'). *The Workshop of Daedalus*, designed by Scholes and Kain as a source-book for *A Portrait of the Artist*, contains important manuscript material, especially the *Epiphanies* and the 1904 essay–story, 'A Portrait of the Artist'. Recently Richard Ellmann has published *Giacomo Joyce*, a brief manuscript completed before 1915 in which Joyce, in the manner of his epiphanies, broods upon vanished youth and the experience of being infatuated with a young girl. Parts of this work were published earlier in Ellmann's biography, *James Joyce*. With the appearance of *Giacomo Joyce* all of Joyce's imaginative works are now available.

An extremely useful anthology of Joyce's major writings is Harry Levin's *Portable James Joyce*, published in England as *The Essential James Joyce*. It contains the complete texts of *Dubliners*, *A Portrait*, *Exiles*, and *Collected Poems*, with useful introductions, as well as selections from *Ulysses* and *Finnegans Wake*. The brief bibliography was brought up to date in 1966 and the text revised to conform with more recent editions

CRITICAL STUDIES AND COMMENTARY

Although Joyce's early works did not receive widespread attention at the time of their publication, the excitement created by the appearance of *Ulysses* in 1922 led to a flood of commentary on all aspects of his life and art. Many of the early reviews and essays now have only an historical interest: concerned with problems of censorship and 'good taste', or designed to defend Joyce against the attacks of reactionary critics, these pieces reveal much about the age in which they were written but offer little practical help to the present-day reader. Most of the important early criticism has been assimilated and extended by recent critics, and in the following section I shall consider only those commentaries of the 1920s and 1930s which are still fresh and suggestive. The best of the essays from 1923 to 1948 have been collected by Seon Givens in *James Joyce: Two Decades of Criticism*.

Those interested in the progress of Joyce's reputation and the contemporary reception of his works should consult Richard Ellmann's *James Joyce* (discussed in BIOGRAPHIES AND LETTERS) and the extremely useful guide by Marvin Magalaner and Richard Kain, *Joyce: The Man, the Work, the Reputation*. This panoramic survey of opinions on Joyce's life and art is now somewhat outdated, but it provides a detailed running account of early reactions to his works and helps us to understand the origins of present-day 'schools' of Joyce criticism.

More recently, Thomas F. Staley has collected seven original essays which survey the current state of critical opinion on Joyce's major works. The essays are extremely uneven in range and quality, but they do serve to emphasize the rapid progress in Joyce studies over the past decade. Clive Hart's chapter on '*Finnegans Wake* in Perspective' is a masterful summary of the problems in interpretation presented by Joyce's last work, as well as a concise account of trends in criticism.

Robert Deming's *James Joyce: The Critical Heritage* reprints most of the major reviews and comments, ranging from the first notices of *Chamber Music* to the earliest reviews of *Finnegans Wake* (1907–1941). Unfortunately, the selections are often badly cut, and presented without adequate context.

Joyce studies came of age with the first attempts to establish a general estimate of his artistic achievement. In *Axel's Castle* (1931) Edmund Wilson undertook to chart the contours of Joyce's career, and his pioneering essay—which emphasizes Joyce's crucial place in the tradition of modern European literature—had a decisive influence on the criticism of the next twenty years. In some ways Harry Levin's *James Joyce* (1941) was an elaboration of Wilson's position. Published in the year of Joyce's death, and subsequently revised, Levin's study was the first to provide a steady perspective for Joyce's entire achievement. Levin demonstrates the thematic and symbolic patterns which link Joyce's works to each other, and is especially good on Joyce's relationship to other modern writers. Although the sections on *Dubliners* and *A Portrait* appear oversimplified in the light of more recent commentary, and the treatment of *Finnegans Wake* has been largely superseded, Levin's study remains one of the best introductions to Joyce's art. Informed by genuine critical ability, and unified by a consistent point of view, Levin's study raised Joyce criticism to a new level of precision and good sense.

The decade of the 1950s produced more tendentious general studies. Tindall's *James Joyce* (1950) stresses the symbolic unity of Joyce's work, and is especially good on Joyce's use of Freudian and archetypal patterns. Like his later *Reader's Guide*, which provides a running explication for the major works, Tindall's *James Joyce* is marked by an unwillingness to distinguish between the important and the trivial, or between reasonable and problematic interpretations. Although filled with illuminating comments, neither book provides a satisfying and reliable approach to Joyce's entire career.

Many of the same qualifications apply to Hugh Kenner's *Dublin's Joyce*. A brilliant and idiosyncratic study, written in a rather disjointed style, *Dublin's Joyce* is packed with shrewd comments and convincing explications of particular passages. The treatments of Joyce's attitude toward Stephen Dedalus, and of the Homeric framework in *Ulysses*, have been especially influential. None the less, the study's general approach will strike many readers as a dogmatic distortion of the complex and often paradoxical attitudes which inform Joyce's major works. By insisting upon an irony that is almost wholly critical and destructive, and by limiting the range of Joyce's human sympathies, Kenner has produced a portrait of the artist that many readers will find at variance with their own responses to the works. In contrast to *Dublin's Joyce*, Kenner's later criticism (especially the sections in *The Pound Era*) yields a rich and humane sense of Joyce's complex realism and of his place in the modern tradition.

Four useful general studies of Joyce's art have appeared in the last decade: Goldberg's *James Joyce*, Adams's *James Joyce: Common Sense and Beyond*, Litz's *James Joyce*, and John Gross's brief study in the 'Modern Masters' series. Goldberg is especially good on the early works and on Joyce's youthful aesthetic, while his section on *Ulysses* —like his earlier full-length study of the work—is marked by a fine regard for its dramatic and 'human' qualities. Unfortunately, Goldberg is completely out of sympathy with Joyce's aims in *Finnegans Wake*, and his last chapter is a bad-tempered dismissal of Joyce's last work. When confronted with *Finnegans Wake* Goldberg is unable to achieve his persistent aim, which is to save Joyce from himself.

Adams and Litz present more balanced, and perhaps more conventional, surveys of the major works. Both authors supply a great deal of background material, and both attempt to avoid programmatic interpretations or the piling-up of received opinions. Gross's *James Joyce* is a sensitive essay which emphasizes Joyce's place in the modern tradition.

Arnold Goldman's *The Joyce Paradox* is an interesting attempt to reconcile some of the divergent critical approaches to Joyce's art. By rehearsing the often conflicting, and sometimes radically opposed, views of Joyce's major critics, Goldman sharpens our sense of the fundamental problems confronted by any reader of Joyce's work. Although the reader may not accept Goldman's own critical synthesis, he will find in *The Joyce Paradox* a valuable context for the reading of individual commentaries. Goldman does not attempt to extend his survey and synthesis beyond *Ulysses*.

Since the mid-1950s studies of Joyce have tended to be more specialized, and I have thought it best to devote the remainder of this section to commentaries on Joyce's individual works. The reader interested in a particular work should also consult the relevant chapters in the general critical studies already discussed. Those who wish to gain a sense of current trends in Joyce studies will find the articles and reviews in the *James Joyce Quarterly* invaluable.

(a) Poetry

Joyce's poetry, slight and conventional though it may be, has not received the attention that it deserves. W. Y. Tindall's edition of *Chamber Music* (see TEXTS AND CONCORDANCES) contains elaborate annotation and commentary, but Tindall's scatological reading of the poems should be heavily discounted. James R. Baker's 'Joyce's *Chamber Music*: The Exile of the Heart' is a convincing discussion of structural and thematic patterns; it shows that as early as *Chamber Music* Joyce was interested in portraying the development of an artistic sensibility. Litz's *James Joyce* contains a section on the poetry.

(b) Dubliners

Dubliners was late in receiving the critical attention it deserves. For many years it was overshadowed by *A Portrait*, which was published at the same time, and Joyce's difficulties with printer and publisher often received more attention than the stories themselves. However, the last decade has witnessed a surprising acceleration in the attention given to *Dubliners*, and some of the best work on Joyce being done today is devoted to the early fiction. This new interest in *Dubliners* reflects, in part, a realization of its importance in the tradition of English fiction, and in part an increasing understanding of the ways in which the stories anticipate Joyce's later techniques.

Brewster Ghiselin's long essay on 'The Unity of Joyce's *Dubliners*' (1956), which emphasizes the symbolic and structural unity of the collection, marked a new stage in *Dubliners* criticism; and it was followed by the detailed commentary of Magalaner's *Time of Apprenticeship* (which also contains a section on *Portrait*). The Viking Critical Edition of *Dubliners*, edited by Litz and Scholes (see TEXTS AND CONCORDANCES), reprints a selection of important criticism. The collection of fifteen original essays edited by Clive Hart, one on each of the stories, contains the best recent criticism of *Dubliners*.

(c) *Stephen Hero* and *A Portrait*

Most of the important criticism of *Stephen Hero* and *Portrait* has appeared in the form of articles, and the best of these have been collected in two recent anthologies: Connolly, *Joyce's 'Portrait': Criticisms and Critiques*; and Morris and Nault, *Portraits of an Artist*. Connolly's anthology contains essays on *Portrait* and the aesthetic theory, while Morris and Nault include more background information and provide a checklist of publications relevant to *Portrait*. Both anthologies reprint the essays by Hugh Kenner and Dorothy Van Ghent, which have become classic studies of the novel. Chester G. Anderson's edition of *Portrait* in the Viking Critical Library also contains a selection of critical articles, as well as notes and background materials.

Since the problem of Joyce's distance from his hero is a crucial one in the interpretation of *Portrait*, biographical and historical materials are of the greatest interest. *The Workshop of Daedalus*, edited by Scholes and Kain (see TEXTS AND CONCORDANCES), includes relevant manuscript materials and a number of selections which illuminate the novel's biographical connections and its artistic milieu. The problem of Joyce's Catholic heritage is raised most acutely by *Portrait*, and two studies have been devoted to this special topic: Morse, *The Sympathetic Alien*, and Noon, *Joyce and Aquinas*. Father Noon's book is the more learned of the two, but it suffers occasionally from special pleading and tends to overemphasize Joyce's debts to Aquinas.

(d) *Exiles*

Exiles has suffered from the deserved reputations of the two works that flank it, *A Portrait* and *Ulysses*. Most of the best commentary on the play will be found in general studies (see especially Kenner, *Dublin's Joyce*). Francis Fergusson's introduction to the play is a fine treatment of its dramatic qualities. Most of the interest in *Exiles* has focused, inevitably, on its autobiographical dimensions, and in this connection Adams's 'Light on Joyce's *Exiles*?' is extraordinary interesting. Adams prints manuscript fragments which seem to represent a 'private' version of the play, and speculates upon the literary and biographical significance of this version.

(e) *Ulysses*

Early criticism of *Ulysses* was clouded by the popular issue of the work's obscenity, and by the need to defend Joyce's status as a serious artist. One of the most frequent charges hurled against the novel was that of 'formlessness', and as a result the early defenders of *Ulysses* went to the opposite extreme of stressing the work's 'order' and intricate structure. In his famous 1923 review, '*Ulysses*, Order, and Myth' (reprinted in Givens, *Two Decades of Criticism*), T. S. Eliot claimed that through use of the Homeric correspondences Joyce had found a way 'of controlling, of ordering, of giving a shape and a significance to the immense panorama of futility and anarchy which is contemporary history'. Rumours concerning Joyce's own *schema* for the novel (his chart outlining the various Homeric and symbolic correspondences for each episode) abetted this interest in structure, and the trend culminated in the publication of Stuart Gilbert's *James Joyce's 'Ulysses'* (1930). Written with Joyce's help and including the famous *schema*, Gilbert's study emphasizes the detailed Homeric analogies and the intricate cross-references which give the novel its mechanical unity. What Gilbert fails to stress are those 'novelistic' qualities which give *Ulysses* its essential life. *James Joyce's 'Ulysses'* is still useful today, but chiefly in its details: the main argument must be seen as an exaggerated reaction to contemporary charges of 'formlessness', and the excessive quotations must be understood as an attempt to communicate the novel's power at a time when it was banned in both England and the US.

Frank Budgen's *James Joyce and the Making of 'Ulysses'*, which followed in 1934, did much to right the critical balance. Budgen knew Joyce better than anyone else during those Zürich years (1918–20) when the novel was nearing completion, and he gives a clear picture of the human as well as the formal values Joyce was seeking to embody. Sensitive, personal, and undogmatic, Budgen's study remains the best introduction to the mind that created *Ulysses*.

Unfortunately, Budgen's work exercised much less influence than

Gilbert's, and during the next two decades most of the important criticism of *Ulysses* centred on its formal qualities. This trend culminated in A. M. Klein's important but little-known articles on the first and fourteenth episodes, which are unmatched in their intricate tracings of allusions and leitmotivs. In his essay on 'The Oxen of the Sun', for example, Klein follows the clues provided in one of Joyce's letters and demonstrates how the entire episode, in its stylistic development, re-enacts the development of the English language, the geological evolution of the earth, the growth of a human foetus, and the progress of *Ulysses* up to that point.

Meanwhile, Kain's *Fabulous Voyager* (1947) and Blackmur's brilliant article on 'The Jew in Search of a Son' (1948) combined analysis of technique with a detailed assessment of the novel's leading themes. Kain's emphasis on the realistic setting and the interaction of characters makes his book still a valuable introduction, although many of his analyses of technique have been superseded. Mention should also be made in passing of W. B. Stanford's *The Ulysses Theme*, which places Joyce's work in the long tradition of interpretations of the *Odyssey* and thereby stresses the more 'human' aspects of Joyce's Homeric structure.

The Homeric parallels have been the point of departure for an important debate—perhaps *the* important debate—in recent criticism of *Ulysses*. Is Joyce's vision essentially humanistic, producing a hero who is a genuine reincarnation of Homer's Ulysses; or is his vision essentially destructive and ironic, intent upon dramatizing the disparities between past and present? Richard Ellmann's *Ulysses on the Liffey* (1972) represents one extreme, while Hugh Kenner's heavily ironic reading in *Dublin's Joyce* represents the other; and between the two lies a whole range of compromised interpretations. In Ellman's recent study (based upon Joyce's original *schema* of 1920, which differs in significant ways from that printed by Stuart Gilbert) the humanism of *Ulysses* is explored through close and sometimes strained attention to the novel's largest symbolic claims. At times, Ellmann seems to lose touch with the realistic action in his determination to establish symmetries and correspondences.

Perhaps the most interesting approach to this problem is that found in S. L. Goldberg's *The Classical Temper*. By minimizing the importance of the more 'mechanical' orders in the novel, and concentrating upon the broad thematic and historical questions which the work poses, Goldberg has produced a controversial and important study which focuses our attention on the 'human validity' of *Ulysses*. *The Classical Temper* is probably the best book yet written on *Ulysses*, in the sense that it deals with the novel's largest claims to greatness and formulates the essential aesthetic questions. Although Goldberg is by temperament unsympathetic to many of Joyce's aims and unwilling to accept the principles of a Symbolist aesthetic, he does more justice to *Ulysses* than many of the work's uncritical admirers. Stanley Sultan's *The Argument of 'Ulysses'*, an extended analysis of narrative structure, complements Goldberg's study in many ways but curiously fails to take *The Classical Temper* into account.

Among more specialized studies, Schutte's *Joyce and Shakespeare* discusses the origins and artistic functions of Stephen Dedalus's Shakespeare theories. It contains a comprehensive listing of Shakespeare allusions in *Ulysses*, and is especially valuable as a guide to the important *Hamlet* motif. Litz's *The Art of James Joyce* contains a discussion of the novel's aesthetic aims based upon a study of Joyce's intricate revisions. Adams's *Surface and Symbol* is an interesting examination of the ways in which Joyce processed his raw materials. Adams attempts to distinguish between those details which are part of the novel's 'naturalistic' surface and those which have been transformed into 'symbol'. Litz and Adams both make use of Joyce's complex notes for *Ulysses*, which provide a fascinating record of his methods of composition; the most important of these notes, now in the British Museum, have been scrupulously edited by Phillip Herring.

Three recent 'guides' deserve special mention. In *The Bloomsday Book* Harry Blamires has produced a running paraphrase, or page-by-page commentary, which can help the unitiated through a first reading. Weldon Thornton's *Allusions in 'Ulysses'* provides detailed annotations on Joyce's more obvious allusions to literature, philosophy, and history. Although many of the obscure allusions are necessarily omitted, and one can quarrel with particular annotations, *Allusions in 'Ulysses'* is extraordinarily useful. The annotations are cross-referenced and keyed to both the old and new Random House editions.

Clive Hart's brief but helpful *James Joyce's 'Ulysses'* is divided into three parts: an examination of the background to *Ulysses*, both in Joyce's environment and his writings; a reading of *Ulysses* itself; and a fine analytic survey of criticism of *Ulysses*, aimed at clarifying the major problems in interpretation. Joyce's complete *schema* is printed as an appendix.

Another brief introduction to the novel is David Hayman's concise and intelligent study, *'Ulysses': The Mechanics of Meaning*. Hayman is especially good on the language of the novel and Joyce's comic vision. Richard Cross's *Flaubert and Joyce*, although it contains

introductory chapters on *Dubliners* and *Portrait*, is most penetrating
on the relations between *Ulysses* and Flaubert's fiction. *Approaches to
'Ulysses'*, edited by Staley and Benstock, gathers together a number
of useful essays on different aspects of the novel, ranging from matters of technique to Joyce's place in the tradition.

(f) Finnegans Wake

The extreme difficulty of *Finnegans Wake*, and the complex evolution
of the text over sixteen years, make the study of this work a world
unto itself. As Clive Hart has pointed out (in Staley's *James Joyce
Today*), the progress of *Finnegans Wake* criticism falls into three
distinct phases. Between 1923 and 1939, when the book was known
as *Work in Progress* and appeared piecemeal in the little magazines,
studies were mainly based upon Joyce's own hints and revelations.
The essays in *Our Exgamination* (Samuel Beckett *et al.*, 1929) were
written under Joyce's direct influence, and must be taken—in spite
of their many useful qualities—as part of the publicity surrounding
Work in Progress.

   With the publication of *Finnegans Wake* in 1939 criticism entered
a second phase. The early reviews by Edmund Wilson ('The Dream
of H. C. Earwicker') and Harry Levin (see the section on the *Wake*
in his *James Joyce*) marked the beginning of systematic study: Wilson
and Levin were working with the full text in front of them, and their
initial reactions were remarkably intelligent and accurate. Both
essays remain useful introductions to *Finnegans Wake*.

   The *Skeleton Key* compiled by Campbell and Robinson (1944)
carried on the task of providing the reader with an overview of
themes and structure. The *Skeleton Key* provides a page-by-page
paraphrase of the *Wake's* 'action', as well as comments on Joyce's
debt to Vico and his general 'archetypal' aims. Although many
experts have attacked the *Skeleton Key* as a lifeless abridgement put
together by an anthropologist and a *Reader's Digest* editor, no other
work has done so much to make *Finnegans Wake* accessible. Most
critics today would caution that the *Skeleton Key* is inaccurate and
distorting, but until a better guide is produced it will be the essential
'first book' for a reader of *Finnegans Wake*.

   W. Y. Tindall's *James Joyce* (1950) continued the synthesizing
work of the *Skeleton Key*, and it was not until the publication of the
first version of Adaline Glasheen's *Census* (1956) that criticism of
Finnegans Wake reached the third stage of specialized and scholarly
study. The *Census*, greatly revised and expanded in 1963, contains a
synopsis of the *Wake* which improves upon that provided at the

beginning of the *Skeleton Key*; a table of 'character' transformations; and a detailed census of proper names, complete with cross-references and critical commentary. The *Census* was followed in 1960 by Atherton's *Books at the Wake*, a fascinating study of Joyce's sources which illuminates the book's structure and meaning, and in 1962 by Hart's *Structure and Motif in 'Finnegans Wake'*, the best survey to date of the *Wake*'s design and major motifs. When used in conjunction with Hart's *Concordance* (see TEXTS AND CONCORDANCES), these studies open *Finnegans Wake* to serious literary criticism.

Since Joyce re-made *Finnegans Wake* time and again during the process of composition, often altering the emphasis in particular sections, studies of his revisions have proved extremely illuminating. Litz's *The Art of James Joyce* discusses Joyce's stylistic aims as reflected in the evolution of the *Wake*. Higginson's edition of the successive drafts of *Anna Livia Plurabelle* presents the reader with a graphic example of Joyce's methods, while Hayman's *First-Draft Version* provides transcriptions of the earliest manuscript versions of each episode.

Hodgart and Worthington's *Song in the Works of James Joyce* indexes and identifies songs and musical allusions throughout Joyce's works, but most of its references are to *Finnegans Wake*. It is a valuable handbook, as are the recent guides to Scandinavian, German, and Gaelic materials in the *Wake* (Christiani, *Scandinavian Elements*; Bonheim, *A Lexicon of the German*; O Hehir, *A Gaelic Lexicon*). The present phase of highly technical studies will probably continue for some time; the great need would seem to be for general works, on the order of the *Skeleton Key*, which can assimilate the vast amount of specialized information uncovered during the past decade.

The *Wake Newslitter*, founded in 1962 under the editorship of Clive Hart and Fritz Senn, is a lively journal which publishes specific explications and carries on a running debate concerning methods of interpretation. If *Finnegans Wake* is a work of the rational imagination, as it certainly is in its design if not in all its details, then guidelines must be established to limit the free-association, 'anything goes' approach which vitiated so much early criticism. *A Wake Digest*, edited by Hart and Senn, draws together many of the best papers from the *Wake Newslitter* and includes original studies by regular contributors.

BIOGRAPHIES AND LETTERS

Since all of Joyce's work is 'autobiographical' in one fashion or another, problems of biographical interpretation have loomed large in the history of Joyce studies. The obvious connections between

Joyce's life and that of his *persona*, Stephen Dedalus, prompted a great deal of fanciful speculation during Joyce's lifetime, and he did little to correct the legends and myths which grew up around the known facts of his career. The authorized biography by Herbert Gorman, written with Joyce's permission and under his scrutiny, conceals as much as it reveals. Gorman was never fully taken into Joyce's confidence; he was unable to use any information that might offend his subject; and Joyce used his review of the proofs to add personal details and settle old accounts. The result was a slapdash job that furnished a great deal of new material (such as the early aesthetic notebooks) but failed to establish a realistic outline of Joyce's life. Gorman often fell victim to the myths and legends, so that from time to time he appears to be writing the life of Stephen Dedalus, not James Joyce.

The publication of *Letters of James Joyce* (1957), edited by Stuart Gilbert, provided the reader with his first opportunity to check Gorman's story against the facts of Joyce's life. The first volume of the *Letters* was followed in 1959 by Richard Ellmann's monumental biography, which made use of much unpublished material to present for the first time a dispassionate and well-proportioned account of Joyce's life. Ellmann had access to major collections of letters, and he combined this information with the memories of surviving family and friends to produce the one indispensable work of Joyce scholarship. One can often quarrel with Ellmann's handling of evidence, especially his tendency to rely heavily on the memories of interested parties, but the fact remains that without his work much of the best criticism of the past decade could not have been written. The most interesting part of Ellmann's biography is the first half, which deals with Joyce's career up to 1914. After the publication of *Dubliners* and *A Portrait* Joyce's life became more and more a history of his evolving works, first *Ulysses* and later *Finnegans Wake*; and in handling this period Ellmann occasionally falls victim to the triviality or repetitiveness of his material. But perhaps the greatest fault of the biography is its lack of a proper index: the index of proper names is of little help to the reader who wishes to follow the recurrent themes of Joyce's life.

Ellmann's work on the biography led naturally into the difficult task of editing Joyce's letters, and in 1966 he produced volumes ii and iii of the *Letters*. At the same time, Gilbert's original volume was republished with corrections by Ellmann. It is unfortunate that the publishers were not able to integrate the letters from volume i into volumes ii and iii. At present volumes ii and iii run chronologically from 1900 to 1941, with elaborate annotation, biographical inter-chapters, and a full index. In contrast, the important letters of volume i, ranging from 1901 to 1940, have sparse annotation and a totally inadequate index of proper names. Until this situation is corrected the reader who wishes to follow Joyce's career in his letters must scuttle back and forth between the volumes.

In addition to Ellmann's *James Joyce* and the *Letters*, anyone inter-ested in Joyce's early life (and its bearing on *Portrait*) should consult Sullivan's *Joyce among the Jesuits*. This account of Joyce's education at Clongowes Wood, Belvedere, and University College establishes Joyce's actual (as opposed to his fictional) relationship with the Jesuit order. Forrest Read's *Pound/Joyce*, which prints Pound's letters to Joyce and the relevant critical essays, is a fascinating record of Joyce's emergence as the master of 'modernism'. Pound was the first critic to identify the major issues in Joyce's art, and his comments in the period 1914–1922 set the pattern for much subsequent criti-cism.

Among the published reminiscences of friends and family, Stanis-laus Joyce's *Diary* and his memoir, *My Brother's Keeper*, are of great interest. Taken together, these two works cover the first twenty-three years of Joyce's life. The *Diary* is perhaps the more reliable, since *My Brother's Keeper* was written after many years of virtual estrangement, but the combination of exasperation and affection which is the hall-mark of the latter work should not put off the reader. In the early years Stanislaus knew his brother better than anyone else, and *My Brother's Keeper* remains, for all its special pleading, an invaluable document. When Stanislaus died in 1955, leaving the book unfin-ished, he had carried the story up to James Joyce's twenty-second year.

Two other memoirs should be singled out for special attention. Constantine Curran, one of Joyce's close friends at University Col-lege, has recorded with fairness and sympathy Joyce's social behavi-our and the events which led up to his departure from Dublin. In its picture of life at University College, *James Joyce Remembered* under-lines the differences between Joyce's actual experiences and their por-trayals in his art. Curran is especially good on Joyce's reading and the intellectual influences that shaped his early life. In *Our Friend James Joyce* Mary and Padraic Colum, who knew Joyce both in the Dublin of 1901–4 and the Paris of 1921–39, have recorded a series of vignettes.

Since Joyce spent most of his exiled life recreating among alien landscapes the solid Dublin of his youth, pictorial biographies pro-vide a sense of place that adds to our pleasure and understanding in reading his works. Patricia Hutchins's *James Joyce's Dublin* is an illustrated account of the places and people that figured in Joyce's life to 1904, while her later *James Joyce's World*—although less well illustrated—is a topographical–biographical guide to Joyce's entire life. Chester Anderson's *James Joyce and His World* combines handsome illustrations with a readable and popular account of Joyce's life drawn mainly from Ellmann's biography.

BIBLIOGRAPHY

The Slocum and Cahoon *Bibliography of James Joyce* (1953) remains the standard description of Joyce's own publications. The sections on books, pamphlets, and articles by Joyce are reasonably complete, although some new information has come to light over the past fifteen years. The sections on translations, manuscripts, and musical settings are, of course, completely outdated. The extent, location, and importance of Joyce's manuscripts were not fully understood in 1953. The great Joyce collection at the University of Buffalo had only recently been formed; the huge collection of *Finnegans Wake* materials sent to Harriet Weaver by Joyce had been given to the British Museum but not yet catalogued; the Cornell Joyce collection, which contains most of the important early letters and manuscripts, was not yet in existence, and these documents were still in private hands. Therefore the 'Manuscripts' section of Slocum and Cahoon should be supplemented by Spielberg's catalogue of the Buffalo collection, Robert Scholes's description of *The Cornell Joyce Collection*, and the 'Draft Catalogue' of the British Museum collection printed as an appendix to Hayman's *First-Draft Version of 'Finnegans Wake'* (see CRITICAL STUDIES AND COMMENTARY).

Although unsatisfactory in many ways, Deming's *Bibliography of James Joyce Studies* superseded all previous listings of Joyce criticism. Deming includes most of the major items published before December 1961, and the entries—some accompanied by brief descriptions—are grouped into useful categories. Thus one can see at a glance the major publications on any story in *Dubliners*, or any section of *Ulysses*. The reader should be warned that Deming's references are sometimes inaccurate, and that his brief annotations are not always to be trusted. For studies published since 1961, as well as a selective view of the whole of Joyce criticism, the student should consult the revised *Modern Fiction Studies* checklist, 'Criticism of James Joyce', compiled by Beebe, Herring, and Litz. Supplemental checklists of Joyce studies are published from time to time in the *James Joyce Quarterly* (see CRITICAL STUDIES AND COMMENTARY) by Alan M. Cohn, and the reviews in the *Quarterly* cover most of the important books.

BACKGROUND READING

Joyce and Yeats stand as the two most important figures in modern literature, and their relationship—both personal and intellectual—is examined by Richard Ellmann in *Eminent Domain*. For a sense of Joyce's place in the Paris literary world of the 1920s and 1930s the reader should consult Sylvia Beach's *Shakespeare and Company*, which is focused on the long struggle to get *Ulysses* into print.

The Irish background of Joyce's works is often a puzzle to readers. In his chapter on Joyce in *The Irish Writers*, Herbert Howarth sketches in Joyce's reactions to Irish Nationalism and provides a superb discussion of Parnell as 'mythic' hero. Howarth's entire book illuminates the intellectual and political environment of the young James Joyce. A similar function is performed by Kain's study of *Dublin in the Age of William Butler Yeats and James Joyce*, which traces the history and cultural achievements of the Irish Renaissance. The chapter on 'Politics' is an especially useful summary, and the book contains a chronology of the landmarks in Irish literature, 1885–1941.

REFERENCES

TEXTS AND CONCORDANCES

C. G. Anderson (ed.), *A Portrait of the Artist as a Young Man* (New York, 1964; 'Compass' paperback).

—— *A Portrait of the Artist as a Young Man: Text, Criticism, and Notes* (New York, 1968; 'Viking Critical Library' paperback).

—— *Word Index to James Joyce's 'Stephen Hero'* (Ridgefield, Conn., 1958).

J. S. Atherton (ed.), *A Portrait of the Artist as a Young Man* (London, 1964).

P. Colum (ed.), *Exiles* (New York, 1951).

P. A. Doyle, *A Concordance to the 'Collected Poems' of James Joyce* (New York and London, 1966).

R. Ellmann (ed.), *Giacomo Joyce* (New York, 1968).

D. Gifford, *Notes for Joyce* (paperback, New York, 1967).

L. Hancock, *Word Index to James Joyce's 'Portrait of the Artist'* (Carbondale, Ill., 1967).

M. L. Hanley, *Word Index to James Joyce's 'Ulysses'* (Madison, Wis., 1937, 1951).

C. Hart, *A Concordance to 'Finnegans Wake'* (Minneapolis, Minn., 1963).

James Joyce, *Collected Poems* (New York, 1937).

—— *Pomes Penyeach* (paperback, London, 1966).

—— *Ulysses* (New York, 1934, 1961; London, 1937, 1960).

—— *Finnegans Wake* (New York and London, 1939, 1958, 1964).

G. Lane (ed.), *Word Index to James Joyce's 'Dubliners'* (New York, 1972).

H. Levin (ed.), *The Portable James Joyce* (New York, 1947, 1966); this anthology appeared in England (London, 1948) under the title *The Essential James Joyce.*

E. Mason and R. Ellmann (edd.), *The Critical Writings of James Joyce* (New York, 1959).

R. Scholes (ed.), *Dubliners* (New York and London, 1967).

—— and R. M. Kain (edd.), *The Workshop of Daedalus* (Evanston, Ill., 1965).

—— and A. W. Litz (edd.), *Dubliners: Text, Criticism, and Notes* ('Viking Critical Library' paperback, New York, 1969).

T. Spencer (ed.), *Stephen Hero* (New York, 1944, 1963).

W. Y. Tindall (ed.), *Chamber Music* (New York, 1954).

CRITICAL STUDIES AND COMMENTARY

R. M. Adams, *James Joyce: Common Sense and Beyond* (paperback, New York, 1966).

—— "Light on Joyce's *Exiles*? A New MS, a Curious Analogue, and Some Speculations', *Studies in Bibliography*, xvii (1964).

—— *Surface and Symbol: The Consistency of James Joyce's 'Ulysses'* (New York, 1962).

J. S. Atherton, *The Books at the Wake* (London and New York, 1960).

J. R. Baker, 'Joyce's *Chamber Music*: The Exile of the Heart', *Arizona Quarterly*, xv (1959).

S. Beckett *et al.*, *Our Exgamination Round his Factification for Incamination of Work in Progress* (Paris, 1929).

R. P. Blackmur, 'The Jew in Search of a Son', *Virginia Quarterly Review*, xxiv (1948).

H. Blamires, *The Bloomsday Book* (paperback, London, 1966).

H. W. Bonheim, *A Lexicon of the German in 'Finnegans Wake'* (Berkeley, Calif., 1967).

F. Budgen, *James Joyce and the Making of 'Ulysses'* (London, 1934).

J. Campbell and H. M. Robinson, *A Skeleton Key to 'Finnegans Wake'* (New York, 1944).

D. B. Christiani, *Scandinavian Elements of 'Finnegans Wake'* (Evanston, Ill., 1965).

T. E. Connolly (ed.), *Joyce's 'Portrait': Criticisms and Critiques* (paperback, New York, 1962).

—— (ed.), *Scribbledehobble: The Ur-Workbook for 'Finnegans Wake'* (Evanston, Ill., 1961).

R. K. Cross, *Flaubert and Joyce: The Rite of Fiction* (Princeton, N.J., 1971).

R. H. Deming (ed.), *James Joyce: The Critical Heritage*, 2 vols. (London and New York, 1970).

R. Ellmann, *Ulysses on the Liffey* (London and New York, 1972; corrected paperback, 1973).

F. Fergusson, 'A Reading of *Exiles*', in *Exiles* (Norfolk, Conn., 1945).

B. Ghiselin, 'The Unity of Joyce's *Dubliners*', *Accent*, xvi (1956), 75–88 and 196–213.

S. Gilbert, *James Joyce's 'Ulysses'* (London, 1930, 1952).

S. Givens (ed.), *James Joyce: Two Decades of Criticism* (New York, 1948, 1963).

A. Glasheen, *A Second Census of 'Finnegans Wake'* (Evanston, Ill., 1963).

S. L. Goldberg, *The Classical Temper* (London, 1961).

—— *James Joyce* (paperback, Edinburgh and New York, 1962).

A. Goldman, *The Joyce Paradox* (London and Evanston, Ill., 1966).

J. Gross, *James Joyce* (London and New York, 1970).

C. Hart, *James Joyce's 'Ulysses'* (Sydney, 1968).

—— *Structure and Motif in 'Finnegans Wake'* (London, 1962).

—— (ed.), *James Joyce's 'Dubliners': Critical Essays* (London and New York, 1969).

—— and F. Senn, *A Wake Digest* (paperback, Sydney, 1968).

D. Hayman, *A First-Draft Version of 'Finnegans Wake'* (Austin, Texas, 1963).

—— *'Ulysses': The Mechanics of Meaning* (New York, 1970).

P. F. Herring (ed.), *Joyce's 'Ulysses' Notesheets in the British Museum* (Charlottesville, Va., 1972).

F. H. Higginson (ed.), *Anna Livia Plurabelle: The Making of a Chapter* (Minneapolis, Minn., 1960).

M. J. C. Hodgart and M. P. Worthington, *Song in the Works of James Joyce* (New York, 1959).

James Joyce Quarterly (The University of Tulsa, Okla., 1963–   ).

R. M. Kain, *Fabulous Voyager* (Chicago, 1947; New York, 1959).

H. Kenner, *Dublin's Joyce* (Bloomington, Ind., 1956).

—— *The Pound Era* (Berkeley, 1971).

A. M. Klein, 'The Black Panther', *Accent*, x (1950), 139–55.

—— 'The Oxen of the Sun', *Here and Now*, i (1949), 28–48.

H. Levin, *James Joyce* (Norfolk, Conn., 1941, 1960).

A. W. Litz, *The Art of James Joyce* (London and New York, 1961, 1964).

—— *James Joyce* (New York, 1966, 1972).

M. Magalaner and R. M. Kain, *Joyce: The Man, the Work, the Reputation* (New York, 1956).

—— *Time of Apprenticeship: The Fiction of Young James Joyce* (New York, 1959).

W. E. Morris and C. A. Nault (edd.), *Portraits of an Artist* (paperback, New York, 1962).

J. M. Morse, *The Sympathetic Alien* (New York, 1959).

W. Noon, *Joyce and Aquinas* (New Haven, Conn., 1957).

B. O Hehir, *A Gaelic Lexicon for 'Finnegans Wake', and Glossary for Joyce's Other Works* (Berkeley, Calif., 1967).

W. J. Schutte, *Joyce and Shakespeare* (New Haven, Conn., 1957).

T. F. Staley (ed.), *James Joyce Today* (Bloomington, Ind., 1966).

—— and B. Benstock (edd.), *Approaches to 'Ulysses'* (Pittsburgh, Pa., 1971).

W. B. Stanford, *The Ulysses Theme* (Oxford, 1954).

S. Sultan, *The Argument of 'Ulysses'* (Columbus, Ohio, 1965).

W. Thornton, *Allusions in 'Ulysses'* (Chapel Hill, N.C., 1968).

W. Y. Tindall, *James Joyce: His Way of Interpreting the Modern World* (New York, 1950).

—— *A Reader's Guide to James Joyce* (New York, 1959).

A Wake Newslitter (University of Essex, Colchester, March 1962–   ).

E. Wilson, 'The Dream of H. C. Earwicker,' in *The Wound and the Bow* (New York, 1947).

—— 'James Joyce', in *Axel's Castle* (New York, 1931).

BIOGRAPHIES AND LETTERS

C. G. Anderson, *James Joyce and His World* (London, 1967).

M. Colum and P. Colum, *Our Friend James Joyce* (New York, 1958).

C. P. Curran, *James Joyce Remembered* (New York and London, 1968).

R. Ellmann, *James Joyce* (New York, 1959).

—— (ed.), *Letters of James Joyce*, vols. ii and iii (New York, 1966).

S. Gilbert (ed.), *Letters of James Joyce*, vol. i (New York, 1957; new edition corrected by R. Ellmann, 1966).

H. Gorman, *James Joyce* (New York, 1939, 1948).

P. Hutchins, *James Joyce's Dublin* (London, 1950).

—— *James Joyce's World* (London, 1957).

S. Joyce, *My Brother's Keeper* (London and New York, 1958).

—— *The Dublin Diary of Stanislaus Joyce*, ed. G. H. Healey (Ithaca, N.Y., 1962).

F. Read (ed.), *Pound/Joyce* (New York, 1967).

K. Sullivan, *Joyce among the Jesuits* (New York, 1958).

BIBLIOGRAPHIES

M. Beebe, P. F. Herring, and A. W. Litz, 'Criticism of James Joyce: A Selected Checklist', *Modern Fiction Studies*, xv (1969).

R. H. Deming, *A Bibliography of James Joyce Studies* (Lawrence, Kans., 1964).

R. Scholes, *The Cornell Joyce Collection* (Ithaca, N.Y., 1961).

J. J. Slocum and H. Cahoon, *A Bibliography of James Joyce* (New Haven, Conn., 1953).

P. Spielberg, *James Joyce's Manuscripts and Letters at the University of Buffalo* (Buffalo, N.Y., 1962).

BACKGROUND READING

S. Beach, *Shakespeare and Company* (New York, 1959).

R. Ellmann, *Eminent Domain: Yeats among Wilde, Joyce, Pound, Eliot and Auden* (New York, 1967).

H. Howarth, *The Irish Writers: Literature and Nationalism, 1880–1940* (paperback, New York, 1959).

R. M. Kain, *Dublin in the Age of William Butler Yeats and James Joyce* (Norman, Okla., 1962).

NOTES ON THE CONTRIBUTORS

Miriam Allott is Reader in English Literature at Liverpool University. Her books include *Novelists on the Novel, Elizabeth Gaskell,* and casebooks in the Macmillan Casebook Series on *Wuthering Heights* and on '*Jane Eyre*' *and* '*Villette*'.

W. E. K. Anderson, Headmaster of Abingdon School, is the author of *The Written Word: Some Uses of English* (1963) and editor of *The Journal of Sir Walter Scott* (1972).

Martin C. Battestin, Professor of English Literature at the University of Virginia, has published numerous studies of Fielding's fiction and is editing the novels for the Wesleyan Edition. His book, *The Providence of Wit: Aspects of Form in Augustan Literature and the Arts,* will be published in 1974 by the Clarendon Press.

Jerome Beaty is Professor of English at Emory University. His books include '*Middlemarch*' *from Notebook to Novel: a Study of George Eliot's Critical Method* (1947), and *Poetry, from Statement to Meaning* (1965).

Bradford A. Booth was Professor of English at the University of California, Los Angeles, until his death in 1968. He was the founder and for twenty years the editor of *Nineteenth-Century Fiction.* He published widely on the nineteenth-century novel, including a critical study of Anthony Trollope (1958), and the edition of Trollope's letters (1952).

Malcolm Bradbury is Professor of American Studies at the University of East Anglia. His critical books include *The Social Context of Modern English Literature* (1971); *Possibilities: Essays on the State of the Novel* (1973); the Prentice-Hall Twentieth Century Views volume on E. M. Forster; and the Macmillan Casebook on *A Passage to India.* He has also published two novels, *Eating People is Wrong* (1959), and *Stepping Westward* (1965).

John Carroll is Professor of English at the University of Toronto. He has edited *Selected Letters of Richardson* (1964) and *Richardson: Twentieth Century Views,* a critical anthology.

J. A. V. Chapple is Professor of English at the University of Hull. He is co-editor of *The Letters of Mrs. Gaskell* (1966) and author of *Documentary and Imaginative Literature 1880–1920* (1970).

Duncan Isles is a Lecturer in English at the University College of Wales, Aberystwyth. He has published critical discussions of Pope, Richardson, Johnson, and Charlotte Lennox, and has edited the Lennox Collection of eighteenth-century correspondence.

Lewis M. Knapp is Professor Emeritus of English at the Colorado College in Colorado Springs. In 1949 he published the now standard biography, *Tobias Smollett, Doctor of Men and Manners.* His edition of *Humphry Clinker* was published in 1966 and *The Letters of Tobias Smollett* in 1970. His numerous articles in various scholarly journals are listed in *Tobias Smollett, Bicentennial Essays*, which was presented to him in 1971 as a Festschrift.

Louis A. Landa is Professor of English at Princeton University. Among his books are *Swift and the Church of Ireland* (1954), the Riverside edition of *Gulliver's Travels*, and (with J. Tobin) *Jonathan Swift: A List of Critical Studies Published from 1895 to 1945* (1971).

A. Walton Litz is Professor of English at Princeton University. Among his books are *The Art of James Joyce* (1961), *Jane Austen: a Study of Her Artistic Development* (1965), *James Joyce* (1966), and *Introspective Voyager: The Poetic Development of Wallace Stevens* (1972).

M. E. Novak is Professor of English at the University of California, Los Angeles. He has written *Economics and the Fiction of Daniel Defoe* (1962), *Defoe and the Nature of Man* (1963), and *William Congreve* (1971). He edited volume X of the California *Works of John Dryden* and is a general editor of the Augustan Reprint Society.

F. B. Pinion, Reader in English (Division of Education) and Sub-Dean (Faculty of Arts) at the University of Sheffield, is the author of *A Hardy Companion* (1968) and *A Jane Austen Companion* (1973). With Evelyn Hardy he edited Thomas Hardy's letters to Mrs. Henniker (*One Rare Fair Woman*, 1972).

Arthur Pollard is Professor of English in the University of Hull. He has written on Crabbe, Mrs. Gaskell, and Charlotte Brontë, among others, and has edited a volume on *The Victorians* and also *Webster's New World Companion to English and American Literature*.

S. Gorley Putt, Fellow and Senior Tutor of Christ's College, Cambridge, was Chairman of the English Association from 1964 to 1972. His book *The Fiction of Henry James* was reprinted by Penguin (Peregrine series) in 1968.

Roger Sharrock is Professor of English Language and Literature at King's College, London; before this he was Professor of English at Durham and edited the *Durham University Journal*. His books include *John Bunyan* (1954), the Oxford English Texts of *Grace Abounding* and *The Pilgrim's Progress*, and the *Pelican Book of English Prose*.

Michael Slater is a Lecturer in English at Birkbeck College, London, and has been editor of *The Dickensian* since 1968. He has edited Dickens's *Christmas Books* and *Nicholas Nickleby* and a collection of centenary essays, *Dickens 1970*. He is at present preparing for publication a catalogue of the Suzannet Dickens Collection now held by the Dickens House Museum, London.

Brian Southam is Editorial Director of Routledge and Kegan Paul. His books include studies of Jane Austen, Tennyson, and T. S. Eliot.

Mark Spilka, chairman of the English Department at Brown University from 1967 to 1973, is managing editor of *Novel: A Forum on Fiction*. He has written and edited books on Lawrence and is the author also of *Dickens and Kafka* (1963).

THE EDITOR

A. E. Dyson is Senior Lecturer in English at the University of East Anglia. His books include *The Crazy Fabric* (1965), *The Inimitable Dickens* (1970), and *Between Two Worlds: Aspects of Literary Form* (1972). He is co-editor of the *Critical Quarterly*.